Creating Cool MINDSTORMS® NXT Robots

Daniele Benedettelli

Creating Cool MINDSTORMS® NXT Robots

Copyright © 2008 by Daniele Benedettelli

ISBN-13 (paperback): 978-1-59059-966-2

ISBN-13 (electronic): 978-1-4302-0599-9

Printed and bound in the United States of America 9 8 7 6 5 4 3 2

Lead Editor: Jeffrey Pepper
Technical Reviewer: Claude Baumann
Developmental Editor: John R. Vacca
Editorial Board: Clay Andres, Steve Anglin, Ewan Buckingham, Tony Campbell, Gary Cornell, Jonathan Gennick, Matthew Moodie, Joseph Ottinger, Jeffrey Pepper, Frank Pohlmann, Ben Renow-Clarke, Dominic Shakeshaft, Matt Wade, Tom Welsh
Project Manager: Beth Christmas
Copy Editor: Susannah Davidson Pfalzer
Associate Production Director: Kari Brooks-Copony
Production Editor: Kelly Winquist
Compositor: Kinetic Publishing Services, LLC
Proofreader: April Eddy
Indexer: Becky Hornyak
Artists: April Milne, Dina Quan
Cover Designer: Kurt Krames
Manufacturing Director: Tom Debolski
Distributed to the book trade worldwide by Springer-Verlag New York, Inc., 233 Spring Street, 6th Floor, New York, NY 10013. Phone 1-800-SPRINGER, fax 201-348-4505, e-mail orders-ny@springer-sbm.com, or visit http://www.springeronline.com.

For information on translations, please contact Apress directly at 2855 Telegraph Avenue, Suite 600, Berkeley, CA 94705. Phone 510-549-5930, fax 510-549-5939, e-mail info@apress.com, or visit http://www.apress.com.

Apress and friends of ED books may be purchased in bulk for academic, corporate, or promotional use. eBook versions and licenses are also available for most titles. For more information, reference our Special Bulk Sales–eBook Licensing web page at http://www.apress.com/info/bulksales.

The source code for this book is available to readers at http://www.apress.com. You will need to answer questions pertaining to this book in order to successfully download the code.

To my brother Alessandro

Contents at a Glance

Contents

PART 1 ■■■ Look, Mom! No Wheels!

PART 2 ■ ■ ■ Back on Wheels

About the Author

DANIELE BENEDETTELLI appeared in this world on December 2, AD 1984 in Grosseto, the capital city of the beautiful Maremma Toscana. While attending high school, apart from his compulsory studies, his main passion was writing music and playing the piano, a passion to which he devoted his childhood. When he was not playing the piano, you could find him playing with LEGOs.

This last passion took a backseat during his "dark age of LEGO," when real-life interests got the better of building plastic creations. In 2000, Daniele scraped enough savings together to get the LEGO MINDSTORMS Robotics Invention System, and from that moment on, a new way of relating to LEGO began: his adult career in the LEGO community started! In 2006, he got a Bachelor of Science degree cum laude in Computer Engineering (Automation concentration) from the University of Siena with a thesis whose approximately translated title is "LEGO MINDSTORMS–based mobile robots team." A toy—a destiny, we could say. Now he's studying for a Master of Science degree in Robotics and Automation at the University of Siena.

In 2006, he was selected by The LEGO Group as member of the MINDSTORMS Developer Program (MDP), and in 2007 as one of MINDSTORMS Community Partners (MCP).

2007 was a turning point for Daniele. He gave birth to a LEGO NXT robot that can solve automatically any 3 × 3 Rubik's Cube in less than a minute. This robot is the mechanical part of the project called the LEGO Rubik Utopy. The world has gone crazy over this wonderful contraption. His activity with LEGO on the NXT line is continuing now with the group called the MINDSTORMS Community Partners 2.0.

About the Technical Reviewer

Since 1999, **CLAUDE BAUMANN** has taught advanced LEGO MINDSTORMS robotics in after-school classes and maintains the related widely known web site http://www.convict.lu/Jeunes/RoboticsIntro.htm. He participated in beta testing of the ROBOLAB software that originated at Tufts University. He also has been in charge—in collaboration with Professor Chris Rogers— of the creation of ULTIMATE ROBOLAB, a cross-compiler environment that allows graphical programming of RCX firmware, and of a unique RCX self-replicating program (also called a "virus"). Claude has been the assessor of various high-school robot projects (among which is the famous LEGO humanoid robot GASTON). He is the author and coauthor of several related articles and conference presentations, and he was the technical reviewer of *Extreme NXT: Extending the LEGO MINDSTORMS NXT to the Next Level* by Michael Gasperi et al. (Apress, 2007). In 2004 and 2005, he was guest speaker at the annual ROBOLAB Conference in Austin, Texas. He's married and has three children, is the director of a boarding institution in Luxembourg, and is the radio amateur LX1BW.

Acknowledgments

I always find reading a book's Acknowledgments section interesting: it is a sort of back stage, where you can get an idea of the work hidden behind these pages.

As is customary, let me first thank all my family. In particular, a thanks goes to my father for the support and inspiration through the development process of the robotic creations in this book. Also, the one-way chats with my mother led me to think aloud and solve many tricky building and programming issues: thanks to her for listening to my incomprehensible ponderings! Thanks to my brother Alessandro, talented guitarist, who spurred me on with suggestions such as "Go and do something serious, instead of playing!" However, this English translation is just a pale rendering of the Italian "*Ma vai a lavoro!*"

Now, I have to thank and acknowledge a lot of people who helped me, more or less directly, during the creation of this book. Forgive me if one name happens to appear before another. Keeping the list in chronological order is as good a rule as another.

I wish to thank Mario Ferrari, major author of well-known LEGO books, who guided my first steps in the LEGO community, since the LEGO Fest where I met him and the members of ITLUG, the Italian LEGO Users Group.

I wish to acknowledge the great work of John Hansen, programmer and MDP/MCP fellow. He is the creator of Not eXactly C (NXC), the powerful textual programming language for the NXT that has been used for the robots of this book. Also, he wrote a number of utilities to interface the LEGO bricks to the computer. One above all, Bricx Command Center (BricxCC), is the environment you'll use to program your robots in NXC. Thanks, John. You gave me the words to instruct my robots!

In this book, you'll enjoy hundreds of detailed building instruction step images, the result of many, many hours of hard work that's not only mine. In fact, the LDRAW system, which I used to draw the 3D CAD models of my robots, is powered by many people who made up the LEGO elements' virtual counterparts. A huge thanks go to all the authors of the parts and of the software: talented people who built up the LDRAW system as we know it today. In particular, I wish to thank the ones who designed the NXT parts you'll see in the following pages: Steve Bliss, Matthias Paul Scholz, and Marc Klein. I myself contributed a little bit, making an early version of the Ultrasonic Sensor front shell.

Philippe Hurbain and Kevin Clague are among those parts' authors, and deserve special thanks. Philippe Hurbain (Philo) is another MDP member and Apress author, who took price-less time to design great-looking CAD versions of most parts of the NXT system. Above all, his masterpieces are the NXT brick, the Sound Sensor, the servomotors, and the BIONICLE claw weapon.

Kevin Clague—MDP member, book author, and creator of many inspiring LEGO bipeds—wrote some really useful programs that I used to assemble the layouts for the building instructions: LEGO Publisher (LPUB) and LEGO Synth, a LEGO bendable parts synthesizer, used to draw the flexible cables. He helped me in learning LPUB, during a period of testing and debugging of the software. Kevin, thank you for your great patience!

Speaking of patience, another person I really want to thank is Claude Baumann, the technical reviewer of this book. My gratitude goes to him for many reasons. First, he believed in my Rubik Solver robot, and invited me, in Luxembourg, to The Science Circus. There I had occasion to see his skill for instruction and passion for teaching. I am glad he accepted the position of my technical reviewer. Apart from the mere technical reviewing of the programs and robots in this book, I wish to thank him for having tried to teach me how to teach. I say "tried" because I was not the ideal pupil! Anyway, your words of advice are precious. Thank you.

Thanks also to the Apress staff, whose names were reported a few pages ago. In particular, thanks to editor Gary Cornell: my brief e-mail was enough for him and his staff to believe in this book that did not exist at that time, except in my head. So, Apress, thanks for having believed in the robots shown on my web page and the material for a book! Thanks to Jeffrey Pepper, lead editor. Thanks to Beth Christmas, my kind project manager, who kept order in my (sometimes) messy material submissions, and John Vacca for his work in getting the "English" into English. On the writing side, thanks to Susannah Davidson Pfalzer, copy editor, who made my style fluent and grammar-examination–proof!

The photos of JohnNXT and the NXT AT-ST robots on the book cover are by Benjamin Maier, professional photographer and friend of mine. I hope he enjoyed spending his time finding my robots' best side and lighting direction. Anyway, I won't steal his time again, so he can direct another feature film—then I'll have the occasion to compose another soundtrack. Thanks, Ben!

I conclude with a little note of regret, while I thank Narendra Sakharam Gaonkar, my native-English-speaking friend and linguistic consultant. Narendra, if only one of the epic and far-reaching alternative titles we conceived for this book had been accepted!

Introduction

You are a LEGO MINDSTORMS NXT owner, aren't you?

If you have this book in your hands, maybe you've already tried (and maybe exhausted) the possibilities offered by the NXT retail set, and the building and programming guides. If not, I recommend that you use those official LEGO guides to start. So, you should have at least a basic idea of what a robot is—otherwise I suspect that you would not even have thought about reading this book!

I began to think of this book as a way to introduce LEGO users to some advanced topics of robotic programming, always keeping it simple, without scaring anyone. In the few theoretical discussions you'll find, you won't have time to get bored: all the theory is explained in order to understand the practice better.

This book is divided into two parts. With the first, I want to break away from the same boring wheeled robots—there are too many of them around. We're used to vehicles; we want to move on legs! So, this part is devoted to walking robots—bipeds in particular. In Chapter 1, I tried to summarize the state of the art for LEGO bipedal walkers. Subsequent Chapters 2, 4, and 5 present three biped robots in order of complexity. Chapter 3 is the only real theoretical chapter, where you learn the finite state machine software technique to give your robot personality and autonomous behaviors. In Chapter 6, the NXT Turtle is described. This is a quadruped robot, featuring a funny autonomous behavior.

The second part is about wheeled robots. I could not write a book without them. That's also because, apart from the Mine Sweeper (an object-collecting vehicle), the other wheeled robot is the great JohnNXT: a replica of Johnny 5, robot star from the *Short Circuit* 1980s movies. I haven't counted the number of people who directly contacted me to ask for JohnNXT instructions, but they are in the hundreds. So, JohnNXT could not be missing from this book.

Except for Chapters 1 and 3, the other chapters containing a robot are organized as follows. At the beginning, the robot is introduced and its capabilities are described. Then, the Not eXactly C (NXC) programs to implement those capabilities are reported and described in detail. Various arguments are deepened, taking advantage of the occasion to discuss programming techniques that arise over and over. The building section is at the end of the chapter. This placement avoids chopping the reading flow in two. The building instructions are introduced first with a detailed bill of materials; then, each step is commented to help with the building. At the end of some chapters, you might find a few exercises, meant to be inspirational cues.

Who Is This Book For?

Mainly, this is a book that should entertain everyone. If the reading will add something to your knowledge, so much the better! So, this book is for the following:

- Those from 6 to 106 years old, wishing to build cool LEGO robots to have fun, without being expert programmers.

- Those who want to build a Johnny 5 replica (more than you might think!).

- Those who need inspiration for their own new creations.

- Those who are tired of exploring the equivalent area of hundreds of computer screens occupied by the graphical NXT-G block programs, who want to change radically the way to program the NXT.

- Those wishing to learn a textual C-like programming language without getting frustrated by complicated useless programs for novices, or bored by abstract exercises. Every program in this book produces visible results.

- Those wishing to learn new programming techniques.

Children, remind your parents that LEGO MINDSTORMS is not their exclusive toy. Ask them for help if you want—you'll have a great time! Parents and grandparents, you can use this book as an excuse to start playing seriously with LEGO robots, while spending time with your kids and grandkids. But let go of that NXT brick—let 'em play too!

What You Need to Use This Book

You can build all the robots using the parts from a single LEGO MINDSTORMS NXT retail set (code number 8527), except the last big one, JohnNXT, and the remote control. So you can enjoy the building and relax—you won't find out that you're missing a needed part when you're a step from the end! If you plan to build and control JohnNXT remotely, I suggest you find all the parts first: you need three NXT sets, and many other extra parts, all listed in the appropriate bills of materials in Chapters 8 and 9.

Then you need a computer to write and send the programs to your NXT robots. The software I used runs on Windows. Mac and Linux releases of the NXC compiler exist, but you'll have to find an alternative Integrated Development Environment (IDE) for the handy Bricx Command Center (BricxCC).

To enjoy this book, you do not have to be a programmer, although it can help you learn the basics to become a programmer. *You can also follow the building instructions and then download the programs provided to your robots, without having to write a single line of code.*

About the software: you should already have the NXT-G program provided by LEGO in your retail set. The other software is the BricxCC IDE and the NXC compiler, both downloadable from `http://bricxcc.sourceforge.net/` and `http://bricxcc.sourceforge.net/nbc/`.

When facing a new programming topic, I recommed that you keep an eye on the complete *Not eXactly C (NXC) Programmer's Guide* by John Hansen, which you can download from http://bricxcc.sourceforge.net/nbc/nxcdoc/NXC_Guide.pdf. To get an idea of what the NXC language looks like, you can also read the tutorial I wrote, *Programming LEGO NXT Robots using NXC*. This paper is available for free at http://bricxcc.sourceforge.net/nbc/nxcdoc/NXC_tutorial.pdf.

Source Code and Extras for This Book

You can download the complete source code for the programs from the Source Code/Download area on the Apress web site, at http://www.apress.com. Also, you can visit the web site http://robotics.benedettelli.com.

PART 1

■ ■ ■

Look, Mom! No Wheels!

After building your first wheeled robots, you can feel bored. Okay, they're built for precision, you can make them go exactly where you want, at the speed you want . . . but they still use wheels! LEGO itself, planning a new MINDSTORMS line, never thought about a wheeled robot becoming its logo and NXT mascot—months before the product release, the figure of Alpha Rex filled every advertising space. In this first section of the book, you'll discover how to leave the wheels behind and get moving on legs.

CHAPTER 1

■ ■ ■

Building Biped Robots

I can imagine your impatience—the urge to skip this introduction chapter altogether, and go directly to building the robots that are shown in the next chapters of this part, which are entirely devoted to walker robots. However, you would entirely miss the essentials necessary to understand why the walkers presented in this book actually work; you would miss finding out how to let your robots leave the wheels behind them and get on their own two feet.

This chapter will present the state of the art in LEGO walking biped robots. I'll introduce some basic notions of that branch of physics called statics (balancing forces) to help you develop steady biped robots that do *not* need to use any advanced sensor to balance, such as accelerometers, tilt sensors, or gyroscopes. The stability of those robots is guaranteed only by the hardware configuration.

LEGO Bipedal Walking: The State of the Art

It has been almost ten years since LEGO MINDSTORMS users like you developed various bipedal walking techniques. The numerous biped robots, created fairly successfully during those years, can be categorized as follows:

- Interlacing legs bipeds

- Jerky center of gravity (COG from now on) shifting bipeds

- Smooth COG shifting bipeds

I'll describe these categories in detail, focusing on their level of complexity and the mechanical solutions used, with the help of some visual examples. In the next chapters you'll find the practical examples of this categorization: Quasimodo (Chapter 2) is an interlacing legs biped, *Star Wars* AT-ST chicken walker (Chapter 4) is a jerky COG shifting biped, while the Omni-Biped (Chapter 5) is a smooth COG shifting biped.

Interlacing Legs Bipeds

Robots that fall in the category of interlacing legs bipeds generally use the simplest walking technique. In other words, you must figure out what is the best way to put one foot in front of another. The solution is usually a cam shaft (see Figure 1-4c, d, and f). With the parts provided in the NXT retail set, you can easily build a cam shaft using the holes in the 24-tooth or the 40-tooth gear (see Omni-Biped's legs in Chapter 5). You must attach the legs to an off-center hole to achieve what's called *eccentric motion*. As an alternative, you can use the black 3-long liftarms (as in Quasimodo, Chapter 2).

The particular shape of the feet stabilize a robot of this category (see Figure 1-1a)—feet interlace each other (hence the name of this category). Usually, in this kind of robot, the center of gravity is not shifted from side to side. So, you must pay close attention to designing the structure in such a way that the COG projection on the ground always falls inside the area that supports the feet, during each phase of walking. This condition must hold when the feet are on the ground together, but also when one of them is lifted from the ground.

Figure 1-1 shows the various walking phases. In *a*, both feet are on the ground; in *b* and *c*, the right foot begins to step forward and is lifted from the ground, leaving all the weight loaded on the left foot and reducing the support area to only the left foot; in *d* both feet are on the ground again. Next, the process starts again with the left foot leaving the ground and stepping forward.

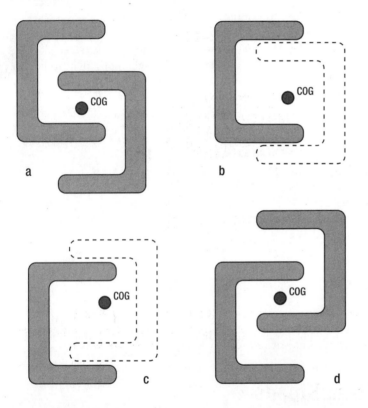

Figure 1-1. *Interlacing legs biped footprints in the various phases of walking*

The preceding approach suffers from the slackness of the LEGO joints: the legs tend to bend inside and the feet do not lift completely from the ground. To solve this problem, you can place a wedge in the inner side of the feet as shown in Figure 1-2c, or you can provide your biped with a sort of "hip tendon" made with rubber bands or LEGO parts, as shown in Figure 1-2d. All bipeds in nature have similar muscles to keep their equilibrium, so that they can walk steadily.

LEGO veteran users tend to be purists and quite conservative. They might consider it a sacrilege to use non-LEGO parts in your robot building. If you are willing to use rubber bands, you should use original LEGO rubber bands, although it is not the most elegant solution.

However, the best solution is to keep the whole leg frame short and rigid by using cross-bracing. The weaker parts of the leg are usually the moving joints, at the ankle and hip level.

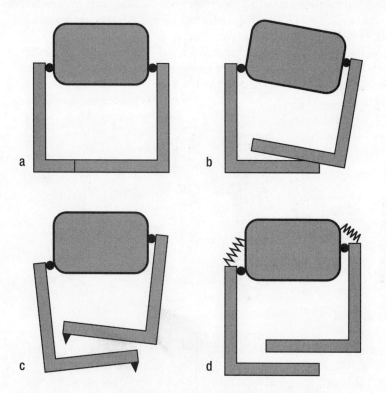

Figure 1-2. *Solving the problems related to LEGO joints' flexible nature*

All this might seem a bit abstract to you, but it will all come clear when you build your own Quasimodo—a biped, and the subject of the next chapter. In Chapter 2, I'll emphasize the defects of this particular walking mechanism and will cover the remedies step by step.

Jerky COG Shifting Bipeds

If you want to get really serious, or if your robot begins to get heavier, you should start thinking about COG shifting. As the term implies, the robot shifts its weight on the foot that remains on the ground, and unloads the other foot that is in the flight phase.

The adjective "jerky" implies that shifting the COG and stepping forward occurs in distinct stages. It also implies that it is done with different motors.

You can accomplish weight shifting while moving the whole mass (RCX or NXT, where most weight resides) from side to side, or by bending the legs at the ankle, knee, or hip level (see Figure 1-3).

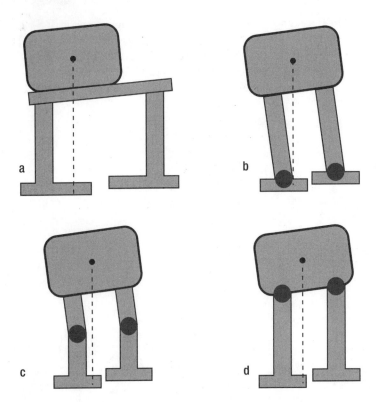

Figure 1-3. *Weight shifting methods*

You can achieve stepping by rotating the legs or *translating* them, keeping them parallel to each other (see Figure 1-4*a*, *b*, and *e*). In these cases, if the feet are moved while they are both touching the ground, the resulting effect is that the robot turns slightly in place. You'll use this feature in the AT-ST biped to make it turn (see Chapter 4).

Figure 1-4 from *c* through *f* shows various stepping solutions. In these pictures, just one leg is shown for clarity: you must attach the hidden one (grayed in *c* and *d*) on the other side of the robot 180 degrees out of phase. For example, in Figure 1-4*c* and *d*, you should attach the legs, on the opposite sides of the robot, at the leftmost position on the cam (the white circle), so that one leg is ahead of the other one. You must apply the same concept when attaching the other leg in elements *e* and *f*.

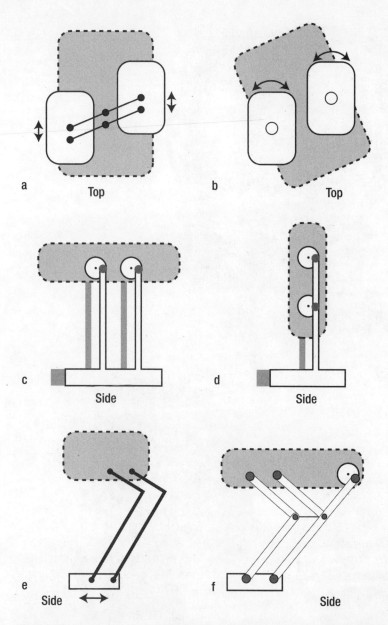

Figure 1-4. *Various stepping methods: a) this top view shows that the legs are translated, keeping them parallel each other; b) another top view where the legs are rotated together; c) side view showing a cammed mechanism keeping the body horizontal; d) a similar side view showing a cammed mechanism with the body kept vertical; e) this side view shows another solution for stepping; f) this cammed mechanism works like the one in c but is better looking.*

As shown in Figure 1-5, many of the bipeds I've built follow this line, such as the Matrix APU (February 2004), the OWL (May 2004), and the RCX-based AT-ST (December 2004). The new NXT AT-ST that you will find in Chapter 4 falls in this category. The dates in parentheses are the construction dates, showing the month in which these creations were published on the Web.

Figure 1-5. *RCX-based jerky COG shifting bipeds: a) Matrix APU, b) OWL, c) AT-ST*

Smooth COG Shifting Bipeds

I prefer smooth COG shifting bipeds due to their speed and smoothness—you probably will, too. They use a single motor to achieve both weight shifting and stepping; hence you need a refined mechanism.

In Figure 1-6, you can see the biped robot that I built in August 2004. This particular robot could only walk straight using COG shifting, and was meant to be a prototype for future bipeds that could also turn.

Figure 1-6. *COG-shifting Biped I*

My Advanced COG Biped (dated October 2004), shown in Figure 1-7, features a smooth walking gait and can turn thanks to a motorized rotating ankle. The left foot includes a motor to allow it to turn, while the other foot is built of normal parts (in the Robotics Invention System kit, there were only two motors), trying to balance the other foot's weight. On each foot, a touch sensor lets the robot know which foot is touching the ground.

The robot uses this sequence for turning: when the left foot is lifted from the ground, it is swung outside at a little angle; then the robot steps to load the weight on the foot, to bring it onto the ground. The ankle is then rotated back in its place and the whole robot turns left.

You can repeat this routine as many times as needed to turn in place, and you can modify it slightly to turn in the other direction.

Figure 1-7. *Advanced COG Biped*

Summary

In this introductory chapter, you saw various approaches to bipedal walking. You were shown some startup ideas that might shed light on the mystery of how to develop a biped that not only walks, but can also turn.

To make a biped that walks without resembling a drunken sailor (and that is not at risk of falling down with every step it takes), the clever designer should try to bind the COG projection inside the area supporting the feet. You should do this during every phase of the walking cycle, when both feet are touching the ground and when one of them is in flight phase, leaving the other to support the whole robot's weight. This condition is essential for creating a biped without advanced sensors such as accelerometers or gyroscopes. Such a robot is a static one, because dynamic effects are not taken into account. Stability is guaranteed only by hardware structure, with no need of sensor feedback.

In the next chapters, you'll create three bipeds using all these techniques.

CHAPTER 2

■ ■ ■

Quasimodo

The hunchbacked biped described in this chapter fits our educational purposes perfectly. By building it, you'll get to see in practice all the theoretical tips, tricks, and rules explained in Chapter 1 about the stability of biped robots.

I decided to call this biped Quasimodo (after the hunchback of Victor Hugo's famous book *Notre-Dame de Paris*), because of its particular shape and the funny way it walks. When you build it, you'll see what I mean. You can get an idea of how Quasimodo looks in Figure 2-1.

I recommend that you read the following sections with a bookmark in Chapter 1, as you'll see that the practical examples of this chapter and the theory that lies behind them (in Chapter 1) correspond.

Throughout this book, in chapters where a model is being built, the chapters will be organized the same way. The first part of the chapter will discuss key features of the model, and its overall function; the second part will discuss the program that has been created to make the model run; and the third part shows the building instructions, part by part, so that you can create the given model yourself.

Figure 2-1. *The NXT biped of this chapter, Quasimodo*

Applying What You Learned

Quasi (to his friends) is an interlacing legs biped, the simplest approach you can adopt for a biped. When designing such a biped, you might start thinking about the leg shape and the cammed mechanism needed to step forward. You can choose two paths: should the cams be aligned in a horizontal or vertical position (as shown in Figure 1-4c and d, respectively)? Placing the geartrain on a vertical beam yields a much higher and more unstable biped, because the motor and the NXT would be placed in a vertical position. It would be more difficult to design the structure to have the NXT center of gravity (COG) inside the feet area. The COG itself would be placed higher, so a slight oscillation due to leg joint flexibility would result in a large oscillation at the top of the robot, causing the COG to go outside the feet area and the robot to fall. For these reasons, I chose to settle the motor, the geartrain beam, and the NXT horizontally.

After I had designed the legs and the motor placement, I didn't know where to put the NXT brick itself. I ended up putting it on the robot's back, just like a hump, and attaching it to the legs so that it swings left and right as the legs move. This way I also achieved COG shifting (as explained in Chapter 1), with surprising ease. Often you have to think hard about a satisfactory solution, but in some rare cases, as here, things seem to work out by themselves.

Let me guide you through the design process that led to the final look of Quasi. This biped is meant to be an educational model, to help me to emphasize the defects and problems you could encounter while designing your first bipeds. The leg attachment to the cams is the weak part of this interlacing legs biped, because the cam pins fit a bit loosely in the leg beam holes. As you'll see, you can solve these problems to result in a biped that walks well.

Caution When I talk about LEGO parts' flexibility, I do not mean that LEGO beams actually bend. *Do not try to force LEGO parts, or you might risk breaking something!* Here, I mean the looseness of the parts shown in certain assemblies, due to their construction tolerance and material. Examples of this slackness are the pins, which don't fit tightly inside the beam holes, making the leg structure not perfectly rigid.

The feet are shaped as shown in Figure 1-1, to let the COG projection always fall inside the supporting area of the feet. You attach the legs to the motor geartrain by a cammed shaft that keeps them 180 degrees out of phase; this simply means that when one leg is up, the other is down; when one is forward, the other is back.

Unfortunately, as you might expect, such a structure is so loose that it risks falling apart. Figure 2-2 shows what I mean. As already explained in Chapter 1, the weaker points of such a biped are the attachments at the hip and ankle levels.

Figure 2-2. *The biped from behind (with the NXT on top removed) shows the looseness of the structure at hip level. The ankle is quite rigid instead.*

It's easy to run into similar problems when working with LEGO parts. Having such a loose structure is a problem that can arise, but don't worry. You can solve it as indicated in the schematic shown in Figure 1-2c, by adding the wedges in the inner side of the feet beams. The result of our biped is shown in Figure 2-3.

Figure 2-3. *Putting wedges in the inner side of both feet compensates for the leg joints' slackness.*

Even after the wedge additions, the hip joint still tends to be quite loose (it's made with long gray pins, which connect the cam to the leg). To solve this tricky issue, I adopted the hip tendons shown in Figure 1-2*d*, a matter that could have been obscure to you just after reading Chapter 1. Don't worry though, it will become clear now.

Compare Figure 2-4 (before the treatment) with Figure 2-5 (after the treatment). Notice how this elegant solution with the tendons made from LEGO steering links with ball joints, prevents the legs from bending. This last idea of creating tendons is particularly good because it does two things for the price of one: it solves the looseness problem and allows us to connect to the NXT brick in an original way.

Figure 2-4. *Tendons are not attached yet.*

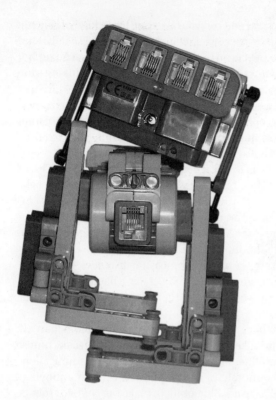

Figure 2-5. *Tendons are now attached.*

Because the tendons are connected to the legs, they swing the NXT in harmony with Quasimodo's gait, and the NXT seems as light as a butterfly. Don't forget that our beloved programmable brick acts as a hump here! I came up with this COG shifting mechanism almost without noticing it, and I must admit this combination of technique, inspiration, and luck is rare. Such a mix makes this robot special. In its simple shape, it summarizes a lot of theory about an unusual way of walking. Ah, I almost forgot: Quasimodo can only walk straight. To create a biped that turns, read the following chapters.

Introducing NXT Technology

Before going on, it's worth introducing the LEGO MINDSTORMS NXT technology briefly. In your NXT retail set, you have LEGO parts, of course, but also some electronic devices that make the NXT system special: three interactive servomotors, a Touch Sensor, a Light Sensor, an Ultrasonic Sensor, and the NXT programmable brick itself. In addition, you have a user guide, and the LEGO software CD-ROM, which allows you to program the NXT using the NXT-G graphical programming language.

The LEGO elements are well assorted, so that you can start creating every kind of robot at once, without having to look for additional spare parts. The set includes LEGO TECHNIC studless elements, except for a few parts. Unlike the common LEGO studded bricks, you do not have to place one brick on another, like building a wall, but you have to start thinking more three-dimensionally, attaching beams and liftarms using pins.

The *NXT servomotors* are different from the common LEGO motors. They are interactive, meaning that they include a Rotation Sensor (optical encoder) that allows you to control interactively the shaft position with 1 degree of resolution, and to set the rotation speed from −100 to 100. A whole shaft rotation is equal to 360 degrees.

The *Touch Sensor* gives your robots the sense of touch: it detects when it is pressed or released, returning a Boolean reading that can be 1 or 0. The *Light Sensor* can distinguish between light and dark colors, measuring the amount of light reflected by the surface illuminated by its LED; it can also measure the light intensity in the environment with the LED off. The *Sound Sensor* makes your robot hear, measuring the sound intensity in decibels. Its readings go from 4 in a silent room to 100, corresponding to people shouting or loud music.

The *Ultrasonic Sensor* enables your robot to see obstacles, measure distances, and detect movement. This digital sensor measures the distance from an object like a bat does, calculating the time needed by an ultrasonic sound wave to hit the object and return. It can measure distances from 0 to 255 centimeters, with an error of **5** 3cm.

Finally, the brain of your robot is the *NXT brick*. It is a microcomputer, programmable with a PC, that lets your LEGO robots come alive, just like JohnNXT (see Chapter 8). You can connect the NXT brick to your PC using a USB cable or Bluetooth. Bluetooth wireless communication is useful if you want to control your robots remotely, or just program it without annoying cables around. You can also connect more NXTs using Bluetooth, to make big complex robots. The NXT has three output ports for attaching motors and four input ports to connect sensors; it has a large dot-matrix screen to display text, numbers, and images. Also, your robots can produce sounds, because the NXT features a loudspeaker to play tones and WAV-like sound files. Two microprocessors are at the base of the NXT brick. The main processor is an Atmel ARM7 (like the one you might have in your mobile phone), and works at 48 MHz, on 32 bits. This allows your robots to deal with large numbers, making calculations at a high speed. The NXT has 256KB of nonvolatile memory; you can store files into it and they won't be erased, even if you remove the batteries.

Oh, I forgot! The NXT needs six AA batteries to work, but can also be powered by the LEGO Li-Ion rechargeable battery. For other details, you can always consult the NXT User Guide included in your retail set.

Meeting the NXT-G Software

Before starting programming at full throttle in NXC, it will help you to get familiar first with NXT programming. The first programming environment you will meet is the official LEGO NXT-G software, the one you should have installed from the CD-ROM included in the NXT retail set. If you haven't done so yet, install this software now.

Connecting the NXT for the First Time

If you've never connected your NXT to a PC before, perform the following steps. You can connect the NXT using the USB cable or using Bluetooth. To find out if your Bluetooth dongle or integrated device is compatible with the NXT, check the LEGO MINDSTORMS official page at `http://mindstorms.lego.com/Overview/Bluetooth.aspx`.

1. Open the NXT-G software and create a new blank program, by clicking the Go button in the Start New Program panel, as shown in Figure 2-6.

Figure 2-6. *The startup panel of the NXT-G software*

2. In the NXT controller (see Figure 2-7), click the top left button to open the NXT window, shown in Figure 2-8.

Figure 2-7. *The NXT controller, which you can find in the right bottom of the software main window*

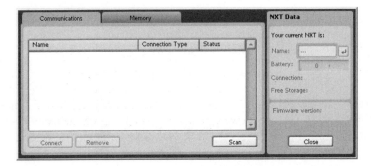

Figure 2-8. *The NXT window, without any NXT devices listed*

3. Connect the NXT to the PC using the USB cable. Otherwise, you can turn on the Bluetooth radio of the NXT brick using its menu. Be sure also to turn on the NXT Bluetooth visibility; use the NXT User Guide as a reference. Then, click the Scan button on the NXT window in Figure 2-8. If you're using a USB connection, it should find the NXT at once; scanning takes a bit more time, if you're searching the NXT using Bluetooth. Once the NXT has been found, it shows up in the list, as you can see in Figure 2-9.

Figure 2-9. *The NXT named "book" has been found using Bluetooth.*

4. Click the Connect button, and you're asked for a passkey in the Enter Passkey dialog (see Figure 2-10). Use the default number 1234 and click OK. The NXT makes a sound, asking for the passkey. Confirm the connection on the NXT brick, using the same passkey as before.

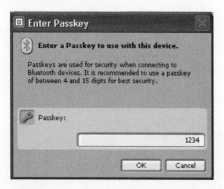

Figure 2-10. *Dialog asking for the passkey for the Bluetooth connection*

5. Once the connection is established, the NXT window looks like the one shown in Figure 2-11; the NXT is reported twice in the list in that figure, because both USB and Bluetooth found it. Once an NXT has been connected, it will be present in the list unless you remove it by clicking the Remove button. As you can see, in this panel you can rename your NXT by typing a new name in the appropriate text field and clicking the Enter button. This window also shows some diagnostic information, such as the battery level, the free FLASH memory amount, and the firmware version. Close the panel and you can start programming your robot.

Figure 2-11. *The NXT is connected.*

Programming Quasimodo Using NXT-G

Quasimodo has only one motor and one Ultrasonic Sensor. The robot walks straight until it sees a near obstacle; it moans and backs up until the sight line is free again, repeating this in a loop. You can code this simple sequence of actions using NXT-G software; the result is shown in Figure 2-12.

In Figure 2-12a you can see how the program looks when completed. Build the program as follows:

1. Start adding the Loop (b) and set it to run forever.

2. Add a Motor block (c), with the following settings:

   • Port: A

   • Direction: Forward

   • Power: 55

   • Control: Motor Power checked

   • Duration: Unlimited

3. Add a Wait block (d), with the following settings:

   • Control: Sensor

   • Sensor: Ultrasonic Sensor

   • Port: 4

   • Until distance < (less than) 20 (cm)

4. Add a Motor block (e), with the following settings:

   • Port: A

   • Direction: Stop

   • Next Action: Brake

5. Add a Sound block (f), with the following settings:

   • Action: Sound File

   • Control: Play

   • Volume: 75

   • File: Woops

   • Wait for Completion checked

6. Add a Motor block (g), with the following settings:

   • Port: A

   • Direction: Reverse

- Power: 55

- Control: Motor Power checked

- Duration: Unlimited

7. Add a Wait block (*h*), with the following settings:

- Control: Sensor

- Sensor: Ultrasonic Sensor

- Port: 4

- Until distance > (greater than) 30 (cm)

The program is ready to be downloaded to the NXT. As shown in Figure 2-7, you can click the Download button (bottom left) or the Download and Run button (center) on the NXT controller. You can also save the program for future use.

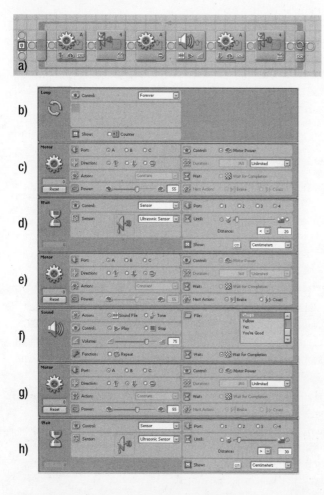

Figure 2-12. *The NXT-G program for Quasimodo*

Now that you know how to connect the NXT to a PC and how to write and download programs using NXT-G software, you can take the next step. From now on, we write the programs for the robots only in the NXC language, using BricxCC as the Integrated Development Environment (IDE). To get started with BricxCC, read Appendix A.

The Shortest Program in the Book

You can translate the program for Quasimodo described earlier into the NXC code in Listing 2-1. Try to single out the correspondences between the NXT-G blocks and the NXC statements.

Listing 2-1. *The Program for Quasimodo*

```
task main ()
{
   SetSensorLowspeed(IN_4);
   while (true)
   {
      // walk forward
      OnFwdReg(OUT_A,55,OUT_REGMODE_SPEED);
      // wait for an obstacle to come near
      while (SensorUS(IN_4)>20);
      // stop walking
      Off(OUT_A);
      // moan
      PlayFile("uuu.rso");
      Wait(800);
      // walk backward
      OnRevReg(OUT_A,55,OUT_REGMODE_SPEED);
      // wait for the obstacle to get far
      while (SensorUS(IN_4)<30);
   }
}
```

Note The #include "NXCDefs.h" statement was used at the top of NXC programs to tell early Beta versions of the NXC preprocessor to include this header file, which was needed to translate every NXC statement into low-level assembly language for the NXT. The latest versions of the NXC compiler (Beta 29 and later) no longer need this preprocessor directive because that file is automatically included at the time of program compilation.

In your program, you use only the main task. Remember that you'll have to put a task named main in every NXC program you'll write. This task is the first one to be executed when the program is run, so you must put it inside all the actions you want your robot to do. Here, you set the input port to 4 to manage the Ultrasonic Sensor using this code:

```
SetSensorLowspeed(IN_4);
```

You start an infinite loop (at least, until the batteries run out, the automatic NXT power-off feature turns it off, or you just stop the program), inside of which you can make the robot do whatever you want. How is this infinite loop done?

Normally, using the following statement, the program will execute the code you put inside the { } braces, while the Boolean condition is true, checking this condition at every loop iteration.

```
while ( condition )
{
    //your code here
}
```

Well, using while (true), the program executes what's inside the braces forever, because its condition never becomes false. The true constant means, in fact, true (not hard to believe!), and the loop goes on forever.

The first three lines of code inside the loop start the motor attached on output port A at 55 percent of full speed, regulating its speed precisely:

```
OnFwdReg(OUT_A,55,OUT_REGMODE_SPEED);
while (SensorUS(IN_4)>20);
Off(OUT_A);
```

The code then waits for the sensor reading to become less than 20cm (an obstacle comes near), using a while loop without the { } braces. Finally, the motor is stopped.

Normally, a while loop is written as shown before, with some code inside the braces. However, in this case you're interested in waiting for something, not in repeating some conditional action. So you start the motor and you wait (doing nothing) until the Ultrasonic Sensor sees something near; the motor will run until it is explicitly stopped by the Off statement. This waiting is accomplished simply by writing the desired condition (as the sensor reading) inside the while loop ( ) brackets, with no additional code inside the { } braces. So, you can remove those last braces and just put in the semicolon after the condition. When an obstacle is seen, the program flow breaks out the while loop, and the Off statement is executed, stopping the motor.

■**Note** Remember, the while (condition); waits for the condition to become false. The until (condition); waits for the condition to become true. This implies that the while(condition) is equivalent to an until(!condition), where ! is the unary logic negation operator NOT. Remember that every line of code must end with a semicolon (;).

The central chunk of code simply plays a file; here, I chose a self-made audio file that I recorded, compressed, and converted to the NXT standard format: RSO. However, you can use any file you want, or you can simply comment out these statements by putting // before the lines of code.

■**Note** The compiler ignores lines preceded by // or enclosed inside the /* and */ couple; for example:

```
//this is a comment until the end of line
statement;
statement;
/* this is a comment
   on multiple lines
*/
```

Warning! The /* */ cannot be nested! So, the following is wrong:

```
/* extern comment
/* inner comment
   whatever
*/ end of inner comment
*/ end of extern comment
```

■**Tip** You can find the custom sounds I made with the book's source code. You can find the RSO default sound files in the \engine\Sounds folder of your official NXT retail or educational version software (for example, C:\Program Files\LEGO Software\LEGO MINDSTORMS NXT\engine\Sounds). You must download the sound files into the NXT memory for the program to find and play them. You can download sounds to the NXT following the directions in Appendix A.

The Wait statement does what it says: it waits for a given number of milliseconds. If you want to play a file without any other action, Wait is needed because the program flow does not wait for a sound file to be played until the end, and it goes on executing the next instruction even if the sound has not been completely played (this holds for PlayTone too).

The third and last chunk of code starts the motor in reverse to let the robot walk away from the obstacle:

```
OnRevReg(OUT_A,55,OUT_REGMODE_SPEED);
while (SensorUS(IN_4)<30);
```

Another while loop is now used to wait for another condition to become false; you want to wait for the Ultrasonic Sensor reading to become greater than 30cm. As soon as the obstacle is far enough, the action sequence starts from the beginning of the loop.

Although simple, this first program is useful as an introduction to the NXC language, and to demonstrate how you can translate a program made with NXT-G blocks using a few lines of code, which are much faster to write. You've seen some basic flow-control statements of the NXC language, as while/until loops, and some NXT-specific Application Programming Interface (API) functions, to move motors and to read sensors.

Building Your Belfry Hunchback

It's time to build this model now. Quasimodo is the simplest robot of the whole book. It will take just few minutes to build this robot, made only out of parts from the NXT retail set. You can check the bill of materials in Figure 2-13 and Table 2-1.

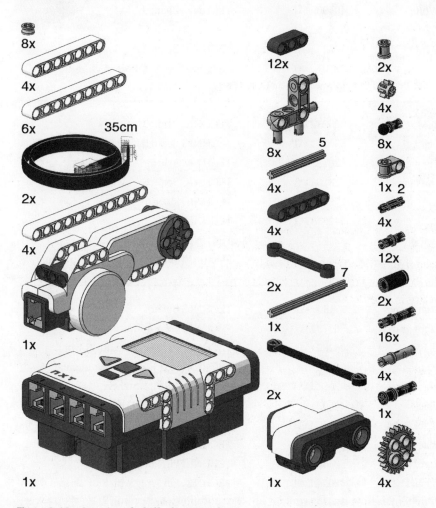

Figure 2-13. *Quasimodo bill of materials*

Table 2-1. *Quasimodo Bill of Materials*

Quantity	Color	Part Number	Part Name
8	Light gray	32123.DAT	TECHNIC Bush 1/2 Smooth
4	White	32524.DAT	TECHNIC Beam 7
6	White	40490.DAT	TECHNIC Beam 9
2		55805.DAT	Electric Cable NXT 35cm
4	White	32525.DAT	TECHNIC Beam 11
1		53787.DAT	Electric MINDSTORMS NXT Motor
1		53788.DAT	Electric MINDSTORMS NXT
12	Dark gray	32523.DAT	TECHNIC Beam 3
8	Light gray	55615.DAT	TECHNIC Beam 5 Bent 90 (3:3) with 4 Pins
4	Light gray	32073.DAT	TECHNIC Axle 5
4	Dark gray	32316.DAT	TECHNIC Beam 5
2	Dark gray	2739B.DAT	TECHNIC Steering Link
1	Light gray	44294.DAT	TECHNIC Axle 7
2	Black	32293.DAT	TECHNIC Steering Link 9L
1		56467.DAT	Electric MINDSTORMS NXT Ultrasonic Sensor
2	Light gray	3713.DAT	TECHNIC Bush
4	Light gray	3647.DAT	TECHNIC Gear 8 Tooth
8	Black	6628.DAT	TECHNIC Friction Pin with Towball
1	Light gray	6536.DAT	TECHNIC Axle Joiner Perpendicular
4	Black	32062.DAT	TECHNIC Axle 2 Notched
12	Black	4459.DAT	TECHNIC Pin with Friction
2	Black	75535.DAT	TECHNIC Pin Joiner Round
16	Black	6558.DAT	TECHNIC Pin Long with Friction and Slot
4	Light gray	32556.DAT	TECHNIC Pin Long
1	Black	32054.DAT	TECHNIC Pin Long with Stop Bush
4	Light gray	3648.DAT	TECHNIC Gear 24 Tooth

118 parts total (all included in the NXT retail set)

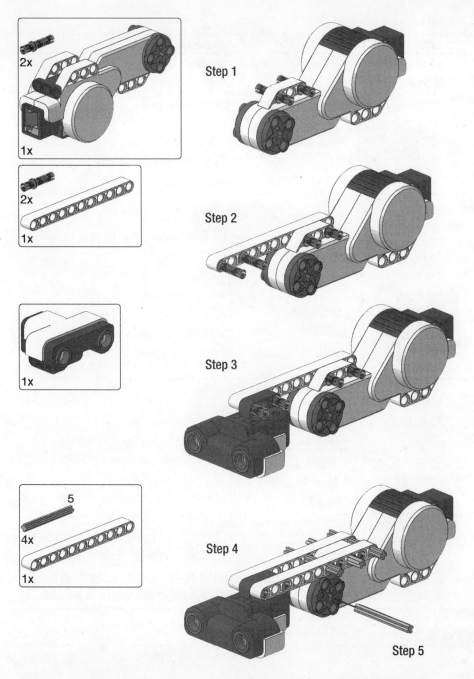

Step 1

Step 2

Step 3

Step 4

Step 5

Start building Quasimodo's body. As you can see, the motor is laid horizontally with respect to the ground. In Step 2, use an 11-long beam. In Step 3, add the Ultrasonic Sensor that forms the robot head, and then insert the 5-long axles into their places. You must insert one of the 5-long axles in the motor shaft hole.

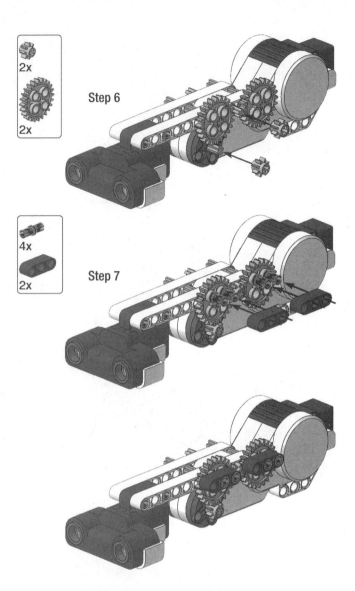

Add the first row of gears, the black pins, and then the 3-long beams. Be sure to align the cams correctly, so that they are parallel. To do this, check the gear meshing. The cams will make the leg move in a circle.

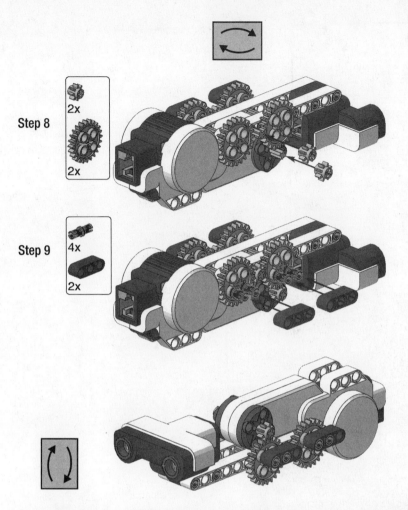

Step 8

2x

2x

Step 9

4x

2x

Rotate the model and place the second row of gears, as you did for the ones already in place.
Then add the cams on this side, making sure to place them 180 degrees out of phase; that is,
rotated half a turn with respect to the other side ones.

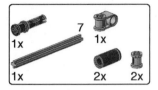

Step 10

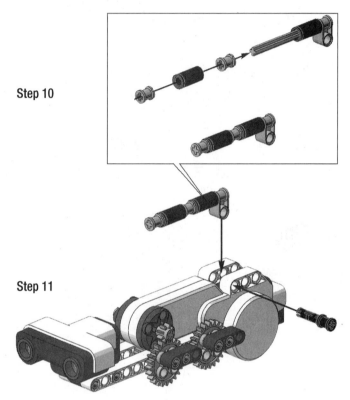

Step 11

The robot main body is complete. Skip this step if you are going to use the NXT rechargeable battery pack instead of regular batteries. Build the submodel of this step if you're going to use normal batteries. In fact, the NXT battery pack protrudes one LEGO unit out of the normal NXT profile; to get this extra battery thickness, needed to have the robot walk smoothly, you have to build this offset part.

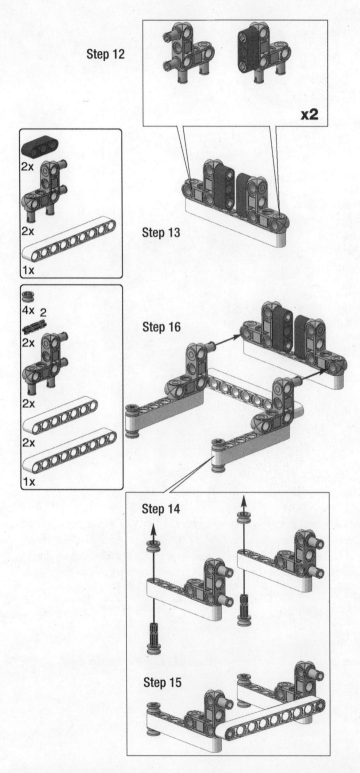

Step 12

x2

2x

2x

1x

Step 13

4x 2

2x

2x

2x

1x

Step 16

Step 14

Step 15

Start building the left leg.

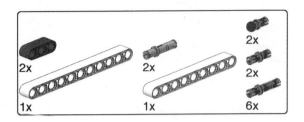

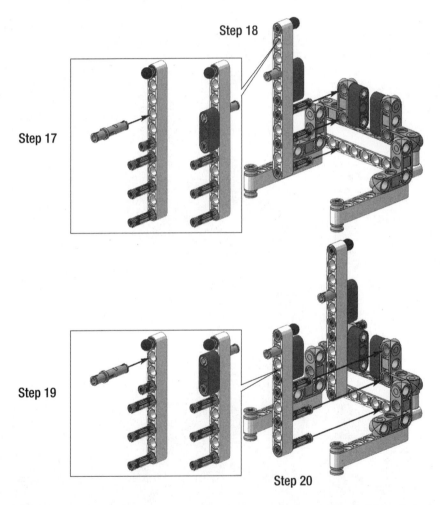

Assemble the vertical beams of the leg. The first is 11 holes long; the second is 9 holes long.

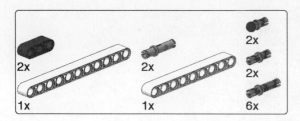

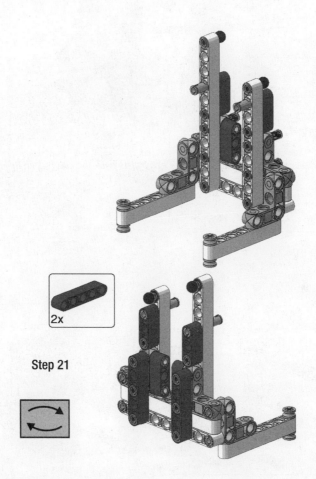

Step 21

The left leg is completed.

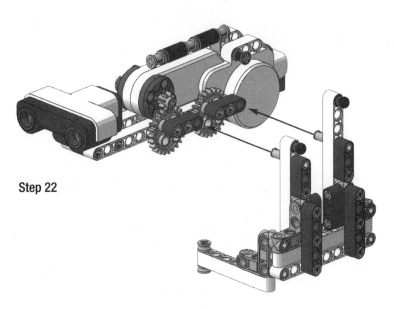

Step 22

Attach the left leg to the robot body, inserting the gray pins into the cam's free holes.

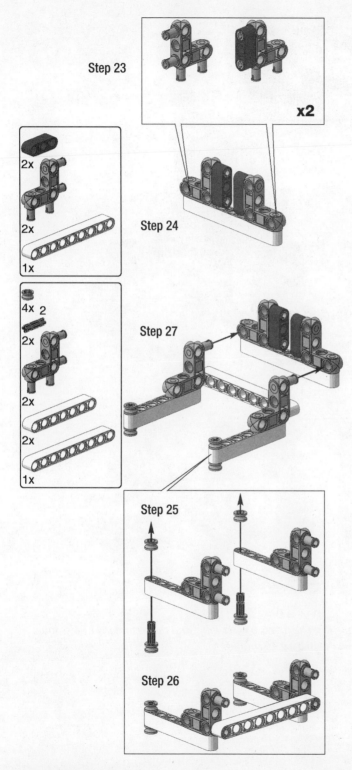

Step 23

Step 24

Step 27

Step 25

Step 26

x2

2x

2x

1x

4x 2

2x

2x

2x

1x

Start building the right leg.

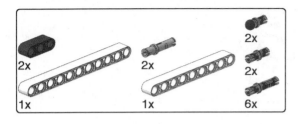

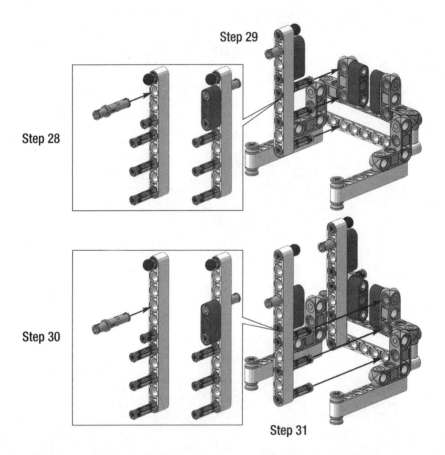

Assemble the vertical beams of the leg. The first is 9 holes long, and the second is 11 holes long; this is the only difference between the two leg assemblies.

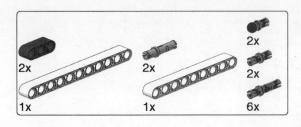

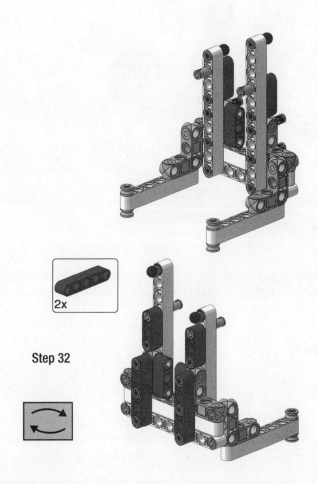

Step 32

The right leg is completed.

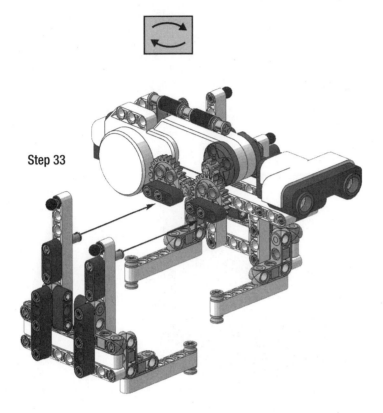

Step 33

Turn the model and attach the right leg to the robot. Notice that, if you built the cams correctly, the legs are out of phase—one forward, the other backward. Quasimodo should now stand on its own feet.

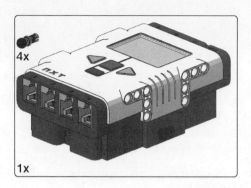

Step 34

Step 35

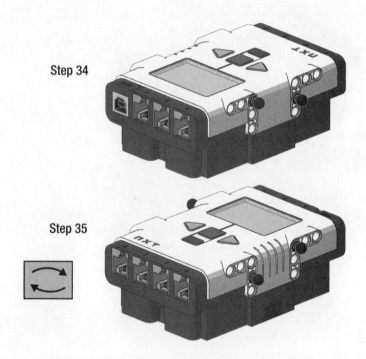

Here you are building the NXT subassembly that forms the hump.

Step 36

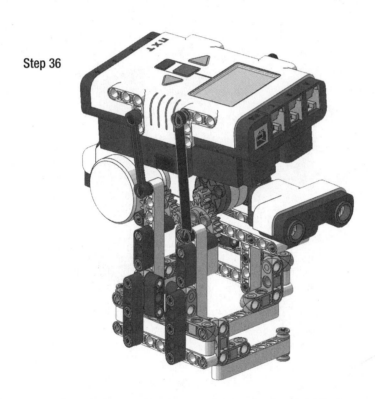

Put the NXT on the robot's top and attach two hip tendons to the right leg.

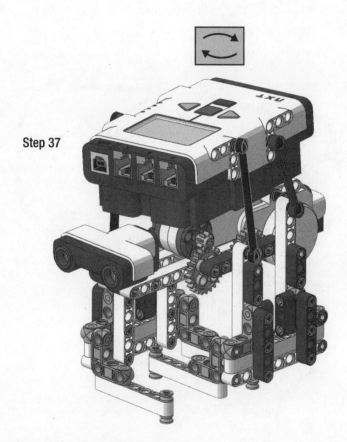

Step 37

Turn the model and attach the other two tendons.

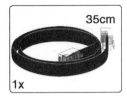

Step 38

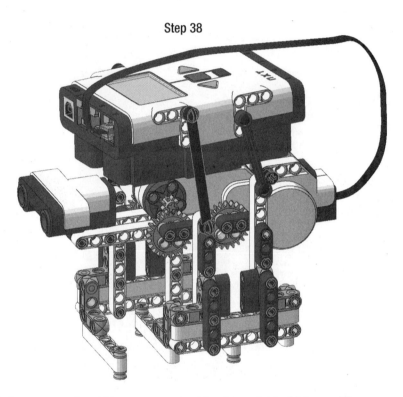

Connect the motor to the NXT output port A with a 35cm (14 inch) long cable.

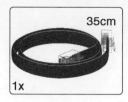

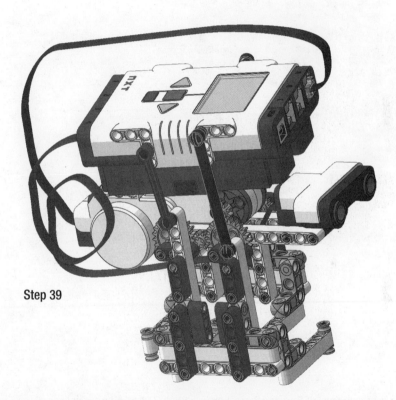

Step 39

Connect the Ultrasonic Sensor NXT input port 4 with a 35cm (14 inch) cable. Try to make the cable pass between the main body beams, as shown.

A view of the robot's back, showing the sensor cable attachment

Here you can see how Quasimodo looks once completed.

Summary

You've made it through the first chapter with building instructions. You should feel satisfied—you've just built a biped that uses many of the techniques described in Chapter 1. This robot is representative of the first category I discussed in this book: interlacing legs bipeds. In addition, I've also given you the first smattering of NXC programming. Not so scary, is it? After learning some more theory in Chapter 3, you'll be able to build and program a scale-sized replica of the imperial AT-ST in Chapter 4: the All Terrain Scout Transport walker from the *Star Wars* saga.

■ ■ ■

Finite State Machines

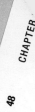

Most simple robots don't show much interesting behavior. Usually, a sequential program flow regulates their actions: the robot walks until it sees an obstacle, it backs up and turns, and then starts walking forward again in a loop.

What do you do if you desire more interesting behavior? How would you give your creature a spark of life, by making it act as if it had its own motivations?

Finite state machines (FSMs) provide the answers to the preceding questions. FSMs are a software technique that you can use to model simple behavior for robots. I'll briefly discuss these FSMs in theory and then you'll apply your understanding in a practical example. Later in this chapter, I'll show you a general way to implement such FSMs. The NXT Turtle in Chapter 6, as well as JohnNXT in Chapter 8, use this technique to feature autonomous behaviors. Finally, you'll learn an elegant implementation of a particular kind of FSM—decision tables.

Finite State Machines in Brief

Let me introduce a bit of the theory behind FSMs. I promise I'll be brief; however, some definition is needed here for you to understand what you'll put in practice later.

A *finite state machine* or *finite state automaton* (plural *automata*) is a model of behavior composed of a finite number of internal states (or simply states), the transitions between these states, the set of events that can occur, and actions performed. The internal state describes the machine's situation, based on past events or actual input signals, thus reflecting the history of what happened from system startup until now. However, in some simple cases, all the things we should know about the machine's past are condensed in just the last state. The state transitions are not physically tangible: when an event occurs in a certain state, the variable that represents the state changes accordingly. When events cause state changes, our particular FSM is called *event-driven*. The actions the machine performs in its different states determine its visible behavior. Therefore, the most expressive way to represent FSMs is the *state diagram*, as shown in Figure 3-1.

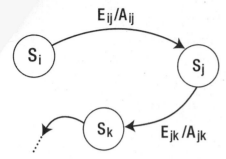

Figure 3-1. *A general FSM diagram*

The circles (nodes) with a name inside represent the states (S_i, S_j, and S_k in Figure 3-1). The oriented arcs going from one state to another represent the transitions between these states. Arcs are marked with the pairs E_{ij}/A_{ij} and E_{jk}/A_{jk}, where E_{jk} is the event that caused the state transition from state *j* to *k*. A_{jk} is the action to be performed (reflected by a change of an external state of output) before changing the internal state.

Notice that the arcs can also close back on the actual state (see S_k), meaning that it is not compulsory to change state while doing external (visible) actions (A_{k1},...,A_{kn}). The automaton will remain in the same state, as shown in Figure 3-2.

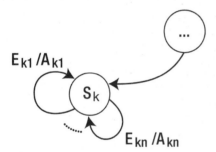

Figure 3-2. *An FSM with many transitions closing back to the same state*

We'll focus on the description of machines' simple behaviors using these automata. You might wonder how these kinds of automata would work in your everyday life. For example, think about an elevator in a building of n floors. In this case, the state contains information about the floor f where the elevator is, and the busy state b (running=1/still=0) x = [f,b], where f = {0,1,2,...,n} and b = {0,1}. When people call the elevator to a floor by pushing the button, an event e is generated, where e = {0,1,2,...,n} containing the floor number. The elevator ignores the event if it is already running (b flag equal to 1); otherwise it will go up or down according to the actual floor and the event: the actions of our system are {go up, go down}. For example, if the state is x=[1,0] and the event was generated from a request on floor 2, the elevator will go up; if it was called from floor 0, it will go down one floor.

Now you should have the background to understand the following example.

Saturating Counter

Now, I'll show you a simple FSM: a saturating counter. This example is useless for making a robot live and enjoy its artificial life, but don't worry—we'll work on something more "robotic" and useful later in the book. For the time being though, a saturating counter is a counter that stops counting when it reaches its bounds. You certainly can implement this without summoning FSMs, but I'll do it this way, because it serves as a basic clear example. The state diagram for this automaton is shown in Figure 3-3.

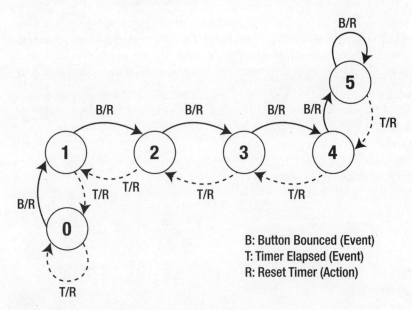

Figure 3-3. *The state diagram of a saturating counter*

In this example, if the user clicks a button, the counter will increment one unit until it reaches five, but if there is no input from the user within a certain timeout, the counter will decrement one unit at a time until zero, and remains there until the user starts clicking the button again.

Inside the circles, as shown in Figure 3-3, you can see the state names that are just numbers from 0 to 5. On the arcs, there are the labels describing the events (T, B) and the actions (R). Figure 3-3 shows that every state can have more than one transition to other states: as many outgoing arcs as the number of the events possible in that state.

Our counter can count up to five (to keep the whole thing small), but we could easily go beyond this limit. When the system starts, the FSM is in state 0 (this is the *entry state*). When the event T (the timer elapsing) occurs in state 0, the state remains the same (the transition arc closes back on state 0) and the timer is reset. In all the states, the clicking of the orange button (the event called B) can cause a transition to the next-numbered state together with a timer reset action. The state 5 is an exception, because more button clicks cause only the timer to reset, but the state remains the same. The other event T can cause transitions to a lower-numbered state—back to state 0, in which more timer elapsing does not change the state, as previously mentioned.

All the intense activity described here could happen with no external visual feedback, but where would the fun be? So, the program that implements this FSM provides visual feedback showing the state transitions, with a level meter made of a bar of black squares. This bar shows what state the FSM is in. See the code for the main task of the saturating counter program in Listing 3-1.

Listing 3-1. *The Main Task of the FSM Example*

```
task main()
{
    short state = STATE_0;  //entry state
    short event;
    while(true)
    {
        switch(state)
        {
            case STATE_0:
                ClearScreen();
                //wait for events
                event = WaitEvent();
                if (event == TOUCH) state = STATE_1;
                if (event == TIMER_ELAPSE) state = STATE_0;
                ResetTimer();
                break;
            case STATE_1:
                ClearScreen();
                Meter(1);
                event = WaitEvent();
                if (event == TOUCH) state = STATE_2;
                if (event == TIMER_ELAPSE) state = STATE_0;
                ResetTimer();
                break;
            case STATE_2:
                ClearScreen();
                Meter(2);
                event = WaitEvent();
                if (event == TOUCH) state = STATE_3;
                if (event == TIMER_ELAPSE) state = STATE_1;
                ResetTimer();
```

```
            break;
        case STATE_3:
            ClearScreen();
            Meter(3);
            event = WaitEvent();
            if (event == TOUCH) state = STATE_4;
            if (event == TIMER_ELAPSE) state = STATE_2;
            ResetTimer();
            break;
        case STATE_4:
            ClearScreen();
            Meter(4);
            event = WaitEvent();
            if (event == TOUCH) state = STATE_5;
            if (event == TIMER_ELAPSE) state = STATE_3;
            ResetTimer();
            break;
        case STATE_5:
            ClearScreen();
            Meter(5);
            event = WaitEvent();
            if (event == TOUCH) state = STATE_5;
            if (event == TIMER_ELAPSE) state = STATE_4;
            ResetTimer();
            break;
        }
    Wait(100);
    }
}
```

■Note The constants STATE_0, STATE_1, and so on that you find in the program are just aliases defined at
the top of the program using the preprocessor directive #define STATE_0 0. The aliases mean that when
the compiler finds STATE_0 later in the program, it will view it as if it were the number 0. It is not essential,
but it's a commonly used practice in programming to write constants with all capital letters.

An FSM code skeleton is a switch statement nested inside an infinite loop. The switch
variable is the state variable itself (called—no surprise—state); it's the variable that contains
the actual state value (defined at the top of the program).

In our example, the states have unimaginative names; for every state we find a case <value>:
label. The code to be executed in this state is included between the case <value>: label and
the break statement.

■**Tip** The switch statement is equivalent to a series of if/else statements, resulting in more efficient compiled code. The break keyword makes the program flow out of the switch statement body once the part of code that's of interest has been executed. Consult the NXC Programming Guide for details.

The code can perform output actions, and also change the internal state, by simply assigning a new value (among the ones defined in the program) to the state variable. Confused? Let's see an example, say state 4, in detail.

```
case STATE_4:
    Meter(4);
    event = WaitEvent();
    if (event == TOUCH) state = STATE_5;
    if (event == TIMER_ELAPSE) state = STATE_3;
    ResetTimer();
    break;
```

At the actual loop iteration, the switch(state) brought us to the case labeled STATE_4. This means that in the previous loop iteration, the state variable was assigned the STATE_4 value. The whole switch body is equivalent to this:

```
while(true)
{
    if (state == 0) //case STATE_0
    {
        //do something in state 0
    } //break
    else if (state==1)
    {
        //do something in state 1
    } //break
    else if (state==2)
    {
        //do something in state 2
    } //break
    [...]
    //as many states as you want
}
```

First, you invoke the Meter(4) function to draw a bar with four black squares on the NXT display (the code of the Meter function is in Listing 3-3), then you use the WaitEvent() function to wait for the timer to elapse or for the button to be clicked (pressed and released). This function returns a value to let the main task know which event occurred.

■**Note** I omit here and later, on purpose, the code to read and reset the timer, to focus your attention better on the current topic. You'll learn how to use the timer in Chapter 6, on the NXT Turtle.

If the timer had elapsed, the state variable would be assigned the value of the lower STATE_3 (remember we are in state 4). But if the button was clicked, the next state would be the highest, STATE_5. At this point, the timer is reset and the program flow breaks out the switch, ready for another ride. On the next loop, the switch statement executes the code corresponding to the case labeled with the value just assigned to the state variable.

In Figure 3-4, you can see the two transitions described in the last paragraph: both the transition from state 4 to 5 (the button was pressed), and the transition from state 4 back to state 3 (the timer has elapsed).

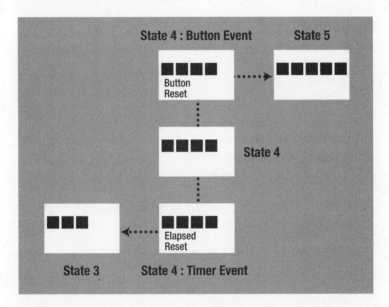

Figure 3-4. *Some NXT display outputs of the saturating counter*

The program starts with a blank screen; if you don't do anything, you'll see the message "Elapse—Reset" flashing periodically. This means you are in state 0, and when the timer elapses, it is reset, while the state remains at 0.

If you try clicking the NXT orange button quickly (the interval between two clicks has to be less than the program-defined timeout), you'll see the number of squares increase. The message "Button—Reset" indicates that action R (see Figure 3-3) is performed, as a result of a button click event B. When in state 5, pressing frequently on the button maintains the counter in its top state. If you stop pressing the button, the bar decreases every time the timer elapses, back to state 0.

The NXC language and NXT firmware don't manage events directly (using interrupts), so you can implement waiting for events with the WaitEvent() function (see Listing 3-2).

Listing 3-2. *The WaitEvent() Function Code*

```
short WaitEvent()
{
   short event = 0;
```

```
    while ( event==0 )
    {
        if (ButtonPressed(BTNCENTER,true)==1)
        {
            event = TOUCH;
            while(ButtonPressed(BTNCENTER,true)==1);
            TextOut(5,LCD_LINE6,"Button");
            break;
        }
        else if (CurrentTick() > time_offset + TIMEOUT)
        {
            event = TIMER_ELAPSE;
            TextOut(5,LCD_LINE6,"Elapse");
            break;
        }
    }
    return event;
}
```

The WaitEvent() function waits for two kinds of events: for the timer to elapse and for someone to click the orange button. It polls continuously whether the orange button has been clicked or if the timer has run out; when one of these events has occurred (the event variable is assigned a value other than 0), the function returns a different number (the constants TOUCH or TIMER_ELAPSE) according to the event that occurred.

Before going forward, as a curiosity, look at Listing 3-3, which draws the bar on the NXT screen.

Listing 3-3. *The Code to Draw a Bar of Filled Squares on the NXT Display*

```
sub Meter(short level)
{
    ClearScreen();
    for(short i=0; i<level; i++) //draw filled rectangles
    {
        //RectOut(MARGIN+OFFSET*i,LCD_LINE4,LENGTH,LENGTH,false);
        for (short j=0; j<=LENGTH; j++)
        {
            LineOut(MARGIN+OFFSET*i+j,LCD_LINE4,MARGIN+OFFSET*i+j,LCD_LINE4+LENGTH);
        }
    }
}
```

The NXC language provides us with many high-level graphic functions to exploit all the NXT screen capabilities. For example, we can use the RectOut function inside a for loop to draw the number of empty squares specified by level, or we can use the LineOut function inside a nested for loop to get a square filled with black pixels. You can obtain filled squares by drawing as many lines as the length of the square. On the other hand, by removing the comment on the RectOut function line and commenting out the nested for loop, you can draw empty squares, thus speeding up the NXT screen redrawing.

FSM General Implementation

Now that you have seen a particular FSM implementation, you might wonder how to program
any FSM you like. I'll explain that after the skeleton code in Listing 3-4.

Listing 3-4. *General Structure to Implement an FSM*

```
task main()
{
   //Initialization of hardware and state variables
   //main exits, leaving space in scheduler for other tasks
}

//sensor monitoring tasks
task SensorMonitor()
{
   Follows(main);  //tells the NXT to execute this task after the main has exited
   while(true)
   {
      //read sensors
      //modify global variables to make state transitions
   }
}

task FSM()
{
   Follows(main);  //tells the NXT to execute this task after the main has exited
   while(true)
   {
      switch ( state )
      {
         case STATE_ONE:
            //actions to be performed in this state

            //the state transition is made
            //assigning a new value to the state variable
            state = ANOTHER_STATE;
            break;

         case STATE_TWO:

   [...]

            break;

         case STATE_THREE:

   [...]
```

```
        break;

    //put how many states you want

    }
  }
}
```

In the code in Listing 3-4, the main task simply performs sensor and variable initialization, and then exits, leaving the execution to all the other tasks. You could use separate tasks to monitor the sensors continuously, to refresh the NXT display, and to run the FSM itself. In a more general situation than the one in the saturating counter example, a program that implements an FSM can be composed of more tasks running simultaneously.

Note You'll learn about multitasking programs in Chapter 5, when I discuss the Omni-Biped software.

The sensor-monitoring tasks would communicate with the FSM task by using global variables, via function calls, or by passing variables as arguments. The most important task is the one implementing the FSM: the whole behavior of our FSM is in fact coded inside this task.

My purpose was just to whet your appetite; I won't show any other example here. I'll discuss an FSM implementation in detail in the program for the NXT Turtle, described in Chapter 6.

Decision Tables

For completeness, a final topic remains to be explained. For example, consider the problem pictured in Figure 3-5. You have a motorized arm that can swivel around by a maximum of 90 degrees. At the lower limit of its run, it has a limit switch, so that the arm can be brought to its zero position at every system startup. The arm has only four allowed positions, or states:

- 0: full down (limit switch pressed)

- 1: down

- 2: mid

- 3: up

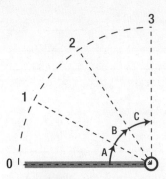

Figure 3-5. *The robotic arm of the decision table example*

Now, let the angle between state 0 and 1 be A, the one between 1 and 2 be B, and the last between 2 and 3 be C. You would want to move the arm around these allowed states, having as a sensor only the servomotor's internal encoder. You can use the limit switch, which is pressed when the arm is in state 0, to reset the incremental encoder. This encoder is a sensor built inside the NXT servomotors, and is called incremental (or relative): it can measure the shaft angle relative to program startup or to a software reset command, although it cannot measure angles with respect to an absolute reference position. Every time the system is turned on, the encoder does not know the motor shaft position relative to a world reference system. The encoder starts measuring the shaft relative position from the startup angle, in a relative way. In our example, we want to measure the arm angle using as a reference the downmost position, corresponding to the state 0. So, at the beginning of the program, we have to bring the arm down until the limit switch is closed; when the arm is in this downmost position, we can issue a reset command for the encoder.

Now you know the hardware framework. The problem is how to write a piece of software to move the arm between any two states of the allowed ones. For example, knowing that the arm is in state 0 and wanting to reach state 3, you should rotate the arm by an angle equal to A+B+C. To move from state 2 to 1, the arm should be rotated by an angle equal to –B. Finally, to go from state 2 to 0, the angle should be –A–B.

You can implement the solution to this problem as an FSM in many ways, by using the common NXC control flow structures if–then–else or switch–case. If there are 4 allowed states, as shown in this simple example, you should write a total of 16 different functions to go from any state to another—taking also into account the cases in which you move from a state to come back to itself. This can be at least tiring, not to mention tricky and messy.

This is why *decision tables* were created. Decision tables are a precise, compact, and elegant way to model complicated logic. You use them to associate conditions (the actual state) with actions to perform.

For the preceding example, the decision table contains the angles by which the servomotor must rotate to move the arm from the actual state to the new state. The system knows that the initial state is 0, after you've brought the arm to its zero position by using the limit switch. You can write the decision table as shown in Table 3-1.

Table 3-1. *The Decision Table to Manage the Robotic Arm*

New State	0	1	2	3
State				
0	0	A	A+B	A+B+C
1	-A	0	B	B+C
2	-A-B	-B	0	C
3	-A-B-C	-B-C	-C	0

Obviously, if the new state is the same as the actual state, the angle is null. Also, the actions are reversible. So, the angle to go, say, from state 3 to 0, is the opposite of the one to go from 0 to 3. The table is thus anti-symmetric, with the diagonal filled with zeroes.

Practical examples of decision tables are in the AT-ST program to control the legs and the head position, and in JohnNXT to move the head, the arms, the torso, and the laser. Yes, every JohnNXT moving part (except the treads) is regulated by its own state variable, by using these decision tables.

Summary

In this chapter, you got a smattering of information about FSMs: theoretic models used to give robots a simple behavior. I've analyzed the situation focusing on the aspects most relevant to our goals, and coupled the analysis with some practical examples. In the next chapter, you'll build the AT-ST biped, with leg movements and general behaviors that are regulated with FSMs and decision tables.

CHAPTER 4

■■■

NXT AT-ST

Also known as "chicken walker," because of its shape and walking motion, the All Terrain Scout Transport (AT-ST) is a bipedal war craft employed by the Galactic Imperial Forces in the *Star Wars* saga.

In this chapter, you'll build the AT-ST biped shown in Figure 4-1, guided by detailed building instructions. You'll program it to walk around, and by the end of this chapter, you'll have at your command one of the most famous battle robots in the history of cinema.

Figure 4-1. *The impressive-looking NXT AT-ST*

Design Thoughts

AT-STs were seen in the *Star Wars* movies in the Battle of Hoth in *The Empire Strikes Back* and the Battle of Endor in *Return of the Jedi*. The AT-ST has chin-mounted double laser cannons, a concussion grenade launcher on the right side of its head, and a blaster cannon on the left. The bipedal propulsion system is the strength of the *Star Wars* AT-ST, allowing it to move its weaponry across uneven terrain that a wheeled unit would not be able to traverse. This craft can carry one pilot and one gunner, with a maximum speed of 90km/h. Even though it's not as imposing as its larger All Terrain Armored Transport (AT-AT) quadruped walker cousin, the AT-ST serves as a sort of robotic cavalry to the Imperial side on the battlefields of the *Star Wars* films.

The NXT AT-ST walker shown in Figures 4-1 and 4-2 is mainly built with NXT retail set parts, but includes a few extra parts, needed just to improve the design. These additional parts aren't structural, so don't worry if you don't have them in your LEGO spare reserves. You'll be guided in how to build the alternative retail-set-only version in the building section of this chapter.

Figure 4-2. *Another view of the NXT AT-ST*

I tried hard to reproduce all the AT-ST features in a well-proportioned way, from the particular leg shape to the head profile. As you might guess, the robot you're going to build cannot move across uneven terrain; on the contrary, the surface to walk on must be smooth and plain. Also, the robot cannot carry humans and won't hurt anybody, because the weapons have been replaced by the Sound Sensor and the Ultrasonic Sensor.

This model wasn't designed in a day! It was difficult to get to the final shape. In Figure 4-3, you can see the AT-ST in one of its early stages of development. The legs were not at all similar to the final ones, and the head was disproportionate. On both feet, I used a Touch Sensor to know which side the robot was leaning on; this feature proved to be useless in the final robot version due to a new, timed approach. Also, notice the tendon made with the ball joint steering link that prevents the hip from bending (as in Quasimodo in Chapter 2). Although a bit raw, this old prototype already featured all the key ideas that brought me to the final AT-ST presented here.

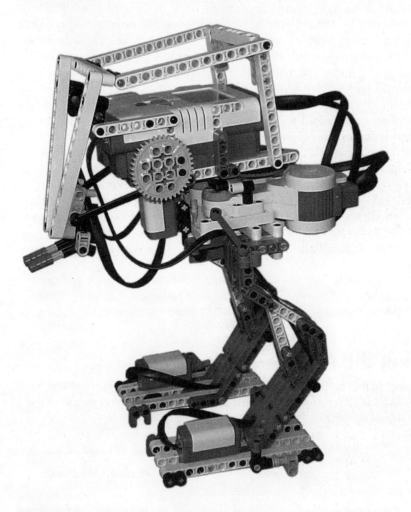

Figure 4-3. *An early prototype of the NXT AT-ST*

This LEGO MINDSTORMS biped perfectly fits in the jerky COG shifting category introduced in Chapter 1. It uses only two motors to accomplish the needed movements, while other robots fitting in this category, which you might have seen on the Web, generally use three motors. Here, one motor shifts the weight (mostly concentrated in the head) by turning the neck turntable, while the other motor rotates the legs in sync, as shown in the plan back in Figure 1-4*b*. Because these movements are done one after another, the gait of this biped is jerky.

Using only two motors allowed me to lighten the whole structure a bit, so that the legs of the AT-ST, accurately reproduced in all their slimness, could support the upper body weight. You can understand what I mean here by "accurately" by looking at Figure 1-5*c* in Chapter 1. The AT-ST I made with the RCX had squat, boxy legs, not at all similar to the real leg shape or the elegance of the legs of the actual NXT version.

I tried to keep the feet as small as possible, always bearing in mind, however, that small feet yield poor stability. On the internal side of both feet, I placed two wedges that are the only touch point of the feet when the head is perfectly centered. When the head turns to the side, only one of the feet will touch the ground with the wedges and with the external rubber edge. If the feet were totally flat (entirely touching the ground), the AT-ST would have needed another mechanism to bend the ankles. With this solution, the legs can be made strong and rigid, because they have no moving joints. The robot walks straight by shifting the head weight aside and suddenly stepping forward, when the loaded foot is touching the ground with wedges and rubber elements, and the other is off the ground.

Turning is a little more complicated, and the performance might vary according to the nature of the surface the robot is walking on. Carpets are the worst surface you can imagine, while flat, smooth surfaces such as tables or parquet are perfect. For example, let me explain how the robot turns right. First, it rotates the legs while they are both on the ground (the head is centered), so that the right foot is in front of the left one. Then, the weight is shifted to the right, and the left foot is suddenly brought forward to get aligned with the right foot again. Repeating this many times, the AT-ST can turn right; and, doing the opposite, it can turn left. This can sound complicated, but don't worry if you don't have a clear understanding of what is going on here. Once you see the robot walking, driven by the program you'll learn later, all the confusion will melt away.

The head contains all the sensors: the side weapons are the Sound Sensor and the Ultrasonic Sensor. A Touch Sensor is used to detect if the head has reached its turning limits; this sensor is hidden (not so well, actually!) under the AT-ST face.

Programming the AT-ST

The program discussed in this section gives your robot the ability to walk everywhere, by avoiding obstacles. Download the sound files provided, together with the source code, to the NXT using BricxCC, so that the NXT can play them.

■**Tip** You can find the files in the Source Code/Download area on the Apress web site at http://www. apress.com. Use Appendix A as a guide for downloading files to the NXT.

When you start the AT-ST program, it aligns the legs and the head in the center. Then the AT-ST starts walking straight as described earlier, until it sees an obstacle. At this point, it produces a twin-laser sound, it chooses a random turning direction, and starts steering. It should turn changing its direction by about 90 degrees, although this depends on the slipperiness of the surface it is walking on. Then it starts walking straight, as before.

"Again? Another walker with obstacle avoidance?" you say. Well, again: having well-performing hardware doesn't mean that making it work well is easy. Therefore, here I'll focus attention on the routines that manage the mechanical parts to allow the robot to walk correctly. This is not at all a trivial issue, especially concerning the right timing of the motor movements. Also, the legs and the head orientation are regulated by FSMs. So, this is the perfect occasion to see in practice what you read about in the previous chapter. Once you have this core software ready to work, you can adapt the program to do anything you want—even control the robot remotely.

As with any NXC program, the declaration of all the constants and macros used in the program appears at the top of the code, shown in Listing 4-1.

■**Note** A *macro* is an operation defined inside a #define directive. Before the NXC compiler starts to translate your code into instructions readable by the NXT processor, the NXC preprocessor expands the macro as follows. If the macro has no arguments, such as #define NEAR 20, the preprocessor will replace NEAR with the constant 20 every time it encounters the word NEAR. If the macro has arguments, such as #define TWO_TIMES(x) 2*(x), then the argument x will be replaced with the argument inside the brackets of a call, such as y = TWO_TIMES(3). So, the preceding will be expanded into y = 2*(3), storing the result 6 inside the variable y. Notice that you could also call y = TWO_TIMES(3+4), which would be expanded into y = 2*(3+4), yielding 14. If you omitted the parentheses in the macro, the expression would be wrongly translated as y = 2*3+4, yielding 10 as a wrong result. Writing macros in all capital letters isn't strictly required, but it is a useful convention. When you see a word with all capital letters, it is probably defined as a macro.

Listing 4-1. *The AT-ST Program Definitions*

```
#define TOUCH IN_3 //short cable
#define SONAR  IN_1 //mid cable
#define MIC IN_4 //mid_cable
#define LEGS OUT_C
#define HEAD OUT_A

#define NEAR 20
#define LEFT 0
#define CENTER 1
#define RIGHT 2
#define TURN_RIGHT 1
#define TURN_LEFT -1
#define WALK 0
#define STOP 5

#define OBSTACLE (SensorUS(SONAR)<NEAR)
```

The main task code is shown in Listing 4-2.

Listing 4-2. *The main Task Code of the AT-ST Program, After Declaring Global Variables*

```
// global variables
int weightState, legsState, runState;
[...]
task main ()
{
   ATST_init();
   int action;

   while (true) {

      if(OBSTACLE)
         runState = 1-2*(Random(2)); // 1, -1
      else
         runState = WALK;

      switch(runState) {
         case TURN_RIGHT:
            TurnRight(9);
            break;
         case TURN_LEFT:
            TurnLeft(9);
            break;
         case WALK:
            GoStraight();
            break;
      }
      CenterHead();
      CenterLegs();
   }
}
```

Outside every task, function, or subroutine, you see three *global* variables declared; every function in the program can access these variables. By contrast, a variable declared inside a function (for example the action variable inside the main task) is called *local* and can be used only by the function inside which it is declared. If any other function tries to use that local variable inside its body, it would cause a compiler error. In fact, the compiler would complain about the presence of an Undefined Identifier action, because it would not know what action is.

At the start, the ATST_init() function is called to perform hardware initialization; in this case, to tell the NXT where each sensor is attached and to reset the head and the legs to their zero position. These operations are not trivial, as you will see later. Next, the program enters an infinite loop, as was the case for Quasimodo (see Chapter 2). Inside this loop, the whole basic AT-ST behavior is expressed. Let's analyze the code by breaking it into smaller chunks:

```
if(OBSTACLE)
    runState = 1-2*(Random(2)); // 1, -1
else
    runState = WALK;
```

With if(OBSTACLE), we're checking if the Ultrasonic Sensor is detecting an obstacle. Well, this could be clear already, but how is it done? OBSTACLE is a macro defined previously as follows:

```
#define OBSTACLE (SensorUS(SONAR)<NEAR)
```

This is a common handy way to have a piece of code replaced by an easier-to-remember macro. Every time the compiler meets this constant OBSTACLE later in the program, it will replace it completely with (SensorUS(SONAR)<NEAR).

Note SONAR is another alias that stands for IN_1: the input port constant to which the Ultrasonic Sensor is attached.

So, if(OBSTACLE) becomes if(SensorUS(SONAR)<NEAR) for the compiler, after the preprocessor has finished its work. If the Ultrasonic Sensor reading is less than NEAR (another constant with the value of 20), then the runState variable will be assigned a random value that can be 1 or -1 (corresponding to the right or left direction). Otherwise, it will be assigned the constant value 0 (WALK). The function Random(2) returns a random value that can be 0 or 1. So, runState = 1-2*(Random(2)) assigns the runState variable a value that can be 1-2*(0) = 1 or 1-2*(1) = -1.

Tip The Random(n) function returns a random number between 0 and n-1.

The switch statement then uses the runState variable to decide what to do: to turn right or left, whether runState has the TURN_RIGHT or TURN_LEFT value, or to go straight if it corresponds to WALK. In the turning functions, the number inside the brackets indicates how many times the turning movement pattern must be repeated. If the AT-ST decides to walk straight, it will stop only when it detects an object. After the walk, in whichever direction, the CenterWeight() and CenterLegs() subroutines realign the head and legs.

Now that you know all about the basic behavior of the AT-ST, it's time to see what's inside the subroutines to realign the head and the legs. Let's dissect them by looking at Listing 4-3, for the leg-centering subroutine.

Listing 4-3. *The CenterLegs Subroutine*

```
sub CenterLegs()
{
    int t;
    t = MotorRotationCount(LEGS); //save actual position
    OnFwd(LEGS,65);
```

```
        Wait(100);
        // if position does not change more than specified angle in specified time
        while( abs(t-MotorRotationCount(LEGS))>10 )
        {
            t = MotorRotationCount(LEGS);
            Wait(100);
        }
        Off(LEGS);
        RotateMotor(LEGS,50,-120);
        Wait(200);
        legsState = CENTER;
}
```

The legs have no evident sensor to let the NXT know which direction they are oriented in. Don't forget, we aren't working with mere motors. The NXT motors contain optical encoders to measure the shaft's relative angle. Thus, all the sensors we need are already inside the motors. The motor's actual angle is saved into the variable t and the motor is started to orient the legs to the left. How can you know if the legs have reached their limit position? Here, I adopted a trick to measure the motor shaft's speed: after the motor has started, the NXT continuously checks if the motor shaft is rotating to a minimum number of degrees (10) in a certain period of time (100ms). The small angle and the time interval were chosen appropriately for the application. What I said in words can be translated into this code:

```
while( abs(t-MotorRotationCount(LEGS))>10 )
{
    t = MotorRotationCount(LEGS);   //update starting angle
    Wait(100);   //wait 100ms
}
```

While the angle of the shaft varies more than 10 degrees in the time interval of 100ms, the program doesn't stop the motor. However, if the motor cannot accomplish this angle in this little bit of time, it means that the legs are stopped by something and the motor is stalling, so it is turned off. The shaft speed is measured every 100ms as the difference between the angle stored in the variable t and the angle measured time by time with the MotorRotationCount() function.

Note Measuring an increment of a shaft angle inside a time window means measuring the shaft's speed; in fact <speed> = <angle increment>/<time>, $s = \Delta a/t$. This effective technique is frequently used in robotics but has no common name. Let me give it a pompous name: servomotors automagic built-in limit switch!

Now that the legs are posed in a known direction, you can bring them to their center position with RotateMotor(LEGS,50,-120), where 120 is the measured number of degrees to rotate the legs from the left direction to the center. The legs are now realigned! Let's see how to center the head, where we have a Touch Sensor, by looking at Listing 4-4.

Listing 4-4. *The Subroutine to Center the Head*

```
sub CenterHead ()
{
   #define CNT_SPEED  50
      OnFwd(HEAD,CNT_SPEED);   //bring the head to the right
      Wait(400);
      Off(HEAD);

      if (Sensor(TOUCH)) //head was already at right or center
      {
         OnRev(HEAD,CNT_SPEED);
         while (Sensor(TOUCH));
         Off(HEAD);
         RotateMotor(HEAD,CNT_SPEED,-30);
      }

      else if (!Sensor(touch)) //head was already at left
      {
         OnRev(HEAD,CNT_SPEED);
         until (Sensor(TOUCH));
         Off(HEAD);
         RotateMotor(HEAD,CNT_SPEED,60);
      }

   weightState = CENTER;
}
```

Reading the Touch Sensor only tells you if the head is turned completely to the right or to the left (sensor closed), but gives you no information about the actual head direction. This is not at all a subtle difference; we only know if the head is turned, but not in which direction! Here, only clever programming can get us out of the trouble. Read on carefully to see how, remembering Listing 4-4.

At the beginning, the head is rotated to the right by the motor, without checking the sensor yet. Only after that can the program check whether the Touch Sensor is closed or not. If it is closed, that means the head is now at the right (the initial turning brought it here). In this case, the motor turns the head to the left until the sensor opens again; it stops and turns a little more to compensate for the remaining constant offset to get to the exact center.

If the Touch Sensor is open after the first "blind" turn, we assume (being right!) that the head was initially pointed left. In this case, the motor turns the head to the left until the sensor is closed and the head has reached the full left side, and stops. The last `RotateMotor(HEAD,CNT_SPEED,60)` brings the head to the center from the leftmost known position. Whew, we did it!

Only the functions to make the AT-ST step and lean aside remain to be covered. ("Only" is just a manner of speaking, of course.) These apparently simple routines are worth a lot of attention and explanation. The subroutine to rotate the head implements an FSM using the `if-then-else` statements, while the other subroutine that moves the legs adopts a decision table (explained in Chapter 3) to make the code cleaner and more elegant. Let's deal with the first subroutine right now. Take a look at Listing 4-5, which enables the AT-ST to lean aside, turning the head left and right.

Listing 4-5. *The Code to Lean the Head*

```
sub Lean (int newState)
{
   if ( weightState != newState )
   {

      if (weightState==CENTER) //head is at center
      {
         if (newState==RIGHT) OnFwd (HEAD,LEAN_SPEED);
         if (newState==LEFT) OnRev (HEAD,LEAN_SPEED);
         until (Sensor(TOUCH));
         Off (HEAD);
      }

      if (weightState==LEFT)  //head is at left
      {
         if (newState==CENTER)
         {
            OnFwd(HEAD,LEAN_SPEED);
            while (Sensor(TOUCH));
            Off(HEAD);
            RotateMotor(HEAD,LEAN_SPEED,40);
         }
         if (newState==RIGHT)
         {
            OnFwd(HEAD,LEAN_SPEED);
            while (Sensor(TOUCH));
            until (Sensor(TOUCH));
            Off(HEAD);
         }
      }

      if (weightState==RIGHT) //head is at right
      {
         if (newState==CENTER)
         {
            OnRev(HEAD,LEAN_SPEED);
            while (Sensor(touch));
            Off(HEAD);
            RotateMotor(HEAD,LEAN_SPEED,-30);
         }
```

```
        if (newState==LEFT)
        {
            OnRev(HEAD,LEAN_SPEED);
            while (Sensor(TOUCH));
            until (Sensor(TOUCH));
            Off(HEAD);
        }
    }
    weightState = newState;
  }
}
```

The new desired position for the head is passed on as the newState argument to the Lean subroutine. If newState is equal to weightState (the state variable that keeps track of the head position), nothing has to be done because the head is already in the desired position. If not equal, different actions are performed according to the new state passed to the subroutine. To get the center from a known side, the motor turns until the Touch Sensor is cleared. To lean aside (say to the left), the program checks if the head is actually right or centered. If it is to the right, the Touch Sensor is pressed and the motor turns until the sensor is cleared, and then is pressed again. You use a similar procedure to get to the right from the left.

Tip Using the weightState variable (and state variables in general) allows you to know the direction of the head without reading any sensor, by reading (and trusting) this variable instead.

Listing 4-6 shows the second subroutine to make your imposing AT-ST take steps.

Listing 4-6. *Making the AT-ST Take Steps*

```
sub Step(int newState, bool slow)
{
    int speed = 65;
    if(newState!=legsState)
    {
        if (slow) speed = 45;
        RotateMotorPID(LEGS,speed,legsAngles[newState+3*legsState],30,20,80);
        legsState = newState;
    }
}
```

■Note RotateMotorPID is an advanced version of the NXC function RotateMotor. The basic function is the same, except you can specify three additional parameters: P, I, and D. Leave them for now; we'll come back to them briefly in Chapter 7.

Here you can see a good example of implementing a decision table: a technique associated with FSMs, which you saw in theory in Chapter 3. In fact, the Step subroutine accepts as an argument the variable newState, which is used together with legsState (the variable that keeps track of the legs' state) to index the table legsAngles. Inside this table you find the appropriate angles to rotate legs from legsState to newState. A table can be viewed as an array with two dimensions—in other words, as a matrix. In NXC, you can declare multidimensional arrays. However, working with them is tricky and not worth the effort for this simple application, so it is preferable to implement the decision table as a single dimensional array. The legsAngles decision table and corresponding array declaration are shown in Table 4-1 and Listing 4-7.

Table 4-1. *legsAngles Decision Table with the Angles to Move the Legs*

	newState	LEFT	CENTER	RIGHT
oldState				
LEFT		0	-S	-2*S
CENTER		S	0	-S
RIGHT		2*S	S	0

Listing 4-7. *The Array Implementing Decision Table 4-1*

```
const int legsAngles[] = {       0      , -STEP_TURN, -2*STEP_TURN,
                           STEP_TURN,      0     ,  -STEP_TURN,
                         2*STEP_TURN,  STEP_TURN,      0       };
```

For example, if you want to go from LEFT (which oldState is equal to) to RIGHT (passed as the newState argument), you'd use this code:

```
RotateMotorPID(LEGS,speed,legsAngles[newState+3*legsState],30,20,80);
```

The preceding code rotates the legs' motor by the angle -2*STEP_TURN, which is found in the legsAngles table at row 0 (LEFT is defined as 0; see the program definitions at the beginning of this section) and column 2 (RIGHT is an alias for 2). To be clear, legsAngles is a one-dimensional array, indexed as follows:

legsAngles[column+3*row]

row and column can be 0, 1, or 2. In the case of this example, the index value is 2+3*0 = 2, and shows where to find the needed angle. You can see other example cases in Table 4-2.

Table 4-2. *Examples of How the Stepping Decision Table Works*

Old State	New State	Index Value	Corresponding Angle
LEFT(0)	CENTER(1)	index = 1+3*0 = 1	(-STEP_TURN)
CENTER(1)	RIGHT(2)	index = 2+3*1 = 5	(-STEP_TURN)
RIGHT(2)	LEFT(0)	index = 0+3*2 = 6	(2*STEP_TURN)
CENTER(1)	CENTER(1)	index = 1+3*1 = 4	(0), as one would expect

■**Caution** Array indexes are 0-based; for example, the first element of array is array[0], and the last element is at an index that equals ArrayLen(array)-1.

I find this solution cleaner and more elegant than using a nested if or a switch statement that would result in much messier code. Now you have an idea of how low-level routines (to manage AT-ST mechanics) work. This software represents the skeleton for any program you would write for your AT-ST, without having to worry about low-level mechanical management.

Building Your Personal AT-ST

Before you throw yourself into building a robot, you should read the following brief notes. To get the best robot appearance, I used some extra parts besides the NXT retail set parts. They aren't hard-to-find elements, and they're used just to embellish the model.

Don't worry; the robot's functionality is not compromised if you don't have these elements. Figure 4-4 shows the parts needed, and Table 4-3 points out which parts are not included in the retail set. Follow the instructions carefully to know which steps to skip and which parts to replace.

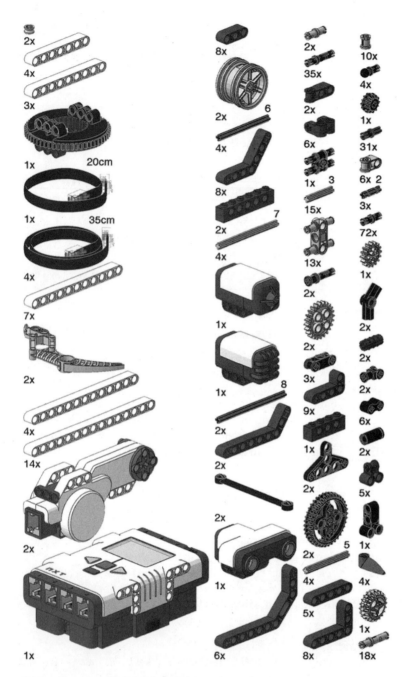

Figure 4-4. *NXT AT-ST bill of materials*

Table 4-3. *NXT AT-ST Bill of Materials*

Quantity	Color	Part Number	Part Name
4	White	32524.DAT	TECHNIC Beam 7
3	White	40490.DAT	TECHNIC Beam 9
1		4845x.DAT	TECHNIC Turntable New
1	Black	55804.DAT	Electric Cable NXT 20cm
4	Black	55805.DAT	Electric Cable NXT 35cm
7	White	32525.DAT	TECHNIC Beam 11
2	Light gray	50914.DAT	TECHNIC Bionicle Weapon Pincer Suukorak
4	White	41239.DAT	TECHNIC Beam 13
11	White	32278.DAT	TECHNIC Beam 15
2		53787.DAT	Electric MINDSTORMS NXT Motor
1		53788.DAT	Electric MINDSTORMS NXT
8	Dark gray	32523.DAT	TECHNIC Beam 3
4	Black	3706.DAT	TECHNIC Axle 6
8	Dark gray	32348.DAT	TECHNIC Beam 7 Liftarm Bent 53.5 (4:4)
2	Dark gray	3894.DAT	TECHNIC Brick 1 × 6 with Holes
4	Light gray	44294.DAT	TECHNIC Axle 7
1		55963.DAT	Electric MINDSTORMS NXT Sound Sensor
1-		53793.DAT	Electric MINDSTORMS NXT Touch Sensor
2	Black	3707.DAT	TECHNIC Axle 8
2	Dark gray	32271.DAT	TECHNIC Beam 9 Liftarm Bent 53.5 (7:3)
2	Black	32293.DAT	TECHNIC Steering Link 9L
1		56467.DAT	Electric MINDSTORMS NXT Ultrasonic Sensor
6	Dark gray	32009.DAT	TECHNIC Beam 11.5 Liftarm Bent 45 Double
2	Light gray	3673.DAT	TECHNIC Pin
33	Black	6558.DAT	TECHNIC Pin Long with Friction and Slot
2	Dark gray	42003.DAT	TECHNIC Axle Joiner Perpendicular with 2 Holes
6	Dark gray	41678.DAT	TECHNIC Axle Joiner Perpendicular Double Split
1	Black	32136.DAT	TECHNIC Pin 3L Double
11	Light gray	4519.DAT	TECHNIC Axle 3
13	Light gray	48989.DAT	TECHNIC Axle Joiner Perpendicular 1×3×3 with 4 Pins
2	Black	32054.DAT	TECHNIC Pin Long with Stop Bush
2	Light gray	3648.DAT	TECHNIC Gear 24 Tooth
3	Black	32184.DAT	TECHNIC Axle Joiner Perpendicular 3L
9	Dark gray	32140.DAT	TECHNIC Beam 5 Liftarm Bent 90 (4:2)

Continued

Table 4-3. *(Continued)*

Quantity	Color	Part Number	Part Name
1	Dark gray	3701.DAT	TECHNIC Brick 1 × 4 with Holes
2	Black	2905.DAT	TECHNIC Liftarm Triangle 5 × 3 × 0.5
1	Black	X344.DAT	TECHNIC Gear 36 Tooth Double Bevel
4	Light gray	32073.DAT	TECHNIC Axle 5
5	Dark gray	32316.DAT	TECHNIC Beam 5
1	Dark gray	32526.DAT	TECHNIC Beam 7 Bent 90 (5:3)
10	Light gray	3713.DAT	TECHNIC Bush
4	Black	6628.DAT	TECHNIC Friction Pin with Towball
1	Black	32270.DAT	TECHNIC Gear 12 Tooth Double Bevel
31	Blue	43093.DAT	TECHNIC Axle Pin with Friction
6	Light gray	6536.DAT	TECHNIC Axle Joiner Perpendicular
3	Black	32062.DAT	TECHNIC Axle 2 Notched
72	Black	2780.DAT	TECHNIC Pin with Friction and Slots
1	Light gray	4019.DAT	TECHNIC Gear 16 Tooth
2	Black	32192.DAT	TECHNIC Angle Connector #4 (135 degree)
2	Dark gray	6538B.DAT	TECHNIC Axle Joiner Offset
6	Black	45590.DAT	TECHNIC Axle Joiner Double Flexible
2	Black	75535.DAT	TECHNIC Pin Joiner Round
5	Dark gray	32291.DAT	TECHNIC Axle Joiner Perpendicular Double
1	Black	32557.DAT	TECHNIC Pin Joiner Dual Perpendicular
1	Light gray	32269.DAT	TECHNIC Gear 20 Tooth Double Bevel
10	Light gray	32556.DAT	TECHNIC Pin Long
2	Light gray	4185.DAT	TECHNIC Wedge Belt Wheel (replaces TECHNIC Gear 36 Tooth Double Bevel)

338 parts total (all included in NXT retail set)

PARTS FOR AESTHETIC ADD-ONS

Quantity	Color	Part Number	Part Name
2	Light gray	32123.DAT	TECHNIC Bush 1/2 Smooth
4	White	32278.DAT	TECHNIC Beam 15
2	Light gray	54087.DAT	Wheel 43.2 × 22 Without Pinholes
2	Black	6558.DAT	TECHNIC Pin Long with Friction and Slot
4	Light gray	4519.DAT	TECHNIC Axle 3
1	Black	X344.DAT	TECHNIC Gear 36 Tooth Double Bevel
2	Black	32039.DAT	TECHNIC Connector with Axlehole
8	Light gray	32556.DAT	TECHNIC Pin Long

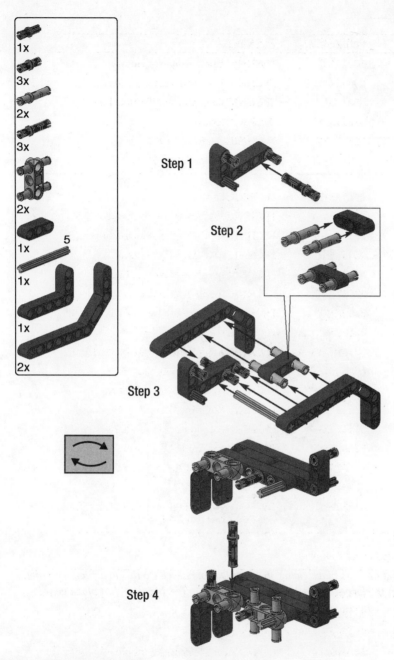

1x
3x
2x
3x
2x
1x   5
1x
1x
2x

Step 1

Step 2

Step 3

Step 4

Start building the left hip.

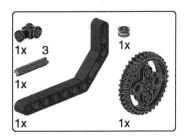

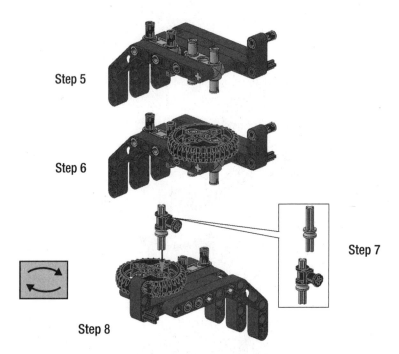

Step 5

Step 6

Step 7

Step 8

Skip Step 8 if you do not have two black Gears 36 Tooth Double Bevel. Do this to achieve symmetry. In fact, you can't mount the large decorative wheel in the other leg, because that black gear is replaced by two gray belt wheels.

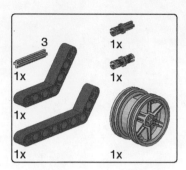

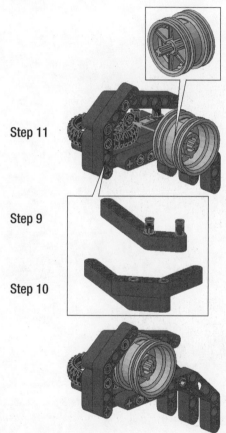

Step 11

Step 9

Step 10

Build the decorative parts of the hip. If you don't have two black gears, don't attach the large decorative wheel for the same reason as before.

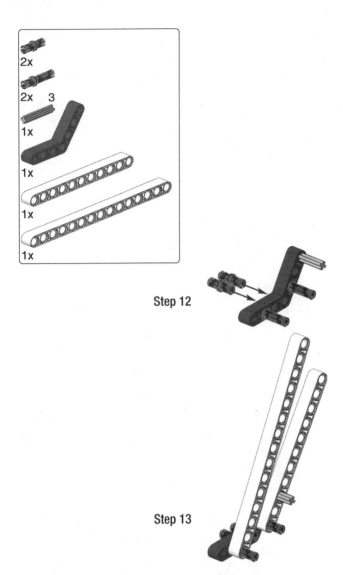

Step 12

Step 13

Start building the part of the leg common to both sides.

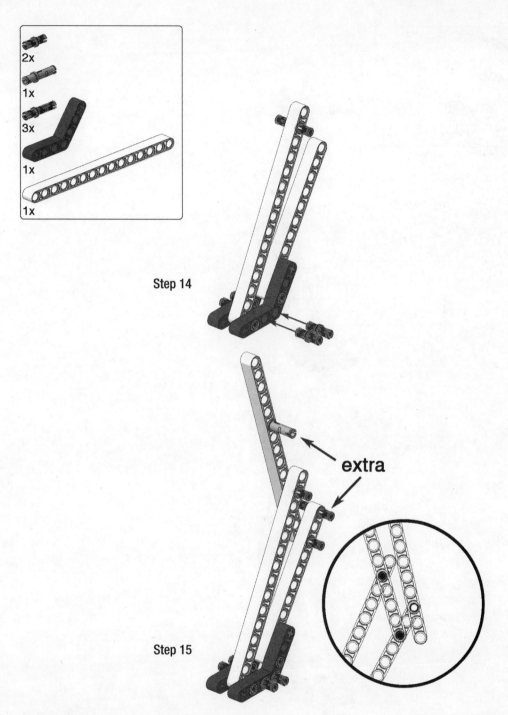

Step 14

extra

Step 15

In Step 15, do not insert the marked pins. In the circle you can see the correct holes in which to attach the upper 15-long beam.

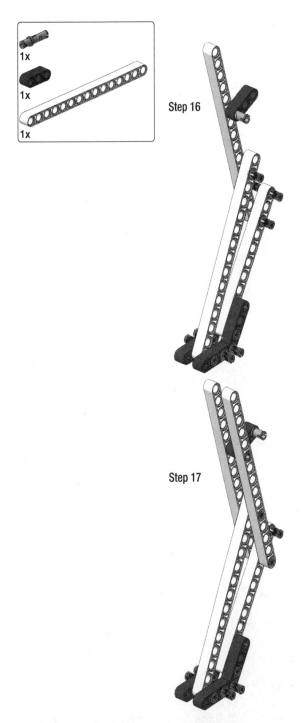

Step 16

Step 17

From here on, you build the decorative part of the leg. If you do not have extra parts, skip Step 16. In Step 17, add just the 15-long beam.

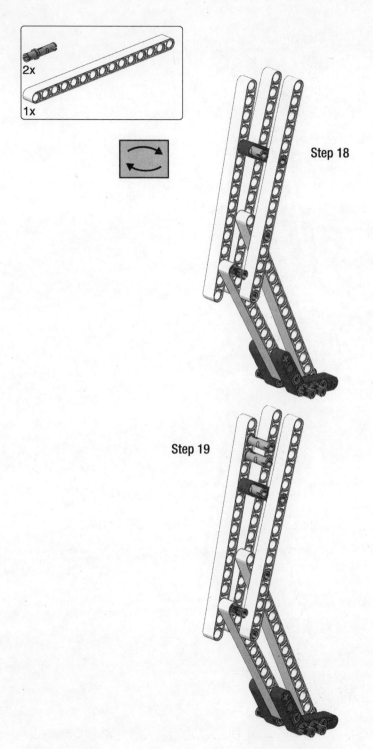

Step 18

Step 19

Continue skipping these steps if you don't have the extra parts.

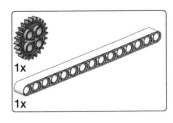

Step 20

Step 21

Continue skipping these steps if you don't have the extra parts. The leg is done.

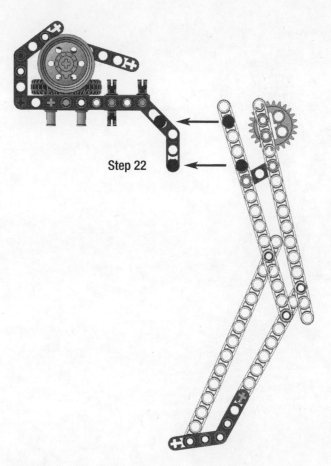

Step 22

The black spots on the leg must meet the spots on the hip.

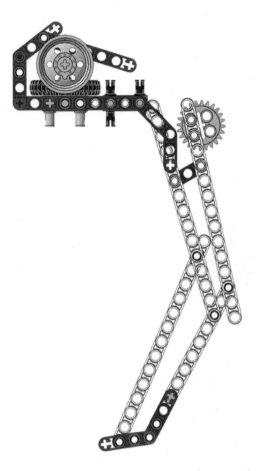

The leg beams must fit in the spaces between the three dark gray bent beams.

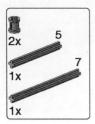

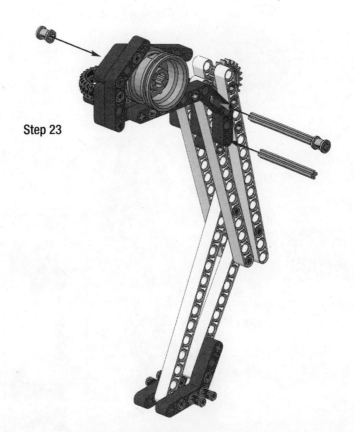

Step 23

This picture shows how the leg should fit in the hip assembly. Insert the axles to hold the leg in place.

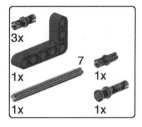

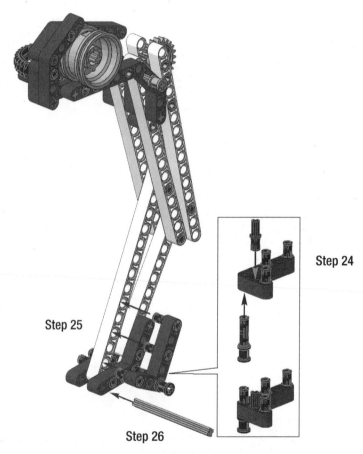

Step 24

Step 25

Step 26

Build the reinforcer that prevents the ankle from bending to the outside too much during stepping. Insert the 7-long axle at the end of the leg.

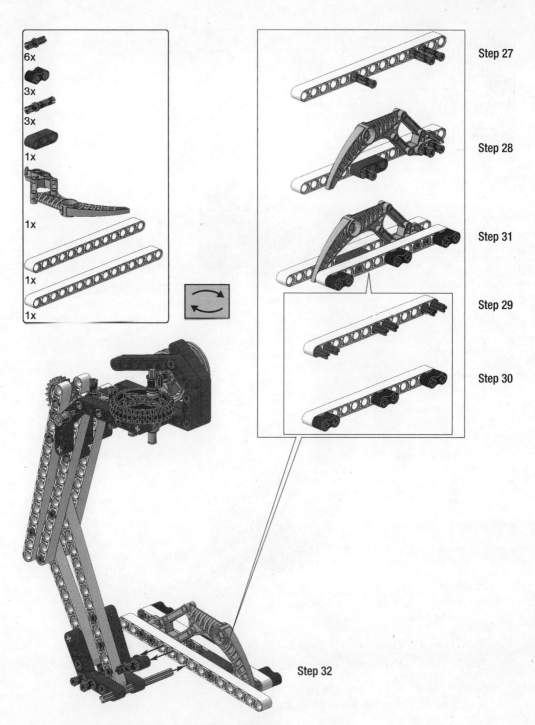

Step 27

Step 28

Step 31

Step 29

Step 30

Step 32

Rotate the assembly and build the external foot.

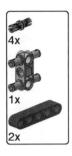

Step 33

Step 34

Step 35

Step 36

Insert the foot pad.

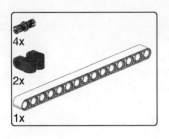

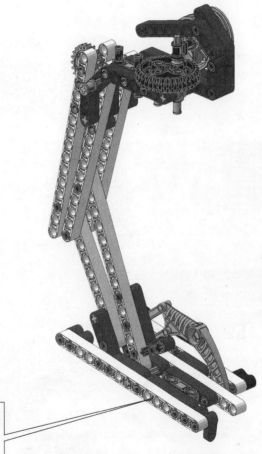

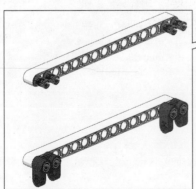

Step 37

Step 38

Step 39

Build the internal side of the foot with wedges.

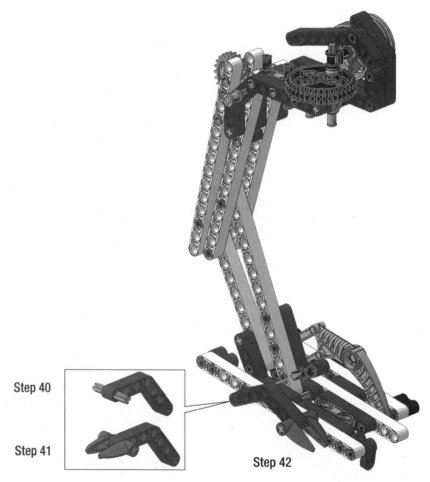

Step 40

Step 41

Step 42

Attach the foot blades.

The left leg is completed.

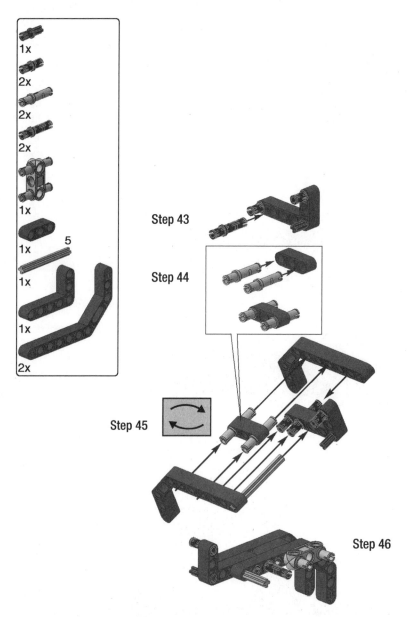

Step 43

Step 44

Step 45

Step 46

Start building the right hip.

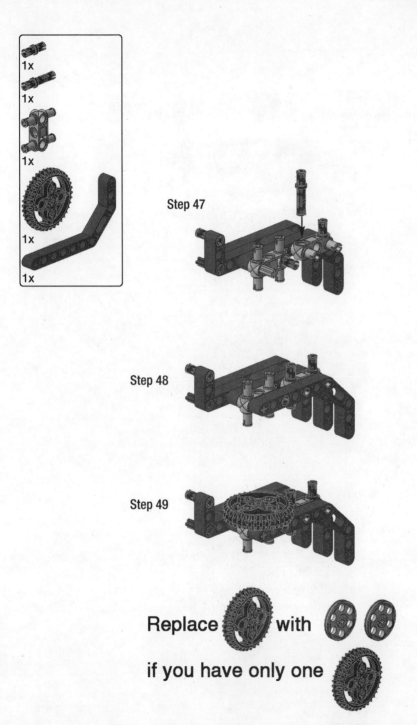

Step 47

Step 48

Step 49

Replace ⬤ with ⬤ ⬤

if you have only one ⬤

In Step 49, if you don't have the extra black gear, replace the black gear with two gray wheels, checking their position in the figure on page 111.

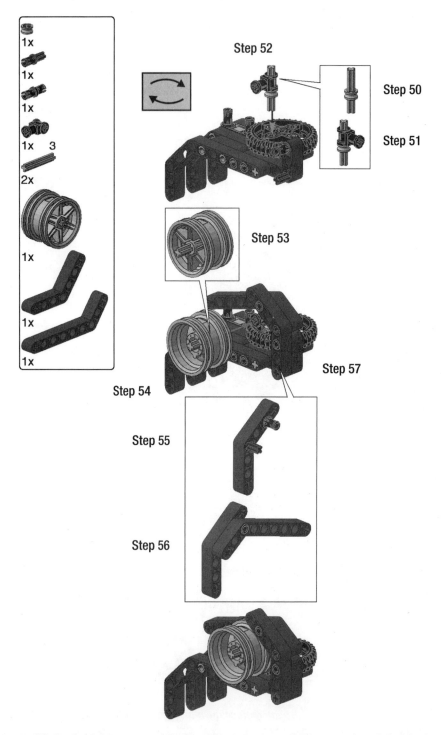

Step 52

Step 50

Step 51

Step 53

Step 57

Step 54

Step 55

Step 56

Build the decorative parts of the hip. Skip Steps 50 to 54 if you replaced the black gear with two gray wheels in Step 49.

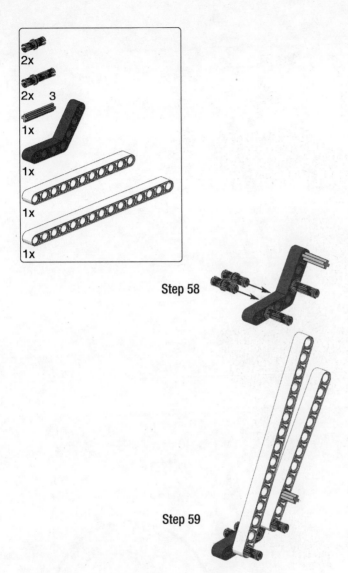

Step 58

Step 59

Start building the part of the leg common to both sides.

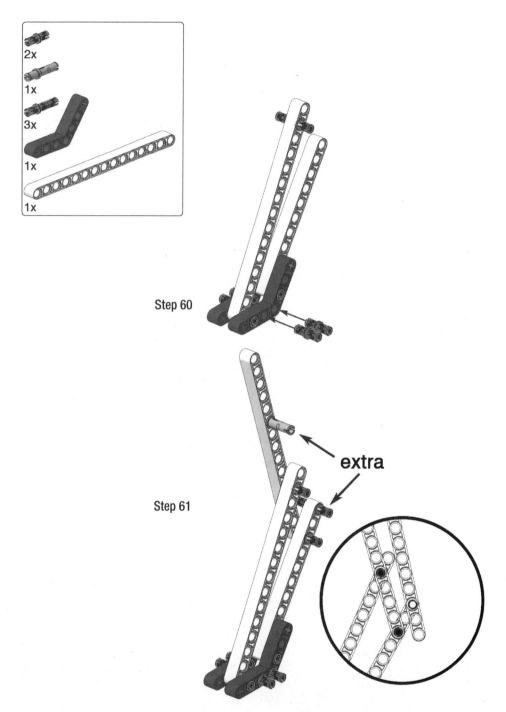

Step 60

Step 61

extra

In Step 61, do not insert the marked pins. In the circle you can see the correct holes where you can attach the upper 15-long beam.

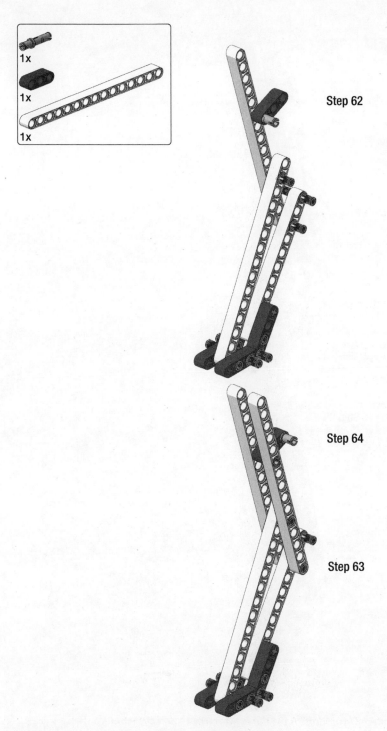

Step 62

Step 64

Step 63

From now on, you'll build the decorative part of the leg. If you don't have the extra parts, skip Step 62, and in Step 64, add just the 15-long beam.

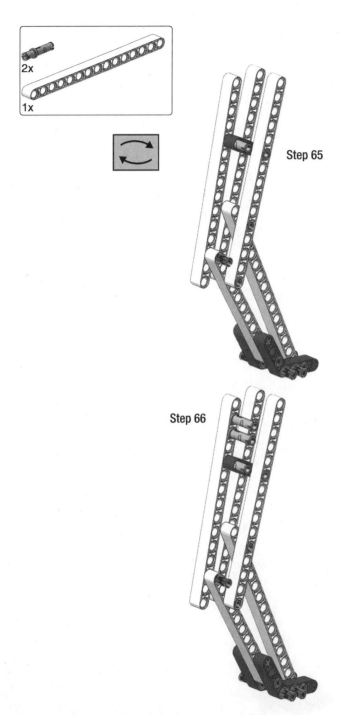

Step 65

Step 66

Continue skipping these steps if you don't have the extra parts.

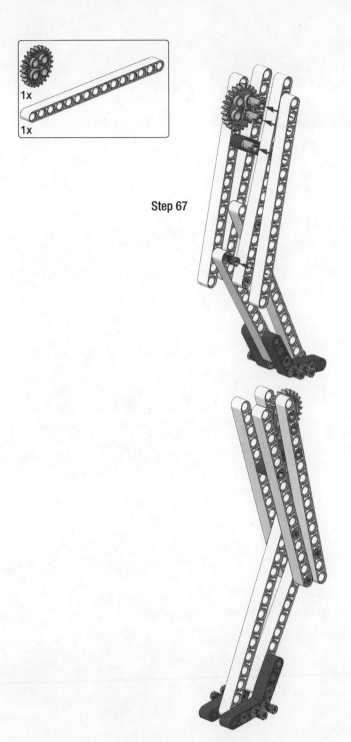

Step 67

Continue skipping these steps if you don't have the extra parts. The leg is done.

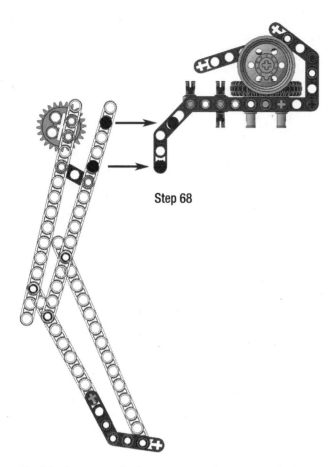

Step 68

The black spots on the leg must meet the spots on the hip.

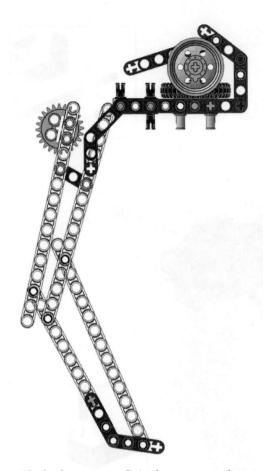

The leg beams must fit in the two spaces between the three dark gray bent beams.

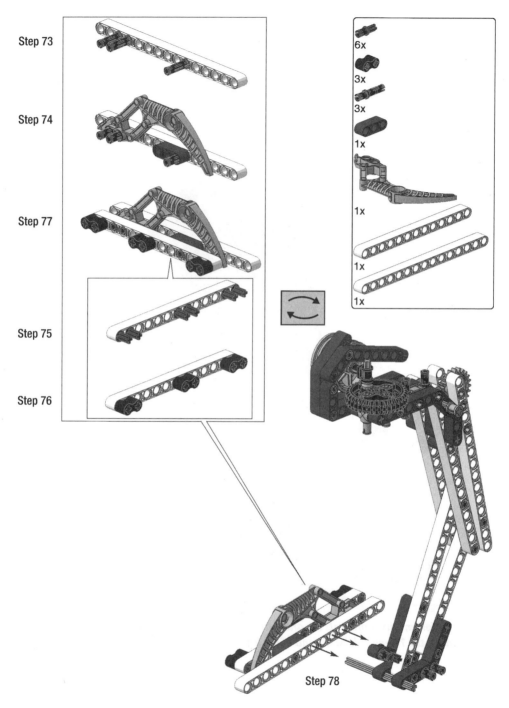

Step 73

Step 74

Step 77

Step 75

Step 76

6x

3x

3x

1x

1x

1x

Step 78

Rotate the assembly and build the external foot.

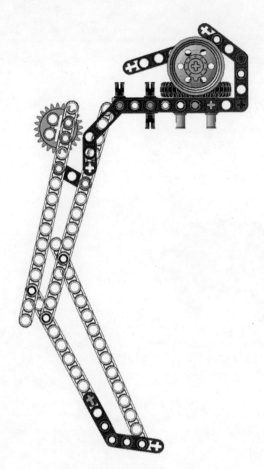

The leg beams must fit in the two spaces between the three dark gray bent beams.

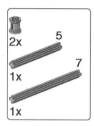

Step 69

This picture shows how the leg should fit in the hip assembly. Insert the axles to hold the leg in place.

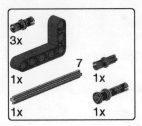

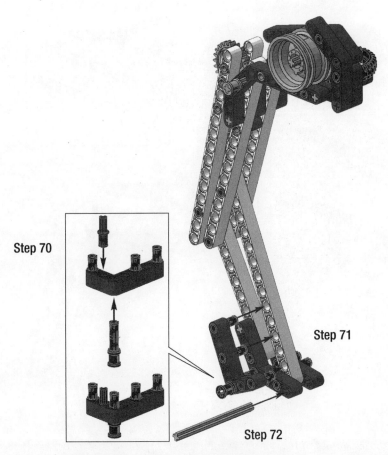

Step 70

Step 71

Step 72

Build the reinforcer, which prevents the ankle from bending too much to the outside during stepping. Insert the 7-long axle at the end of the leg.

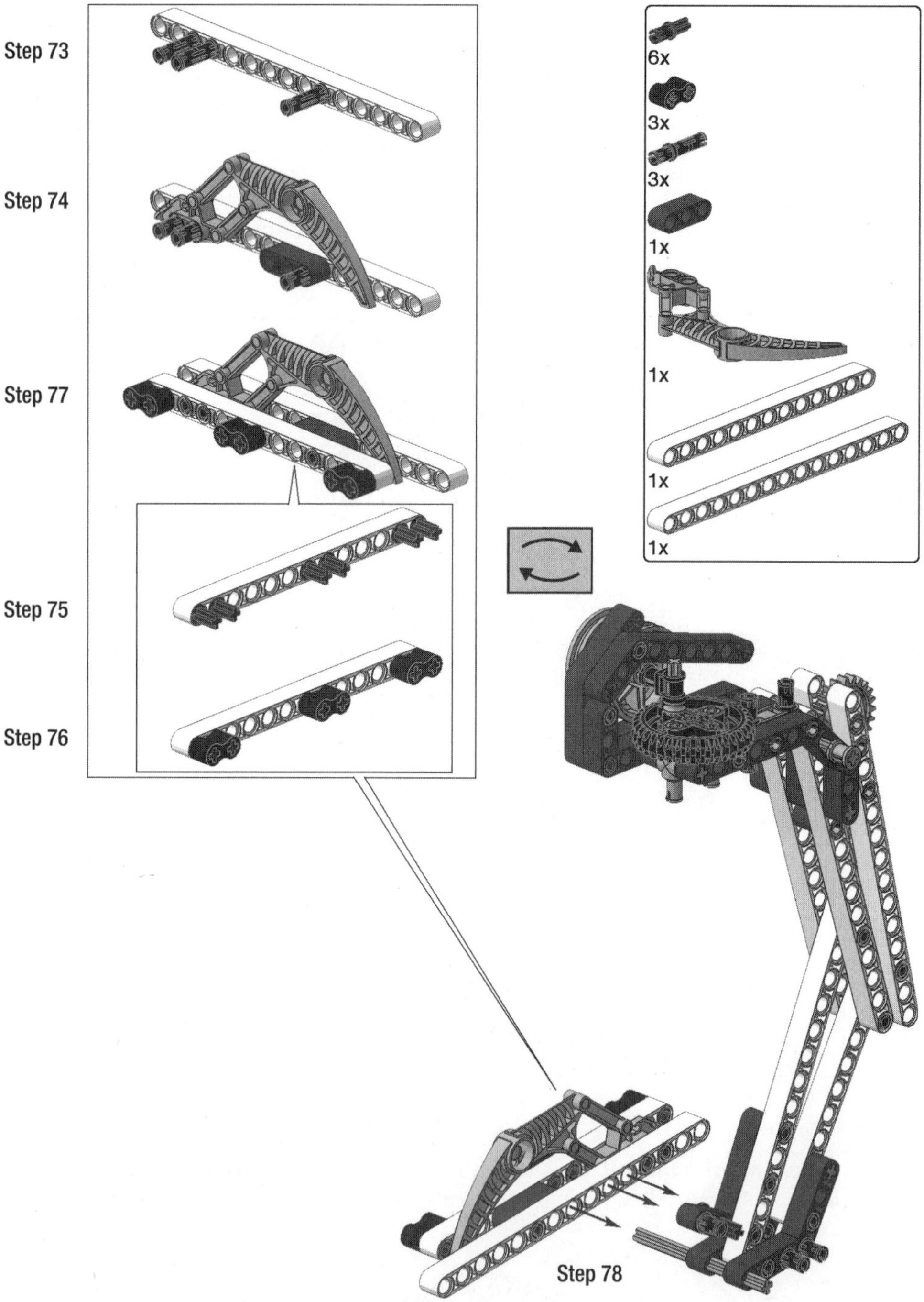

Step 73

Step 74

Step 77

Step 75

Step 76

6x

3x

3x

1x

1x

1x

1x

Step 78

Rotate the assembly and build the external foot.

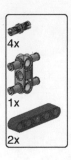

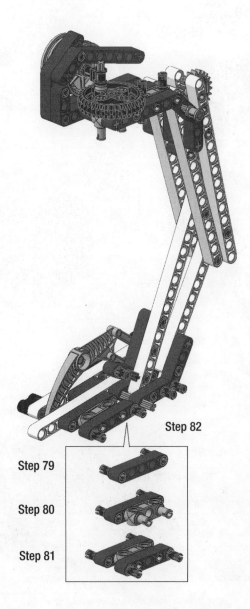

Step 82

Step 79

Step 80

Step 81

Insert the foot pad.

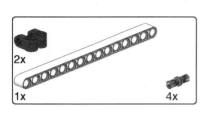

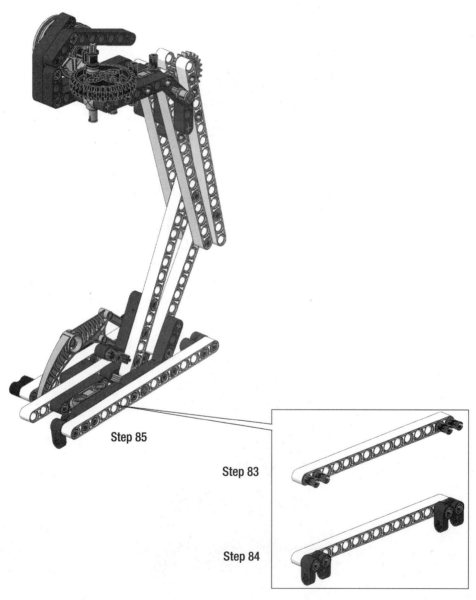

Step 85

Step 83

Step 84

Build the internal side of the foot with wedges.

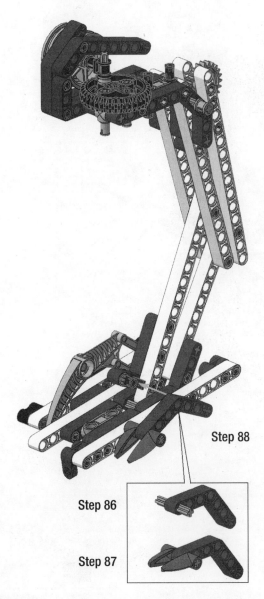

Step 88

Step 86

Step 87

Attach the foot blades.

The right leg is completed.

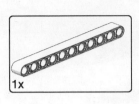

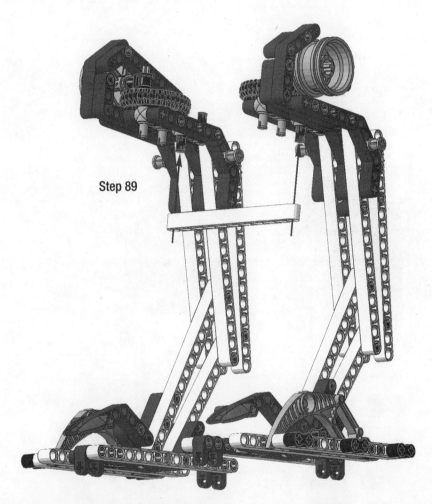

Step 89

Join the completed legs with an 11-long beam.

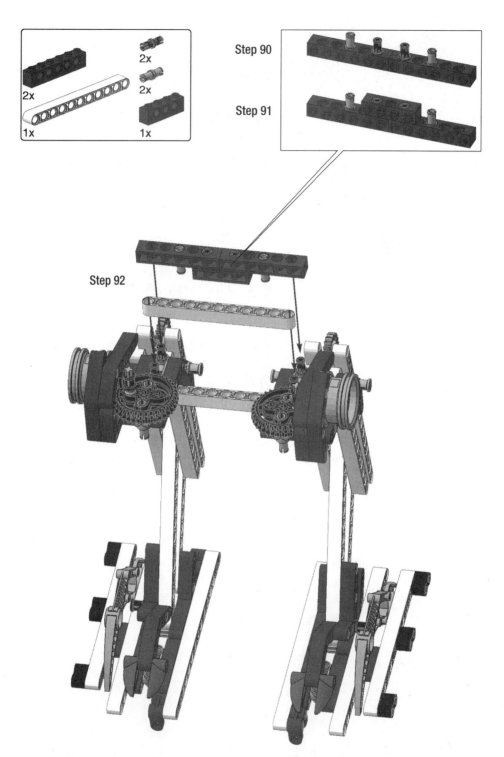

Step 90

Step 91

Step 92

To make the legs move parallel to each other, insert another 11-long beam and the brick assembly.

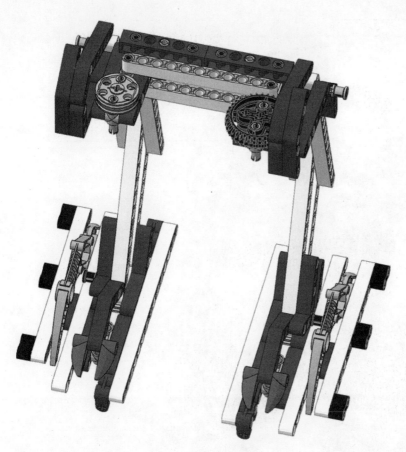

This picture shows how the AT-ST looks when assembled with retail set parts only. Notice the two gray wheels on the right hip assembly and the black gear on the left hip.

This picture shows the AT-ST legs without the additional 15-long beams. You can remove those beams safely, because they aren't structural.

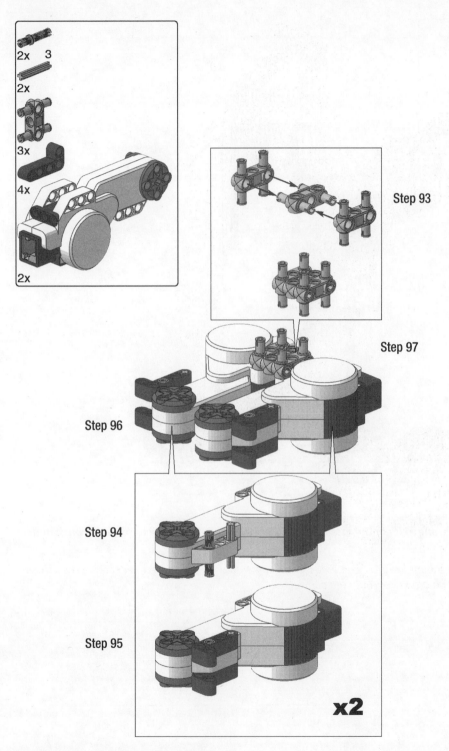

2x 3
2x
3x
4x
2x

Step 93

Step 97

Step 96

Step 94

Step 95

x2

Now build the subassembly for the motors.

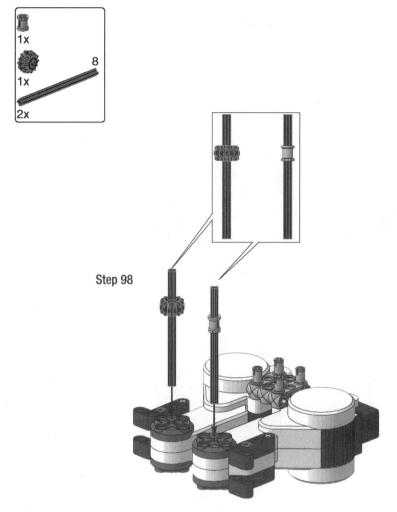

Step 98

Insert two 8-long axles in the motor shafts. The callout shows where to place the bush and the gear.

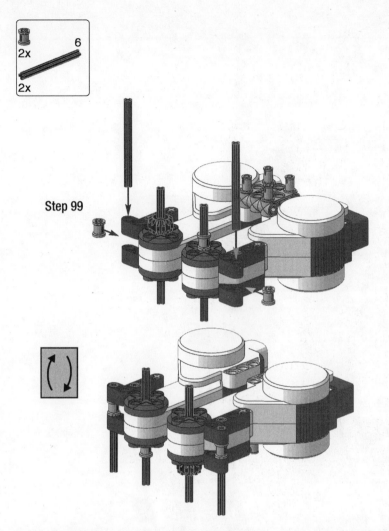

Step 99

Insert the 6-long axles, fixing them with the bushes. Rotate the model and check if you inserted the axles correctly.

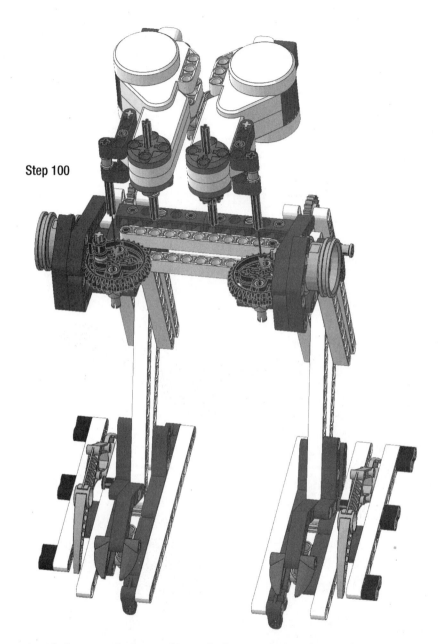

Step 100

Attach the motors' subassembly on the legs. Insert the 6-long axles in the black gear's central hole (left leg) and in the gray wheel's central hole (right leg). However, if you have two black gears, the model looks as in this picture.

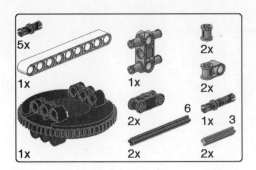

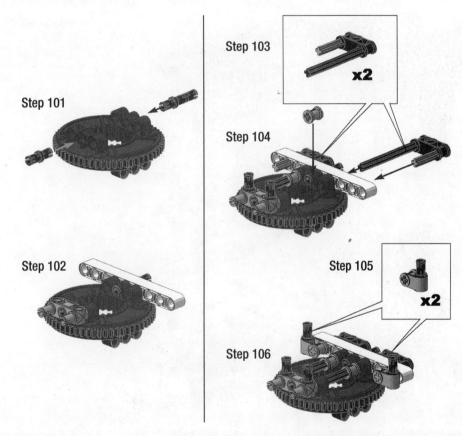

Build the rotating neck.

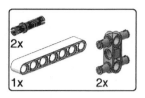

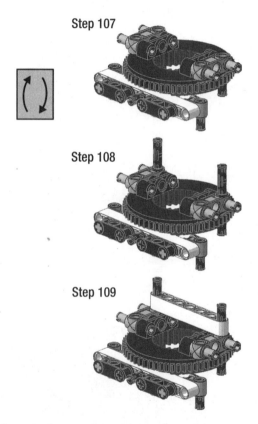

Step 107

Step 108

Step 109

Rotate the model upside down and finish the neck assembly.

Step 110

This graphic shows the motors attached to the legs, and also how to insert the neck in place.

Step 113

Step 111

Step 112

Build the beam that will hold the legs firmly.

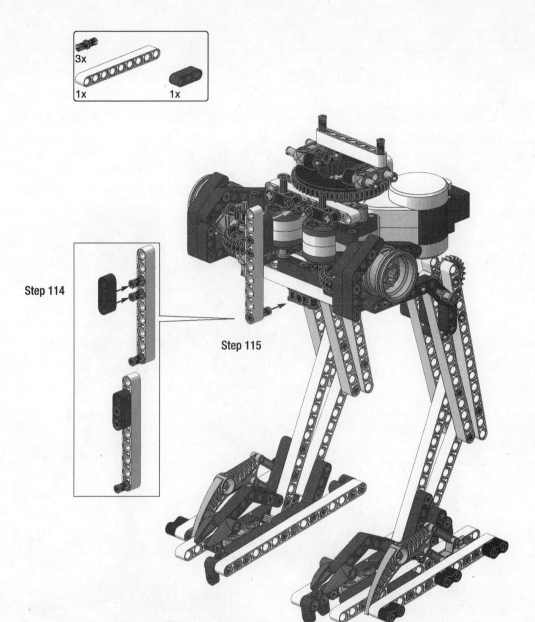

Step 114

Step 115

Insert the cross-bracing beam that holds the legs. Notice that you can't detach the legs from the AT-ST if this beam is in place.

Step 116

Insert the 16-tooth gear and the bush in their places.

*Notice that the right motor gear (on top) engages the neck turntable, while the left motor
12-tooth gear (on bottom) engages the left leg's black gear.*

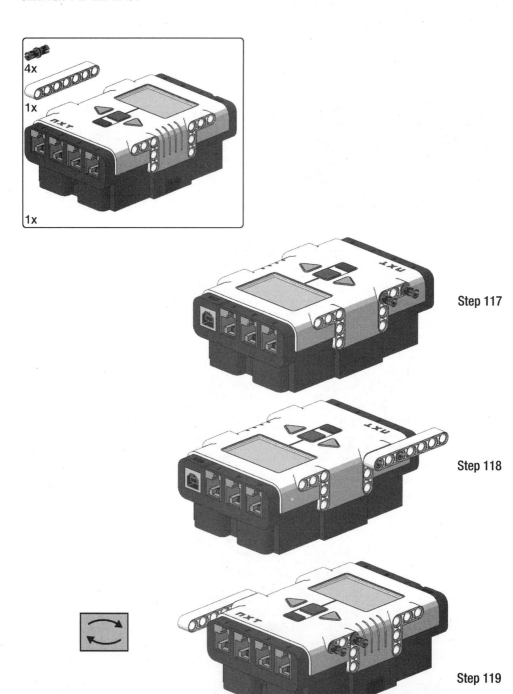

Step 117

Step 118

Step 119

The NXT is used as the AT-ST head.

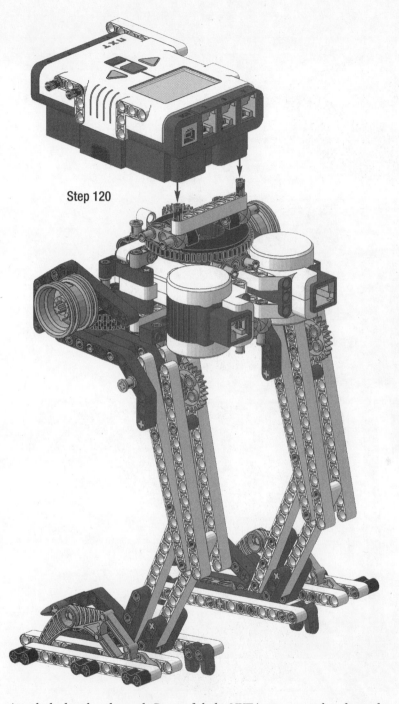

Step 120

Attach the head to the neck. Be careful; the NXT is not secured to the neck yet.

Step 121

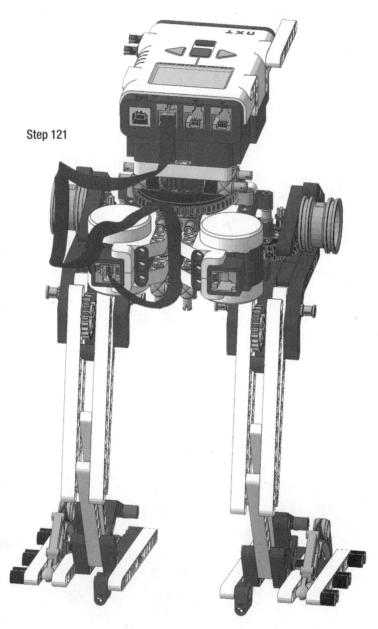

Connect the left motor to NXT output port C using a 35cm (14 inch) cable.

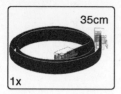

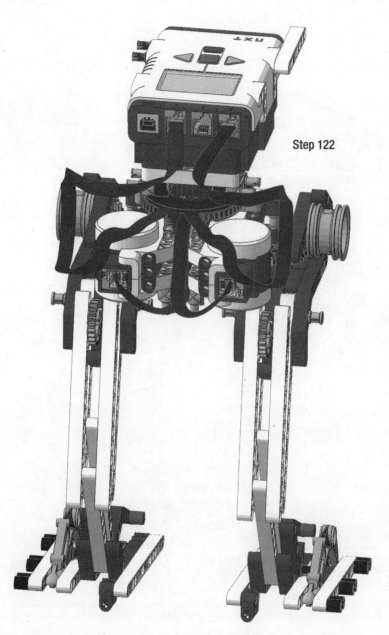

Step 122

Connect the right motor to NXT output port A using a 35cm (14 inch) cable.

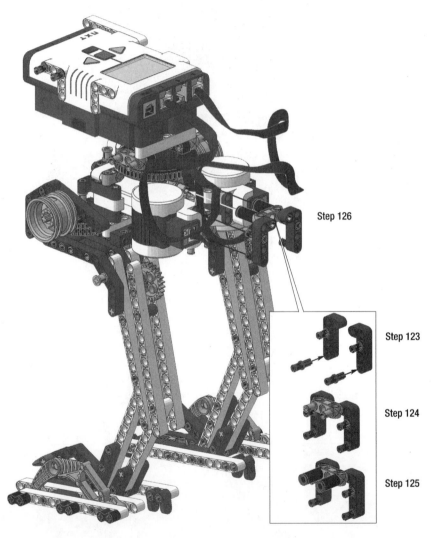

This frame will firmly connect the neck to the motors. Also, this time use the cross-bracing technique.

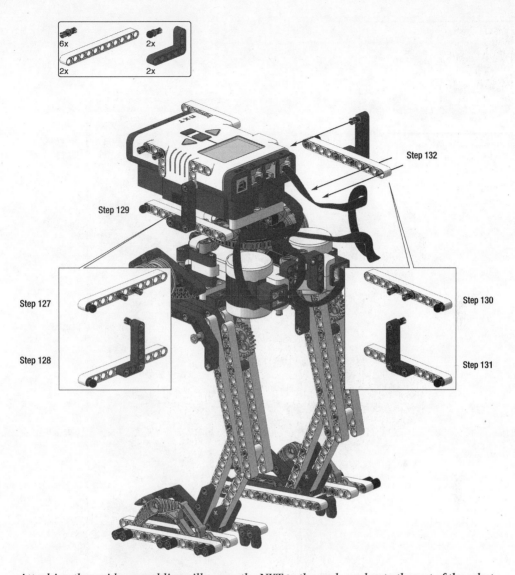

Attaching these side assemblies will secure the NXT to the neck, and so to the rest of the robot.

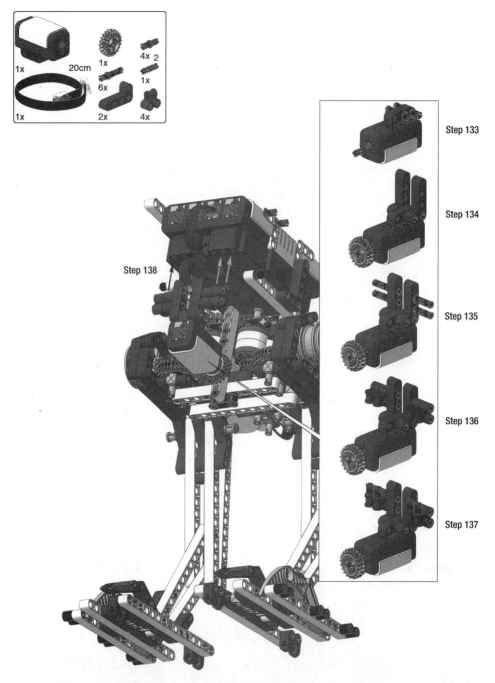

Build the Touch Sensor assembly and attach it under the head. Connect the Touch Sensor to NXT input port 3 using a 20cm (8 inch) cable.

Step 139

Attach a 35cm (14 inch) cable to NXT input port 4 and pass it under the bent beam on the left side of the head.

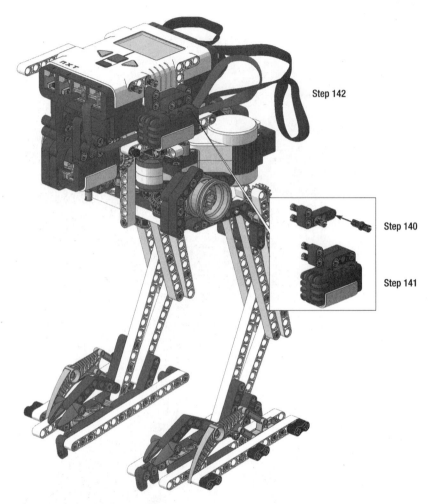

Step 142

Step 140

Step 141

Build the Sound Sensor assembly and attach it to the NXT and to the cable left free in the preceding step.

Step 143

Turn the model and attach another 35cm (14 inch) cable to NXT input port 1, passing it under the bent beam on the right side of the head.

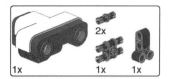

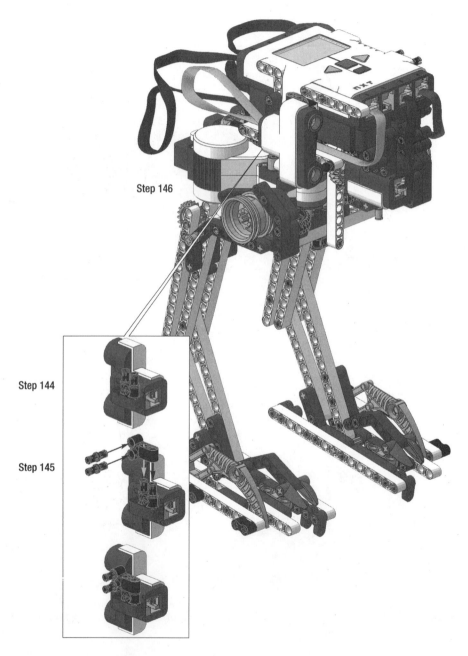

Step 146

Step 144

Step 145

Build the Ultrasonic Sensor assembly and attach it to the NXT and to the cable left free in the preceding step.

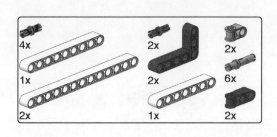

Step 147

Step 148

x2

Step 149

Step 150

Step 151

Step 152

Step 153

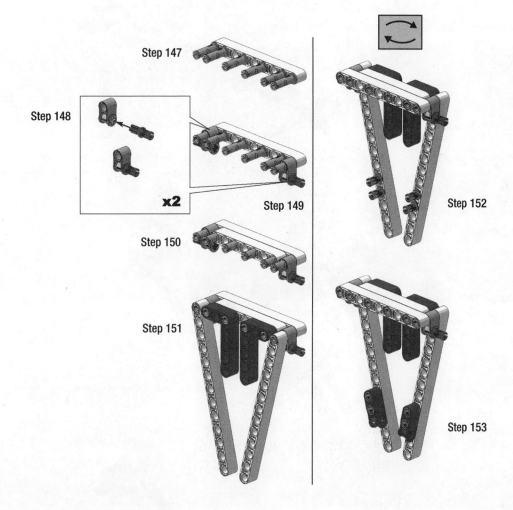

Start building the face of the robot.

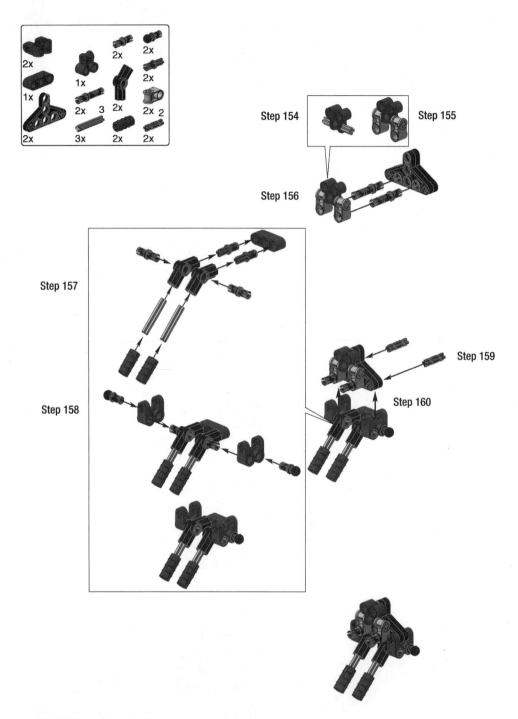

Step 154

Step 155

Step 156

Step 157

Step 158

Step 159

Step 160

Build the chin-mounted laser cannons.

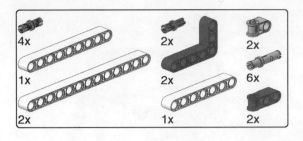

Step 161

Complete the AT-ST face assembly.

Step 162

Attach the face to the rest of the head.

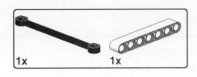

Step 164

Step 163

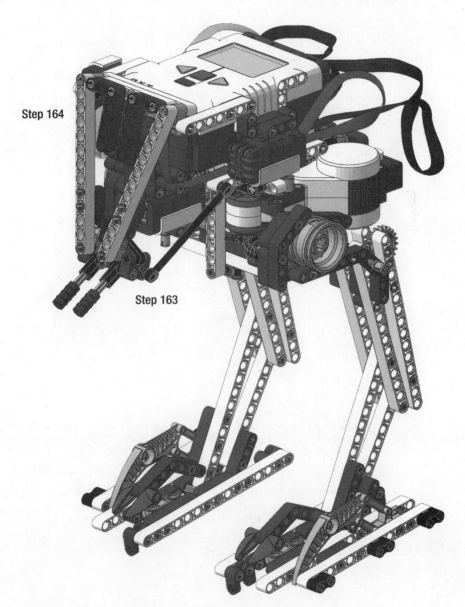

Place a 7-long beam and a black steering link to hold the head.

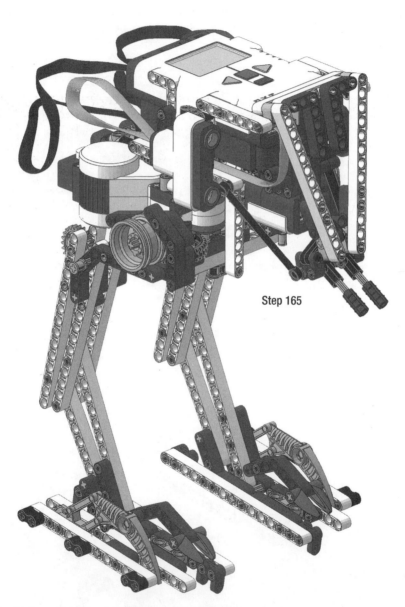

Step 165

Add another link on the right side and the AT-ST is ready for battle!

Summary

In this chapter, you learned about, built, and programmed a jerky COG shifting biped. It's not just any biped, but the famous AT-ST—the walking armored craft seen in the *Star Wars* films.

The model is quite a sculpture in itself; it's elegant, and proportioned to resemble the real AT-ST as closely as possible. The software, at first view, isn't bursting with originality, but it hides a lot of interesting tricks; the "servomotors automagic built-in limit switch" technique is one of them. Another useful idea is the use of state variables to keep track of the position of a robot's moving parts without always having to read the sensors. In the next chapter, you'll see how to build a smooth COG shifting biped.

Exercise 4-1. Further Ideas

- After reading Chapter 9 about remote controlling, write a couple programs to control the AT-ST remotely. You can reuse all the subroutines to manage the mechanics; you just have to call the functions `TurnRight(int times)`, `TurnLeft(int times)`, and `WalkStraight()`. You should manage how to wait for the current walking routine to end before resetting the mechanics and starting another walking routine. For example, if the AT-ST receives a command to turn while it's walking, it would have to finish stepping, to realign the legs and the head, and only then could it turn.

- Change the AT-ST program to make it react to sounds.

CHAPTER 5

Omni-Biped

Alpha Rex is certainly cool. However, the turning mechanism is missing something, don't you think? In this chapter you'll meet the Omni-Biped (see Figure 5-1), a smooth COG-shifting biped that can walk and also turn. It is omni-directional, hence the name. It shares the leg frame shape with Alpha Rex, but uses motors in a whole different way: each motor drives the leg to which it is attached. This feature allows the robot to turn quickly left and right within its own footprint.

Figure 5-1. *Omni-Biped with arms—an aesthetic addition*

History of a Biped

The biped robots that you see in these pages are not the first ones I've made, but they're the result of years of trial and error, and much experience. In 2001, my quest to create the perfect biped started. With good old RCX, I achieved the results that were shown in Chapter 1. However, I was limited by the motors' lack of precision and the everlasting lack of Rotation Sensors. In fact, in the good old Robotics Invention System set, such sensors were not included, but were available only in extension sets. Without Rotation Sensors, the robots' movements could be driven only using precise timing; that is, to make a shaft turn for a small number of degrees, you had to start the motor, wait for an estimated number of milliseconds, and stop the motor. As you can guess, this method is based on the estimation of motor speed (how much will it travel in this lapse of time?), and therefore is rough. The new NXT servomotors integrate the Rotation Sensor (also called encoder) and so solve that old motors' precision problem: now you can rotate a motor shaft by an exact amount of degrees.

As soon as I got the new NXT set, in the early phase of the MINDSTORMS Developer Program (MDP), I didn't even try to build the Tribot—the quick start guide rover bot. I immediately rushed on to the Alpha Rex, due to my curiosity to learn how LEGO designers had created a stable, smooth walking biped.

It was a great-looking robot, indeed! It gave me a bright idea about how to integrate the bulky NXT servomotors inside the legs' frame, and how to use the mass of the NXT brick as a counterweight, thus turning a possible cause of unsteadiness into an advantage. But I have to say that the steering mechanism, based on a rubber gripper, disappointed me. So, I thought up something different.

In the Omni-Biped, each leg is entirely driven by a motor to obtain two coordinated movements: the ankle is bent to shift the robot's center of gravity (COG), and the foot swings back and forth, to achieve stepping. With good reason, this biped belongs to the third of the categories introduced in Chapter 1, the "smooth COG shifting" one.

The hardware configuration secures the stability, just as for the Alpha Rex. Furthermore, the software manages all leg-synchronization hassles, because this robot uses no sensor to know which side it's leaning on or which foot is loaded. Synchronicity between legs is essential for this biped. When both motors turn in the same direction the robot walks straight; when the motors run in opposite directions, the Omni-Biped turns in place.

For the biped to walk and turn correctly, you must make sure to align the legs correctly every time you start the Omni-Biped program. To do this, rotate the bevel gear to align the 5-long beam with the diagonal that connects the 24-tooth gear holes. Adjust the alignment of both legs, using Figure 5-2 as reference.

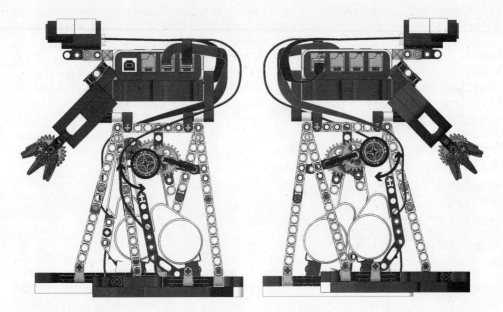

Figure 5-2. *Correct alignment of the legs*

Single-Tasking vs. Multitasking

Before introducing the programs for the Omni-Biped, let's discuss single-task and multitask programs. In the simplest case, a program can be seen as a sequence of actions; for example:

- Go forward for three seconds.

- Turn left for two seconds.

- Wait for an incoming object.

- Go backward until the object goes out of sight.

- And so on . . .

The preceding sequence can be translated into an NXC program that has only one task—the main task, to be more precise. In fact, as you know, the first lines of code to be executed when you start a program are the ones inside the main task. So, single-task programs can have only this task, and the flow of execution is specified by the code inside the main task.

What do you do if you'd like to have more action sequences running together? You would have to use multitasking; that is, writing a program with more than one task, each one containing its own action sequence. For example, you should have a task to read a sensor continuously, another task to manage an animation on the NXT display, one to move the robot around, and one dealing with Bluetooth communication. The main task is always present, of course, and you would have to tell the NXT firmware that you want to run more tasks together. You can do this in two ways. You can add the following statement at the top of main, so that the NXT will execute the tasks listed inside the parentheses:

```
Precedes (task1, task2, ... , taskN);
```

These tasks will be started only when the task that called the Precedes statement has ended its execution. Note that any task, not just main, can call Precedes.

The other way to tell the NXT to run multiple tasks is to add the following statement in every task that must be executed when the tasks listed in parentheses have ended:

```
Follows(main, task1, task2, ...);
```

To start multiple tasks at the beginning of the program, the main task must contain only some initialization code (to initialize sensors or variables) and the Precedes statement. So, the main task exits at once, and the program flow is split up into the other tasks listed inside the Precedes parentheses. The alternative solution is to have an empty main task, and to put a Follows(main) statement in every task you want to run.

In reality, the NXT processor executes one task at a time, switching from one to another so quickly that you have the illusion that all the tasks are running together. To be more precise, the part of the NXT firmware termed *scheduler* is responsible for this task execution switching.

Multitasking is also called *concurrent programming*, if the tasks in execution are sharing some resources, such as a sensor, an output device, a motor, or a display. This resource sharing must be well disciplined to avoid weird and unpredictable behavior in the program; this is the main trap of multitasking.

As an example to make this clearer, imagine a narrow kitchen of a restaurant, equipped with pots, ladles, but only one oven. If only one cook is at work, there's no problem: he can use all the equipment with ease. However, if the restaurant owner decides to improve his kitchen, engaging one more cook and a chef, then things change a lot. In fact, the two cooks must now share the kitchen resources, while moving in such little space, and in particular, dealing with the only oven available. So, the chef would have to schedule the two cooks in the kitchen to avoid their becoming stuck, and would provide them a way to alternate using the oven, eventually making one cook wait if the other one is using it.

Leaving the cooks to their work and coming back to NXC, you must find a way to avoid the scenario that more than one task accesses the same resource at the same time. I said that in reality the processor is executing only a task at a time. However, if the scheduler suspends the running task that is using the common resource, before the task has released the resource, then no other task (awakened by the scheduler) should access that resource.

For example, imagine task 1 playing a high-pitched tone at a certain rate; the sound has not been completely played when the scheduler halts task 1, putting task 2 into execution. Task 2 plays a sound at a different frequency. If the sound output device usage is not properly managed, you would hear the sounds coming out of the NXT without order: the sound played by a task would interrupt the other task sound without waiting for it to finish—without discipline.

The tools that solve the preceding problem are special variables called *semaphores*, or *mutexes* (singular *mutex*, from *mut*ual *ex*clusion). You must use the shared resources only inside so-called *critical sections*—parts of code that must be included between an Acquire(mutex_name) statement and a Release(mutex_name) statement:

```
Acquire (mtx);

/* critical section, where shared resources are used */

Release (mtx);
```

Acquire simply waits for the mutex_name mutex variable to be released, and this waiting avoids conflicts with other tasks that require the shared resource. Release, as the term suggests, releases the mutex, thus allowing other tasks blocked at the Acquire statement line to enter the critical section.

You can recast Acquire as follows:

```
void Acquire (bool &mtx)
{
    while (mtx) Wait(10);
    mtx = true;
}
```

You could replace Release as follows:

```
void Release (bool &mtx)
{
    mtx = false;
}
```

■**Note** The & (ampersand) before the argument name means that it is passed by reference, and thus can be modified by the function code. In NXC, you usually pass arguments by value: the variable x passed by value to myfun(x) is not modified after the myfun call. A temporary copy of the x variable is made instead. For details, check the NXC Programming Guide.

Let's see this technique in practice, with the help of two simple multitasking programs. The programs should do the same thing. They have two tasks running at the same time, one playing a high tone, the other playing a lower tone, alternately: high, low, high, low, and so on. Listing 5-1 shows the first, wrong version of the program.

Listing 5-1. *The Wrong Version of a Simple Multitask Program to Play Sounds*

```
task task1()
{
    while(true)
    {
```

```
        PlayTone(1000,300);
        Wait(600);
    }
}

task task2()
{
    while(true)
    {
        PlayTone(500,300);
        Wait(600);
    }
}

task main()
{
    Precedes(task1,task2);
}
```

Here you can see that the main task is used just to tell the NXT scheduler to execute the tasks named task1 and task2, after the main task itself has finished. Because the Precedes statement is the only thing the main task has to do, it ends at once, leaving space for the other two concurrent tasks. They are concurrent, in fact, because both are trying to play a tone, accessing the NXT loudspeaker as a shared resource. The program does not behave as expected, because the tasks alternate with no discipline about the loudspeaker usage. The sound pattern coming out is random: it could be low, high, high, high, low, low, high, high, low, low, low, low, high . . . , instead of the regular pattern described before, where the high and low tones alternate in an orderly fashion. Now you should realize why you must employ mutex variables. See the correct version of the preceding program in Listing 5-2.

Listing 5-2. *The Correct Version of a Simple Multitask Program to Play Alternating Sounds*

```
mutex sound;

task task1()
{
    while(true)
    {
        Acquire(sound);
        PlayTone(1000,300);
        Wait(600);
        Release(sound);
    }
}

task task2()
{
    while(true)
```

```
    {
        Acquire(sound);
        PlayTone(500,300);
        Wait(600);
        Release(sound);
    }
}

task main()
{
    Precedes(task1,task2);
}
```

The program is the same, but now the critical sections—those parts of the task code where the shared resource is used—are enclosed by the Acquire/Release statements. The mutex variable is called sound, according to the function of the critical section it is meant to discipline. It is declared as a global variable, so that every function or task in the program can see and use it. The sound pattern coming out is the one you desired: high, low, high, low, high, low . . . The first sound to be played is always the high-pitched one, because task1 comes before task2 in the Precedes statement list. The first scheduled task is task1, playing the high tone first. If you swap the task names inside parentheses, such as Precedes(task2,task1), the first sound heard will be the low-pitched one, played by task2.

Now you should have the essential background about multitasking to continue on.

Writing a Single-Task Program

Omni-Biped's behavior is simple. It starts walking straight until it sees an obstacle with the Ultrasonic Sensor; at that point, it stops, realigns the legs, and draws back until the obstacle goes out of view. Then it starts a turning maneuver, choosing the direction randomly. The turning lasts only a few moments, or until another object comes in sight. After the turn, Omni-Biped starts walking straight again.

As explained and shown before in Figure 5-2, the legs must always be aligned correctly before the program is started. The robot will realign the legs automatically after every walk, to bring them back to the starting position.

First, you'll see the single-task program that implements this simple behavior. As usual, the program starts defining the preprocessor macros (see Listing 5-3), useful to maintaining and modifying the program easily.

Listing 5-3. *The Initial Definitions of the Omni-Biped Program and Global Variable Declaration*

```
#define HALF_STEP 540
#define FULL_STEP 1080
#define RIGHT_LEG OUT_B
#define LEFT_LEG OUT_A
#define BOTH_LEGS OUT_AB
#define EYES IN_1
```

```
#define NEAR 12 //cm
#define FAR  40 //cm
#define LEFT -1
#define RIGHT 1
#define FORWARD 0

#define WALK_SPEED 90
#define ALIGN_SPEED 60
#define TURN_TIME 100
#define BACKUP_TIME 800

#define TURN_FILE "Turn.rso"
#define LEFT_FILE "Left.rso"
#define RIGHT_FILE "Right.rso"
#define FORWARD_FILE "Forward.rso"
```

The various subroutines and functions are shown in Listing 5-4. There you can find the functions to initialize the NXT I/O ports, to display text or numbers on the NXT screen, and to realign legs to the ground after every walk.

Listing 5-4. *The Functions of the Omni-Biped Program*

```
sub Biped_init ()
{
   ResetRotationCount (BOTH_LEGS);
   SetSensorLowspeed (EYES);
}

void Smessage( string msg )
{
   TextOut(0,LCD_LINE5,"             ");
   TextOut(0,LCD_LINE5,msg);
}

void Nmessage( int n )
{
   TextOut(0,LCD_LINE5,"             ");
   NumOut(0,LCD_LINE5,n);
}

sub AnnounceDir ( int dir )
{
   if (dir!=0)
   {
      PlayFileEx (TURN_FILE, 4, false);
      Wait(450);
   }
```

```
      if (dir==LEFT)
         PlayFileEx (LEFT_FILE, 4, false);
      if (dir==FORWARD)
         PlayFileEx (FORWARD_FILE, 4, false);
      if (dir==RIGHT)
         PlayFileEx (RIGHT_FILE, 4, false);
      Wait(200);
}

sub RealignLegs()
{
   Smessage("Realigning");
   long right_count, left_count;

   //computes angular distance from the initial leg position
   right_count = abs(MotorRotationCount(RIGHT_LEG) % FULL_STEP);
   left_count = abs(MotorRotationCount(LEFT_LEG) % FULL_STEP);

   //choose the direction to align the right leg,
   //turning motor the least possible
   if (right_count<HALF_STEP)
      OnRev (RIGHT_LEG, ALIGN_SPEED);
   else
      OnFwd (RIGHT_LEG, ALIGN_SPEED);

   //wait for the leg to be aligned
   while (right_count>0)
   {
      right_count = abs(MotorRotationCount (RIGHT_LEG) % FULL_STEP);
   }
   Off(RIGHT_LEG);

   //choose the direction to align the left leg,
   //turning motor the least possible angle
   if (left_count<HALF_STEP)
      OnRev (LEFT_LEG, ALIGN_SPEED);
   else
      OnFwd (LEFT_LEG, ALIGN_SPEED);

   //wait for the leg to be aligned
   while (left_count>0)
   {
      left_count = abs(MotorRotationCount (LEFT_LEG) % FULL_STEP);
   }
   Off(LEFT_LEG);
}
```

The Biped_init() subroutine is in charge of resetting the motor's rotation count registers and setting up the NXT input port to read the Ultrasonic Sensor. You use the two functions Smessage(string msg) and Nmessage(int n) to clear just a line of the NXT screen and to display a text message or a number, respectively. To clear a line, it is enough to output a blank string, such as TextOut(0,LCD_LINE5," "). The AnnounceDir subroutine makes the robot say in which direction it is going to walk.

The most interesting subroutine is the RealignLegs one, used to bring the legs back in the position they were at the program startup; it is worth a detailed explanation. First, you compute the angular distance from the initial shaft position with abs(MotorRotationCount(X_LEG) % FULL_STEP). The binary operator % is called the *modulo* operator, whose result is the remainder of an integer division. For example:

```
3 % 2 = 1 since 3 = 2·1 + 1,
6 % 2 = 0 since 6 = 2·3 + 0,
347 % 5 = 2 since 347 = 69·5 + 2.
```

So, the motor on the leg to be realigned is started in a direction that minimizes the rotation to reach the desired position. This is done simply by checking if the angle is less than half a step, or not: if the first case, the motor is turned on by OnRev, otherwise by OnFwd. After the motor is started, the subroutine uses the modulo operator to check if the leg motor has turned by an angle that is an integer multiple of the degrees needed to make a full step. The condition is verified when MotorRotationCount (RIGHT_LEG) % FULL_STEP becomes 0: when the leg returns back to its starting position, the motor is stopped. Once the right leg is aligned, the subroutine repeats the same procedure for the left leg.

■**Tip** You will notice that the RealignLegs subroutine is executed many times to resynchronize the legs after a stop. Realigning legs one at a time (the program runs a single task) is not the best solution. Instead, you could use two tasks running together to realign the legs simultaneously. This method is shown later in the multitask version of the Omni-Biped program.

Now that you know all the subroutines, look at Listing 5-5 to see how the main task uses them.

Listing 5-5. *The main Task Code for the Omni-Biped*

```
task main ()
{
    int timer = 0, direction;
    //initializes sensors and direction variable
    Biped_init();
    direction = FORWARD;
```

```
while (true)
{
    //tells the direction it is going in
    AnnounceDir(direction);

    //starts walking
    OnFwdSyncEx (BOTH_LEGS, WALK_SPEED, sign(direction)*90, RESET_NONE);
    Wait(SEC_1);
    //waits for obstacle if going forward
    if (direction==FORWARD)
    {
        while (SensorUS (EYES)>NEAR);
    }
    else
    //waits for obstacle or time elapsing if turning
    {
        timer = 0;
        while (SensorUS(EYES)>NEAR && timer<TURN_TIME)
        {
            timer++;
            Nmessage(timer);
        }
    }
    Off (BOTH_LEGS);

    //realigns legs to the ground, as they were at program start
    RealignLegs();

    //if the obstacle is still there, walk backwards...
    if (SensorUS(EYES)<FAR)
    {
        OnRevSyncEx (BOTH_LEGS, WALK_SPEED, 0, RESET_NONE);
        //...until the obstacle goes out of sight
        while (SensorUS(EYES)<FAR);
        Off (BOTH_LEGS);
        RealignLegs();
    }

    //plans to turn in a random direction if the robot was going forward
    //plans to go straight if the robot has just finished turning
    if (direction==FORWARD) direction = 1-2*(Random(2));
    else direction = FORWARD;
}
}
```

You call the `Biped_init` subroutine to configure the Ultrasonic Sensor port and to reset the leg rotation count. The direction local variable is initialized to FORWARD (an alias yielding 0); then the program enters the infinite `while(true)` loop. The robot announces the chosen direction with the NXT speaker and then the motors are started in synchronized mode, meaning they will wait for each other if one of them slows down. The expression `sign(direction)*90` determines the turning ratio. This turning ratio depends on the value of the direction variable, which can assume only the three constant values: FORWARD (0), RIGHT (1), or LEFT(-1). The resulting turning ratio can be 0, and the motors will run synchronized in the same direction. If the resulting ratio is 90 or -90, the motors will run in opposite directions, allowing the robot to turn. If your robot is going straight, as specified by the condition of the first `if` branch, the program will wait until a near object is seen (the NEAR constant is defined in centimeters), but if your robot is turning, the program will wait for an obstacle to be seen within a timeout (see the `timer` variable). Then, both legs are stopped and realigned into the position they had at the start of the program, one at a time.

If the obstacle is still in view, the robot backs up until the obstacle is farther than FAR. If the robot was going straight, a new random direction is chosen to turn the robot away from the obstacle. Otherwise, if it turned and saw an obstacle, it would plan to go straight, and the loop would start over again. The formula to choose a random direction is similar to the one used by the AT-ST, so you can go back to Chapter 4 if you missed it.

Using Hysteresis

You might wonder about the presence of two distance thresholds, NEAR and FAR. Would only NEAR be enough? Maybe yes, but you are doing something cooler: you are using a *hysteresis* cycle. What is hysteresis?

In physics, it is a sort of "memory effect" featured by some magnetic materials. I won't get too in-depth into the topic, because this isn't a physics book. Suffice to say that hysteresis is a natural phenomenon that inspired programmers; it has been translated into a common programming technique used to filter noise in electronic devices or sensor equipment.

Take a look at the example illustrated in Figure 5-3. Consider using the distance measured by the Ultrasonic Sensor to change the value of a Boolean variable from `false` to `true` when an object gets nearer than a threshold distance, and change its value back to `false` when the object is viewed further than the threshold.

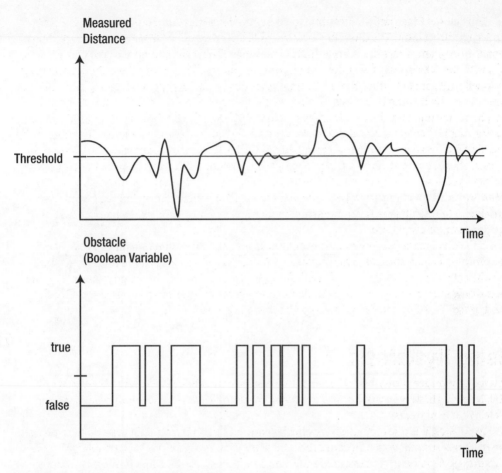

Figure 5-3. *Using a single threshold to determine if an object is near leads to a flickering, unreliable measurement. The first graph shows the sensor distance readings; in the second graph, the value of the Boolean variable is true if the distance is lower than the threshold, and false otherwise.*

As you might have noticed, the distance readings that you get from your Ultrasonic Sensor are flickering. In fact, this sensor measures instant values of distance that change suddenly, moment by moment. Also, the Ultrasonic Sensor could measure a faraway distance even if the object is near, when the object that reflects the ultrasonic bursts has a corrugated surface. So, an object that was seen close a moment ago could not be seen by the sensor in the successive reading. The value of your Boolean variable would change constantly between true and false when the sensor reading is near the threshold value, as the preceding figure clearly shows.

It would be desirable to filter all this flickering using two thresholds instead of one, thus getting a more stable Boolean result. Take a look at Figure 5-4, because a graph is better than a thousand words.

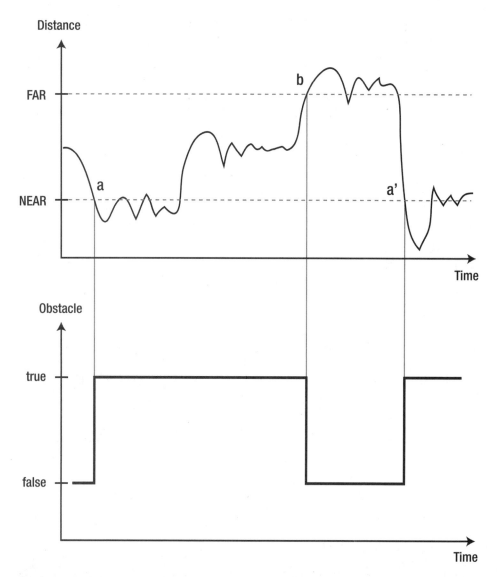

Figure 5-4. *Using hysteresis, you can filter the flickering of the distance measurements.*

This is exactly the solution used in the Omni-Biped program, where you are using two thresholds, NEAR and FAR. In the graph, when the distance reading (top graph) goes below the NEAR threshold, the obstacle Boolean variable (plotted in the bottom graph) becomes true (point *a*). In other words, when the measured distance is low, the robot assumes that an object is near. As you can see, the measurement flickering about the NEAR threshold does not influence the obstacle variable; this holds also for the fluctuation inside the band delimited by NEAR and FAR. The Boolean variable obstacle becomes false only when the distance measure will be higher than the FAR threshold (point *b*). Finally, the obstacle variable again receives the value true only if the distance reading goes lower than the NEAR threshold (*a'* label). This way, you can get a smoother-working system, filtering the measurement fluctuations.

Recall what I said before: a system has hysteresis when the path to go from state A to B is different from the path to go from B to A. Now that you've seen the preceding example, you can understand the graph in Figure 5-5.

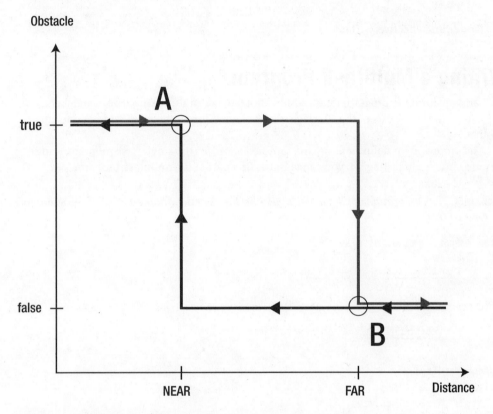

Figure 5-5. *The hysteresis cycle connecting the distance read by the sensor to the obstacle detection variable. The path going from A to B is different from the path going from B to A.*

The x axis shows the distance reading of the Ultrasonic Sensor. The y axis displays the value of the Boolean variable obstacle, which can be true or false.

Imagine that obstacle is initially false and that the distance value is higher than FAR. This means that no object is in sight, and this state is labeled B. So, imagine that you are moving toward 0 along the x axis. According to what you saw before, when the distance goes below the NEAR threshold, the obstacle value switches to true (compare the event labeled *a* in Figure 5-4). You have just traveled from the state B to state A, following the darker oriented path on the graph.

Now imagine starting from state A: the obstacle variable is true and the distance is below the NEAR threshold. Start following the gray path; when the distance increases beyond the NEAR threshold, nothing happens. Only when the distance grows higher than the FAR threshold, obstacle becomes false, and you are back in state B. This corresponds to the event labeled *b* in Figure 5-4.

Finally, it is easier to do it than to say it. The code to implement hysteresis is simple, and reusable with all kinds of sensors.

```
d = SensorUS (EYES);
//hysteresis cycle
if (d < NEAR) obstacle = true;
else if (d > FAR ) obstacle = false;
```

Simple and effective, isn't it?

Writing a Multitask Program

You can transform the program for the Omni-Biped to use multitasking. The overall behavior will remain the same, except that the legs will be aligned simultaneously, and not one after another.

The preprocessor definitions are the same as before for the single-task program, and so they are omitted. In Listing 5-6 you can view the first part of the multitask program.

Listing 5-6. *The Declaration of Global Variables and the Functions of the Multitask Program for the Omni-Biped*

```
mutex Rmotor, Lmotor, display;

bool obstacle, Rreset, Lreset, play;

int direction;

void Smessage(string msg)
{
   Acquire(display);
   TextOut(0,LCD_LINE5,"               ");
   TextOut(0,LCD_LINE5,msg);
   Release(display);
}

void Nmessage(int n)
{
   Acquire(display);
   TextOut(0,LCD_LINE5,"               ");
   NumOut(0,LCD_LINE5,n);
   Release(display);
}

sub AnnounceDir ( int dir )
{
   if (dir!=FORWARD)
   {
      PlayFileEx (TURN_FILE, 4, false);
      Wait(450);
   }
```

```
   if (dir==LEFT)
   {
      PlayFileEx (LEFT_FILE, 4, false);
      Smessage("TURN LEFT");
   }
   if (dir==FORWARD)
   {
      PlayFileEx (FORWARD_FILE, 4, false);
      Smessage("FORWARD");
   }
   if (dir==RIGHT)
   {
      PlayFileEx (RIGHT_FILE, 4, false);
      Smessage("TURN RIGHT");
   }
   Wait(500);
}


sub Biped_init ()
{
   ResetRotationCount (BOTH_LEGS);
   SetSensorLowspeed (EYES);
   obstacle = false;
   Rreset = false;
   Lreset = false;
   play = false;
   direction = FORWARD;
}

sub RealignLegs ()
{
   Rreset = true;
   Lreset = true;
   Smessage("REALIGN LEGS");
   while (Rreset || Lreset) Wait(100);
   Wait(50);
   Smessage("DONE");
}

sub AcquireLegs ()
{
   Acquire(Rmotor);
   Acquire(Lmotor);
}

sub ReleaseLegs ()
```

```
{
    Off (BOTH_LEGS);
    Release(Rmotor);
    Release(Lmotor);
}
```

In the preceding code the global variables are declared, together with the mutex variables that will act as semaphores, to regulate the concurrent tasks' access to the shared resources.

Tip You should note that global variables are a good way to let many tasks communicate with one another. On the other hand, they must be seen as shared resources, so the access to those variables must be well disciplined to avoid corrupting their value, in case more than one task wants to write them. Notice that such a conflict does not exist, if a task only writes a global variable, while the others just read it.

The Smessage and Nmessage functions are a bit different from the previous version, because the NXT display is now a shared output device. So, you must put the TextOut and NumOut API functions inside a critical section, delimited by the Acquire(display) and Release(display) statements. The AnnounceDir and Biped_init functions are pretty much the same as before.

However, the RealignLegs subroutine is completely different. It doesn't move motors directly, but is used to discipline the realignment tasks' access to the motors. Before continuing the discussion, read the code in Listing 5-7.

Listing 5-7. *The main() and Walk() Tasks of the Omni-Biped Multitask Program*

```
task main ()
{
    Biped_init();
}

task Walk ()
{
    int timer;
    Follows (main);
    while (true)
    {
        AcquireLegs();
        AnnounceDir (direction);
        OnFwdSyncEx (BOTH_LEGS, WALK_SPEED, sign(direction)*90, RESET_NONE);
        if (direction==FORWARD)
        {
            while (!obstacle) Wait(50);
        }
        else
        {
            timer = 0;
```

```
        while (!obstacle && timer<TURN_TIME)
        {
            timer++;
        }
    }
    ReleaseLegs();
    RealignLegs();
    if (obstacle)
    {
        Smessage("BACKWARD");
        AcquireLegs();
        OnRevSyncEx (BOTH_LEGS, WALK_SPEED, 0, RESET_NONE);
        while (obstacle) Wait(50);
        ReleaseLegs();
        RealignLegs();
    }
    if (direction==FORWARD) direction = 1-2*Random(2);
    else direction = FORWARD;
    }
}
```

In this multitask program, the main task simply calls the Biped_init subroutine and exits. This leaves space for all other concurrent tasks in the program that contain the statement Follows(main). The concurrent tasks are as follows:

- Sight: Reads the Ultrasonic Sensor continuously and shares information about obstacles using the global variable obstacle, the output of the hysteresis cycle filter.

- Walk: Contains the loop corresponding to the main loop in the single-thread program. The robot goes straight until it sees an obstacle. It then backs up until the obstacle fades away, turns randomly, and then starts the loop again.

- AlignRightLeg *and* AlignLeftLeg: This time, the legs are reset in separate tasks, so that the duties can be accomplished simultaneously, thus saving time.

As mentioned before, some of these tasks share the same resources. In particular, Walk shares the motors with AlignRightLeg and AlignLeftLeg. To avoid conflicts, when one of these tasks wants to use the motors, it must first acquire the corresponding mutex, use the motors inside the critical section, and release the mutex when done. For example, the Walk task calls the AcquireLegs() and ReleaseLegs() functions (see Listing 5-6) to enclose the critical section where it uses the motors. In Listing 5-8, you can see the code of one of the alignment tasks (the code for the other leg is similar and thus omitted).

Listing 5-8. *The Code of the Task to Realign the Right Leg Position*

```
task AlignRightLeg ()
{
    Follows(main);
    long right_count;
    while (true)
```

```
    {
        while (!Rreset) Wait(100);
        Acquire (Rmotor);
        right_count = abs(MotorRotationCount (RIGHT_LEG) % FULL_STEP);

        if (right_count<HALF_STEP)
            OnRev (RIGHT_LEG, ALIGN_SPEED);
        else
            OnFwd (RIGHT_LEG, ALIGN_SPEED);

        while (right_count>0)
        {
            right_count = abs(MotorRotationCount (RIGHT_LEG) % FULL_STEP);
        }

        Off(RIGHT_LEG);
        Release (Rmotor);
        Rreset = false;
        Wait(10);
    }
}
```

These realignment tasks run forever, and they would try to realign the legs continuously, conflicting with the Walk task. So, they must be kept quiet until realignment is required. To accomplish this and also to avoid any unwanted behavior, use the mutex-like Lreset and Rreset Boolean variables.

■**Note** These Lreset and Rreset Boolean variables have a different function from the Rmotor and Lmotor mutexes, because they discipline a larger-scale mechanism: mutexes are used to avoid low-level conflicts, while these Boolean variables prevent the tasks from becoming stuck waiting for one another.

When you want to reset, say, the right leg, you must set the Rreset variable to true, unblocking the realignment task. In fact, the AlignRightLeg task hangs at the while (!Rreset) Wait(100) statement until the RealignLegs function sets Rreset to true (see Listing 5-6). Once free to do its duty, the task acquires the right leg mutex and aligns the leg as described before. When the realignment is completed, the Rreset variable is set to false, so that at the next loop iteration the task will stop, waiting for the Rreset variable to be set to true again.

Finally, the Sight task implements, in its last lines, the hysteresis cycle described in the previous paragraph (see Listing 5-9).

Listing 5-9. *The Code of the Task Used to Measure the Obstacle's Distance Continuously*

```
task Sight ()
{
    Follows(main);
    int d;
    while (true)
    {
        d = SensorUS (EYES);
        Acquire (display);
        TextOut (5, LCD_LINE1, "distance:        ");
        NumOut (70, LCD_LINE1, d);
        Release (display);
        Wait(10);
        //hysteresis cycle
        if (d < NEAR) obstacle = true;
        else if (d > FAR ) obstacle = false;
    }
}
```

■**Tip** Try to set both the FAR and NEAR constant thresholds to the same value, and download the program to the Omni-Biped. You should notice a jerky behavior, meaning that the robot switches constantly from forward to backward motion. This undesirable effect comes about because the hysteresis cycle is made idle by the identical values of the thresholds. After having experimented, fix the program by setting the FAR constant higher than the NEAR constant value.

Building Instructions

I'll stop chattering—it's time to build! You can build Omni-Biped using only the NXT retail set parts. If you stop before building the arms' assembly (Step 70), you'll have a walking base to be freely customized. For example, you could follow the MINDSTORMS retail set instructions to build the Alpha Rex upper body to attach to these legs; otherwise, you can embellish the model with many additions, such as arms, hands, a tail, or whatever you desire. You must pay attention not to upset the equilibrium of the robot and avoid excessively protruding or asymmetric features. To start with, build the body as illustrated in Steps 74–111.

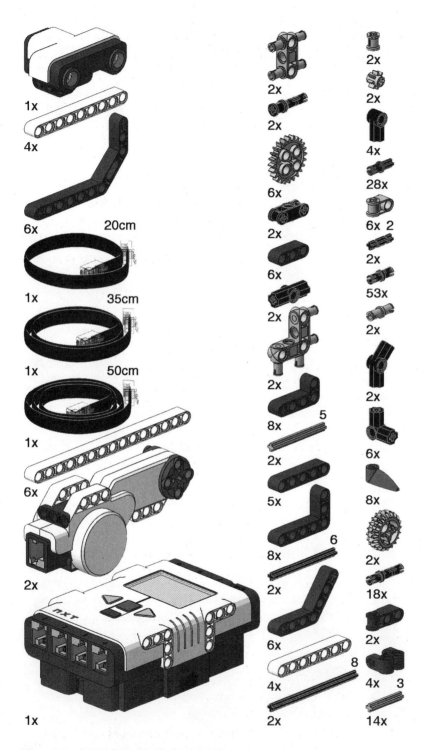

Figure 5-6. *Omni-Biped bill of materials*

Table 5-1. *Omni-Biped Bill of Materials*

Quantity	Color	Part Number	Part Name
1		56467.DAT	Electric MINDSTORMS NXT Ultrasonic Sensor
4	White	40490.DAT	TECHNIC Beam 9
6	Dark gray	32009.DAT	TECHNIC Beam 11.5 Liftarm Bent 45 Double
1	Black	55804.DAT	Electric Cable NXT 20cm
1	Black	55805.DAT	Electric Cable NXT 35cm
1	Black	55806.DAT	Electric Cable NXT 50cm
6	White	32278.DAT	TECHNIC Beam 15
2		53787.DAT	Electric MINDSTORMS NXT Motor
1		53788.DAT	Electric MINDSTORMS NXT
2	Light gray	48989.DAT	TECHNIC Axle Joiner Perpendicular 1×3×3 with 4 Pins
2	Black	32054.DAT	TECHNIC Pin Long with Stop Bush
6	Light gray	3648.DAT	TECHNIC Gear 24 Tooth
2	Black	32184.DAT	TECHNIC Axle Joiner Perpendicular 3L
6	Dark gray	32523.DAT	TECHNIC Beam 3
2	Black	32034.DAT	TECHNIC Angle Connector #2
2	Light gray	55615.DAT	TECHNIC Beam 5 Bent 90 (3:3) with 4 Pins
8	Dark gray	32140.DAT	TECHNIC Beam 5 Liftarm Bent 90 (4:2)
2	Light gray	32073.DAT	TECHNIC Axle 5
5	Dark gray	32316.DAT	TECHNIC Beam 5
8	Dark gray	32526.DAT	TECHNIC Beam 7 Bent 90 (5:3)
2	Black	3706.DAT	TECHNIC Axle 6
6	Dark gray	32348.DAT	TECHNIC Beam 7 Liftarm Bent 53.5 (4:4)
4	White	32524.DAT	TECHNIC Beam 7
2	Black	3707.DAT	TECHNIC Axle 8
2	Light gray	3713.DAT	TECHNIC Bush
2	Light gray	3647.DAT	TECHNIC Gear 8 Tooth
4	Black	32013.DAT	TECHNIC Angle Connector #1
28	Blue	43093.DAT	TECHNIC Axle Pin with Friction
6	Light gray	6536.DAT	TECHNIC Axle Joiner Perpendicular
2	Black	32062.DAT	TECHNIC Axle 2 Notched
53	Black	2780.DAT	TECHNIC Pin with Friction and Slots
2	Light gray	3673.DAT	TECHNIC Pin
2	Black	32192.DAT	TECHNIC Angle Connector #4 (135 degree)
6	Black	32014.DAT	TECHNIC Angle Connector #6 (90 degree)

Continued

Table 5-1. *Continued*

Quantity	Color	Part Number	Part Name
8	Orange	41669.DAT	TECHNIC Bionicle 1 × 3 Tooth with Axlehole
2	Light gray	32269.DAT	TECHNIC Gear 20 Tooth Double Bevel
18	Black	6558.DAT	TECHNIC Pin Long with Friction and Slot
2	Dark gray	42003.DAT	TECHNIC Axle Joiner Perpendicular with 2 Holes
4	Dark gray	41678.DAT	TECHNIC Axle Joiner Perpendicular Double Split
14	Light gray	4519.DAT	TECHNIC Axle 3

237 parts total (all included in the NXT retail set)

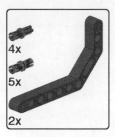

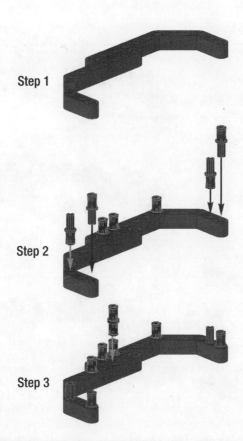

Step 1

Step 2

Step 3

Start building the right foot. In Step 2, insert the blue axle pins at the end of the bent beams.

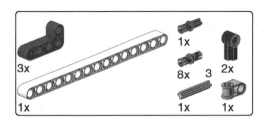

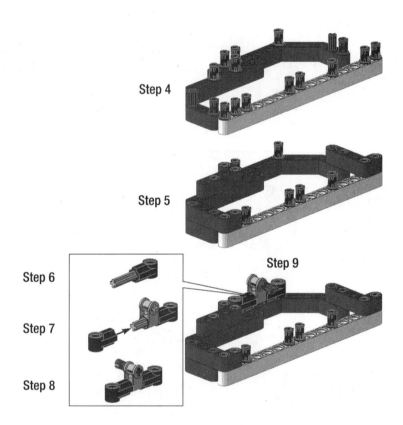

Add a 15-long beam with 8 black pins, then join the foot parts with the dark gray bent liftarms. Finally, add the ankle hinge.

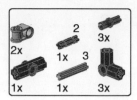

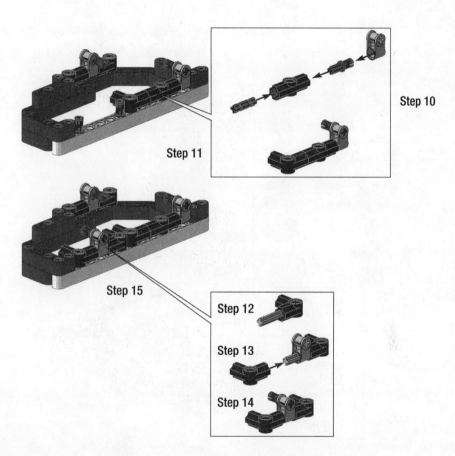

Add the other two ankle hinges that allow the biped to bend the ankle to shift the weight smoothly. The right foot is completed.

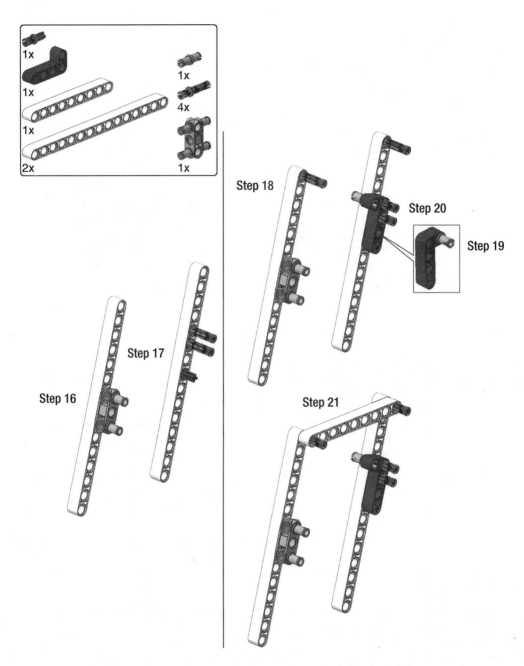

Now build the right leg. Here you must use two 15-long beams and a 9-long beam to join them.

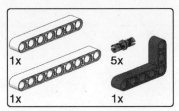

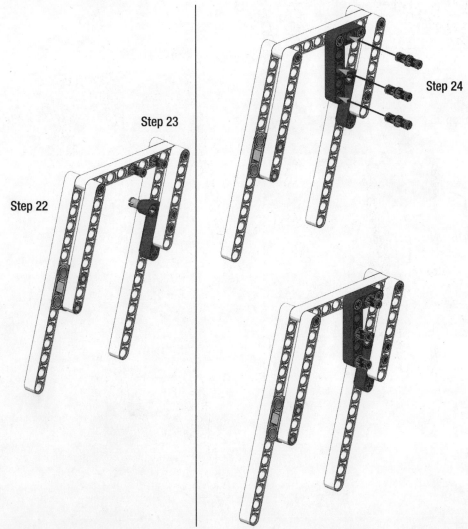

Step 22

Step 23

Step 24

Reinforce the leg using 9-long and 7-long beams. Add the bent beam where the legs' cams will be attached and add the black pins.

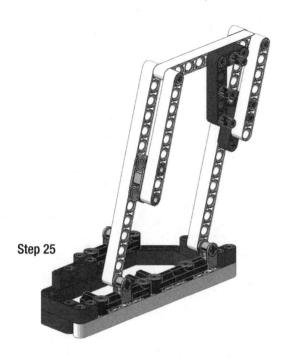

Step 25

The right leg is done.

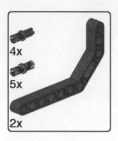

Step 26

Step 27

Step 28

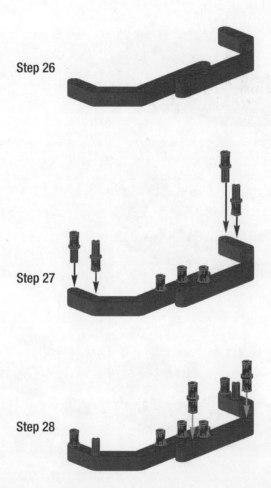

Start building the left foot. In Step 27, insert the blue axle pins at the end of the bent beams.

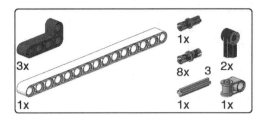

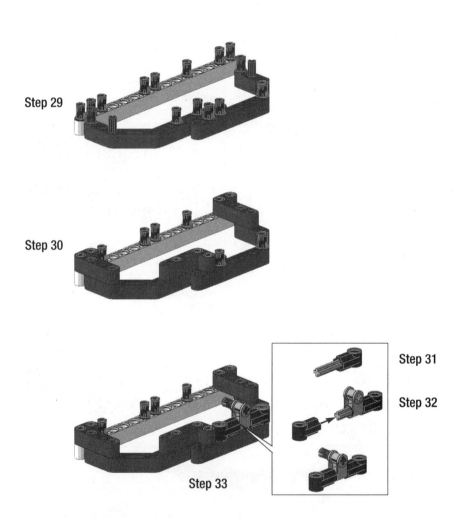

Step 29

Step 30

Step 31

Step 32

Step 33

Add a 15-long beam with eight black pins, then join the foot parts with the dark gray bent liftarms. Finally, add the ankle hinge.

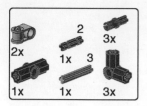

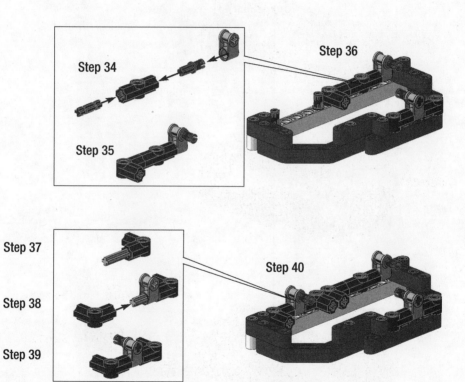

Add the other two ankle hinges. The left foot is completed.

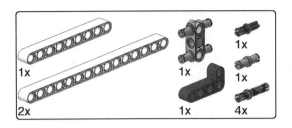

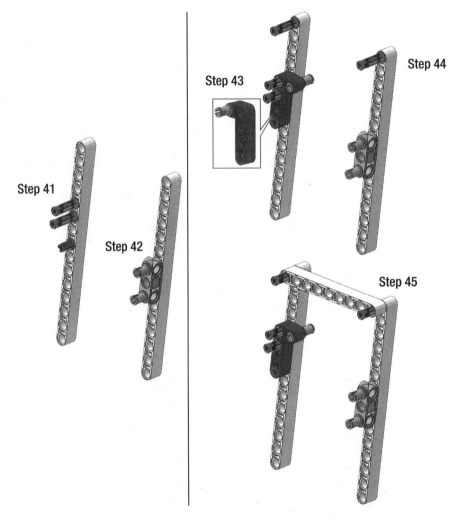

Now build the left leg. Here you must use two 15-long beams and a 9-long beam to join them.

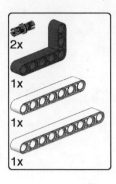

Step 46

Step 47

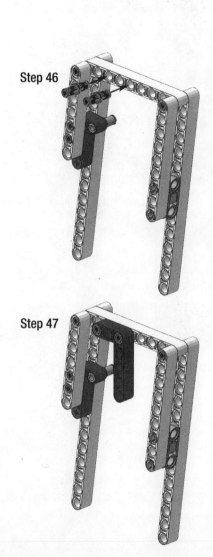

Reinforce the leg using 9-long and 7-long beams. Add the bent beam where the legs' cams will be attached, and the left leg is finished.

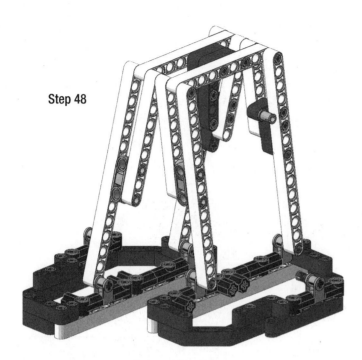

Step 48

Attach the two legs together, using the central dark gray bent beams as a reference. Place the right leg forward and the left leg backward, as shown.

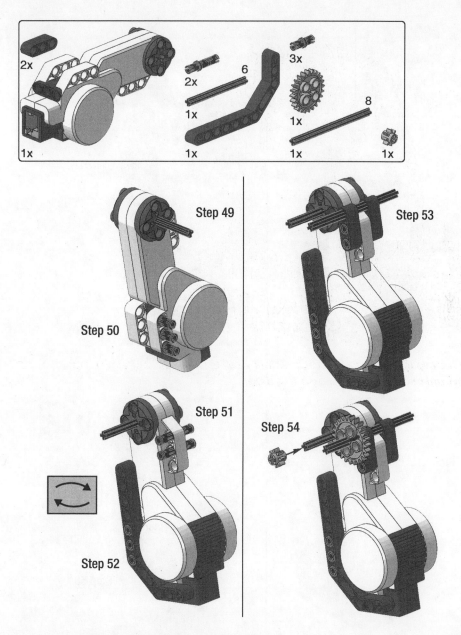

Step 49

Step 50

Step 51

Step 52

Step 53

Step 54

Now you're building the left motor subassembly.

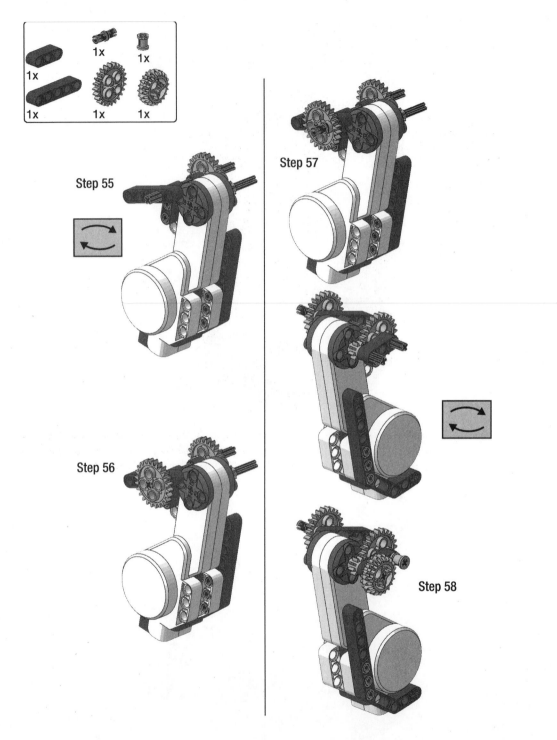

Attach a black pin in a hole of the 24-tooth gear; this gear must be rotated so that two of its holes are aligned with the 5-long beam holes. Use Figure 5-2 as reference.

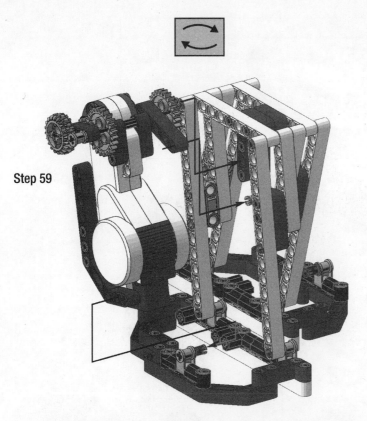

Step 59

Insert the left motor subassembly in place. The cam pin goes in the free hole of the central bent beams of the leg assembly, the last hole of the 5-long beam goes in the gray pin of the leg, and the external ankle hinge pin goes in the first round hole of the motor assembly's bent beam.

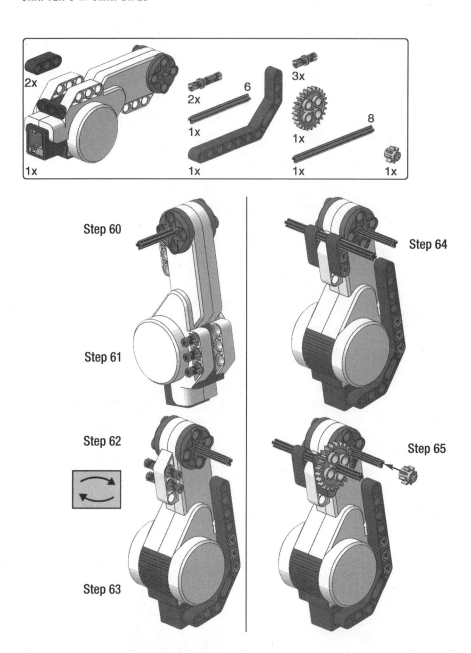

Now you're building the right motor subassembly.

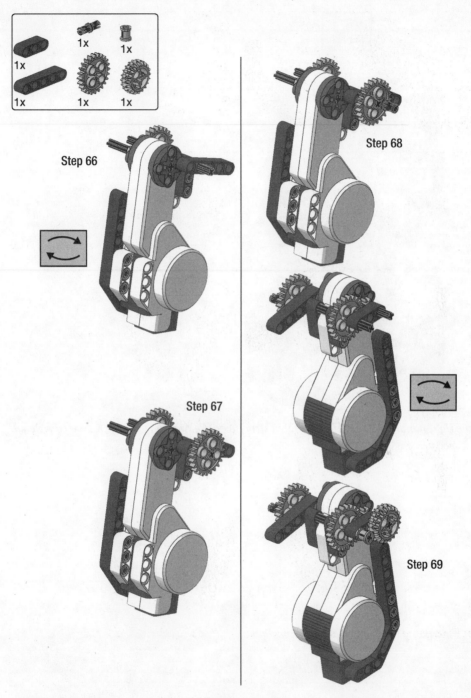

Step 66

Step 67

Step 68

Step 69

Attach the black pin in a hole of the 24-tooth gear, so that it is the opposite hole with respect to where you placed the pin in the other leg cam. This is not crucial now, but the correct alignment of cams and legs is essential later.

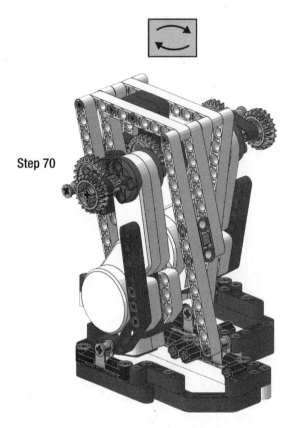

Step 70

Insert the right motor assembly onto the robot structure as before. The walking base is completed.

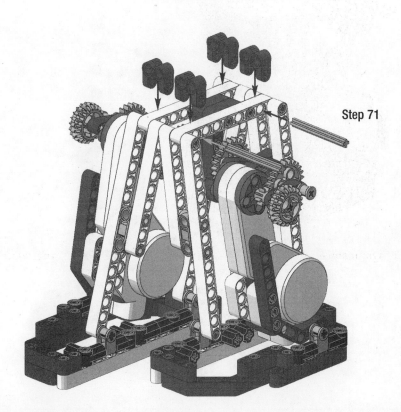

Step 71

From now on, you are building the robot's upper body. You can get creative or continue building as illustrated. Rotate the model and add the perpendicular joiners, blocking them with two 5-long axles.

4x

Step 72

Add four black long pins.

Step 73

Add the 7-long beams.

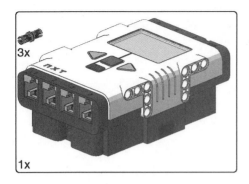

Step 74

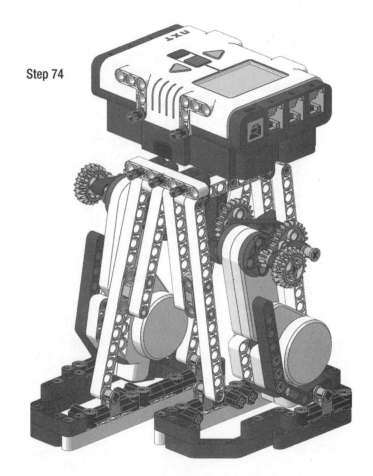

Place the NXT on the legs and put three pins where shown. In the picture you see a "flying" NXT because the instructions are meant for both those who will use normal batteries or the Li-Ion battery pack, which makes the NXT one unit taller than normal.

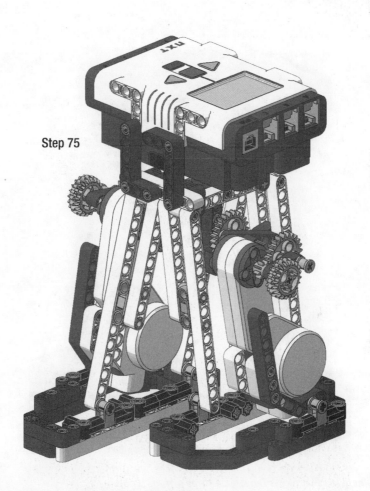

Step 75

Place two bent beams to lock the NXT on this side.

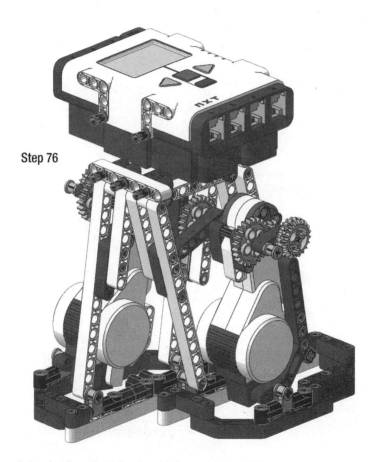

Step 76

Turn the model to see the robot's back. Add three pins as before.

Step 77

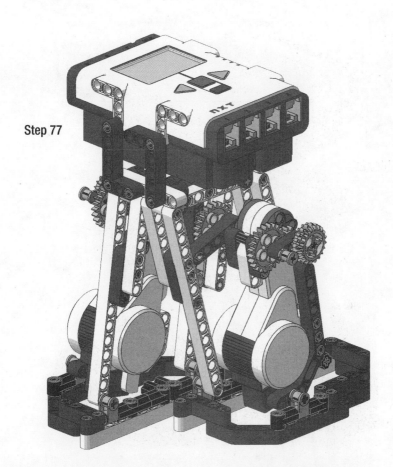

Add two bent beams again and the NXT is now completely locked onto the legs.

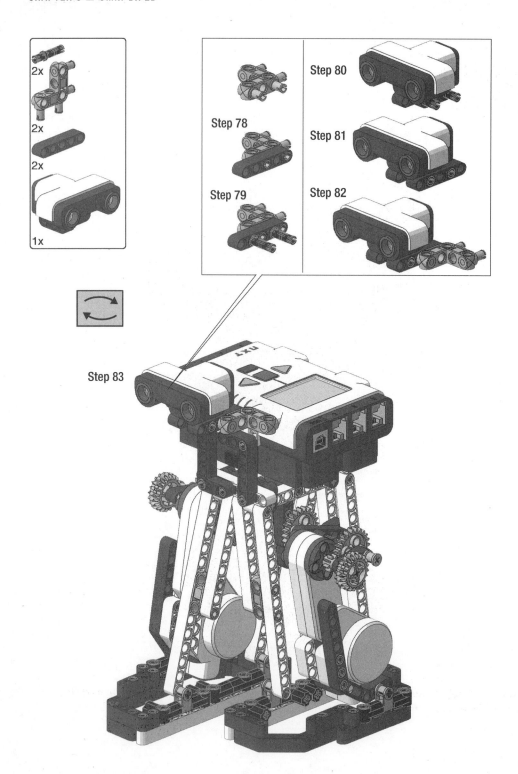

Step 78

Step 79

Step 80

Step 81

Step 82

Step 83

Build the robot's head.

Step 84

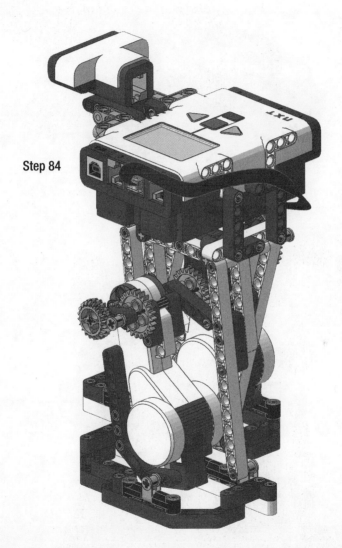

Attach the right motor to NXT output port B using a 50cm (20 inch) cable. See the next step (85)
to see where to pass the cable.

Step 85

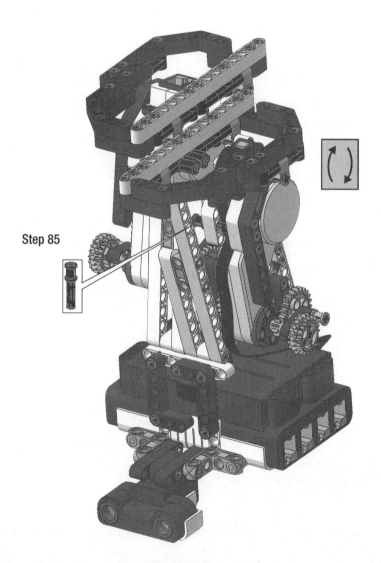

The cable must pass tightly in the space between the motor's white beams, and you must block it there with a long pin with the stop bush. The cable turn in the bottom of the foot must clear the ground or the robot won't walk correctly.

Step 86

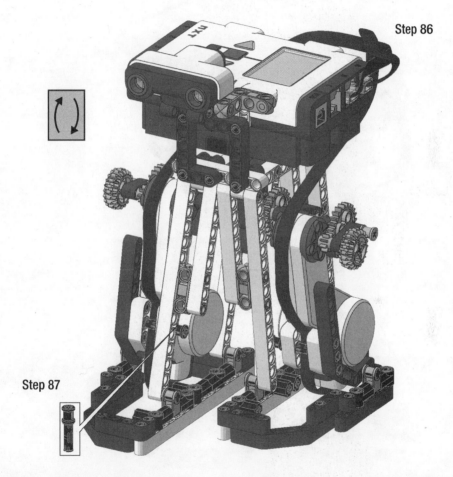

Step 87

Attach the left motor to NXT output port A using a 35cm (14 inch) cable. Pass and block the cable as shown. Check the previous caption as a guide.

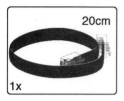

Step 88

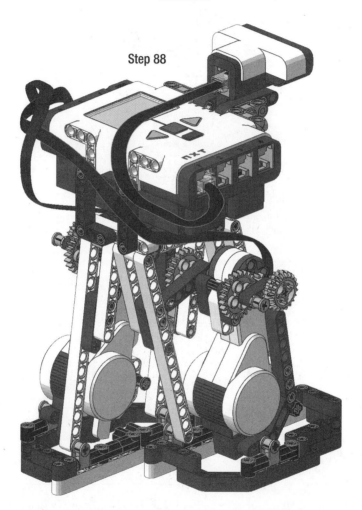

Attach the Ultrasonic Sensor to NXT input port 1 using a 20cm (8 inch) cable.

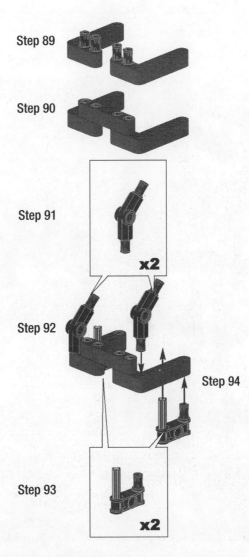

Step 89

Step 90

Step 91

Step 92

Step 94

Step 93

Start building the arms' decorative assembly. This submodel is optional and can be replaced or customized as you want, just paying attention not to compromise the robot's balance.

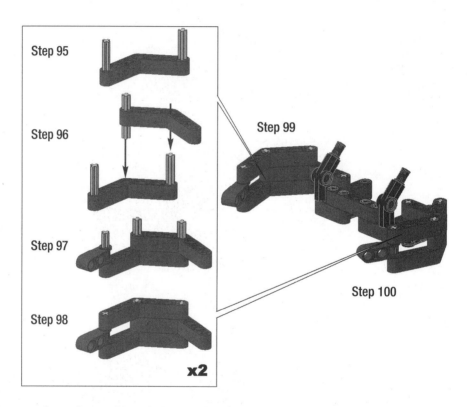

Build the arms themselves and attach them to the rest of the assembly.

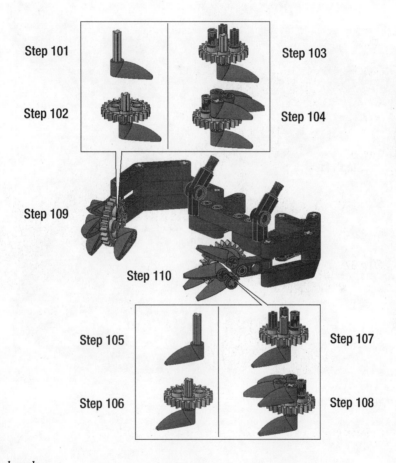

Build the hands.

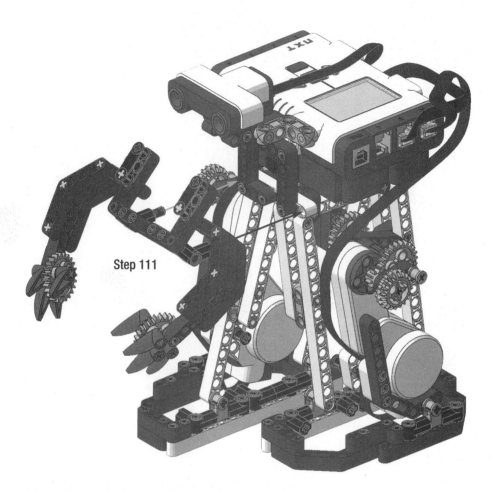

Step 111

Attach the arms' subassembly to the robot.

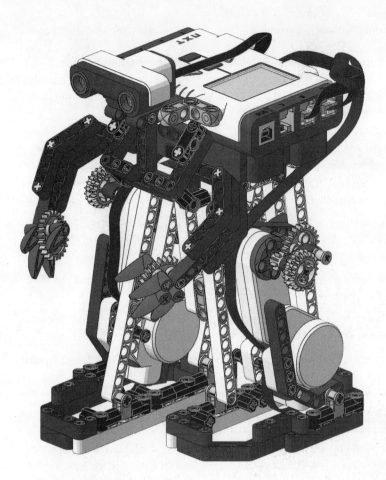

The Omni-Biped is completed.

Summary

In this chapter, you've been introduced to a small and quick biped robot—the walker alternative to the LEGO wheeled Tribot. This is a simple project, with respect to other ones you'll find later in the book. Still, it offers many ideas, and an occasion to show some techniques that could be useful in other situations.

Alpha Rex inspired the Omni-Biped legs' shape, but notice how small but fundamental modifications have notably improved the gait, especially regarding turning. The motor is a mobile part of the leg itself, while in Alpha Rex, motors are hung inside the leg frame and don't move during the gait. Here, every motor drives a whole leg, both stepping and leaning, while in Alpha Rex the motors control different movements of both legs together; that is, one motor controls robot leaning, the other controls the stepping. Furthermore, the turning mechanism is much more elegant in Omni-Biped than in Alpha Rex, whose solution (with rubber grippers) is not realistic.

On the software side, you saw the difference between single-task and multitask programs. We also touched the tip of the iceberg with regards to concurrent programming difficulties and their solution: the mutual exclusion semaphores. Also, the modulo operator (%) could be useful in your future projects. Finally, we analyzed the operation, the uses, and the implementation of the hysteresis cycle.

Having three sensor ports left, there's plenty of space for add-ons and new features. Don't forget the third motor in your box that is waiting for action! The following exercises might also inspire you to build some new type of robot. If your creativity needs to be sparked some more, keep on reading the next chapters.

Exercise 5-1. Hardware Ideas

Rebuild the leg frames to shape a chicken-like leg, with a reverse bent knee. Modify the motor placement accordingly, to keep using the motors as structural support.

Add a tail and a head (like a dinosaur) that would follow the legs' movement, helping the COG shifting. For example, when the robot is leaning left, the tail would be bent left, and the same for the right side, balancing the robot. You might drive the tail with the third motor or use the leg motors themselves.

After having read the AT-ST instructions in Chapter 4, try to add sensors and modify the software to let your robot reset its leg position automatically at program startup.

Don't let that third motor go to waste! After having read Chapter 7, you can use its fetching arm as a starting idea to develop a grabber for Omni-Biped. Could you give it the ability to find objects autonomously?

The world is full of line-following robots on wheels. There aren't that many line-following walkers. There's no need to say a word more. Do it!

Exercise 5-2. Software Ideas

Using the multitask version of the software, add new tasks to play a melody while walking, and display animation. Be careful when using the mutex variables to synchronize display access for animation and string messages, and voice announcements with music.

After having read Chapter 3 about FSMs and Chapter 6 about the NXT Turtle, try to give the Omni-Biped an autonomous behavior. You can use as state names (and corresponding functionality) Lazy, Normal, Worried, and Dancing; transition events among states could be an incoming obstacle, a sharp sound, a sound pattern, or a timer elapsing. The robot in Lazy state could stand still, performing some random movement; when it senses a sharp sound, its state could become Worried and it would walk a bit. If the sounds continue around it, the Dancing state could be triggered, and the robot would eventually start to dance. In Normal state, finally, it could walk, avoiding obstacles. These are just a few ideas, but you can customize the robot's behavior as you prefer.

CHAPTER 6

■ ■ ■

NXT Turtle

After the bipeds, it's time to double the leg count. In this chapter, you'll bring a robotic turtle to life. Once built, it will look as shown in Figure 6-1, if you power the NXT with the LEGO rechargeable battery. The NXT is in fact a LEGO unit that's taller than normal, because the battery pack adds thickness.

Figure 6-1. *The NXT Turtle, in the version including the rechargeable battery*

Quadruped Walking

Balancing a quadruped is simpler than balancing a biped, that's for sure. However, the legs must move in sync to clear the COG bounds that we discussed in Chapter 1. Here we are talking about a generic quadruped robot that uses only its four feet as supporting points—that is a robot, whose legs are long, and whose body is far from the ground.

Figure 6-2 shows the techniques a quadruped robot could use to walk straight—assuming that the legs on each side are synchronized. This means that each front leg is coupled with the back leg on the same side. When one foot is lifted from the ground, the other foot is touching the ground; when a leg moves forward, the other is brought backwards, as shown in Figure 6-3. Every leg is given two degrees of freedom (DOF): the first to move the foot up and down, the second to move the leg back and forth. You can do the coupling using mechanical parts that connect the legs directly or drive the leg motors together, assuming you have separate motors to move them.

About the motors: even if you have to give each leg two DOF (one to raise and lower the leg, one to move the leg back and forth) you don't necessarily need two motors per leg. In fact, you can give each leg two DOF with just a motor, using a particular cammed mechanism, or you can even move the couple of two-DOF legs on the same side with a single motor. The latter is precisely what happens in the NXT Turtle.

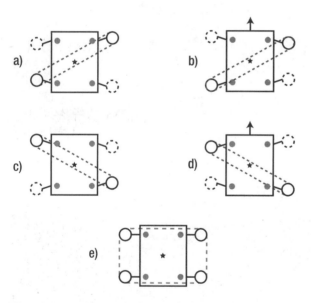

Figure 6-2. *Quadruped robot straight walking scheme*

In Figure 6-2e, the robot has all feet on the ground and the supporting area is wide, containing the COG of the robot (indicated as a star). This is the steadier state of the robot.

The NXT Turtle hides in its simplicity many hardware and software inspirations. Other less realistic approaches to building walking legged robots exist: one motor to lean aside, the others to advance, or a cammed mechanism that keeps legs parallel to the body. The actual mechanism is smooth, effective, and realistic—a pleasure to see working! You can reuse this technique in other walking robots, varying leg angle and length.

On the software side, you were introduced to a good example of how to implement a finite state machine (FSM) (see Chapter 3) to simulate a simple autonomous behavior, so that the turtle can change its mood depending on what's happening, becoming quiet, hungry, scared, or bored. If you annoy it too much, it could decide to run away, but if nothing happens for a while, it will eventually turn around, looking for food. If it gets too bored, it could fall asleep!

Programming the Turtle

The turtle crawls around using the same motor configuration as a wheeled bot. That way, you can start trying your turtle movements with a few lines of code, or the NXT-G Move Blocks. You can even guide the model with a Bluetooth remote application running on a PC, PDA, or cell phone.

After having remote-controlled the turtle a bit, you can turn to something more serious. Now you'll see how to write a program to make the turtle walk while avoiding obstacles. In the second program, you'll see how to make the turtle follow lines. Finally, in the third, complex program, you'll give the turtle a breath of life, implementing an autonomous behavior with a FSM. Your turtle will behave like a real one, plus make some additional unnatural but funny sounds.

Simple Program

The first program for the turtle implements the simple behavior described in the introduction paragraph and shown in the flow chart in Figure 6-4. The turtle walks straight until it sees a near object; it retracts its head and walks backward until the object is far enough away. Once the sight line is clear, the turtle turns in a random direction, gets its head out of its shell, and begins to walk straight again. In Figure 6-4, the gray dashed arrow pointing at the FINISH label means that the loop is perpetual, but the program can be eventually stopped by pressing the dark gray stop button on the NXT, when the NXT power-off timer elapses or the batteries run dry.

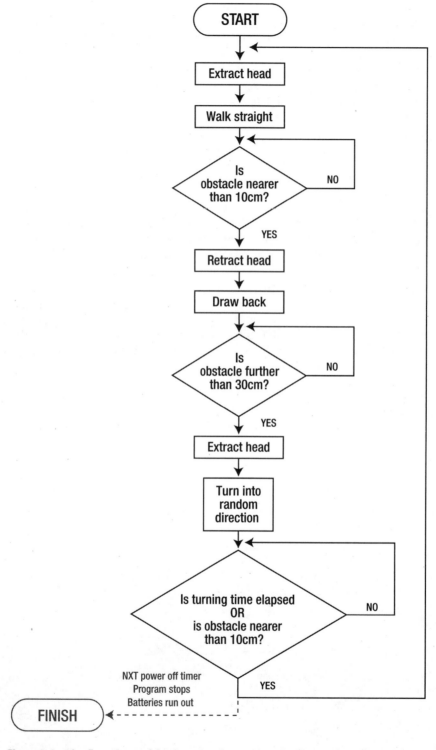

Figure 6-4. *The flow chart of the first simple program for the turtle*

Now you'll see how the behavior described before can be translated into NXC code. In Listing 6-1 you can read the code of this first program for the turtle.

Listing 6-1. *First Program for the Turtle*

```
// aliases
#define R_LEGS OUT_A
#define L_LEGS OUT_C
#define LEGS OUT_AC
#define HEAD OUT_B
#define EYES IN_2
#define MIC IN_1
#define LINE IN_3
#define NEAR 10
#define FAR 30
#define TURN_TIME SEC_4
#define IN -1
#define OUT 1

// global variables
short head_state;
unsigned long start_time;

// Subroutine to move head IN or OUT
sub MoveHead ( short position )
{
    int t;
    // move head only if the desired position
    // is different from the actual state
    if (head_state != position)
    {
        t = MotorRotationCount(HEAD);
        PlayFile("! Blips 19.rso");
        // start motor in desired direction
        OnFwd(HEAD,60*sign(position));
        Wait(80);
        // sense if the motor is stalled
        while( abs(t-MotorRotationCount(HEAD))>7 )
        {
            t = MotorRotationCount(HEAD);
            Wait(50);
        }
        Off(HEAD);

        // update head state with actual position
        head_state = position;
    }
}
```

```
task main(){
    //init sensors
    SetSensorSound(MIC);
    SetSensorLowspeed(EYES);
    SetSensorLight(LINE);

    // extract head
    head_state = IN;
    MoveHead(OUT);

    while (true)
    {
        //go straight
        OnFwdSync(LEGS,100,0);
        ClearScreen();
        TextOut(30,LCD_LINE3,"Go!");

        //wait for an object to come near
        while (SensorUS(EYES) > NEAR);

        //stop and retract the head
        Float (LEGS);
        MoveHead(IN);

        //back up
        OnRevSync(LEGS,100,0);
        ClearScreen();
        TextOut(20,LCD_LINE3,"Run away...");
        Wait(SEC_3);

        //wait for the object to get far enough
        while (SensorUS(EYES) < FAR);

        //stop and extract head
        Float (LEGS);
        MoveHead(OUT);

        // choose a random direction and turn
        if (Random(2)==1)
        {
            ClearScreen();
            TextOut(30,LCD_LINE3,"Turn right");
            OnRevSync(LEGS,100,80);
        }
```

```
    else
    {
        ClearScreen();
        TextOut(30,LCD_LINE3,"Turn left");
        OnRevSync(LEGS,100,-80);
    }

    // save actual time to use as offset later
    start_time = CurrentTick();

    //wait for the timer to elapse or another object to come near
    until ( (CurrentTick()-start_time)>TURN_TIME || SensorUS(EYES) < NEAR );
    Float(LEGS);
  }
}
```

The program starts executing the main task. At the beginning, the input ports are initialized, then the program enters into a perpetual loop. The head is brought out, calling the MoveHead(OUT) subroutine. The legs are started with OnFwdSync(LEGS,100,0), which tells the motors to move synchronized at full speed, with a Turn Ratio equal to zero, because the turtle must go straight. The program flow stops at the while (SensorUS(EYES) > NEAR) statement, checking the specified condition continuously (object seen further than NEAR). When it becomes true, the head is retracted, calling MoveHead(IN), and the legs are told to walk backwards in sync with OnRevSync (LEGS,100,0). Another blocking wait follows. With while (SensorUS(EYES) < FAR) the program waits for the object to be nearer than FAR; at that point, the head is moved out again, and a random turning direction is chosen. The function calling Random(2) generates random numbers that can be 1 or 0, so the condition if(Random(2)==1) can be true or false, allowing a choice between turning left or right. The turning is achieved by starting the legs with the NXC function OnRevSync(LEGS,100,80); the Turn Ratio makes the motors rotate in opposite directions.

Tip Using the OnFwdSync(ports, speed, turn_ratio) and OnRevSync(...) functions, the NXT starts two motors (OUT_AB, OUT_BC, OUT_AC), controlling their relative speed, specified by the turn_ratio argument. With a turn_ratio equal to 0, the motors' speeds are controlled to be perfectly equal and a wheeled robot would go straight. With a negative turn_ratio, the robot would turn in one direction; with a positive value, the robot would turn in the other direction. The turn_ratio can be any value from -100 to 100. Check the NXC Programming Guide for further details.

After the legs are started, the actual system time is saved into the start_time variable, an unsigned long integer variable with values from 0 to $2^{32}-1$. This action corresponds to a timer reset.

TIMERS

It's worth saying a few words about the timer provided by the NXT brick. Although RCX standard firmware provides three one-hundredth of a second resolution timers, NXT has only one timer, with a one-thousandth of a second resolution. That timer can count up to 2^{32} milliseconds. This corresponds to 49 days, 17 hours, 2 minutes, 47 seconds, and 296 milliseconds of continuous operation. I think this is quite enough for anyone's needs.

Why should you use a timer when the easy `Wait` function is available? Simple: by using `Wait`, the program flow would stop for a specified number of milliseconds, during which you could not check for other occurring events. In this case you want to continue checking for events while waiting for the time to elapse, and these events would stop the waiting, even if the time has not passed yet. To do this, you should replace the `Wait(TURNING_TIME)` statement with the following:

```
until ( (CurrentTick()-start_time)>TURN_TIME || SensorUS(EYES) < NEAR );
```

You can check both the timer elapsing and the occurrence of other events, like an object approaching or sounds occurring. In the preceding statement, you can check simultaneously if the timer has elapsed or if the object has gone out of view. It's enough for one condition to become `true` to break out of the loop. The `until()` loop will stop waiting if the time difference `CurrentTick()-start_time` grows bigger than `TURN_TIME` (first condition), or if the obstacle comes closer than `NEAR` (second condition).

The only two system calls to access the system timer are `FirstTick()`, which returns the ticks from the NXT startup to program start, and `CurrentTick()`, which returns ticks from the NXT startup to the actual system call moment. In the preceding wait loop, the following difference is checked against `TURN_TIME`:

```
(CurrentTick()-start_time)
```

`CurrentTick()` minus `start_time` yields the time elapsed from the time contained in the `start_time` variable. Before the loop, you saved the actual system time in that variable, so you are checking for the time elapsed from the statement that performs the "timer reset." If the time elapsed is more than `TURN_TIME`, the condition will be `true`, and this will be sufficient to stop waiting in the loop.

On the other hand, if the other condition (`SensorUS(EYES) < NEAR`) becomes `true`, the waiting will stop, even if the `TURN_TIME` has not elapsed.

In general, to add other conditions into this special wait loop, it is enough to add them inside the parentheses, by using the suitable logical operators (logical *AND* &&, logical *OR* ||, and logical *NOT* !). To see how the Boolean operators AND, OR, and NOT work, check out the sidebar "Boolean Operators."

BOOLEAN OPERATORS

How do you express complicated logical conditions for `if`, `while`, and `until` statements?

If you want to check for two conditions to be verified together, use the AND operator &&. For example, you can translate the condition "if the sun is shining and the temperature is warm, go out without an umbrella" as follows:

```
if ( sun == SHINING && temperature > TWENTY_DEGREES )
{
    // go out without an umbrella
}
```

If you want to check if any of the conditions are verified, you have to use the operator OR ||. To negate a condition, use the operator NOT (represented by the exclamation mark !). For example, if your condition is "if the sun is not shining or the temperature is cold, wear a sweater," you have to use the operator NOT ! and the operator OR ||, and the code would be as follows:

```
if ( sun != SHINING || temperature < TEN_DEGREES )
{
    // wear a sweater
}
```

You can put the negation operator (!) before a condition or a Boolean variable to negate it, transforming it to `true` if it was `false`, and vice versa. For example, the condition (`sun != SHINING`) is equivalent to `!(sun == SHINING)`.

Furthermore, two important laws hold about Boolean algebra: the De Morgan Laws. Let A and B be two Boolean conditions. These two laws follow:

- !(A && B) is equal to (!A || !B)

- !(A || B) is equal to (!A && !B)

For example, let's see how to apply the second law to the preceding expression:

```
until( (CurrentTick()-start_time)>TURN_TIME || SensorUS(EYES)<NEAR );
```

Remembering that `until(condition)` is equal to `while(!condition)`, the preceding is equal to the following:

```
while( !( (CurrentTick()-start_time)>TURN_TIME || SensorUS(EYES)<NEAR ) );
```

Applying the second De Morgan Law, you can transform it into this:

```
while ((CurrentTick()-start_time)<=TURN_TIME && SensorUS(EYES)>=NEAR);
```

Try to replace it in the first program for the turtle and verify that it works exactly the same.

Finally, when the waiting is done, the head is brought out again, and the program restarts from the beginning of the external `while(true)` loop.

Line Following

The second program is a nice application for a walker vehicle of a line-following algorithm, well-known to many long-standing LEGO MINDSTORMS users. The weird thing is that the algorithm presented here allows the turtle to follow the lines only going backward. This isn't surprising. In fact, the Light Sensor used to detect the black line on the white surfaces is mounted in the back of the turtle—behind its turning center.

Start thinking about following a path going forward, but say you have your eyes on the nape of your neck: you would see what's behind you, not what's coming in front of you! Your turtle is the same way, because the Light Sensor to see the black line is on the back. Thus, it can follow lines only walking backwards. At the beginning of the program, you are asked to set two thresholds. Pressing the NXT left arrow, you store the low threshold; pressing the right arrow, you store the high threshold; and pressing the orange button, you accept the settings. Only at this point does the line-following algorithm start.

To understand how the line-following algorithm works, look at Figure 6-5. This composite figure shows how the two thresholds low and high are used (see Figure 6-5a), and the value of the Light Sensor reading, depending on its position.

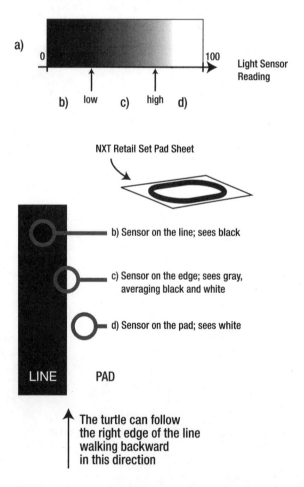

Figure 6-5. *Composite figure to explain the line-following algorithm*

The turtle follows the black line going backward. It turns right if the color seen by the sensor is black (Figure 6-5b), it goes straight if the reading is gray (Figure 6-5c), and turns left if the reading is white (Figure 6-5d). This way, the turtle can follow the right edge of a black line on white ground, or the left edge of a white line on dark ground. The line-following program is shown in Listing 6-2.

Listing 6-2. *The Program for the Turtle to Do Line-Following*

```
#define R_LEGS OUT_A
#define L_LEGS OUT_C
#define LEGS OUT_AC
#define LIGHT IN_3
#define TOLERANCE 3

// this macro clears a line of the display
#define ClearLine(line)  TextOut(0,line,"                    ")

int low=30, high=50;

void Tracking_init ()
{
   bool done = false;
   SetSensorLight(LIGHT);
   ClearScreen();

   // display menu
   TextOut(0,LCD_LINE6," Set         Set");
   TextOut(0,LCD_LINE7,"dark   OK  light");

   until(done)
   {
      TextOut(0,LCD_LINE2,"Reading:       ");
      NumOut(50,LCD_LINE2,Sensor(LIGHT));

      // if you press the NXT left arrow button...
      if (ButtonPressed(BTNLEFT,true))
      {
         // ...you are setting the low threshold
         low = Sensor(LIGHT) + TOLERANCE;
         ClearLine(LCD_LINE8);
         NumOut(8,LCD_LINE8,low);
         NumOut(75,LCD_LINE8,high);
         while (ButtonPressed(BTNLEFT,true));
      }
```

```
        // if you press the NXT right arrow button...
        if (ButtonPressed(BTNRIGHT,true))
        {
            // ...you are setting the high threshold
            high= Sensor(LIGHT) - TOLERANCE;
            ClearLine(LCD_LINE8);
            NumOut(8,LCD_LINE8,low);
            NumOut(75,LCD_LINE8,high);
            while (ButtonPressed(BTNRIGHT,true));
        }
        // if you press the NXT orange button, you accept the changes
        if (ButtonPressed(BTNCENTER,true)) done = true;
        Wait(10);
    }
    Wait(1000);
    ClearScreen();
}

task main ()
{
    int reading;

    // call the initialization function to set the thresholds
    Tracking_init();

    while (true)
    {
        // read the Light Sensor
        reading  = Sensor(LIGHT);

        // if the sensor sees white (pad)
        if ( reading >= high )
        {
            TextOut(5,LCD_LINE3,"WHITE");
            Float(LEGS);
            // the turtle turns right
            OnRev(L_LEGS,100);
        }
```

```
    // if the sensor sees gray (line edge)
    if ( reading < high && reading > low )
    {
        TextOut(5,LCD_LINE3,"GRAY  ");
        // the turtle goes straight
        OnRevSync(LEGS,100,0);
    }
    // if the sensor sees black (line)
    if ( reading <= low )
    {
        TextOut(5,LCD_LINE3,"BLACK");
        Float(LEGS);
        // the turtle turns left
        OnRev(R_LEGS,100);
    }
    // display the actual sensor reading
    TextOut(0,LCD_LINE2,"Reading:          ");
    NumOut(50,LCD_LINE2,reading);
    Wait(100);
    }
}
```

At the beginning of the program, the main task calls the Tracking_init() function. This function is used to ask the user to set the two thresholds high and low, explained before (see Figure 6-5a). The TOLERANCE value (set to 3), added to the low threshold and subtracted from the high threshold, is used to narrow the range of values seen as gray, to compensate for the flickering measurements of the sensor. For example, if during the initial setup, the sensor reading stored for the black color is 35, the algorithm will classify as black every reading less than 38 (35+3). Assuming you stored a reading of 51 for the white color, the algorithm will classify as white every reading greater than 48 (51-3). So, the TOLERANCE value represents the tolerance used when discerning sensor readings (a tautology!). Once you press the orange button, the Tracking_init() function returns, and the line-following algorithm starts. The algorithm works as explained earlier, running forever inside the while(true) loop.

Autonomous Behavior Simulation

It's time to give your pet the spark of life! You'll see how to model an autonomous behavior for the turtle, to make it resemble a real one. Read the following description while looking at Figure 6-6, where you can see a comprehensive diagram of the turtle's behavior.

NXT Turtle Autonomous Behavior

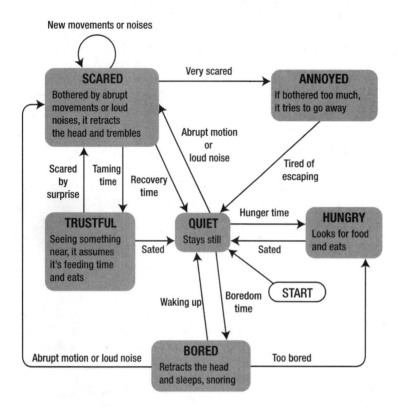

Figure 6-6. *The diagram of the FSM implemented to simulate the turtle's behavior. The named boxes describe the moods, and the arrows represent state transitions caused by events.*

When the program starts, the turtle is in QUIET mood, and stands still in place. After a while, if you don't come close to its eyes, or if you don't scare it with loud noises, it could become bored or hungry. In BORED mood, the turtle decides to have a nap: it retracts its head and snores loudly. It wakes up on its own after a while, returning to QUIET, but could also be awakened suddenly by a loud noise, leading to a SCARED mood. Imagine how nervous you'd be, awakened suddenly by a giant alarm clock! After a few naps, the boredom is so oppressive that it gets HUNGRY: it turns around, bites (fictional) grass, chews, and gulps. After quickly digesting, it burps unceremoniously.

As said before, there are two ways to scare the turtle: coming too close to its head, and producing a loud noise. These two disrespectful actions cause the turtle to get SCARED—to retract its head inside the shell and shiver with fright. If you continue to scare it, it will get ANNOYED and try to escape. Unfortunately, its laziness will soon get the better of it, and the turtle will slow down and stop after a few steps.

However, your turtle is easy to tame. When it is in SCARED mood, try to keep your hand near its eyes, so it can see you. When a certain amount of time has passed, it recovers from the fright and tries to pull its head out slowly, because it begins to trust you. Don't let it down, poor shy turtle! If you scare it with a noise during this taming phase, the turtle will get back in SCARED mood. If this delicate phase passes with success, the turtle is TRUSTFUL and will eat directly from your hand. Of course, this is fiction: the NXT Turtle can *not* eat any grass, and the fact that it eats when tamed is just an imitation of what a real turtle would do.

Explaining the turtle's behavior in words is easy, while its software implementation requires a bit of patience. In Listing 6-3 is the turtle program, which shapes the behavior described earlier. The program uses multitasking and is a practical example of an FSM, explained in Chapter 3.

This long program is commented to help the understanding. It is divided into many sections, labeled with commented headings:

- *Timer-related functions*: Here you can see the functions to generate random times and to reset the timer, using the technique you saw in the first turtle program.

- *Subroutines to walk*: Here are the simple subroutines to make the turtle walk and turn, using the OnFwdSync/OnRevSync NXC API functions.

- *Subroutines to move the head, to eat, and to tremble*: The subroutine to move the head is the same as the one seen in the simple program for the turtle. The eating sequence is written to be as realistic as possible: the turtle produces biting, chewing, gulping, and burping sounds to accompany the neck movements. The shivering is obtained by switching leg motors into forward and reverse quickly.

- *Functions to initialize the turtle and show its mood*: The initializing function is used to set up input ports, to move the head out, and to set the turtle's initial mood. The mood is shown by the appropriate function that prints information on the NXT screen.

- *Subroutines describing actions for the various moods*: The turtle executes different actions in each mood it can have. In this section, the actions for every mood are coded into their corresponding subroutine. You'll find their structure quite similar to one another: at the beginning, new random times are generated, to trigger the timed events (such as *boredom time, hunger time, recovery time* in Figure 6-6). Then, the actions involving the motors are performed. You can also find while/until loops, used to wait for multiple events, such as the timer elapsing or the sensor readings loud_noise or near_object. Then the mood variable is changed according to the occurred events, for the FSM to work.

- *Turtle tasks*: In this last section you find the code of the various tasks. There is the main task, the task that implements the FSM, the task to monitor the Ultrasonic Sensor readings, the one for the Sound Sensor, and the last used just to display the turtle's "biological clock" NXT screen. In effect, the time shown is the TIMER macro value that holds the difference between the current system time and the timer_start value. The value of this last variable is updated with the actual system time (as the "timer reset" action explained in the first program) before any waiting performed in the various states.

Listing 6-3. *The NXC Program for the Turtle That Implements the Autonomous Behavior*

```
// I/O aliases
#define LEGS OUT_AC
#define HEAD OUT_B
#define EYES IN_2
#define MIC IN_1
#define LINE IN_3

// various constant definitions
#define NEAR 10
#define FAR 30
#define IN -1
#define OUT 1
#define SOUND_HEAD_OUT 1
#define SOUND_HEAD_IN 2
#define SOUND_YAWN 3

// mean times definitions
#define BOREDOM_MEAN_TIME    8
#define TURN_MEAN_TIME       4
#define SLEEP_MEAN_TIME      4
#define WANDER_MEAN_TIME     10
#define RECOVERY_MEAN_TIME   3
#define TAMING_MEAN_TIME     3
#define HUNGER_MEAN_TIME     6

// possible moods of the turtle
#define QUIET      0
#define BORED      1
#define SCARED     2
#define ANNOYED    3
#define HUNGRY     4
#define TRUSTFUL   5

// macros
#define ClearLine(line)    TextOut(0,line,"                    ")
#define TIMER (CurrentTick()-timer_start)

// global variables
bool near_object, loud_noise;
mutex sound_sem;
unsigned long timer_start;
short head_state, times_bored, times_scared, mood;
```

```
//===================================================================//
//                    TIMER-RELATED FUNCTIONS                        //
//===================================================================//

int RandomTime( int mean, int variation, int scale )
{
   // generates a random number with given mean
   // and given variation
   // for example: variation = 2
   // possible outputs = scale*{mean-2, mean-1, mean, mean+1, mean+2}
   return ( mean + ( variation - Random(2*variation+1) ) )*scale;
}

void ResetTimer()
{
   timer_start = CurrentTick();
}


//===================================================================//
//                    SUBROUTINES TO WALK                            //
//===================================================================//

sub GoStraight( int speed )
{
   OnFwdSync(LEGS,speed,0);
}

sub GoBack( int speed )
{
   OnRevSync(LEGS,speed,0);
}

sub TurnRight( int speed )
{
   OnRevSync(LEGS,abs(speed),80);
}

sub TurnLeft( int speed )
{
   OnRevSync(LEGS,abs(speed),-80);
}
```

```
//=====================================================================//
//              SUBROUTINES TO MOVE THE HEAD, EAT, or TREMBLE          //
//=====================================================================//

// subroutine to move head IN or OUT
sub MoveHead ( short position, bool scared )
{
    int t;
    // move head only if the desired position
    // is different from the actual state
    if (head_state != position)
    {
        // play a sound only if the turtle
        // is moving the head because it is scared;
        // this is controlled by the scared parameter
        if ( scared )
        {
            if(position==IN)
                PlayFile("falling.rso");
            else
                PlayFile("raising.rso");
        }

        t = MotorRotationCount(HEAD);
        // start motor in desired direction
        if ( scared )
            OnFwd(HEAD,80*sign(position));
        else
            OnFwd(HEAD,55*sign(position));

        Wait(80);
        // detect if the motor is stalled
        while( abs(t-MotorRotationCount(HEAD))>4 )
        {
            t = MotorRotationCount(HEAD);
            Wait(50);
        }
        Off(HEAD);

        // update head state with actual position
        head_state = position;
    }
}
```

```
// the turtle eats
sub Eat()
{
   repeat(Random(3)+1)
   {
      repeat(3)
      {
         // biting
         PlayFile("chew.rso");
         OnFwd(HEAD,50);
         Wait(200);
         Float(HEAD);
         // chewing
         Wait(RandomTime(2,1,100));
      }
      until(SoundFlags()==SOUND_FLAGS_IDLE);
      Wait(400);
      // gulping
      PlayFile("gulp.rso");
      until(SoundFlags()==SOUND_FLAGS_IDLE);
      Wait(RandomTime(2,2,100));
   }
   // and burping
   Wait(RandomTime(1,1,1000));
   PlayFile("burp.rso");
   until(SoundFlags()==SOUND_FLAGS_IDLE);
   Wait(10);
}


// the legs tremble when the turtle is in SCARED mood
sub Tremble( int times )
{
   repeat( times )
   {
      OnFwd(LEGS,100);
      Wait(70);
      Off(LEGS);
      OnRev(LEGS,100);
      Wait(70);
      Off(LEGS);
   }
}
```

```
//=====================================================================//
//       FUNCTIONS TO INITIALIZE THE TURTLE AND SHOW ITS MOOD          //
//=====================================================================//

void Turtle_init ()
{
   TextOut(0,LCD_LINE1,"Initializing...");
   SetSensorSound(MIC);
   SetSensorLowspeed(EYES);
   // initial mood
   mood = QUIET;
   MoveHead(OUT,true);
   Wait(500);
   ClearScreen();
}

// displays the mood of the turtle on NXT screen
void ShowMood(short m)
{
   TextOut(20,LCD_LINE1,"NXT Turtle");
   TextOut(0,LCD_LINE3,"mood:            ");
   TextOut(0,LCD_LINE4,"----------------------");
   switch(m)
   {
      case QUIET:   TextOut(30,LCD_LINE3,"QUIET   "); break;
      case BORED:   TextOut(30,LCD_LINE3,"BORED "); break;
      case SCARED:  TextOut(30,LCD_LINE3,"SCARED "); break;
      case HUNGRY:  TextOut(30,LCD_LINE3,"HUNGRY "); break;
      case ANNOYED: TextOut(30,LCD_LINE3,"ANNOYED "); break;
      case TRUSTFUL: TextOut(30,LCD_LINE3,"TRUSTFUL"); break;
   }
}

//=====================================================================//
//       SUBROUTINES DESCRIBING ACTIONS FOR THE VARIOUS MOODS          //
//=====================================================================//

sub QuietMoodActions()
{
   int boredom_time, hunger_time;
   bool event = false;
   int bored_or_hungry;
   // turtle can get bored or hungry
   bored_or_hungry = Random(3);
   // random time after which turtle gets bored
   boredom_time = RandomTime(BOREDOM_MEAN_TIME, 2, SEC_1);
   // random time after which turtle gets hungry
```

```
hunger_time = RandomTime(HUNGER_MEAN_TIME, 4, SEC_1);

// turtle stays still...
MoveHead(OUT,false);

ResetTimer();
until (event)
{
    // ... hungry (with probability 1/3)...
    if (bored_or_hungry == 1 && TIMER > hunger_time )
    {
        mood = HUNGRY;
        event = true;
    }
    // ...until it gets bored (with probability 2/3)
    else if ( TIMER > boredom_time )
    {
        mood = BORED;
        event = true;
    }
    // ...or a frightening event occurs
    if (near_object || loud_noise)
    {
        mood = SCARED;
        event = true;
    }
}
}

sub HungryMoodActions()
{
    int turn_time;
    // reset boredom counter
    times_bored = 0;
    MoveHead(OUT,false);
    ResetTimer();

    // turns randomly to look for grass
    turn_time = RandomTime(TURN_MEAN_TIME, 4, MS_500);
    if(Random(2)==1)
        TurnRight(80);
    else
        TurnLeft(80);
    Wait(turn_time);
    Float(LEGS);

    Eat();
```

```
      // and then returns in QUIET mood
      mood = QUIET;
}

sub BoredMoodActions()
{
   int sleep_time;
   bool event = false;
   short sweet_waking = 0;

   // increase the boredom counter and show it
   times_bored++;
   TextOut(0,LCD_LINE5,"bored:             ");
   NumOut(40,LCD_LINE5,times_bored);

   // turtle yawns and prepares to sleep
   PlayFile("yawn.rso");
   until(SoundFlags()==SOUND_FLAGS_IDLE);
   MoveHead(IN,false);

   // turtle sleeps until sleep_time has elapsed
   // or a loud noise occurs
   sleep_time = RandomTime(SLEEP_MEAN_TIME, 2, SEC_1);
   PlayFileEx("snore.rso",4,true); // playing a loop

   ResetTimer();
   until (event)
   {
      if (TIMER>sleep_time)
      {
         event = true;
         // too much boredom makes the turtle hungry
         if (times_bored>1)
            mood = HUNGRY;
         else
            mood = QUIET;
      }
      // if the turtle wakes up suddenly, it gets scared
      else if (loud_noise)
      {
         mood = SCARED;
         event = true;
      }
   }
   StopSound(); //stop snoring
   ClearLine(LCD_LINE5);
}
```

```
sub ScaredMoodActions()
{
    int recovery_time;
    MoveHead(IN,true);
    times_scared++;
    // increase the scares counter and display it
    TextOut(0,LCD_LINE5,"scared:            ");
    NumOut(43,LCD_LINE5,times_scared);

    // time to recover from scare
    recovery_time = RandomTime(RECOVERY_MEAN_TIME, 1, SEC_1);
    //while the time to recover from scare has not passed
    until (TIMER>recovery_time)
    {
        Tremble(Random(2)+2);
        Wait(200);
        // if the scares rage on...
        if( loud_noise )
        {
            ResetTimer();
            // increase the scares counter and display it
            times_scared++;
            TextOut(0,LCD_LINE5,"scared:            ");
            NumOut(43,LCD_LINE5,times_scared);
        }
    }

    // if the sight is clear, turtle returns in QUIET mood
    if (near_object)
        mood = TRUSTFUL;
    // else if someone is near, it becomes a bit less shy
    else
        mood = QUIET;
    // however, if too scared, it decides to escape
    if (times_scared>2)
        mood = ANNOYED;
    ClearLine(LCD_LINE5);
}

sub TrustfulMoodActions()
{
    int eating_max_times = Random(2)+1;
    int eating_counter = 0;
    short event = 0;
    OnFwdReg(HEAD,5,OUT_REGMODE_SPEED);
    ResetTimer();
    // turtle tries to get the head out in a shy way
```

```
    while( event == 0  )
    {
        if (TIMER>2500)
        {
            event = 1;
        }
        // but you can scare it again
        if (loud_noise)
        {
            event = -1;
        }
    }
    Off(HEAD);
    // if the head is completely out before another scare,
    if ( event == 1 )
    {
        MoveHead(OUT,false);
        while (near_object && eating_counter<=eating_max_times)
        {
            // it accepts food from you
            Eat();
            eating_counter++;
        }
        // until you go away
        while(near_object);
        mood = QUIET;
    }
    // if the turtle is scared again while getting the head out,
    // goes in SCARED mood again
    else
    {
        head_state = OUT;
        MoveHead(IN,true);
        mood = SCARED;
    }
}

sub AnnoyedMoodActions()
{
    int turn_time, wander_time;
    // reset the scares and boredom counter
    times_scared = 0;
    // the boredom has passed, reset the counter
    times_bored = 0;
    // the turtle decides to escape
    // it draws back while it sees something near
    GoBack(100);
```

```
     while(near_object);
     Float(LEGS);
     // shakes the head
     MoveHead(OUT,true);
     MoveHead(IN,true);
     MoveHead(OUT,true);

     // then turns randomly
     turn_time = RandomTime(TURN_MEAN_TIME, 2, SEC_1);
     wander_time = RandomTime(WANDER_MEAN_TIME, 3, SEC_1);
     ResetTimer();
     // chooses between right and left
     if(Random(2)==1)
        TurnRight(100);
     else
        TurnLeft(100);

     Wait(turn_time);
     Float(LEGS);

     ResetTimer();
     // ...and walks straight quickly
     GoStraight(100);
     while( TIMER<wander_time/3 && !near_object );
     // but then gets tired,
     GoStraight(70);
     while( TIMER<2*wander_time/3 && !near_object );
     // so tired...
     GoStraight(40);
     while( TIMER<wander_time && !near_object );
     // ...that it stops after a while!
     Float(LEGS);
     mood = QUIET;
}


//======================================================================//
//        TURTLE TASKS: main, finite state machine,  monitors          //
//======================================================================//

task main()
{
   Turtle_init ();
   // exits to the other tasks including Follows(main) statement
}

task FSM ()
{
```

```
    Follows(main);
    // finite state machine loop
    while(true)
    {
        ShowMood(mood);
        // the turtle acts according to its actual mood.
        // The order in which the moods are listed in the
        // switch structure is not relevant
        switch(mood)
        {
            case QUIET:
                QuietMoodActions();
            break;

            case HUNGRY:
                HungryMoodActions();
            break;

            case BORED:
                BoredMoodActions();
            break;

            case SCARED:
                ScaredMoodActions();
            break;

            case TRUSTFUL:
                TrustfulMoodActions();
            break;

            case ANNOYED:
                AnnoyedMoodActions();
            break;
        }
    }
}

// this task monitors the noise level around.
// its reading is used only when the legs' motors
// are still; otherwise their noise would saturate the sensor
// and the turtle would not be able to sense lower noises.
task NoiseMonitor ()
{
    Follows(main);
    int s;
    while (true)
    {
```

```
    s = Sensor(MIC);
    if (s > 75)
    {
        loud_noise = true;
        Wait(200);
        until (Sensor(MIC)<25);
    }
    loud_noise = false;
    TextOut(0,LCD_LINE7,"noise:          ");
    NumOut(35,LCD_LINE7,s);
    NumOut(60,LCD_LINE7,loud_noise);
    Wait(100);
    }
}


// This task monitors the Ultrasonic Sensor.
// Its output is the near_object variable, filtered
// by a hysteresis cycle.
task View ()
{
    Follows(main);
    int d, d1, d2;    // contain the distance readings
    while (true)
    {
        // first reading
        d1 = SensorUS (EYES);
        Wait(50);
        // second reading
        d2 = SensorUS (EYES);
        // d is the average of d1 and d2
        d = (d1 + d2)/2;
        if (d < NEAR)
            near_object = true;
        else if ( d > FAR )
            near_object = false;
        TextOut(0,LCD_LINE6,"distance:          ");
        NumOut(53,LCD_LINE6,d);
        NumOut(80,LCD_LINE6,near_object);
    }
}


// this task shows the turtle's "biological clock"
task ShowTimer ()
{
    string time, sec, sec_tenth;
    Follows(main);
    while(true)
```

```
    {
        time = "bioclock: ";
        sec = NumToStr(TIMER/1000);
        sec_tenth = NumToStr((TIMER%1000)/100);
        // concatenate the strings to show
        // "bioclock: <seconds>.<tenths> s" on screen
        time = StrCat( time, sec, ".", sec_tenth, " s" );
        ClearLine(LCD_LINE8);
        TextOut(0,LCD_LINE8,time);
        Wait(200);
    }
}
```

The FSM task is worth more attention. It resembles the general structure for an FSM, like the one seen in Chapter 3, in Listing 3-4. Listing 6-4 displays the FSM task code.

Listing 6-4. *The Code of the Task Implementing the Turtle's FSM*

```
task FSM ()
{
    Follows(main);
    // finite state machine loop
    while(true)
    {
        ShowMood(mood);
        // the turtle acts according to its actual mood.
        // The order in which the moods are listed in the
        // switch structure is not relevant
        switch(mood)
        {
            case QUIET:
                QuietMoodActions();
            break;

            case HUNGRY:
                HungryMoodActions();
            break;

            case BORED:
                BoredMoodActions();
            break;

            case SCARED:
                ScaredMoodActions();
            break;
```

```
    case TRUSTFUL:
        TrustfulMoodActions();
    break;

    case ANNOYED:
        AnnoyedMoodActions();
    break;
        }
    }
}
```

The task contains the Follows(main) statement, telling the system to execute this task after the main has exited. Then there is a perpetual loop, and inside the loop is a switch structure. The variable that enables the various cases of the switch is the mood variable; it represents the actual turtle mood, set as QUIET in the Turtle_init() function and then changed by every different mood-related subroutine. The various cases are labeled with the allowed values that the mood variable can assume. As you can guess from the capital letters, those are human-readable aliases, standing for constant numbers defined at the top of the program in Listing 6-3.

The code of this task is quite clean because, instead of placing the statements to be executed in the various moods between the case and break keywords, those statements have been moved into their corresponding subroutines. In every case body, those subroutines are called. The order in which the cases appear in the switch is irrelevant: the actions inside every case are executed only if the mood variable has the same value as the case label. Writing modular code helps you maintain and modify your programs.

For example, to add another mood to the turtle's behavior, you just have to add another case to the switch and write the corresponding subroutine for it. Pay attention to planning the whole state machine so as to assure that the every state is *not absorbing*, meaning that once the machine has entered that state, it will never abandon it. This condition is easily verifiable in the diagram in Figure 6-6, in which every state has arrows that arrive and arrows that leave from it.

This concludes the description for the third complex program for your turtle. Now you're ready to build it, and to have fun with your new robotic pet. It doesn't need any food and it doesn't leave any dirt around. Just remember to provide it with fresh batteries!

Building Your Pet

The model requires about an hour to build with ease. In any case, building LEGO models is a relaxing activity; why would you ever build something in a hurry?

I also provided you with a solution to use the NXT rechargeable battery that protrudes by a LEGO-unit out of the NXT's normal height. Just follow the alternative instructions to place the NXT a bit higher, and hold it with the illustrated frame subassembly. Adding the Li-Ion battery doesn't affect the design too much.

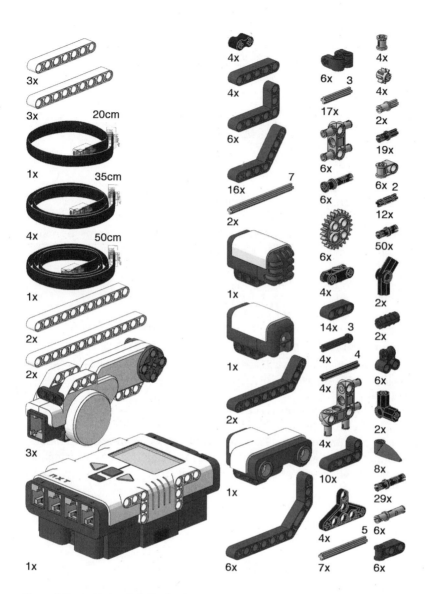

Figure 6-7. *NXT Turtle bill of materials*

Table 6-1. *NXT Turtle Bill of Materials*

Quantity	Color	Part Number	Part Name
3	White	32524.DAT	TECHNIC Beam 7
3	White	40490.DAT	TECHNIC Beam 9
1		55804.DAT	Electric Cable NXT 20cm
4		55805.DAT	Electric Cable NXT 35cm
1		55806.DAT	Electric Cable NXT 50cm
2	White	32525.DAT	TECHNIC Beam 11
2	White	41239.DAT	TECHNIC Beam 13
3		53787.DAT	Electric MINDSTORMS NXT Motor
1		53788.DAT	Electric MINDSTORMS NXT
4	Black	45590.DAT	TECHNIC Axle Joiner Double Flexible
4	Dark gray	32316.DAT	TECHNIC Beam 5
6	Dark gray	32526.DAT	TECHNIC Beam 7 Bent 90 (5:3)
16	Dark gray	32348.DAT	TECHNIC Beam 7 Liftarm Bent 53.5 (4:4)
2	Light gray	44294.DAT	TECHNIC Axle 7
1		55963.DAT	Electric MINDSTORMS NXT Sound Sensor
1		55969.DAT	Electric MINDSTORMS NXT Light Sensor
2	Dark gray	32271.DAT	TECHNIC Beam 9 Liftarm Bent 53.5 (7:3)
1		56467.DAT	Electric MINDSTORMS NXT Ultrasonic Sensor
6	Dark gray	32009.DAT	TECHNIC Beam 11.5 Liftarm Bent 45 Double
6	Dark gray	41678.DAT	TECHNIC Axle Joiner Perpendicular Double Split
17	Light gray	4519.DAT	TECHNIC Axle 3
6	Light gray	48989.DAT	TECHNIC Axle Joiner Perpendicular 1×3×3 with 4 Pins
6	Black	32054.DAT	TECHNIC Pin Long with Stop Bush
6	Light gray	3648.DAT	TECHNIC Gear 24 Tooth
4	Black	32184.DAT	TECHNIC Axle Joiner Perpendicular 3L
14	Dark gray	32523.DAT	TECHNIC Beam 3
4	Dark gray	6587.DAT	TECHNIC Axle 3 with Stud
4	Black	3705.DAT	TECHNIC Axle 4
4	Light gray	55615.DAT	TECHNIC Beam 5 Bent 90 (3:3) with 4 Pins
10	Dark gray	32140.DAT	TECHNIC Beam 5 Liftarm Bent 90 (4:2)
4	Black	2905.DAT	TECHNIC Liftarm Triangle 5 × 3 × 0.5
7	Light gray	32073.DAT	TECHNIC Axle 5

Continued

Table 6-1. *Continued*

Quantity	Color	Part Number	Part Name
4	Light gray	3713.DAT	TECHNIC Bush
4	Light gray	3647.DAT	TECHNIC Gear 8 Tooth
2	Tan	3749.DAT	TECHNIC Axle Pin
19	Blue	43093.DAT	TECHNIC Axle Pin with Friction
6	Light gray	6536.DAT	TECHNIC Axle Joiner Perpendicular
12	Black	32062.DAT	TECHNIC Axle 2 Notched
50	Black	2780.DAT	TECHNIC Pin with Friction and Slots
2	Black	32192.DAT	TECHNIC Angle Connector #4 (135 degree)
2	Dark gray	6538B.DAT	TECHNIC Axle Joiner Offset
6	Dark gray	32291.DAT	TECHNIC Axle Joiner Perpendicular Double
2	Black	32014.DAT	TECHNIC Angle Connector #6 (90 degree)
8	Orange	41669.DAT	TECHNIC Bionicle 1×3 Tooth with Axlehole
29	Black	6558.DAT	TECHNIC Pin Long with Friction and Slot
6	Light gray	X783.DAT	TECHNIC Pin Long
6	Dark gray	42003.DAT	TECHNIC Axle Joiner Perpendicular with 2 Holes
Battery holder parts (included in the set)			
4	Black	6558.DAT	TECHNIC Pin Long with Friction and Slot
8	Black	2780.DAT	TECHNIC Pin with Friction and Slots
2	Dark gray	32523.DAT	TECHNIC Beam 3
2	Dark gray	32526.DAT	TECHNIC Beam 7 Bent 90 (5:3)
2	Dark gray	3894.DAT	TECHNIC Brick 1×6 with Holes

331 parts total (all included in NXT retail set)

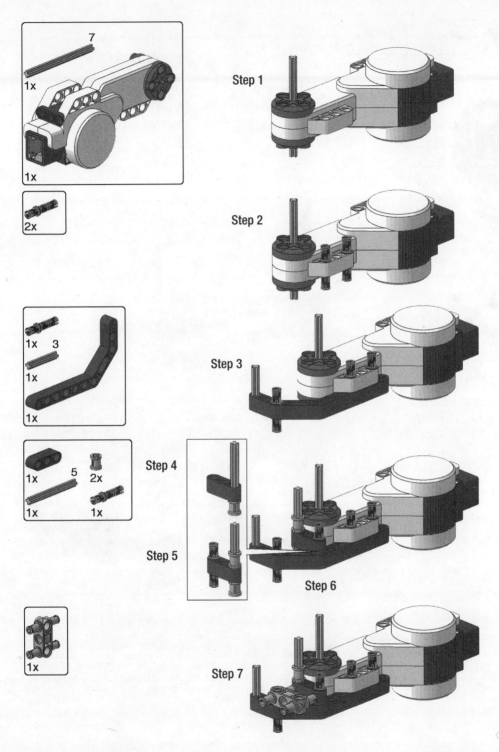

Step 1

Step 2

Step 3

Step 4

Step 5

Step 6

Step 7

Start building the right legs' assembly.

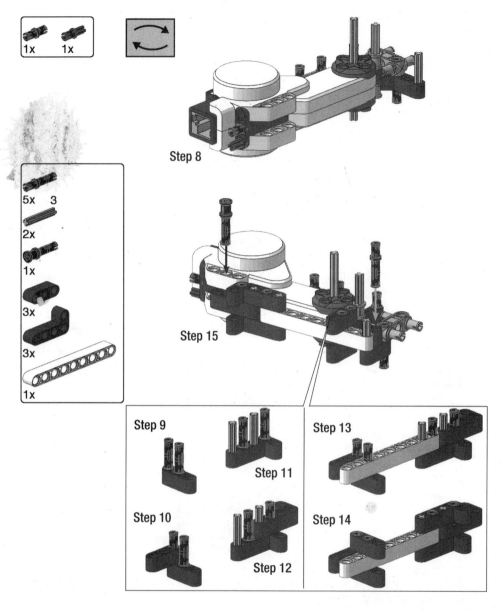

Step 8

5x 3

2x

1x

3x

3x

1x

Step 15

Step 9

Step 11

Step 10

Step 12

Step 13

Step 14

Rotate the model and add a black pin and a blue axle pin in the motor's rear holes. Then build the attachment frame for the legs.

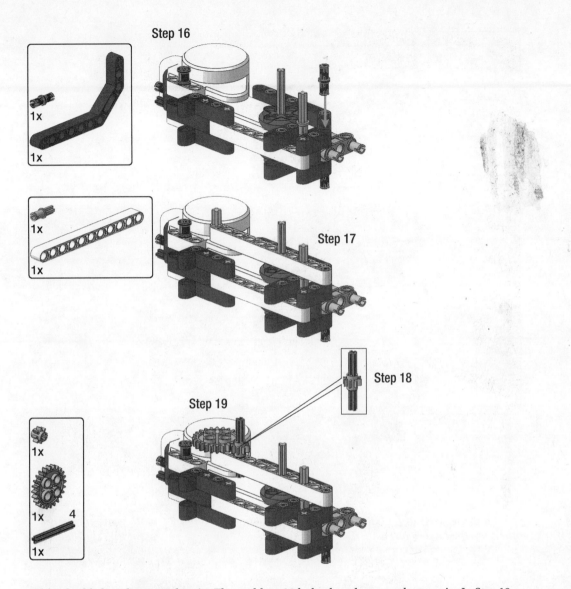

Step 16

Step 17

Step 18

Step 19

Add a double bent beam and a pin. Then add an 11 holes-long beam and a tan pin. In Step 19, add an 8-tooth and a 24-tooth gear.

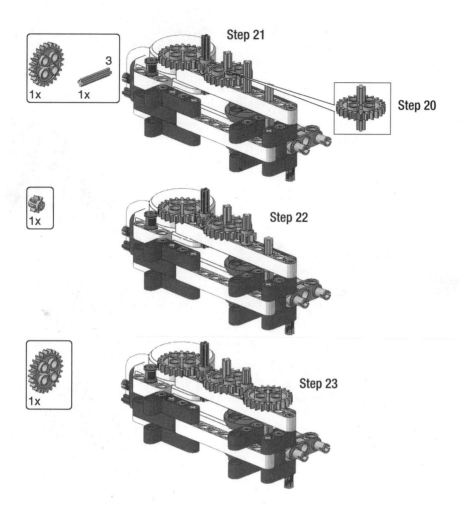

Complete the geartrain. In Step 23, make sure to align the outer 24-tooth gears correctly, otherwise the turtle won't walk as expected.

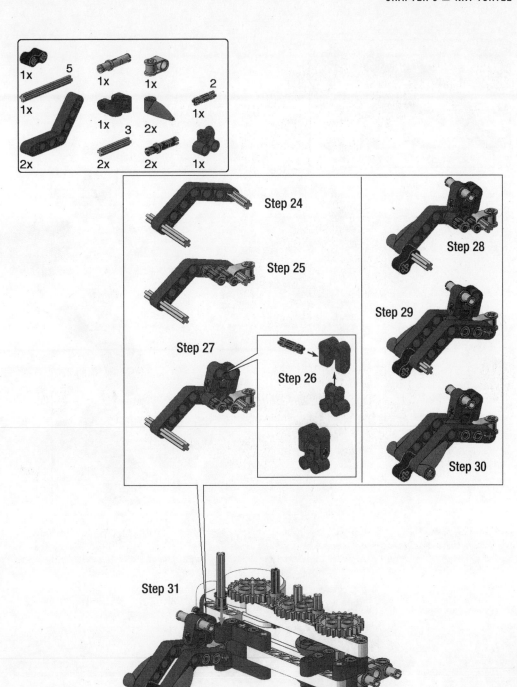

Build the right rear leg and attach it to the frame using a 3-long axle.

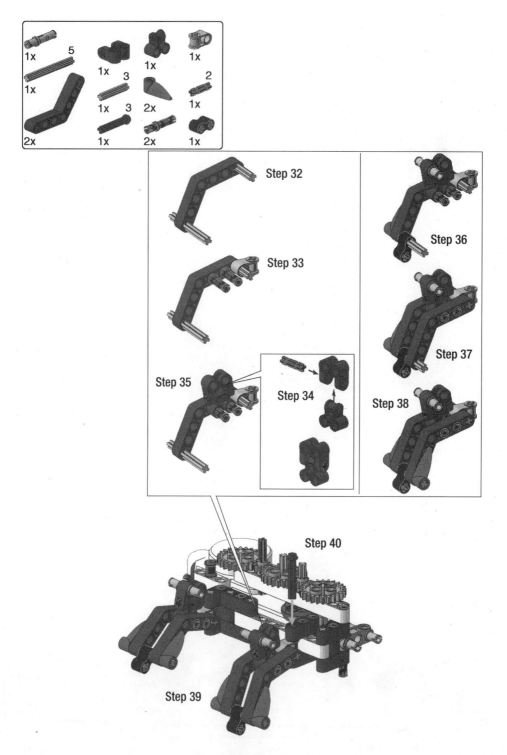

Build the right front leg and attach it to the rest of the assembly using a 3-long axle with stud.

Step 41

Step 42

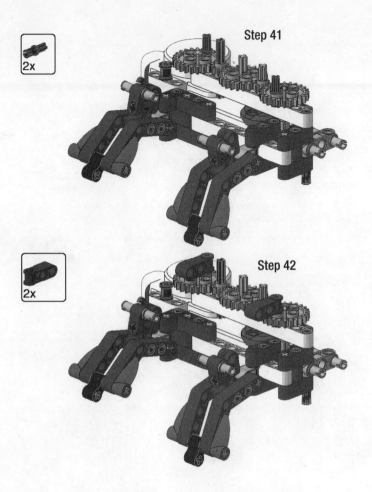

Insert two blue pins in the outer 24-tooth gears. Make sure to attach them 180 degrees out of phase: in Step 41, one is in the hole closer to the front leg, and the other pin is closer to the motor's round part.

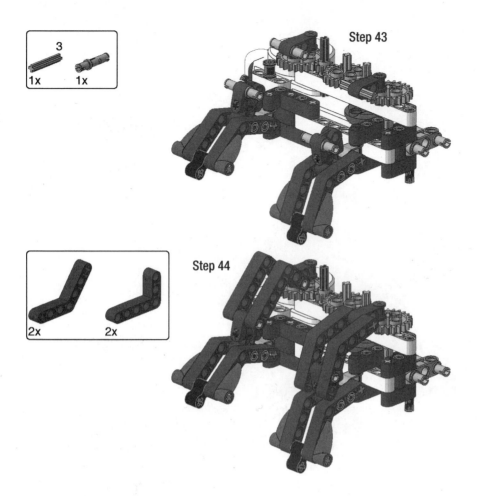

Add the 3-long axle and the long gray pin to the perpendicular joiners. Add the bent beams to complete the right legs' assembly.

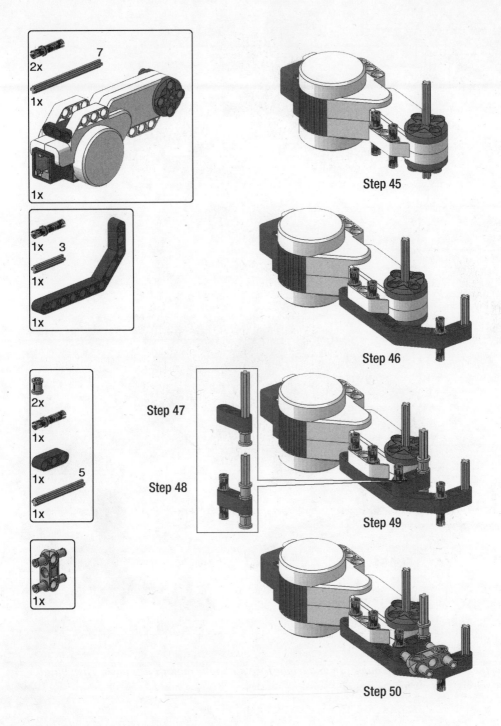

Step 45

Step 46

Step 47

Step 48

Step 49

Step 50

Start building the assembly for the left leg.

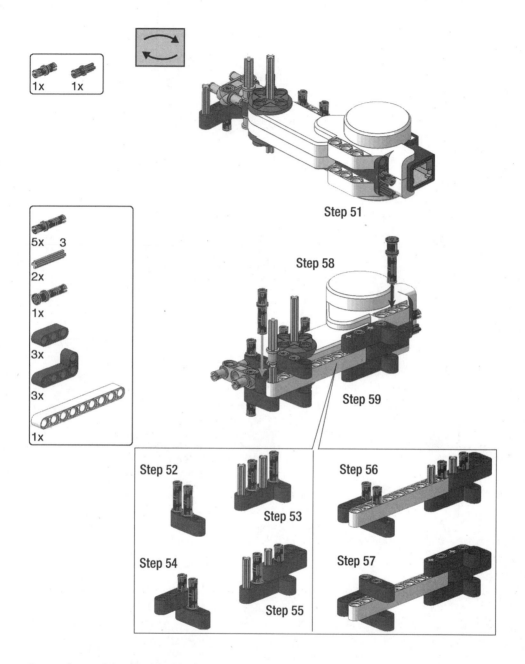

Step 51

Step 58

Step 59

Step 52

Step 53

Step 54

Step 55

Step 56

Step 57

Rotate the model and add a black pin and a blue axle pin in the motor's rear holes. Then build the attachment frame for the legs.

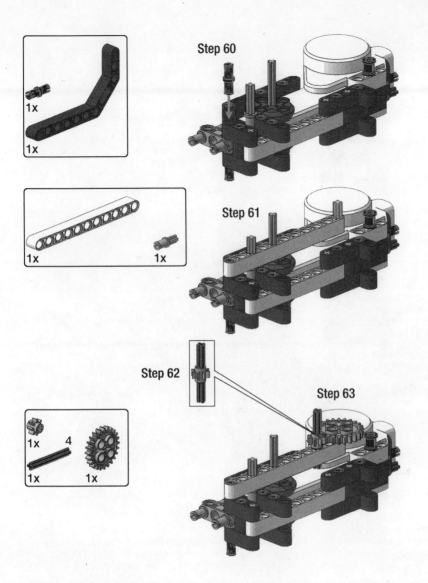

Step 60

Step 61

Step 62

Step 63

Add a double bent beam and a pin. Then add an 11 holes-long beam and a tan pin. In Step 63, add an 8-tooth and a 24-tooth gear.

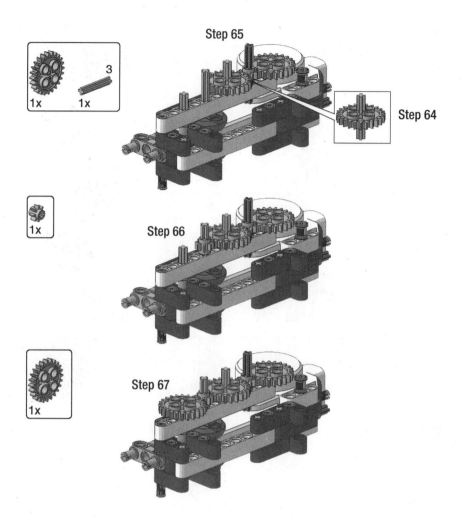

Step 65

Step 64

Step 66

Step 67

Complete the geartrain. Make sure to align the outer 24-tooth gears correctly, otherwise the turtle won't walk as expected.

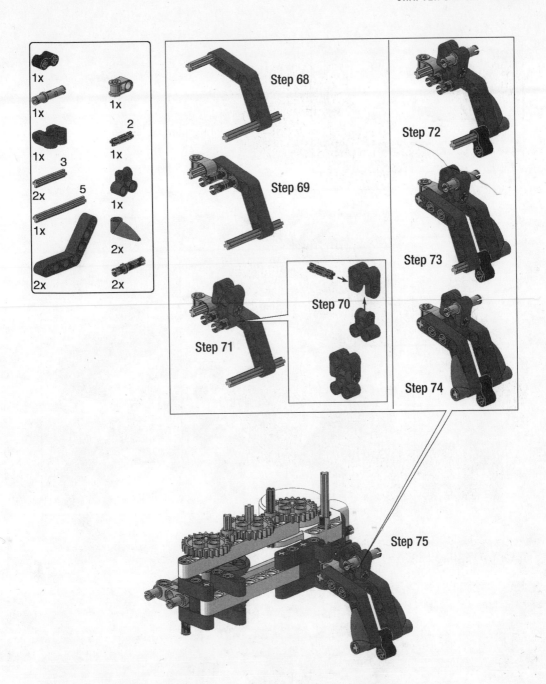

Step 68

Step 69

Step 70

Step 71

Step 72

Step 73

Step 74

Step 75

1x

1x

1x

3

2x

1x

2x

1x

1x

2

1x

1x

2x

2x

5

Build the left rear leg.

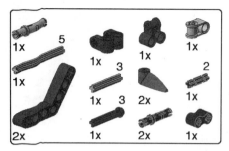

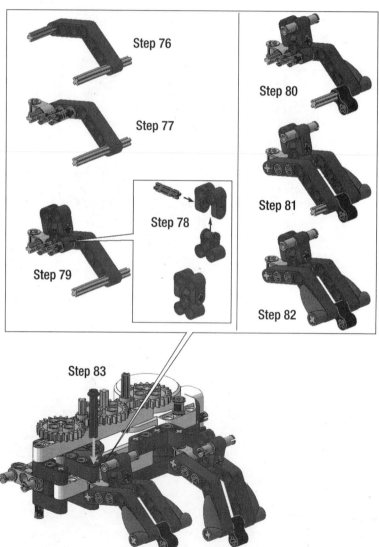

Build the left front leg.

Step 84

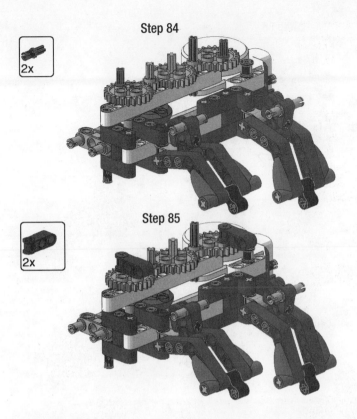

Step 85

Insert two blue pins in the outer 24-tooth gears. Make sure to attach them 180 degrees out of phase. One pin is in the hole closer to the back leg, and the other pin is in the hole further from the front leg.

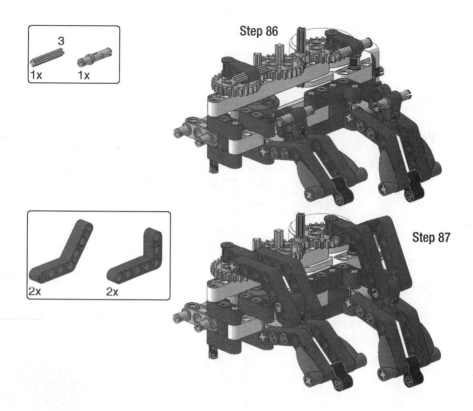

Step 86

Step 87

Add the 3-long axle and the long gray pin to the perpendicular joiners. Add the bent beams to complete the assembly for the right leg.

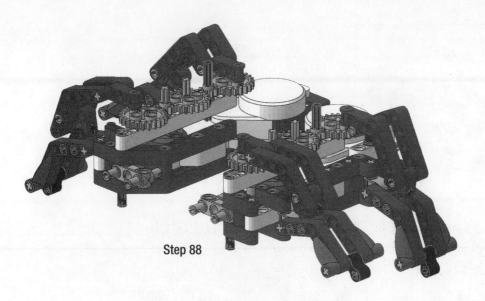

Step 88

Place the assemblies for the two legs close to each other.

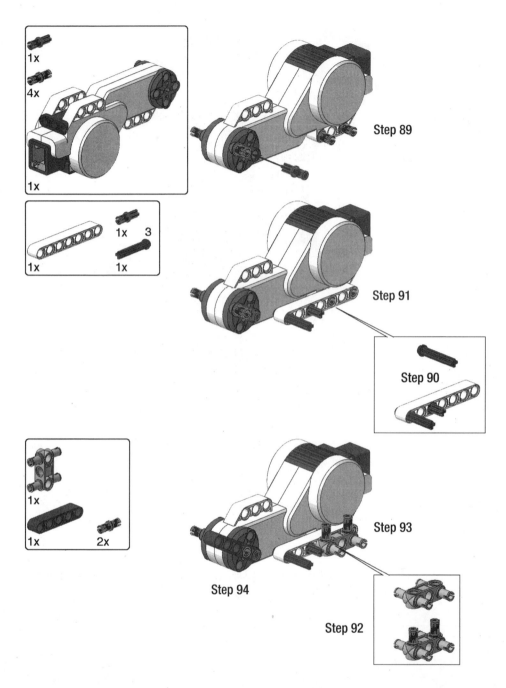

Step 89

Step 91

Step 90

Step 93

Step 94

Step 92

Start building the head assembly. In Step 89, insert a blue pin in the motor shaft's hole.

Add the left neck subassembly. Then turn the model and add two black pins. In Step 100, insert a blue axle pin in the motor shaft's central hole.

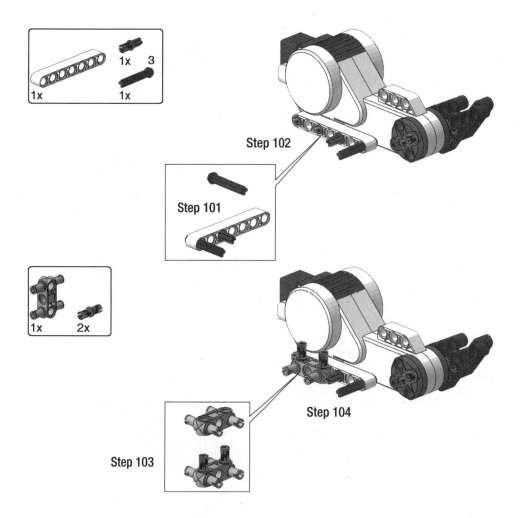

Add the indicated parts to the right side of the motor. In Step 101, use a 3-long dark gray axle with a stud.

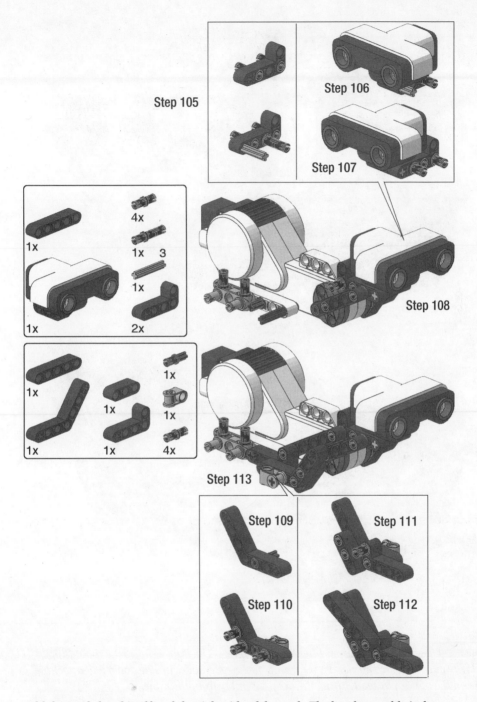

Step 105

Step 106

Step 107

Step 108

Step 113

Step 109

Step 110

Step 111

Step 112

Add the turtle head itself and the right side of the neck. The head assembly is done.

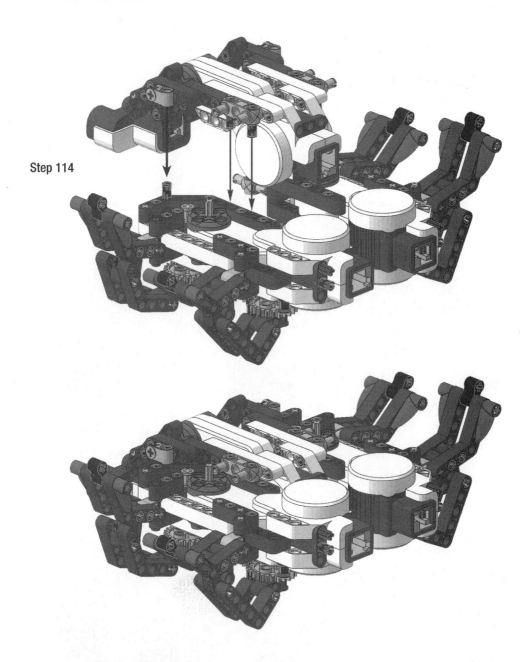

Step 114

Attach the head assembly to the assemblies for the two legs. The image shows the robot flipped just for clarity purposes. I recommend not turning the leg assemblies upside down, but attaching the legs from the bottom instead, lifting the head assembly from the table.

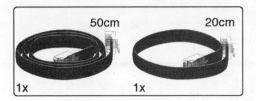

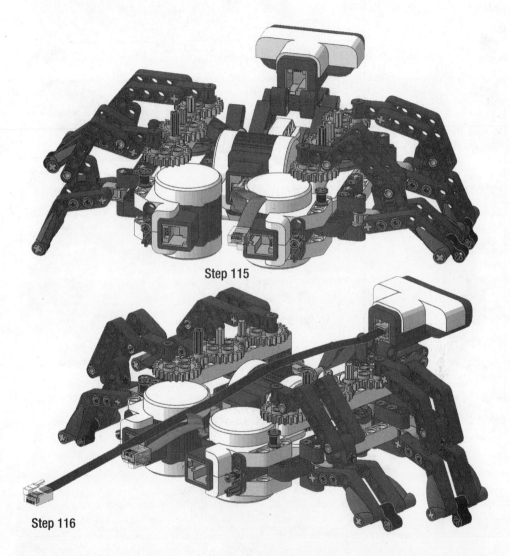

Step 115

Step 116

First, attach a 20cm (8 inch) cable to the head motor. Then, attach a 50cm (25 inch) cable to the Ultrasonic Sensor. Let these cables pass between the legs' motors and come outside from the back. You'll attach them to the NXT ports later.

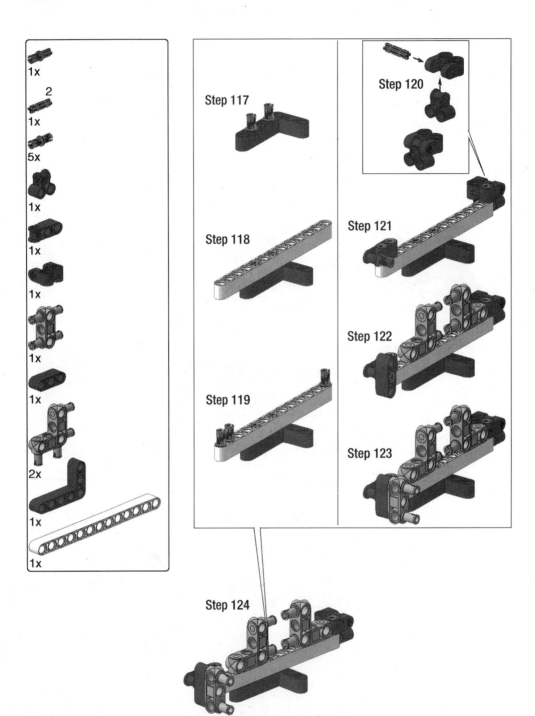

Start building the turtle's shell.

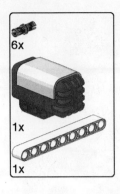

Step 125

Step 126

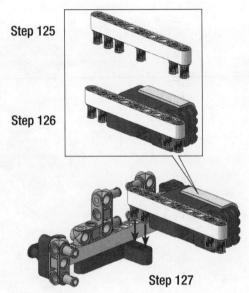

Step 127

Build the Sound Sensor assembly.

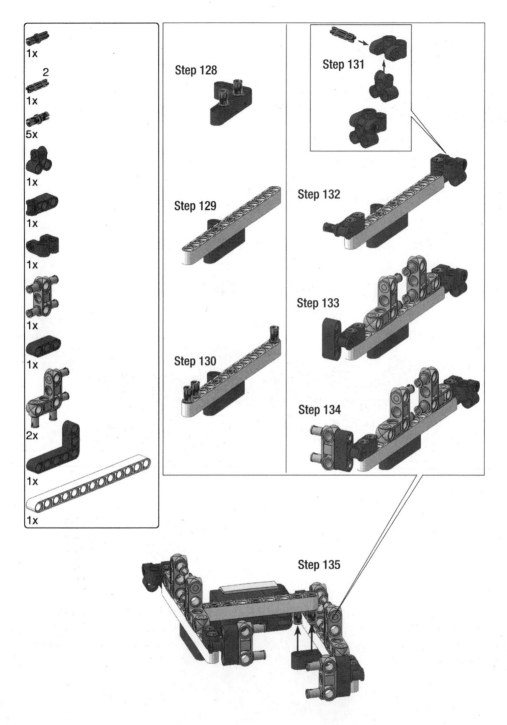

Build the other side of the shell and attach it to the rest of the assembly.

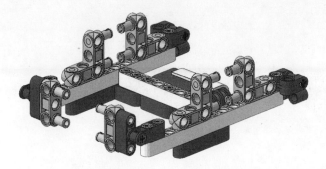

The shell is finished.

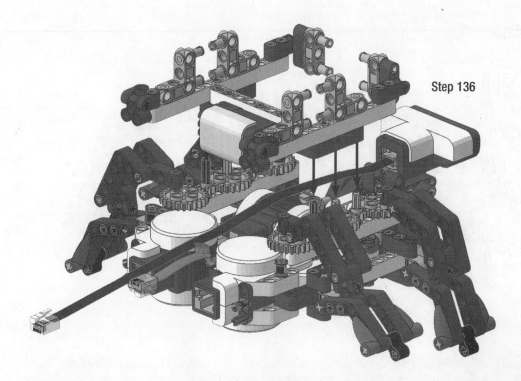

Step 136

Put the shield on the turtle, making sure to insert the geartrain axles for the legs into the dark gray bent beam holes of the shield. In this way, cross-bracing will keep the whole structure together. Arrange the head sensor cable between the legs' motors, so that it can slide freely while the head goes in and out.

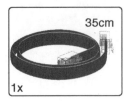

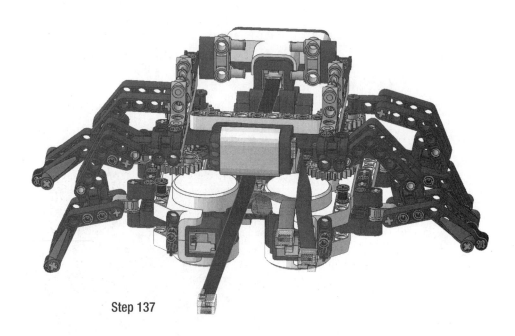

Step 137

This foreshortening of the turtle's back shows how to connect a 35cm (14 inch) cable to the Sound Sensor. You'll attach this cable to the NXT later.

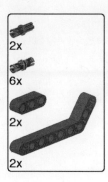

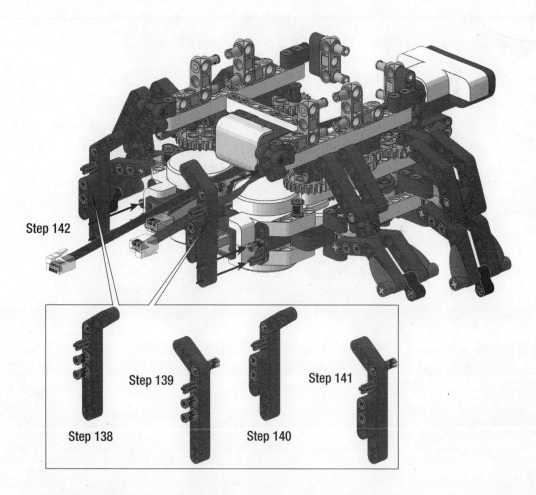

Step 142

Step 138

Step 139

Step 140

Step 141

Build the back frame that holds the motors together with the shell. Notice how the cross-bracing technique is employed to strengthen the model.

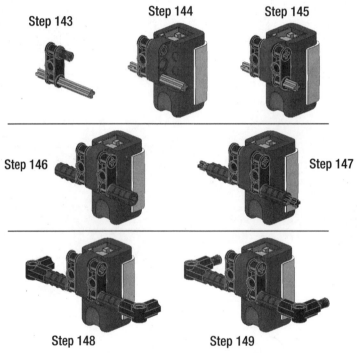

Step 143

Step 144

Step 145

Step 146

Step 147

Step 148

Step 149

Build the back Light Sensor assembly. It will be used to follow lines.

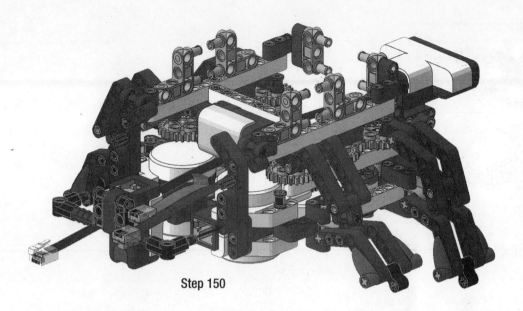

Step 150

Attach this sensor assembly to the turtle's back.

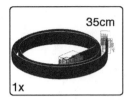

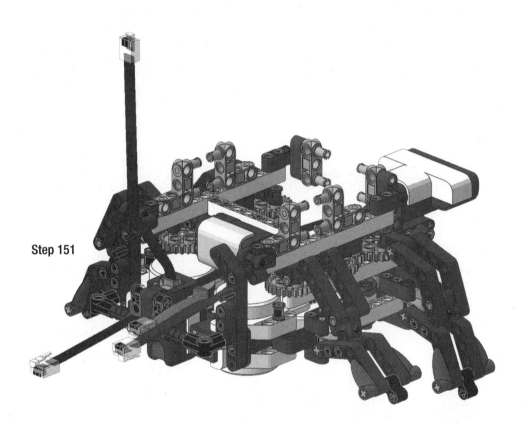

Step 151

Attach a 35cm (14 inch) cable to the Light Sensor.

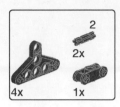

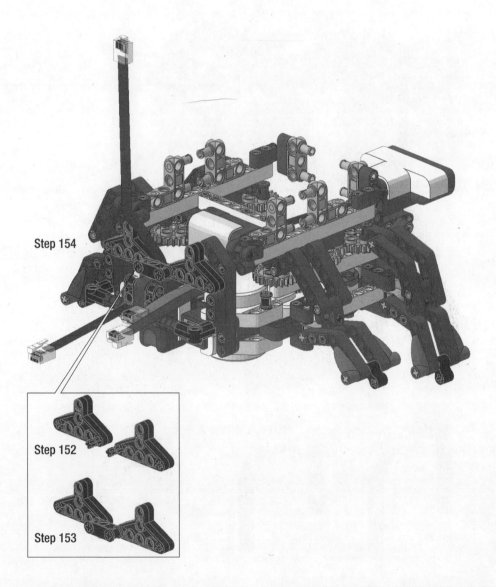

Step 154

Step 152

Step 153

Build the reinforcement frame and attach it to the turtle. Pass the head sensor cable over this frame, and not below.

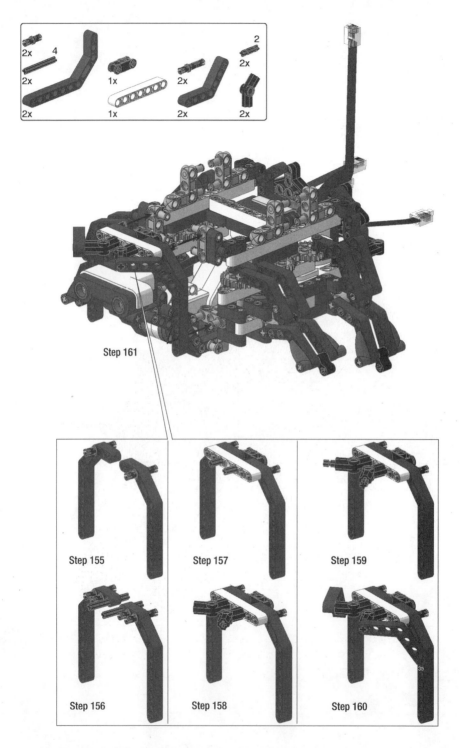

Step 161

Step 155

Step 157

Step 159

Step 156

Step 158

Step 160

As you did in the back, now build the cross-bracing structure in the front of the turtle. This assembly shapes the front of the turtle's shell and holds the whole thing together.

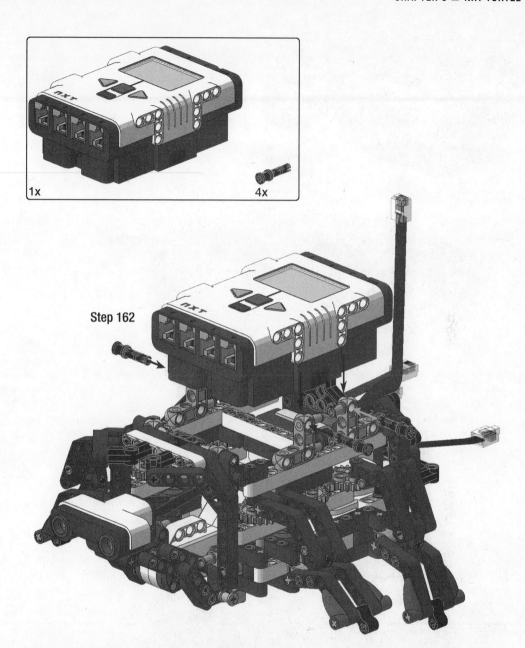

Step 162

1x   4x

If you're going to use normal batteries, follow this version. Remember to insert batteries in the NXT before attaching it to the shield. To change batteries, you just have to pull the long pins away, without disassembling the turtle.

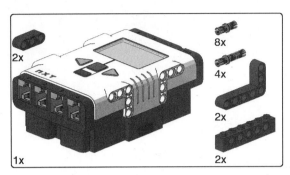

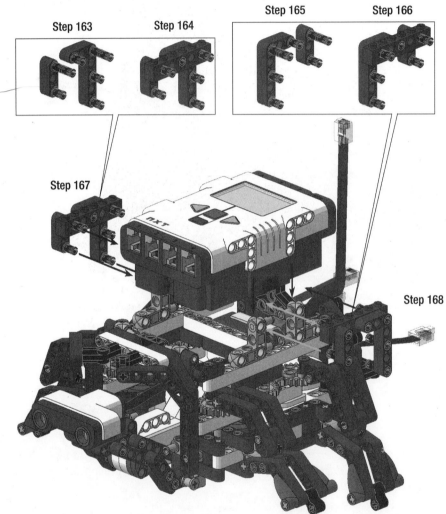

If you have the Li-Ion battery pack, then follow these instructions to build the blocks that will hold the NXT. The battery makes the NXT thicker, so a different structure is needed to hold it in place.

This illustration shows how the frames holding the side together look when assembled. Attach the cables to the NXT input ports as shown in the next step.

Step 169

The building process continues the same way, no matter how you connected the NXT to the robot, depending on what kind of batteries you are using.

This page shows how to attach the sensor cables to the NXT. You must connect the Sound Sensor to input port 1, the Ultrasonic Sensor to port 2, and the Light Sensor to port 3. Curl the Light Sensor cable to shorten it. If you are using the rechargeable battery and thus you have built the side frame to hold the NXT, you can pass the cables where shown in Figure 6-1.

Step 170

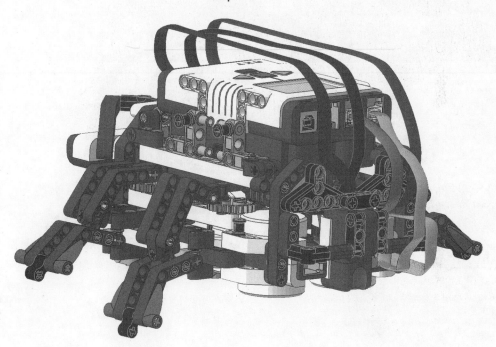

Turn the turtle and attach the right motor to NXT output port C with a 35cm (14 inch) cable, rolling it two times around the back sensor frame. Attach the head motor cable to NXT output port B.

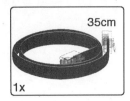

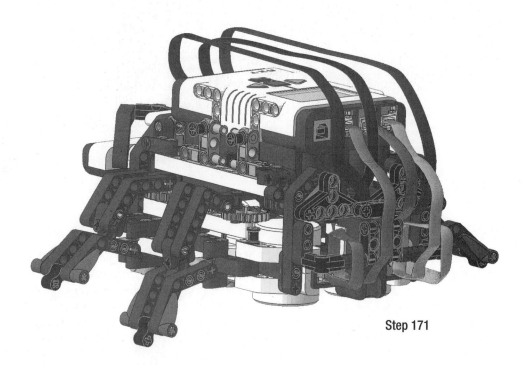

Step 171

Attach the left motor to NXT output port A with a 35cm (14 inch) cable, rolling it two times as before.

The turtle is finished!

Design Thoughts

This model hit the Web in April 2006 and a bunch of heavily inspired copies popped up right away. It was a sign of great appreciation! The turtle's head was originally different. At the beginning, there was no Ultrasonic Sensor, and the motor formed the head itself. Then, due to this web cross-inspiration, I came upon the actual shape, including an Ultrasonic Sensor.

The turtle is designed to go slowly, just as the real ones do. You can dramatically redesign the legs to move more quickly. You can do this by removing the gear reduction and coupling the motor shaft directly to the cams made with the 24-tooth gears.

I tried hard to keep the shell profile low because lifting too much of the NXT brick (even if it were useful to make room for sensors and mechanisms) would result in a bulky turtle—a box with legs attached! I designed the leg shape in one try and tuned the position of the rubber fingers for the best grip.

The shell shape passed through many refinements, as the NXT brick was rotated by 90 degrees as compared to the first prototype, to fit better on the turtle and reduce the overall size. As you'll notice, the robot frame is strong. Cross-bracing parts hold the leg subassemblies to the head motor and the rest of the upper body.

Summary

This turtle-shaped quadruped robot shows off many hidden and interesting aspects in its simplicity. The hardware features a smooth mechanism to walk in a realistic way, while the software tries to emulate autonomous behavior by using an FSM. Finally, the moving head is a nice touch.

Exercise 6-1. Further Ideas

Try to develop a strategy to follow lines going forward, by keeping the Light Sensor where it actually is. If that's not possible, try to place the Light Sensor in the front of the robot.

Replace the Light Sensor with a Touch Sensor to let the turtle sense whether it has been lifted from the ground, and act correspondingly. You can add this event among those that are causing the turtle to get scared.

Change the gearing to speed up the walking gait (suggestion: the legs' frame must be shifted with respect to the motor, to attach one of the gear cams directly to the shaft).

Replan the FSM to make your pet less lazy and a bit more enterprising (idea: rebuild the head so it can't retract anymore, using the motor to bite instead!).

PART 2

■ ■ ■

Back on Wheels

After discussing the walker robots in Part 1, let me lead you back to wheels. The robots in this part are not mere wheeled robots. The first one I present (just as a warm-up) is the Mine Sweeper: a robot with a two-degrees-of-freedom grabber arm driven by just one motor.

The last robot of this book is JohnNXT, a detailed replica of the famous robot from the *Short Circuit* movies. As the real Johnny Five does, its NXT counterpart moves on triangular treads, and features a rotating head, lifting torso, grabbing hands, and a moving laser. Also, he needs input, of course!

CHAPTER 7

■ ■ ■

Mine Sweeper

The protagonist of this chapter is a compact wheeled robot equipped with a frontal double-sensor scanner and a grabbing arm. Its design will show you how a single motor can accomplish more than a single function. In Figure 7-1, you can see the Mine Sweeper with the abyss-avoidance sensor mounted. In the frontal scanner a Light Sensor is used to detect dark LEGO bricks on white ground. In addition, the Ultrasonic Sensor is mounted downwards as an abyss detector, so if the robot is going to work on upland planes (tables), it won't fall down.

Figure 7-1. *The Mine Sweeper is equipped with a ravine-avoidance sensor. The mines shown here are built using two black 2 × 4 LEGO bricks.*

The robot you are going to build could have been given many other different names: garbage collector, floor sweeper, object collecting contraption, and so on. If "Mine Sweeper" recalls the sadness of some human invention, call the robot whatever else you want, and I won't take offense.

The robot can collect only small objects with a regular shape, distinguished by their dark color on a light ground; it is not able to collect objects of any color and any shape. Because it is specialized for collecting only a precise kind of object, it came to mind to call it a mine sweeper. The real bomb-disposal robots use particular metal detectors to find mines on the ground and collect them using skilled robotic arms; our LEGO Mine Sweeper has a frontal sensor and a grabber arm, and this gave me the idea for the name.

Getting More Actions from a Single Motor

The arm mechanism is designed to grab objects, lift them, and store them into the robot's internal hold, performing all these actions with only one motor. This is particularly interesting, because usually one motor corresponds to one degree of freedom (DOF).

UNDERACTUATION

We talk about underactuation, in robotics, when dealing with mechanical devices that have a lower number of motors than degrees of freedom.

The DOF of a mechanical system is defined as the number of independent parameters needed to characterize its state. In other words, if a motor can drive only a mechanism, a robot must have a motor for each action it can do. For example, in a wheeled robot a motor controls each wheel; in a steering vehicle the motor that drives the wheels cannot also steer; in the official NXT robotic arm, the motor used to grab the balls does not move the arm up and down. However, having an actuator for every DOF can become a problem! In a robotic grasping hand, using an actuator for every phalanx leads to a huge number of actuators: the device's versatility would increase, but its cost, complexity, and weight would become unmanageable.

In the Mine Sweeper's case, its arm can both grab and lift objects. The grabbing is an *underactuated* mechanism, because there is not a specific motor to close the fingers; the actuation is done by the same motor that lifts the whole arm. This solution saves space—*where to fit another motor?*, reduces cost—*simply, we do not have a fourth motor*, and lowers the overall weight. For these reasons, underactuated devices can be more efficient, simpler, and more reliable than their fully actuated alternatives. Of course, for a motor to perform more actions, you must devise a clever mechanism.

LEGO itself produced some official models that use an underactuated mechanism to grab an object first, and then lift it. Among many others, some examples are the yellow submarine 8250/8299 (released in 1997), the barcode truck 8479 (1997), and the alternative model of bulldozer 8275 (2007). How can a single actuator decide in which order to perform such different tasks—to grab and then to lift?

The submarine has a pneumatic hand that grabs and then lifts a barrel. Talking informally, in the submarine detail shown in Figure 7-2, the grasping is a lighter operation than the lifting. When the pneumatic piston shortens, it runs into the mechanical opponent force of the spring (the LEGO shock absorber) and then closes the grabber. Once the grabber is fully closed, the movement is blocked so the piston can't help but raise the arm. When the piston lengthens, the arm is lowered first and then the grabber is opened. Also at this time, the spring that forces the arm down does the lowering. Something similar happens both in the barcode truck and in the bulldozer alternative model, but this time, the opposing force is gravity.

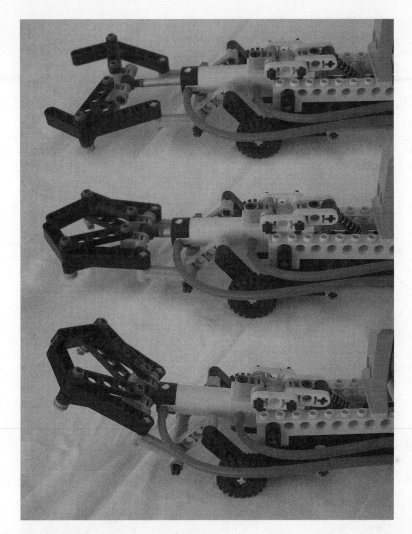

Figure 7-2. *The underactuated grabber mechanism of the LEGO submarine 8299. The piston first closes the grabber and then raises it.*

Now you know the state-of-the-art in underactuated LEGO grabbers. Among the many unofficial LEGO robots featuring underactuated grabbers are Ben Williamson's FetchBot (1998), Jonathan Knudsen's Minerva (1999), and Philippe Hurbain's Barrel Collector Robot (2003), all based on the RCX system.

The Mine Sweeper becomes part of that unofficial LEGO robots rank—it uses the same principle as the barcode truck. The arm grabs, lifts, and brings the mine up to the opening of the hold if the motor is turning forward. It then releases the mine into the hold and comes back down if the motor's turning direction is reversed. The easiest and most direct way to understand how this double action is achieved is to build the robot and observe it in action; see the photos in Figure 7-3.

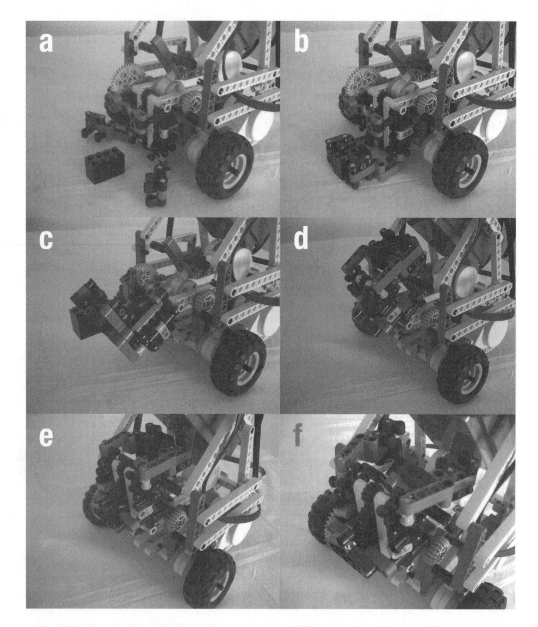

Figure 7-3. *The Mine Sweeper's grabbing sequence (the frontal scanner is removed)*

Now, take a look at Figure 7-4. Here you can see the arm mechanism extracted from the robot context. At the base of the actions' switching stands an opposing force. Here the force is gravity, while in the submarine, the force was produced by the compressed spring.

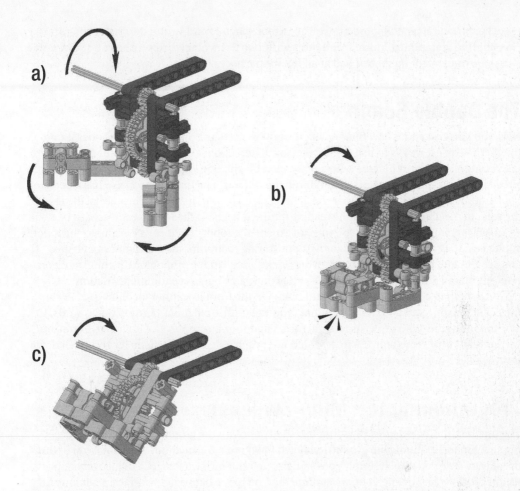

Figure 7-4. *The Mine Sweeper's grabber arm is extracted from the robot's context. The sequence of actions is determined by the force of gravity and by the limited run of the fingers.*

In Figure 7-4*a*, the arm is hanging vertically and the motor starts to move in the direction specified by the arrow; the light-colored parts are the ones that can move freely. The axle that transmits the driving torque is not integral with the 7-long white beams that form the arm frame; the axle rotates freely in the beam holes, and the geartrain brings its movement to the fingers. The arm is prevented from lifting by the force of gravity, which has no influence on the fingers' movement. So, the driving torque flows towards the fingers, because they are completely free to move. In Figure 7-4*b*, the fingers are completely closed, and the driving torque is thus redirected to raise the arm. In Figure 7-4*c*, the axle has become integral with the arm frame, because the geartrain is blocked by the closed fingers. The axle can't help but lift the whole structure. This sequence *a–b–c* in Figure 7-4 is matched with the photos *a–b–c* of Figure 7-3. If the sequence ends here, the robot has collected an object: reversing the motor direction, the object will be lowered and released. To store the mines into the hold, the sequence must be completed, as shown in Figure 7-3, photos *d*, *e*, and *f*.

The dark objects collected are stored into a space found in the depths of the robot. Considering a standard "mine," one built with two 2×4 black bricks, the robot can collect more than ten of them. Not bad at all for our purposes!

The Double Scanner

Now, you know all about how the robot collects and stores the objects. But, how does it find them? The easiest way is to use a Light Sensor to detect dark objects on lighter ground by measuring the amount of light reflected by the objects. The Light Sensor is equipped with a red Light Emitting Diode (LED) that illuminates objects. The Light Sensor also has a detector (a phototransistor) that can measure the light reflected by the surface of the objects: the lighter the color of the object, the higher the reading returned by the Light Sensor, expressed in percent.

Using a third-party color sensor, you can expand the robot's abilities. For example, the robot could pick up bricks of a certain color without storing them (the short sequence of Figure 7-4) and accumulate them in a pile, as a moving brick sorter. On the other hand, it could work on uneven colored ground, overcoming the actual dark-and-light recognition restriction.

As anticipated at the beginning of this chapter, the frontal scanner includes two sensors: the Light Sensor, used to detect the mines, and the ultrasonic radar pointed downwards, to give the robot the ability to avoid the ravines. The robot interprets as a ravine an Ultrasonic Sensor reading of more than 35cm. It would not be a big deal if our expensive robot fell down from a table!

Programming the Mine Sweeper

The program presented gives the robot the ability to clean the ground of the bricks, proceeding straight and scanning the ground as shown in Figure 7-5. The robot does not know about the already explored area. It simply goes straight, unless a ravine avoidance maneuver changes its direction. As said before, here we assume that the robot is on a light surface, searching for dark mines.

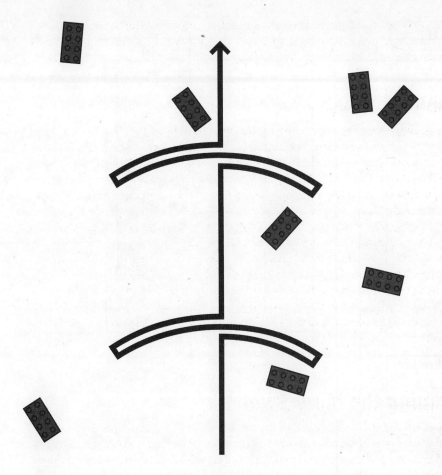

Figure 7-5. *The path taken to search for mines*

How do we obtain that particular searching path? Take a look at the flow chart in Figure 7-6. The overall working is given by the actions' sequence: search the mine, estimate the mine center, grab the mine. The ravine avoidance maneuver is activated only in case of emergency, during the search.

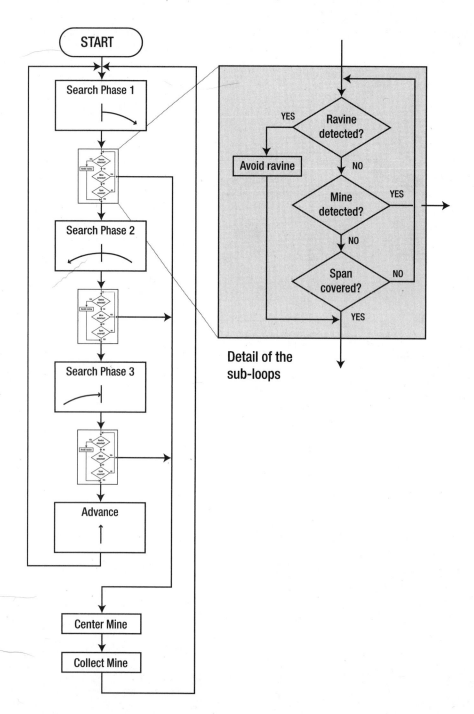

Figure 7-6. *The flow chart of the Mine Sweeper program*

The ground scanning is divided into three steps. First, the robot spins in place clockwise, until a ravine or a mine is detected, or a limited span has been covered (phase 1); then, the robot spins counterclockwise to reach the symmetric position, under the same conditions as earlier (phase 2); finally, it spins back to its original heading (phase 3) and advances a bit. The waiting for the three events that can stop the spinning (ravine detection, mine detection, and angle limit) is represented inside the subloop inserted between the "search phase N" blocks, whose detailed structure is shown in Figure 7-6, inside the gray rectangle.

If a ravine is detected when the Ultrasonic Sensor measures a big distance, the searching is suspended, the robot spins to change its heading, and then the searching is resumed. If a mine is detected, the search loop is interrupted, the mine size is measured to find its center of mass, and then it is collected. After the mine is stored inside the robot's hold, the searching loop restarts from the beginning (phase 1).

Now you are ready to be introduced to the NXC program that implements the working just described. The program is divided into many subsections, labeled by commented headings; the various parts will be discussed separately. The program for the Mine Sweeper is in Listing 7-1.

Listing 7-1. *The Complete Mine Sweeper Program*

```
// NXT ports aliases
#define LIGHT           IN_1
#define USONIC          IN_4
#define WHEELS          OUT_AC
#define GRABBER         OUT_B
#define LEFT_WHEEL      OUT_A
#define RIGHT_WHEEL     OUT_C

#define SEARCH_WIDTH    100
#define SEARCH_SPEED    25
#define SEARCH_TIMEOUT  2000
#define CW 1      // clockwise
#define CCW -1    // counterclockwise

// detection events definitions
#define NONE            0
#define MINE_EV         1
#define RAVINE_EV       2
#define TIMEOUT_EV      3
#define EDGE_EV         4

// mine centering algorithm definitions
#define TOP             1
#define BOTTOM          -1
#define RIGHT           1
#define LEFT            -1
#define APPROACHING     1
#define DISMISSING      0
```

```
// macros
#define RAVINE_DETECTED (SensorUS(USONIC)>35)
#define MINE_DETECTED   (Sensor(LIGHT)<threshold-8)
#define MINE_LOST       (Sensor(LIGHT)>threshold-4)

// global variables
int threshold;
bool found;


//======================================================================//
//                        ROBOT INITIALIZATION                          //
//======================================================================//
sub GrabberZeroPosition()
{
   // bring the grabber to its zero position,
   // with the arm down and the grabber opened.
   int t;
   t = MotorRotationCount(GRABBER);
   // run the grabber motor
   OnRev(GRABBER,40);
   Wait(400);
   // while it is not stalled
   while( abs(t-MotorRotationCount(GRABBER))>14 )
   {
      t = MotorRotationCount(GRABBER);
      Wait(50);
   }
   // and stop it
   Off(GRABBER);
   Wait(50);
   Float(GRABBER);
}


sub MineSweeper_init()
{
   // initialize sensor ports
   SetSensorLight(LIGHT);
   SetSensorLowspeed(USONIC);
   // measure the ground color:
   // the robot must be started with no mine
   // under the detector
   threshold = Sensor(LIGHT);
   // show the threshold, given by the light color
   // of the ground, according to which dark mines are detected
   TextOut(5,LCD_LINE1,"Threshold: ");
   NumOut(70,LCD_LINE1,threshold);
   // close the grabber a bit to avoid forcing
   // the geartrain
```

```
   RotateMotorExPID(GRABBER,60,180,0,false,false,20,20,50);
   // and then reset its position
   GrabberZeroPosition();
   TextOut(5,LCD_LINE1,"                         ");
}


//=====================================================================//
//                    SUBROUTINES FOR SPINNING                         //
//=====================================================================//
sub AvoidRavine()
{
   // avoid the ravine by spinning,
   // to change the robot heading
   // to the opposite direction
   Off(WHEELS);
   RotateMotorEx(WHEELS,80,550,-100,true,true);
   OffEx(WHEELS,RESET_ALL);
}


sub Spin( short dir )
{
   // this is called during the search phases
   // to start the robot spinning
   // the parameter dir indicates the
   // spinning direction (CW or CCW)
   OnFwdReg(LEFT_WHEEL, sign(dir)*SEARCH_SPEED, OUT_REGMODE_SPEED);
   OnFwdReg(RIGHT_WHEEL, -sign(dir)*SEARCH_SPEED, OUT_REGMODE_SPEED);
   Wait(50);
}


//=====================================================================//
//                      SEARCHING PHASES                               //
//=====================================================================//
bool SearchPhase ( byte phase )
{
   // the research is divided into 3 phases:
   // 1 - the robot scans the ground spinning clockwise
   // 2 - the robot scans the ground spinning counterclockwise
   // 3 - the robot spins back to get the initial heading
   // this function returns true if the mine has been found,
   // and false otherwise
   byte detection;
   bool result;
   short span;

   detection = NONE;
   result = false;
```

```
// start spinning according to the search phase
if (phase == 1)
{
   Spin(CW);
   span = SEARCH_WIDTH;
}
if (phase == 2)
{
   Spin(CCW);
   span = 2*SEARCH_WIDTH;
}
if (phase == 3)
{
   Spin(CW);
   span = SEARCH_WIDTH;
}
// the following loop is interrupted when
// a ravine is detected
// a mine is found
// the robot has covered the current search width
while ( detection == NONE )
{
   if (RAVINE_DETECTED)
   {
   // if a ravine is detected, avoid it
   // and break out of this loop
      detection = RAVINE_EV;
      AvoidRavine();
   }
   else if (MINE_DETECTED)
   {
   // if a mine is detected, set result to true
   // and break out of this loop
      detection = MINE_EV;
      result = true;
   }
   else if (abs(MotorTachoCount(LEFT_WHEEL))>span)
   {
   // if the span has been covered,
   // break out of this loop
      detection = TIMEOUT_EV;
   }
}
```

```
   OffEx(WHEELS, RESET_NONE);

   return result;
}


//=====================================================================//
//                        SEARCH THE MINE                              //
//=====================================================================//
sub SearchMine()
{
   byte detection;
   // initialize "mine found" flag to false
   found = false;
   TextOut(0,LCD_LINE5,"SEARCHING MINE     ");
   // repeat the procedure until a mine is found
   until (found)
   {
      // phase 1 : search the mine spinning clockwise
      found = SearchPhase(1);

      if (!found) // do this if the mine has not been found yet
      {
         // phase 2 : search the mine spinning counterclockwise
         found = SearchPhase(2);
      }

      if (!found) // do this if the mine has not been found yet
      {
         // phase 3 : spin back to center
         found = SearchPhase(3);
      }

      if (!found) // do this if the mine has not been found yet
      {
         // advance a bit
         OffEx(WHEELS, RESET_ALL);
         RotateMotorEx(WHEELS,50,40,0,true,true);
      }
   }
}
```

```
//===================================================================//
//                DETECT MINE EDGE, MEASURE MINE LENGTH              //
//===================================================================//

/*
        top
        ___
      |0)0)|.              ^
      |0)0)|| right        |
 left |0)0)||          length
      |0)0)||              |
      \___\|               v

       bottom


     <-width->
*/

byte WaitEdge( byte mode )
{
   // wait for the sensor reading to change
   byte event = NONE;
   unsigned long time = CurrentTick();

   while(event == NONE)
   {
      if ( (CurrentTick()-time) > SEARCH_TIMEOUT )
      {
         event = TIMEOUT_EV;
      }
      else if ( mode == DISMISSING )
      {
      // detect the transition from black to white
         if (MINE_LOST) event = EDGE_EV;
      }
      else if ( mode == APPROACHING )
      {
      // detect the transition from white to black
         if (MINE_DETECTED) event = EDGE_EV;
      }
   }

   return event;
}
```

```
int FindMineLength( short edge )
{
    // this function returns the left wheel rotation count (angle)
    // used to measure the mine length as the
    // distance between top and bottom edge
    int y;
    byte ev;
    // save start position
    y = MotorRotationCount(LEFT_WHEEL);

    OnFwdSync(WHEELS,sign(edge)*30,0);

    if (edge == BOTTOM)
    {
        // ignore the first edge found (the top one)
        WaitEdge(APPROACHING);
    }

    // wait for mine dismissing with timeout constraint
    ev = WaitEdge(DISMISSING);
    Off(WHEELS);
    if (ev == EDGE_EV)
    {
        // if the edge was found, save position
        y = MotorRotationCount(LEFT_WHEEL);
    }
    return y;
}


//====================================================================//
//                        CENTER THE MINE                             //
//====================================================================//
sub CenterMine()
{
    int length;
    // this file should be present in the NXT memory
    // if you have downloaded the latest complete firmware
    PlayFile ("! Attention.rso");
    TextOut(0,LCD_LINE5,"CENTERING MINE   ");

    // find top and top and bottom edges of the mine
    // to measure its length
    TextOut(0,LCD_LINE6," TOP EDGE     ");
    length = FindMineLength(TOP);
    TextOut(0,LCD_LINE6," BOTTOM EDGE ");
    length = length - FindMineLength(BOTTOM);
    // and then center the mine
```

```
    RotateMotor(WHEELS,40,length/2);
    //
    // HERE YOU CAN ADD A SIMILAR PROCEDURE TO
    // MEASURE THE MINE WIDTH
    //
    // clear line 6 of the screen
    TextOut(0,LCD_LINE6,"              ");
}


//=======================================================================//
//                        COLLECT THE MINE                               //
//=======================================================================//
sub CollectMine()
{
    TextOut(0,LCD_LINE5,"COLLECTING MINE   ");
    // move forward to get the mine between the claws
    RotateMotorEx(WHEELS, 50, 115, 0, true, true);
    ResetAllTachoCounts(WHEELS);
    StopSound();
    // grab the mine and lift it
    RotateMotorPID(GRABBER,90,1460,30,30,60);
    // release the mine into the hold, and lower the arm again
    RotateMotorExPID(GRABBER,-100,1000,0,false,false,30,20,50);
    GrabberZeroPosition();
}


task main ()
{
    // call the initialization subroutine
    MineSweeper_init();

    // execute the sequence of actions forever
    // using the preceding subroutines
    while ( true )
    {
        SearchMine();
        CenterMine();
        CollectMine();
    }
}
```

The program starts, as always, by executing the main task, which is the only task running in this program. In main, the MineSweeper_init() subroutine is called to perform robot initialization. After the sensor ports are configured to read data from the Light Sensor and the Ultrasonic Sensor, the color of the ground is acquired to set the threshold that will be used in the rest of the program to distinguish the dark mines on the ground. Then, the grabber arm is brought into its zero position by the GrabberZeroPosition() subroutine, using the useful motor stall detection algorithm you have seen throughout the book.

After initialization, the program flow comes back to the main task, where a perpetual loop begins: here inside the mine, searching, centering, and collecting procedures are called, one after another. You may begin to compare these parts of the code with the corresponding abstract blocks of the flow chart in Figure 7-6.

Let's dive into the detailed description of these three procedures, proceeding in order. The SearchMine() subroutine contains a loop that sequentially activates phases 1, 2, and 3 of the search, calling the SearchPhase(byte phase) function, passing the phase number as an argument. The program flow breaks out the SearchMine() loop only if a mine is found during one of those phases. Also, notice that the SearchPhase function calls after the first are performed only if the mine has not already been found (and the found variable is false). In fact, when the mine is right under the sensor, the robot must not continue with the successive scanning phases: the SearchMine() subroutine returns, and the main task can call the other subroutines.

The SearchPhase function implements the subloops shown in gray in Figure 7-6, returning a Boolean value that is true if a mine has been detected during the scan, false otherwise. Inside this function, the ravine avoidance maneuver can be eventually triggered. According to the phase argument passed to this function, the robot spins clockwise or counterclockwise, and the span covered is determined by the value of the span variable. Every time that the motors are started, their Tacho Count register is reset. So, the condition abs(MotorTachoCount(LEFT_WHEEL))>span allows you to check if the left wheel has turned by the number of degrees specified by the span variable.

■Caution The motors' Tacho Count registers are always reset by the standard functions such as OnFwd, OnRev, Off, and other functions, unless you use their counterparts with the Ex postfix, as OnFwdRegEx, OnFwdSyncEx, OffEx, and so on. Among the arguments accepted by these extended functions, you can specify which motor-related registers you want to reset, or none of them. For details about all the motors' control registers, consult the NXC Programming Guide.

The Spin(short dir) subroutine simply runs the motors in opposite directions, calling the OnFwdReg NXC function. Using this function, the NXT firmware turns the motors on and regulates their speed precisely.

Once a mine is found, the program flow goes back to main task. Here, the CenterMine() and CollectMine() subroutines are called sequentially. The CenterMine() subroutine attempts to find the mine's center of mass, measuring the mine's length. The program is left open to the development of a more refined centering procedure; for example, also measuring the mine's width. However, given that the size of the collectable objects is almost known, the grabber rarely fails in collecting them, even if they are not precisely aligned with respect to the robot's direction.

You measure the mine length by calling the FindMineLength(short edge) function, passing as an argument the edge constant values TOP and BOTTOM. This function returns the left wheel's motor rotation count at the moment of the edge detection. The information about the other wheel angle is not important, because the motors are running synchronized. You can determine the center of the mine by subtracting the value returned by the second call from the wheel angle that's returned by the first FindMineLength call, and dividing the result by 2. The CenterMine subroutine calculates and uses this value to move the robot forward. Use Figure 7-7 as a reference.

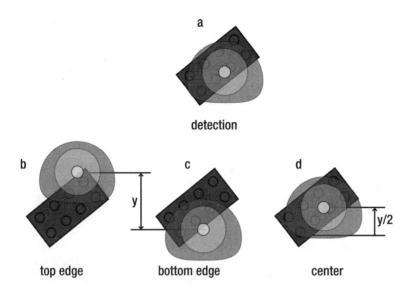

Figure 7-7. *This scheme shows the phases to align the mine before collecting it.*

Once the mine is detected (*a*), its precise position under the sensor is unknown; the only known thing is that the Light Sensor is reading a value well below the threshold value. The function FindMineLength saves the actual left wheel rotation count and, receiving the constant TOP as an argument, moves the robot forward until a transition from black to white occurs (*b*: top edge). This waiting is done by calling the WaitEdge(byte mode) function: the argument mode allows the caller to specify WaitEdge to wait for a black-to-white transition, or for a white-to-black transition, implemented by the two macros MINE_LOST and MINE_DETECTED, respectively. The first waiting mode is associated with the constant DISMISSING, meaning that you want to wait for the mine to go away from the sensor halo; the second mode is given the name APPROACHING, meaning that you want to wait for the mine to approach, until it comes under the sensor halo. To avoid unpredictable color measurement problems making this waiting become infinite, you can use a timeout mechanism. The timeout is detected using the same technique you have encountered in Chapter 6. The constants and macros the WaitEdge function uses are summarized in Table 7-1.

Table 7-1. *Constants Used in the Edge Detection Functions*

Waiting Mode	Macro Used	Expanded Code	Color Transition
APPROACHING	MINE_DETECTED	Sensor(LIGHT)<threshold-8	White to black
DISMISSING	MINE_LOST	Sensor(LIGHT)>threshold-4	Black to white

After an edge is detected or the timeout has elapsed, the WaitEdge function returns a value describing which of the two events has occurred. If the edge was found before the timeout, FindMineLength returns the actual left wheel rotation count, otherwise it returns the value saved before the edge detection.

Once FindMineLength(TOP) returns, the CenterMine() subroutine calls FindMineLength(BOTTOM), to detect the bottom edge (*c*). The only difference, with respect to before, is that receiving

BOTTOM as an argument, FindMineLength() first waits for a transition from white to black—WaitEdge(APPROACHING) —and then for another transition from black to white—WaitEdge (DISMISSING). This is necessary, because the top edge detection implies that the dark mine is not under the sensor anymore: the robot was going forward, and when it stopped after the top edge detection, it surpassed the mine a bit. So, when going backwards, the robot must wait for the mine to be detected again in correspondence with the top edge, and then wait for the bottom edge to be detected. Once the bottom edge is found, in correspondence with a black-to-white transition, the second measurement of the wheel angle is taken.

The CenterMine() subroutine subtracts the two measurements, halves the result, and moves the robot forward (*d*). The mine should be now under the sensor. The CenterMine() subroutine returns, and the next subroutine called by main is the one to grab and store the mine.

The distance from the sensor to the grabber is fixed, determined by the structure of the robot. So, the CollectMine() subroutine makes the robot advance by the amount of space needed to bring the mine between the grabber claws; the grabber motor is rotated by a precise number of degrees, and our good ol' underactuated mechanism does the rest! The mine should be released correctly into the hold opening, shaped to help the mines to fall down, under the central motor. Note that if the mine was placed in an unfavorable way on the ground, an aspect of the whole procedure could go wrong: the mine could not be picked up at all, or could become stuck with the frontal scanner during the lifting, or could remain in the hold opening instead of falling down into the hold.

After the collection, the grabber motor is reversed, to bring the arm back down; the appropriate subroutine brings the grabber into its zero position.

■**Note** RotateMotorEx and RotateMotorExPID are extended versions of the basic RotateMotor NXC function, whose arguments are motor Port, Power, and Angle. With RotateMotorEx, you can rotate two motors together using the Sync feature, and tell the motor to come to a stop after having turned the specified number of degrees. The other function RotateMotorExPID rotates the motor like the preceding functions, but also allows you to change the internal Proportional, Derivative, and Integrative gains of the PID controller that is run by the NXT firmware. The *Proportional* contribution gives promptness to the motor response, the *Integrative* contribution eliminates the steady state error (deviation from the desired position after the motor is stopped), while the *Derivative* contribution compensates for the oscillations generated by the Integrative and Proportional combined contribution, to reach the steady state faster. Consider, however, that the PID control is an argument well worth dedicating entire books to. For details about those NXC functions, check the Programming Guide.

Once the mine has been collected, the loop inside the main task restarts from the beginning, searching for the next mine on the robot's path.

Building the Mine Sweeper

You can build the robot with all the parts from the NXT retail set. After the robot building instructions, you'll see how to prepare four mines of the correct size and color for your robot, using the few retail set parts left. You might also want to prepare some other suitable object to be collected, by using some black 2 × 4 bricks that you might have among your LEGO spares. You can make a mine from two piled bricks. After completing the grabber subassembly (Step 70), you can test the arm mechanism by rotating the bevel gear by hand.

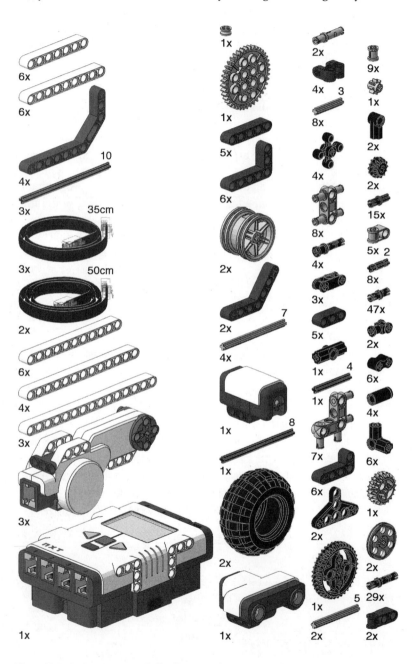

Figure 7-8. *Mine Sweeper bill of materials*

Table 7-2. *Mine Sweeper Bill of Materials*

Quantity	Color	Part Number	Part Name
6	White	32524.DAT	TECHNIC Beam 7
6	White	40490.DAT	TECHNIC Beam 9
4	Dark gray	32009.DAT	TECHNIC Beam 11.5 Liftarm Bent 45 Double
3	Black	3737.DAT	TECHNIC Axle 10
3		55805.DAT	Electric Cable NXT 35cm
2		55806.DAT	Electric Cable NXT 50cm
6	White	32525.DAT	TECHNIC Beam 11
4	White	41239.DAT	TECHNIC Beam 13
3	White	32278.DAT	TECHNIC Beam 15
3		53787.DAT	Electric MINDSTORMS NXT Motor
1		53788.DAT	Electric MINDSTORMS NXT
1	Light gray	32123.DAT	TECHNIC Bush 1/2 Smooth
1	Light gray	3649.DAT	TECHNIC Gear 40 Tooth
5	Dark gray	32316.DAT	TECHNIC Beam 5
6	Dark gray	32526.DAT	TECHNIC Beam 7 Bent 90 (5:3)
2	Light gray	54087.DAT	Wheel 43.2 × 22 Without Pinholes
2	Dark gray	32348.DAT	TECHNIC Beam 7 Liftarm Bent (4:4)
4	Light gray	44294.DAT	TECHNIC Axle 7
1	White	55969.DAT	Electric MINDSTORMS NXT Light Sensor
1	Black	3707.DAT	TECHNIC Axle 8
2	Black	55976.DAT	Tire 56 × 26 Balloon
1	White	53792.DAT	Electric MINDSTORMS NXT Ultrasonic Sensor
2	Light gray	X783.DAT	TECHNIC Pin Long
4	Dark gray	41678.DAT	TECHNIC Axle Joiner Perpendicular Double Split
8	Light gray	4519.DAT	TECHNIC Axle 3
4	Black	32072.DAT	TECHNIC Knob Wheel
8	Light gray	48989.DAT	TECHNIC Axle Joiner Perpendicular 1×3×3 with 4 Pins
4	Black	32054.DAT	TECHNIC Pin Long with Stop Bush
3	Black	32184.DAT	TECHNIC Axle Joiner Perpendicular 3L
5	Dark gray	32523.DAT	TECHNIC Beam 3
1	Black	32034.DAT	TECHNIC Angle Connector #2
1	Black	3705.DAT	TECHNIC Axle 4
7	Light gray	55615.DAT	TECHINIC Beam 5 Bent 90 (3:3) with 4 Pins
6	Dark gray	32140.DAT	TECHNIC Beam 5 Liftarm Bent 90 (4:2)

Continued

Table 7-2. *Continued*

Quantity	Color	Part Number	Part Name
2	Black	2905.DAT	TECHNIC Liftarm Triangle $5 \times 3 \times 0.5$
1	Black	X344.DAT	TECHNIC Gear 36 Tooth Double Bevel
2	Light gray	32073.DAT	TECHNIC Axle 5
9	Light gray	3713.DAT	TECHNIC Bush
1	Light gray	3647.DAT	TECHNIC Gear 8 Tooth
2	Black	32013.DAT	TECHNIC Angle Connector #1
2	Black	32270.DAT	TECHNIC Gear 12 Tooth Double Bevel
15	Blue	43093.DAT	TECHNIC Axle Pin with Friction
5	Light gray	6536.DAT	TECHNIC Axle Joiner Perpendicular
8	Black	32062.DAT	TECHNIC Axle 2 Notched
47	Black	2780.DAT	TECHNIC Pin with Friction and Slots
2	Black	32039.DAT	TECHNIC Connector with Axlehole
6	Black	45590.DAT	TECHNIC Axle Joiner Double Flexible
4	Black	75535.DAT	TECHNIC Pin Joiner Round
6	Black	32014.DAT	TECHNIC Angle Connector #6 (90 degree)
1	Light gray	32269.DAT	TECHNIC Gear 20 Tooth Double Bevel
2	Light gray	4185.DAT	TECHNIC Wedge Belt Wheel
29	Black	6558.DAT	TECHNIC Pin Long with Friction and Slot
2	Dark gray	42003.DAT	TECHNIC Axle Joiner Perpendicular with 2 Holes

266 parts total (all included in NXT retail set)

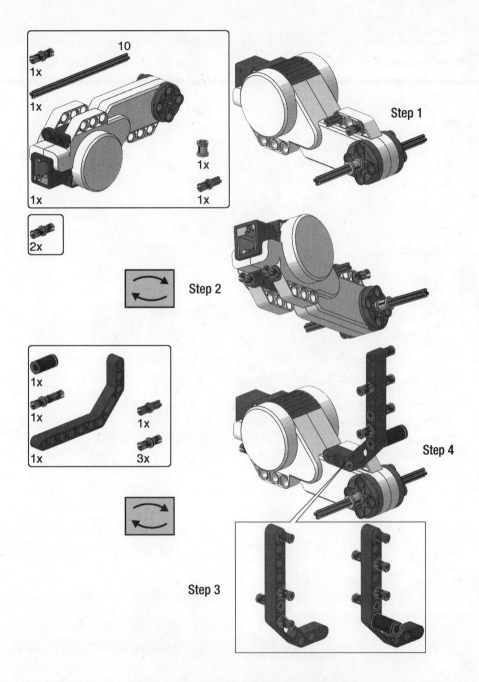

Step 1

Step 2

Step 4

Step 3

Start building the right wheel assembly. In Step 2, insert two black pins in the motor's rear.

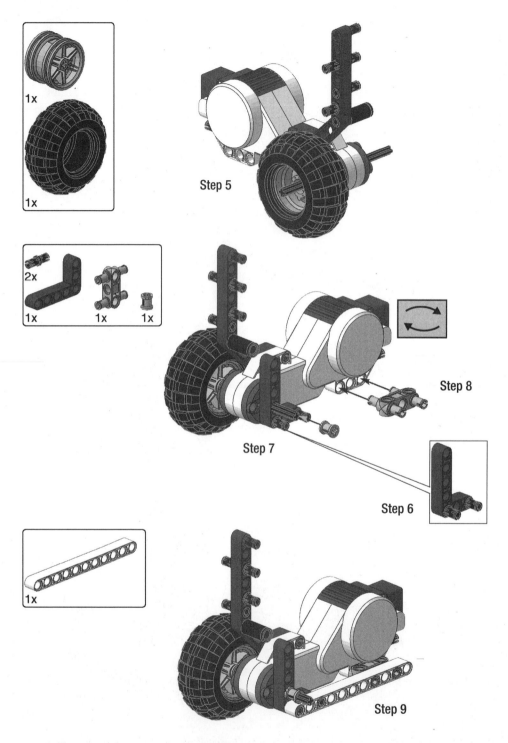

Step 5

Step 8

Step 7

Step 6

Step 9

Attach the wheel, then turn the model and insert the bent beam in the wheel axle, securing it with a bush. Finally, add an 11 holes-long beam.

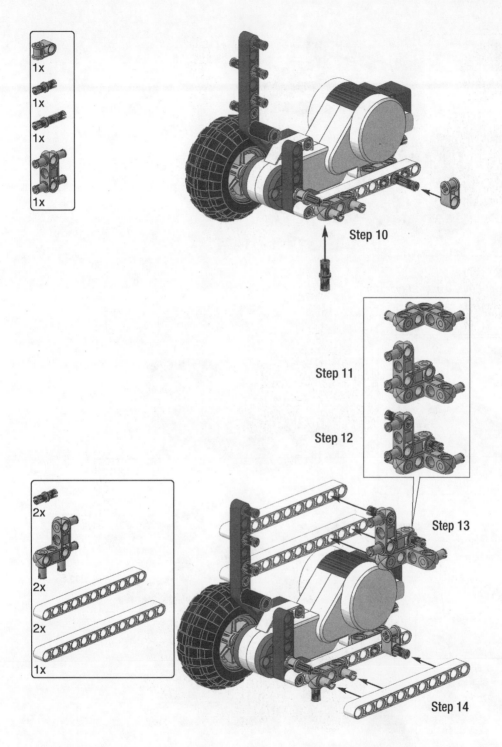

Continue building the structure. In Step 14, place two 11 holes-long beams and a 13-long beam as shown.

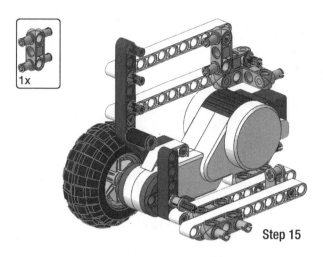

Step 15

The right wheel assembly is done.

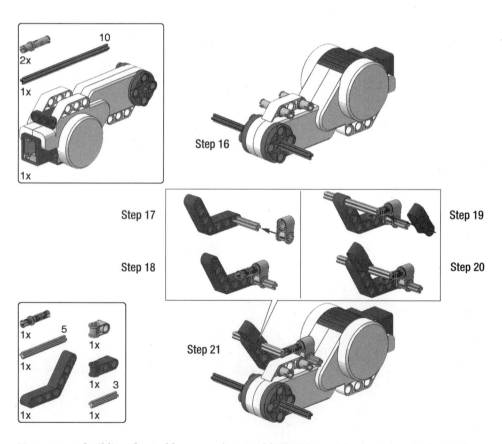

Step 16

Step 17

Step 18

Step 19

Step 20

Step 21

Now you are building the grabber motor's assembly that forms the central part of the robot.

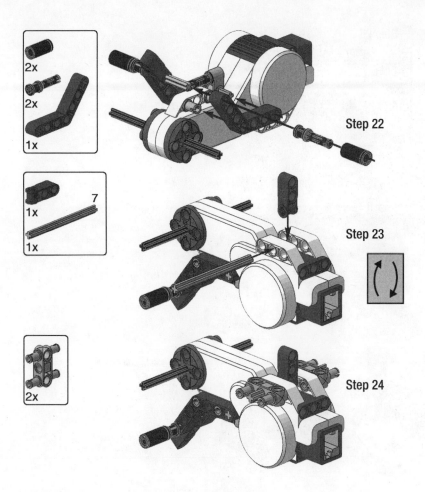

Step 22

Step 23

Step 24

The bent wedge on top of the motor helps the mines to slide down into the robot's hold, once the grabber arm has collected, raised, and released them.

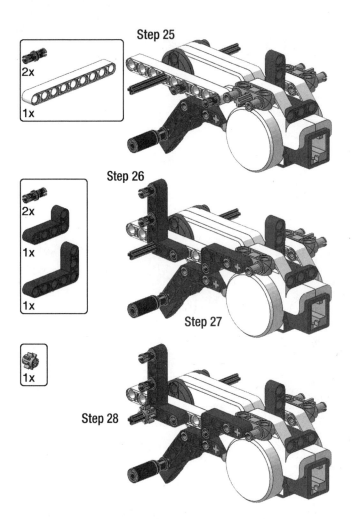

Step 25

Step 26

Step 27

Step 28

The building goes on by placing a 9-long beam and two pins. Then add the bent beams to hold the white beam in place. Finally, add the 8-tooth gear.

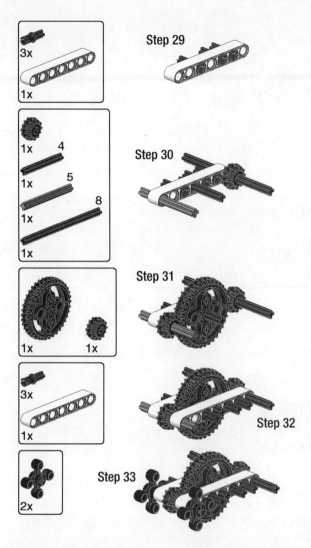

Step 29

Step 30

Step 31

Step 32

Step 33

Start building the grabber arm itself. In Step 29, place the blue axle pins in the 7-long beam as shown. Then add the gears and the other white beam. Lock the structure with two black knob wheels. They are used to trasmit movement at 90 degrees to the grabber fingers, as were gears with just 4 teeth.

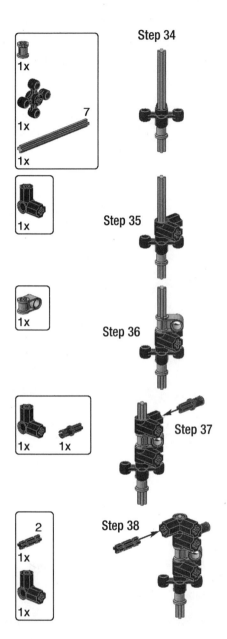

Step 34

Step 35

Step 36

Step 37

Step 38

Start building the right finger subassembly.

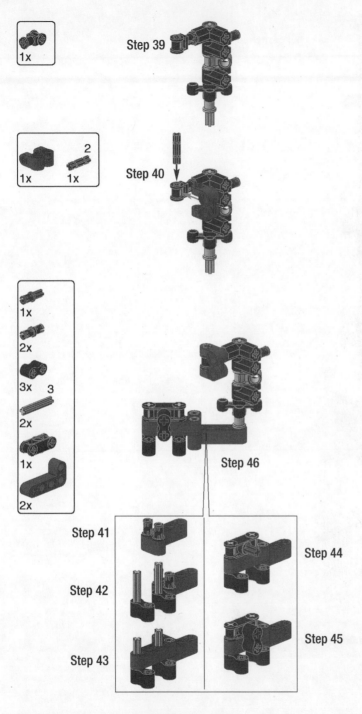

Step 39

Step 40

Step 41

Step 42

Step 43

Step 46

Step 44

Step 45

The right finger subassembly is done.

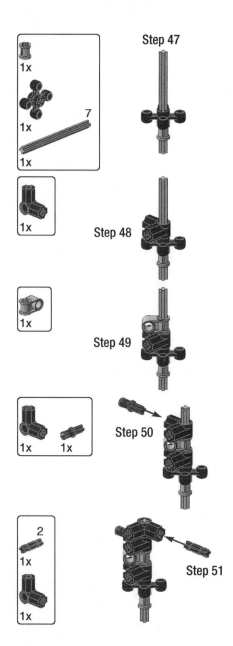

Start building the left finger subassembly.

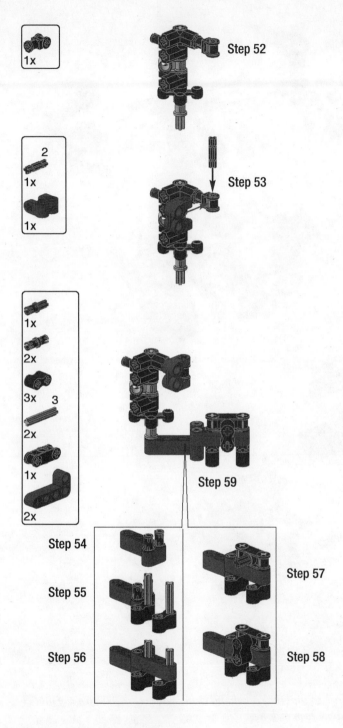

Step 52

Step 53

Step 59

Step 54

Step 55

Step 56

Step 57

Step 58

The left finger subassembly is done.

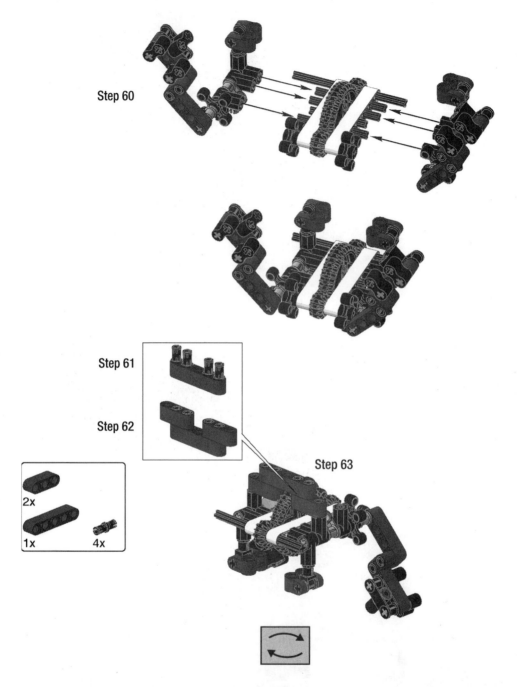

Step 60

Step 61

Step 62

Step 63

2x

1x   4x

Attach the fingers to the grabber arm, so that they open and close symmetrically. Turn the model and add a blocking beam. The grabber arm is done.

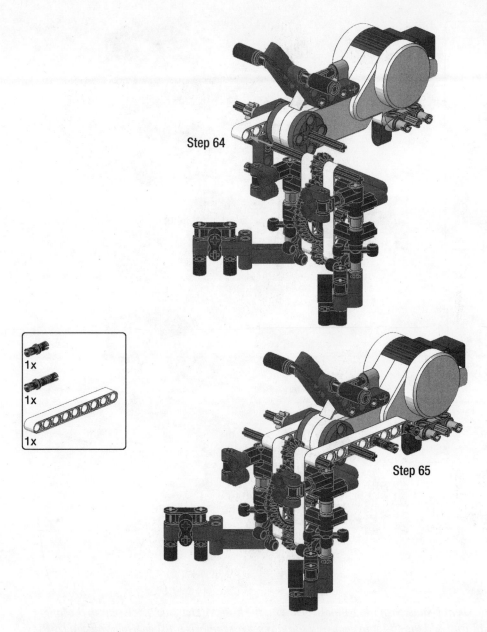

Step 64

1x

1x

1x

Step 65

Insert the grabber arm into its place in the grabber motor assembly. Add a 9-long beam, a black pin, and a long pin.

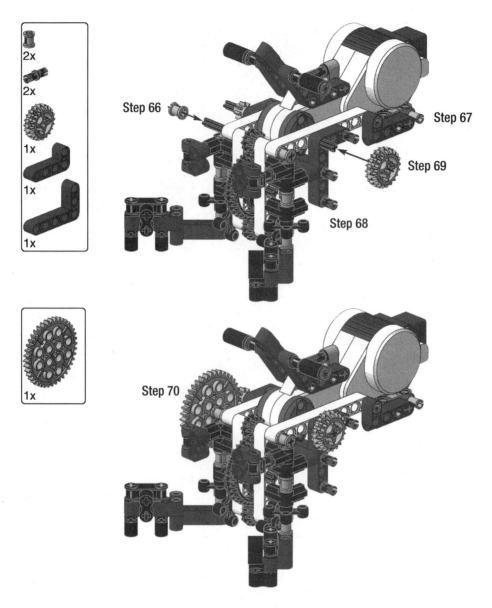

Step 66

Step 67

Step 69

Step 68

Step 70

2x

2x

1x

1x

1x

1x

Add two bent beams, then the 20-tooth gear and the bush. Attach two black pins to the longer bent liftarm. Add the 40-tooth gear, and the grabber assembly is finished. Now you can try the underactuated mechanism, turning the bevel gear by hand.

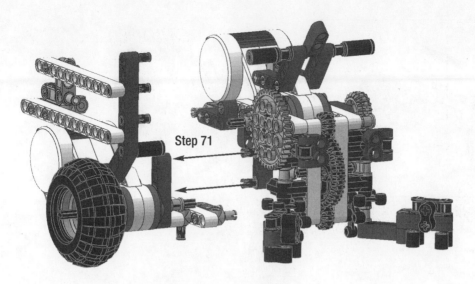

Step 71

Attach the grabber assembly to the right side of the robot.

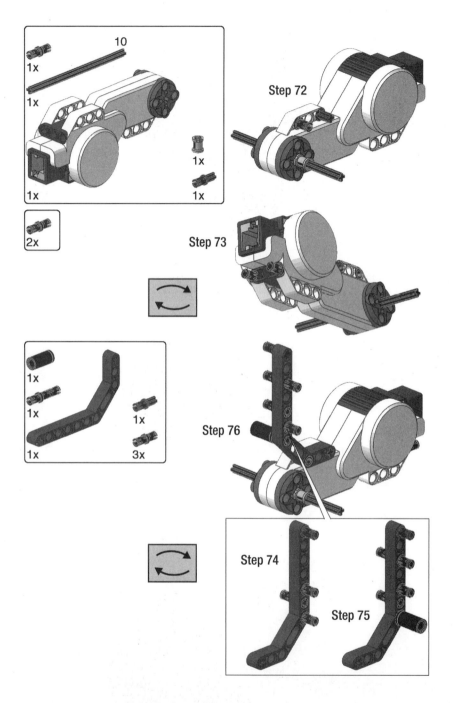

Start building the left wheel assembly. In Step 73, insert two black pins in the motor's rear.

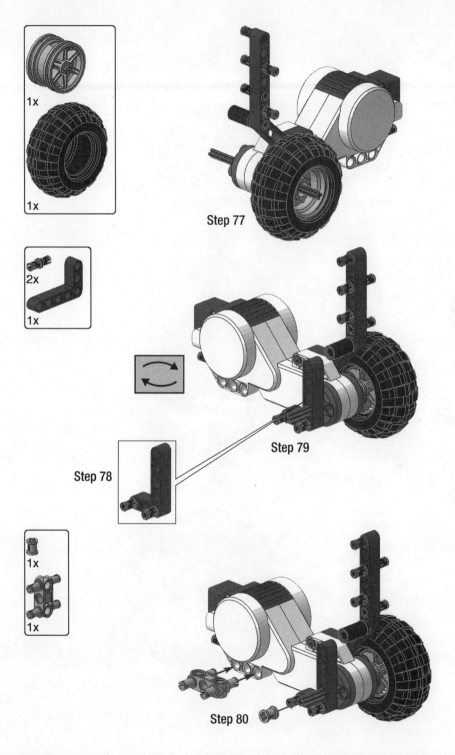

Step 77

Step 78

Step 79

Step 80

Attach the wheel, then turn the model and insert the bent beam in the wheel axle, securing it with a bush.

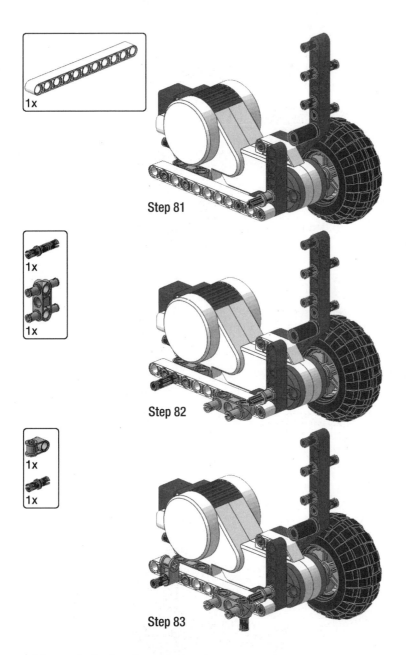

Step 81

Step 82

Step 83

Add an 11 holes-long beam in Step 81.

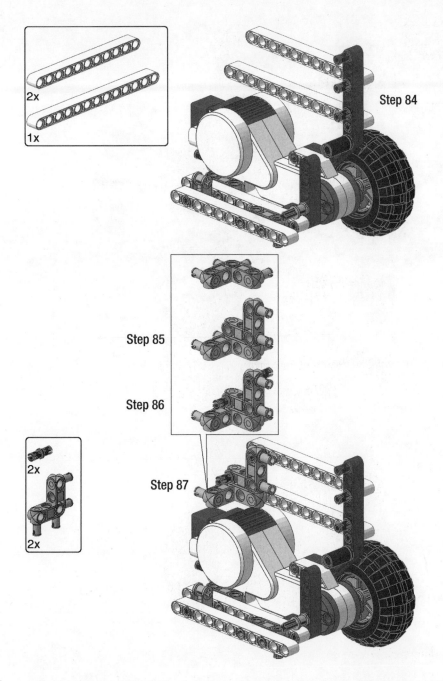

In Step 84, place two 11 holes-long beams and a 13 holes-long beam as shown. The left wheel assembly is done.

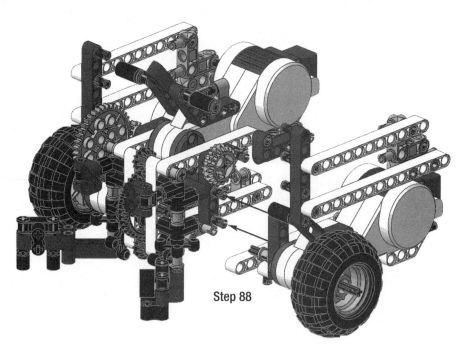

Step 88

Attach the left wheel assembly to the rest of the robot.

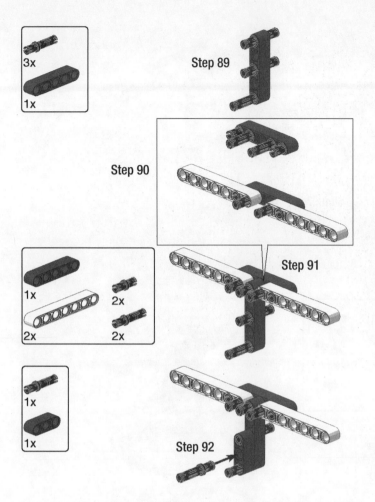

Start building the frame that will be placed in the back of the robot to hold together the three main parts you just built.

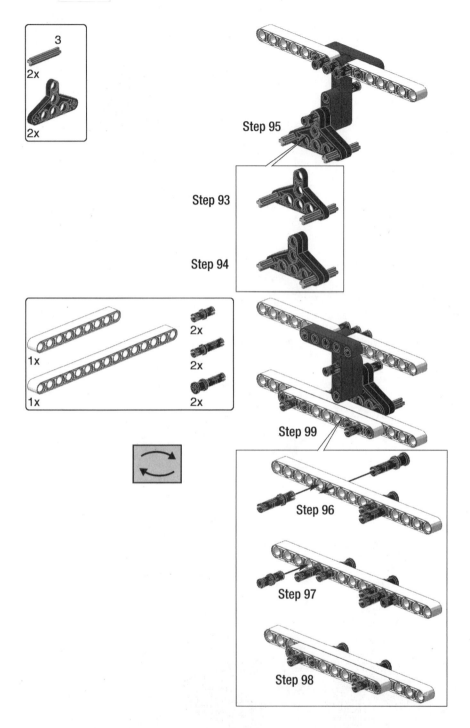

Step 95

Step 93

Step 94

Step 99

Step 96

Step 97

Step 98

Continue building the frame as shown.

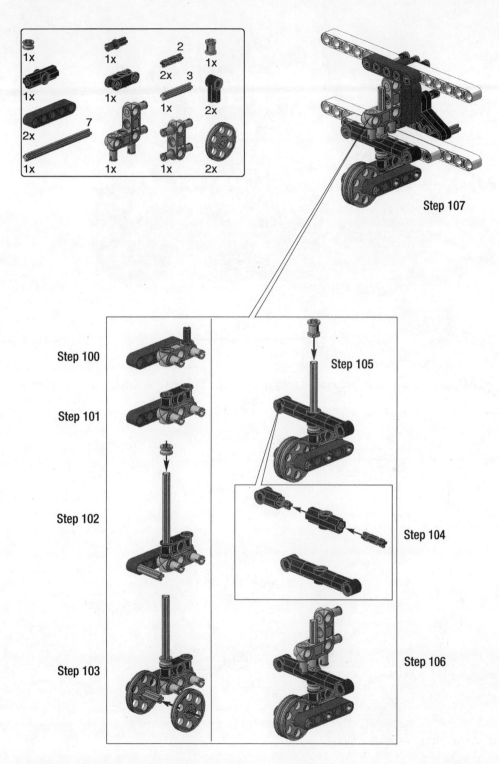

Step 107

Step 100

Step 101

Step 102

Step 103

Step 105

Step 104

Step 106

This frame also holds the rear passive wheel.

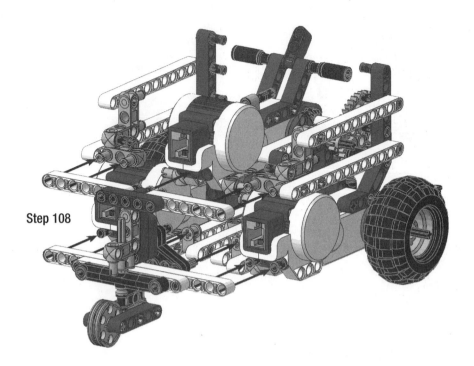

Step 108

Attach the frame on the back of the robot. Step 108 is tricky, because you have to insert 14 pins in their correct holes.

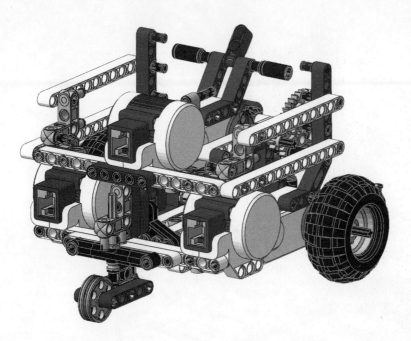

Here you can see how the back frame looks when attached.

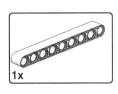

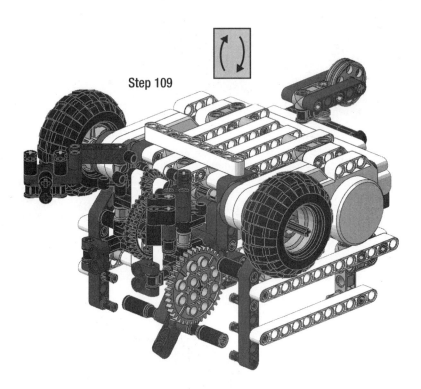

Step 109

Rotate the robot and insert a 9-long beam.

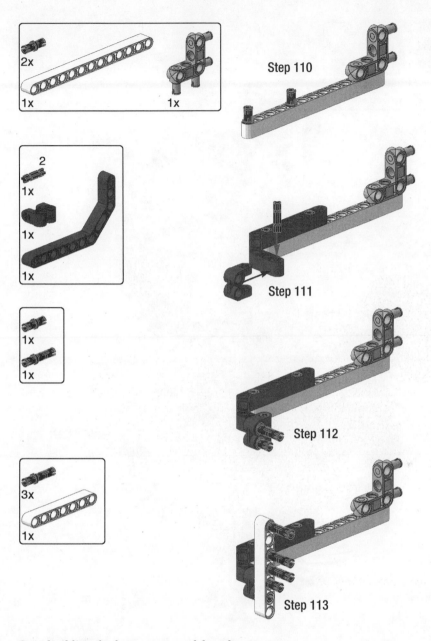

Step 110

Step 111

Step 112

Step 113

Start building the front scanner of the robot.

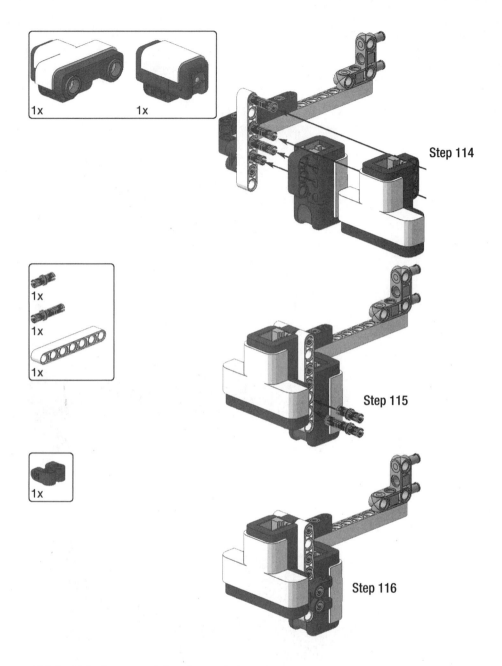

Step 114

Step 115

Step 116

Add the Light Sensor and the Ultrasonic Sensor.

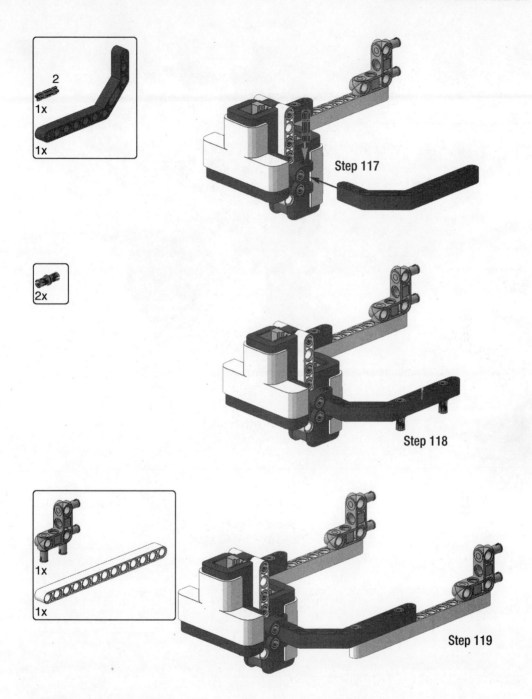

Step 117

Step 118

Step 119

Complete the front scanner.

Step 120

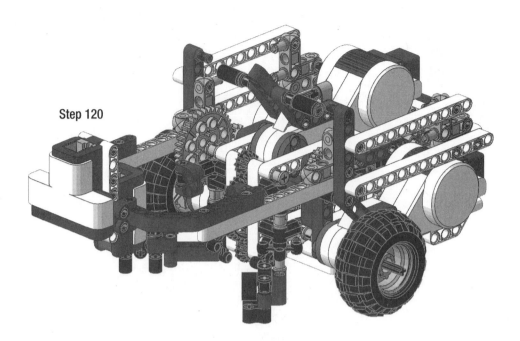

Here's how the robot looks when the front scanner is attached.

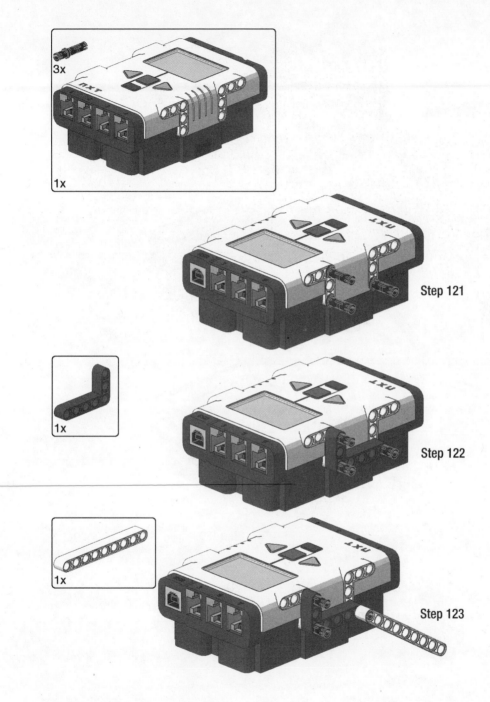

Build the NXT holder frame.

Step 121

Step 122

Step 123

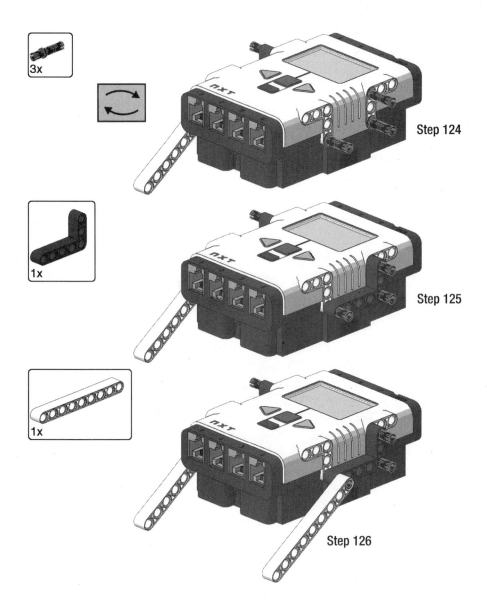

Step 124

Step 125

Step 126

The NXT frame will stand on the top of the robot.

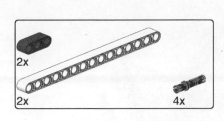

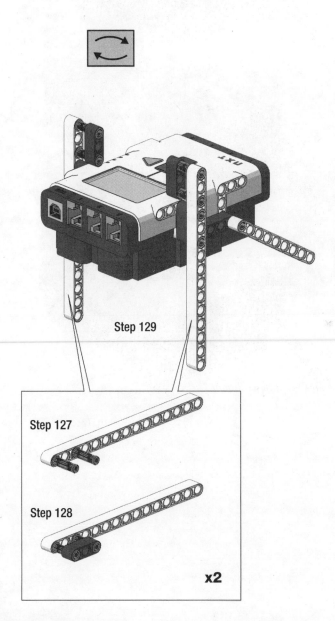

Step 129

Step 127

Step 128

x2

Complete the NXT frame assembly.

Step 130

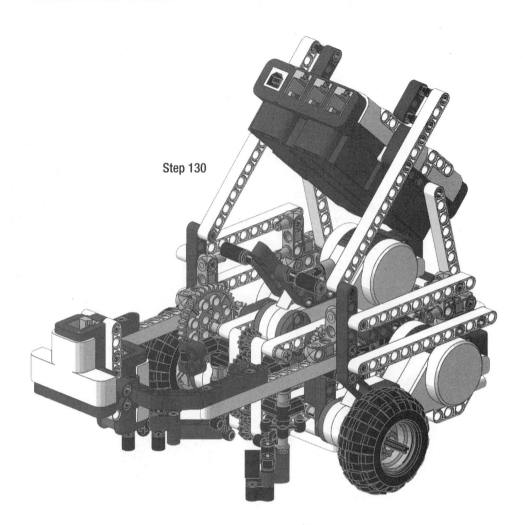

Attach the NXT frame on the robot as shown.

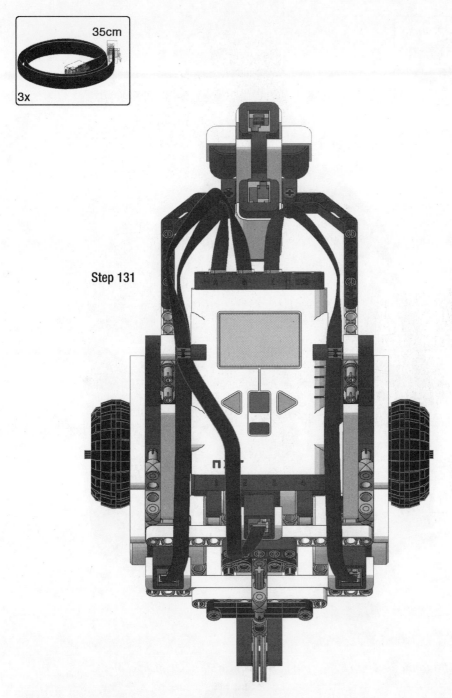

35cm

3x

Step 131

Attach the left wheel motor to NXT output port A, the grabber motor to port B, and the right wheel motor to port C. Use three 35cm (14 inch) cables. Pass these cables through the NXT frame's top beams as shown here and in the next figure.

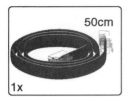

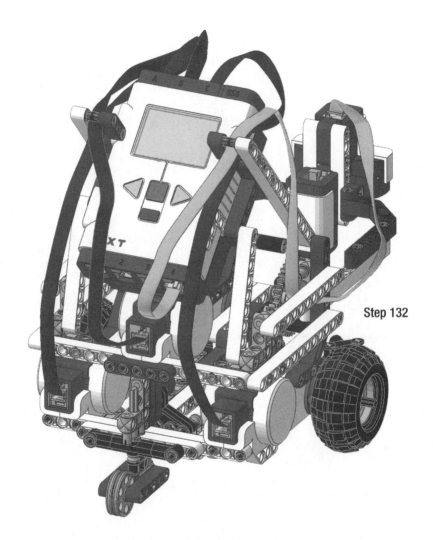

Step 132

Attach the Ultrasonic Sensor to NXT input port 4 using a 50cm (20 inch) cable.

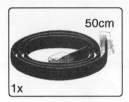

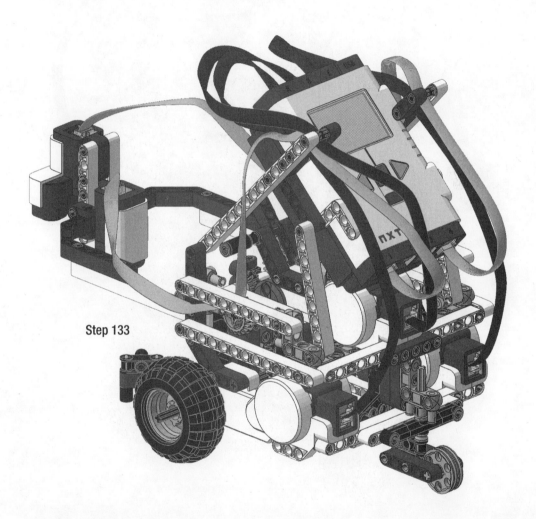

Step 133

Attach the Light Sensor (mine scanner) to NXT input port 1 using another 50cm (20 inch) cable.

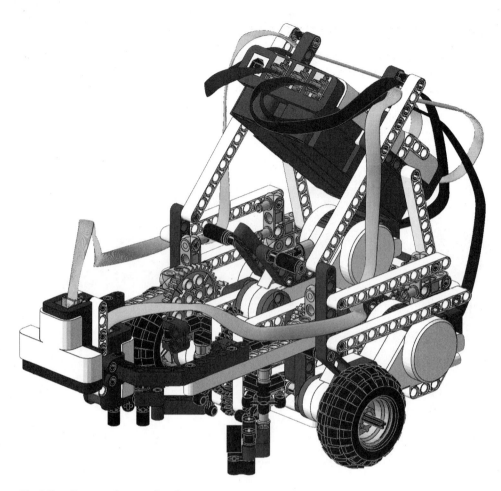

The Mine Sweeper is completed.

Mines Building Instructions

In the NXT retail set there are no 2 × 4 black bricks, which are ideal to build the mines for our robot. So, you'll now see how to build four kinds of mines using the NXT set parts left. These mines are of the right size and color, so that the Mine Sweeper will be able to detect and handle them.

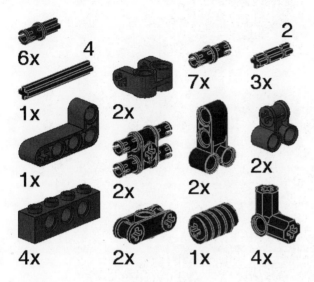

Figure 7-9. *Mines bill of materials*

Table 7-3. *Mines Bill of Materials*

Quantity	Color	Part Number	Part Name
6	Blue	43093.DAT	TECHNIC Axle Pin with Friction
1	Black	3705.DAT	TECHNIC Axle 4
1	Dark gray	32140.DAT	TECHNIC Beam 5 Liftarm Bent 90 (4:2)
4	Dark gray	3701.DAT	TECHNIC Brick 1 × 4 with Holes
2	Dark gray	41678.DAT	TECHNIC Axle Joiner Perpendicular Double Split
2	Black	32136.DAT	TECHNIC Pin 3L Double
2	Black	32184.DAT	TECHNIC Axle Joiner Perpendicular 3L
7	Black	2780.DAT	TECHNIC Pin with Friction and Slots
2	Black	32557.DAT	TECHNIC Pin Joiner Dual Perpendicular
1	Black	4716.DAT	TECHNIC Worm Screw
3	Black	32062.DAT	TECHNIC Axle 2 Notched
2	Dark gray	32291.DAT	TECHNIC Axle Joiner Perpendicular Double

37 parts total (all included in NXT retail set)

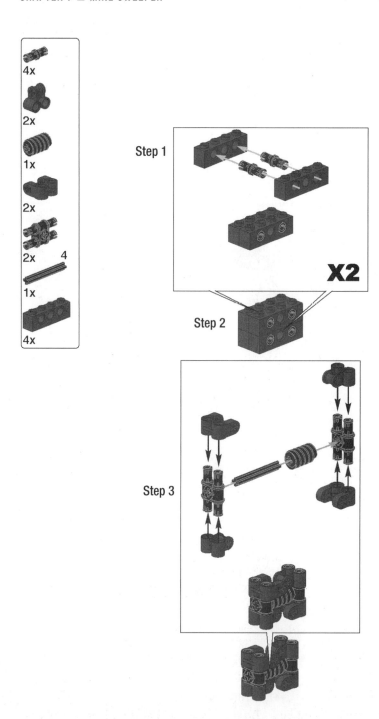

Here you are building both the first and second kind of mine.

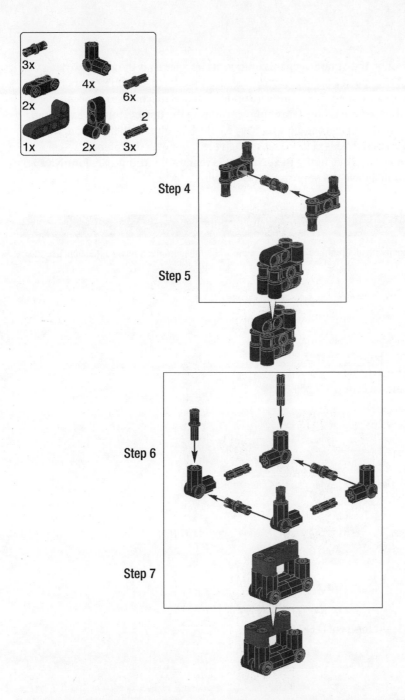

Now you are building the third and fourth kind of mine. Notice that all these mines are made in a color and shape such that the robot can detect and handle them.

Summary

Though it's a wheeled robot, the Mine Sweeper is unique. Its peculiarity is the ability to detect, grab, and store "mines" (two piled 2×4 black bricks are ideal) scattered around its working area. This model has shown you an interesting hardware underactuated mechanism to accomplish two different tasks with the same motor (grabbing and storing the objects into its capacious hold). On the software side, you learned how to drive a wheeled robot with precision, when needed to accomplish refined tasks—in this case, to align the robot with the mine.

The treaded robot you will see in the next chapter is really something else. JohnNXT is a stunning robot, and you'll have the opportunity to see why.

Exercise 7-1. Further Ideas

1. Improve the mine-centering algorithm by adding the mine width measurement. As a suggestion, use the following code:

```
int FindMineWidth( short edge )
{
    int x;
    byte ev;
    unsigned long time = CurrentTick();
    // save start position
    x = MotorRotationCount(LEFT_WHEEL);

    Spin(sign(edge));

    if (edge == LEFT)
    {
        // ignore the first edge found (the right one)
        WaitEdge(APPROACHING);
    }
    // wait for edge, dismissing with timeout constraint
    ev = WaitEdge(DISMISSING);
    Off(WHEELS);
    if (ev == EDGE_EV)
    {
        // if the edge was found, save position
        x = MotorRotationCount(LEFT_WHEEL);
    }
    return x;
}
```

Also, change the CenterMine() subroutine accordingly, adding the code proposed after the first centering procedure:

```
TextOut(0,LCD_LINE6,"  RIGHT EDGE    ");
width = FindMineWidth(RIGHT);
TextOut(0,LCD_LINE6,"  LEFT EDGE     ");
width = width - FindMineWidth(LEFT);
// and then center the mine
RotateMotorEx(WHEELS,80,width/2,-100,true,true);
```

2. It might happen that a mine is not detected even if it falls under the Light Sensor. If this unfortunate case occurs, the mine could end up in the space between the Light Sensor of the protruding scanner and the grabber fingers. Could you plan how to avoid this situation—both by using an additional sensor or thinking about some software security procedure, as a periodic maneuver to free these trapped mines?

3. As is, the Mine Sweeper goes around quite randomly. After any mine collection, you should design a solution to let it find its way again. For example, you can use a third-party digital compass sensor to keep the right direction.

CHAPTER 8

JohnNXT Is Alive!

Here comes the top model of the book. By huge public demand, I'm proud to present JohnNXT! For those who don't know this robot yet, JohnNXT is an accurate desktop-scale–sized replica of the famous robot Johnny 5 from the *Short Circuit* 1980s movies. This is a fairly complex robot: you'll need more parts than the ones included in the two NXT retail sets to build it.

Johnnicle: My LEGO Johnny 5 Chronicle

Johnny 5 is the robot star of the 1986 movie *Short Circuit*. The film became a cult classic, along with its sequel *Short Circuit 2*, which followed in 1988. If you were a kid in the 80s or 90s (like me), you surely know those films. In *Short Circuit,* the robot called Number 5, one of five prototypes built by Nova Robotics for military purposes, is struck by lightning while being recharged and becomes alive, achieving self-consciousness, a sense of humor, and an understanding of the value of life. At the end of the film, he renames himself Johnny 5. I think Johnny 5 is one of the most engaging robots in film history.

Inspired by these movies, I've been trying to build a LEGO Johnny 5 (J5) replica since age 11. I started with plain LEGO bricks. Then, I abandoned the project during my "dark age of LEGO" (a period of time when real-life interests got the better of LEGO play). I came back to this project when I first got my Robotics Invention System MINDSTORMS set, after I found on the Web the amazing two-RCX robot called Cinque (meaning "five" in Italian), a J5 replica built by Mario Ferrari in 2001. You can see this robot at `http://www.marioferrari.org/cinque/cinque.html`. I got inspired both by the general concept of that robot and by the functions it featured. After four draft proto-types, I got to the final shape of the RCX-based J5, which you can see in Figure 8-1.

Figure 8-1. *RCX-based version of LEGO Johnny 5*

This LEGO model resembles the real J5, and already features all the functions that will also be in the NXT version you'll build: moving treads, rotating head, raising torso, and grabbing hands. To drive the six motors with just one RCX, I invented a motor multiplexer to allow the RCX to pilot up to six motors with its three output ports. I also built a homebrew infrared proximity detector in J5's head to let him follow my hand. This detector was built with the kind help of Philippe Hurbain, better known in the LEGO MINDSTORMS community as Philo.

The head is a bit over-dimensioned to feature the expressive poseable eyelids and neck. However, the entire model was *not* designed with regard to the proportions and the body's relative sizes. The head is too big, the base is too short, the shoulders are too large, the tread hubs are too small, and so on. Nonetheless, it remains a good functional J5 replica. I knew myself that I could do better.

The NXT system provided the perfect material to improve the project. As you can guess, the NXT version inherits a lot from the RCX version. In the early design stage, I started studying J5's real dimensions and proportions from all the photos that I found on the Web. From the many captured movie frames, I began to put a 2D CAD project together. I took the best measurements that I could to reproduce the J5 structure. After finishing this CAD drawing, I went on looking for the right LEGO elements to match the scaled-size J5 parts.

As a reference size to choose the scale for the whole robot, I used the dimensions of the NXT Ultrasonic Sensor, which fits perfectly as a J5 head. Since MINDSTORMS NXT's first sightings on the Web, many people have noticed the resemblance between the shape of the Ultrasonic Sensor and the J5 head, so they thought, "Johnny 5 is alive!" I surfed this popular wave of thinking. In Figure 8-2, you can see an early stage of JohnNXT's body development.

Figure 8-2. *An early stage of JohnNXT's body development*

The Ultrasonic Sensor alone was not big enough to shape the head, so I added some LEGO fairing panels. Other J5 parts that immediately followed in the size-matching process were the treads' hubs and passive wheel. The first complete JohnNXT (version 1) still had many defects, mainly regarding the passive wheel and the upper body structure. In Figure 8-3, you can get an idea of what JohnNXT version 1 looked like.

Figure 8-3. *JohnNXT version 1, still missing some parts*

The top tread hubs were made with large black turntables, which are in fact dimensionally perfect when coupled with the 40-tooth gears used as ground hubs. The laser shape was primitive, but already functional. It did not just rotate about a pivot—its movement was *eccentric*:

a combination of a rotation and a translation. This rough model was the starting point that resulted in the making of the second version of JohnNXT, shown in Figure 8-4.

Figure 8-4. *JohnNXT version 2, with one of the NXT microcomputers removed*

The head shape was already the final one, with eyelids and positionable neck pistons. It has not been modified further in successive versions. The fingertips were made with half-cut rubber axle joiners (horror for the purists!) to get more grabbing friction. The main problems raised in this version were the laser shape, the unreliable head-driving mechanism (a slippery rubber band), and the shoulders' shape. The worst problem was the fact that the treads' chains escaped from the largest hubs—the ones made with turntables.

For the third version (see Figure 8-5), the laser was completely redesigned. The lever mechanisms allow it to lower and move toward the shoulder, or to lift and move away from it. The tread hubs were made using 40-tooth gears, sacrificing the design a bit, but eliminating the escaping chain problem. Also, the passive wheel was improved, making it as smooth as possible, to avoid influencing the treads' movements with its friction on the ground.

Figure 8-5. *JohnNXT version 3, featuring new treads and laser. Notice the rubber bands added on both elbows.*

A rubber band was added on both elbows to improve the underactuated two-DOF mechanism that allows the arms and hands to be driven by just one motor. As explained in Chapter 7, with regard to how to get more functions from a single actuator, you need one movement to be done before the other. Here, you need the arms to unfold before the hands open; the rubber band comes into play to help you. In the Johnny RCX version (similar to the Mine Sweeper grabber), the rubber band was not needed. This was because the forearm fell down under the force of gravity, because the whole arm assemblies were roughly vertical. In JohnNXT, the arms are inclined with respect to the ground, so I needed another force to make the forearms move before the hands. You can read the discussion about underactuation back in Chapter 7.

The rubber band used as the transmission to drive the head was replaced with a more reliable gear train. The head motor was built inside the upper body, while the arms' motor is on the side made invisible in the photo, shaping Johnny's typical toolbox. I was still not satisfied with the shoulder shape and the upper body in general. The end result is the final version 4, shown in Figure 8-6.

Figure 8-6. *JohnNXT version 4, with new shoulder shape. The NXTs communicate using Bluetooth. The final version you'll build is identical, but uses the NXT high-speed serial ports to let the two bricks communicate.*

Although many things might seem to appear the same as before, there are significant differences from the previous version. The shoulders are completely redesigned to look like a cylinder. The parallelogram frame of the upper body, used to keep the shoulders and head vertical while JohnNXT raises the torso, is now dimensionally more precise. The head tended to lean backward when the torso was raised, while now the neck axis always remains vertical, whatever inclination the upper body has. The arms' motor now has a structural function in the upper body. The arms' motor and head motor are swapped in position. Also, the head's and arms' geartrains are now different, to fit in the new frame. Finally, the treads have been structurally improved and lightened, by using a triangular frame. Could this version be the last one? Could I stop with version 4? Of course not.

The main reason is that this fourth version of JohnNXT has two NXTs that communicate using Bluetooth. What's wrong with it? Nothing, at first glance. But, wanting to control the whole model remotely using Bluetooth (see Chapter 9), I needed to free the connection and so had to plan a different manner of communication. So, I used the mysterious high-speed serial communication implemented behind port 4 of the NXT. The external shape of JohnNXT remains the same, while a new communication protocol had to be developed to use the serial ports.

So, the final version of JohnNXT, the one you'll build, is version number 5, where the version change is primarily due to the software update. It seems this number was assigned by fate! Our beloved JohnNXT can be controlled remotely via Bluetooth with a mobile phone, a PDA, or the remote control shown in Chapter 9. This concludes the development chronicle for the robot you'll build in this chapter.

JohnNXT Features

Let me try to summarize all the JohnNXT features. From now on, I'll refer to version 5, the final one. This complex robot is a differential drive mobile robot, meaning that it has two independent treads to move around. You can vary its angular speed (rotational speed about its turning center) by driving the treads at different speeds; to drive it straight, the treads must turn at the same speed.

Sensors and Actuators

Check out the following features in Figure 8-7. Two NXT bricks are used to drive six motors. The master NXT, placed in the abdomen, drives the two motors for the treads, as well as the third motor, used to turn the head. The slave NXT, built in the base, controls the other three motors. The fourth motor is used to raise the whole robot's body, both the lower column and the torso; the fifth motor is used to move the arms; and finally the sixth motor is used to arm and disarm the laser.

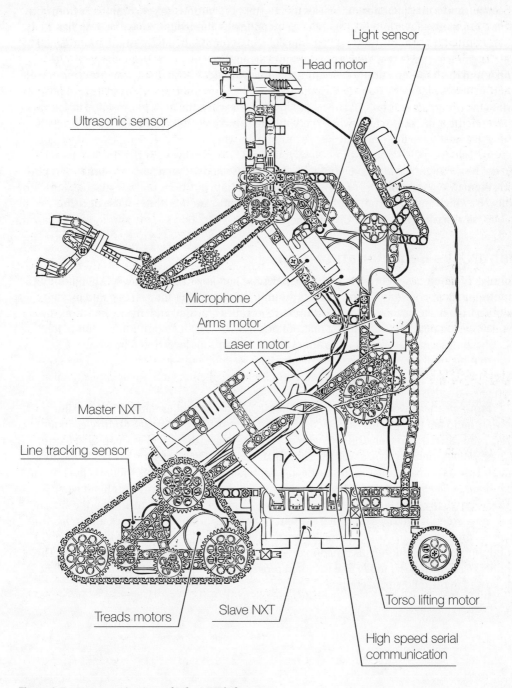

Figure 8-7. *Panoramic view of JohnNXT's features*

JohnNXT senses the world through a down-facing Light Sensor, the Ultrasonic Sensor in the head, and a microphone. It also uses the master NXT buttons to get commands from you. This equipment allows JohnNXT to follow a black line on the ground, to follow your hand, or to react to sounds. He can grab and lift small objects, commanded by a sound-counting FSM.

The moving parts that have a limited moving range—such as the head, the arms, the torso, and the laser (practically everything except the treads)—use the servomotors automagic built-in limit switch technique (see Chapter 4 for details) to reset every part to its zero position when the programs are started. The head's motor feels when the neck has reached its leftmost position, the arms' motor feels when the arms are completely folded, the torso's motor feels the downmost torso limit, and the laser's motor feels when the laser is completely raised or lowered, all using the same method. Now, you should realize how powerful this technique is. To do the same thing without servomotors, I would use many Touch Sensors, sometimes putting them in awkward places. To manage the intermediate positions of these mechanisms—to know by which angle a certain part must rotate to get into another state—I use decision tables, as described in detail in Chapter 3.

JohnNXT's Behavior and Menu

JohnNXT features a simple autonomous behavior, schematized in Figure 8-8. When nothing interesting happens around him, he fools around, by performing some action and playing sounds from his repertoire. If the environment becomes crowded and noisy (the Ultrasonic Sensor sees something near and the microphone measures a loud continuous sound), John-NXT becomes angry, and enters into attack mode: he aims his laser and remains there, threatening, until everything gets calm again. If he sees someone getting near and the noise level is reasonably low, he greets and then asks for input. It enters into the menu as soon as you press the master NXT orange button.

From the menu, you have access to all JohnNXT functionalities: remote control, line following, hand following, arms' sound control, and show off. In the *Remote Controlled* mode (*R/C*), you can fully control JohnNXT with the remote device described in Chapter 9. In the *Line Following* mode, you're asked to calibrate the bottom Light Sensor on the light ground and on the dark line, similar to the Turtle in Chapter 6, and then JohnNXT follows the line. In the *Hand Following* mode, JohnNXT swings his head and moves toward your hand when he sees it near. If the head is centered, he will move straight; if the head is turned on the side, he will move steering on that side; and if the hand is too near, JohnNXT will back up. In the *Arms Control* mode, you can control JohnNXT's arms with repeated sound pulses. In the *Show Off* mode, JohnNXT exhibits all his functionalities, synchronized with a looped soundtrack. The JohnNXT complete user guide and the main programming topics to get him to work will be discussed in the following sections.

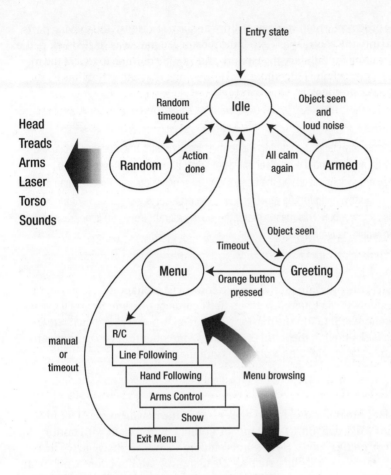

Figure 8-8. *The FSM describing JohnNXT's behavior*

JohnNXT User Guide

Before we get into the programming details, a good user guide to exploit all JohnNXT's features is needed. This section will lead you through all JohnNXT's functions.

Turning It On

Calm down, I'm not teasing you! I know that you know how to turn on two NXTs and how to start the programs! This section explains how to get JohnNXT working, seeing it as a system composed of three NXT bricks. Two of them are locally connected with a 6-wire cable, while the third NXT is the one for the remote control device.

Turn on both the master and the slave NXT in JohnNXT. Then, start the slave program. At the beginning, the slave performs the initialization of the hardware: it resets the torso to its downmost position, folds the arms, raises the laser, and then raises the torso to its middle position again. Only after that can it start receiving and executing the master's commands.

Now run the master program, which starts by telling the slave to reset all the moving parts, and then brings the head into the central position. If the master program was started before the slave, it would hang on, waiting for the slave to respond, and would continue to repeat the message until it received the slave acknowledgement (ack), meaning that the action has been completed. Using this kind of protocol, no command gets lost.

■Note A message-exchanging communication protocol is termed *synchronous*, if the sender is blocked until the receiver responds with an ack, and the receiver is blocked until it receives a message. This protocol guarantees that the two sides are synchronized. On the contrary, if the sender puts the message into a buffer and continues its execution without waiting for the receiver's ack, the protocol is termed *asynchronous*. The protocol used by JohnNXT is *synchronous*. This means that if the slave program (receiver) is not responding, the master program (sender) would become stuck.

After that, you can start the program for the remote control (see Chapter 9); it automatically connects to the master NXT via Bluetooth. If you don't connect the remote, you'll get an error message saying "Remote offline" on the master NXT screen, when trying to activate the R/C item (*Remote Controlled* mode) in the JohnNXT menu. Remember that you cannot control JohnNXT remotely unless you select the *R/C* mode from the menu first.

Autonomous Behavior

Once both master and slave programs are started, they reset all the moving parts of JohnNXT into their zero position. If you leave JohnNXT alone, in a quiet environment with nothing in front of him, he'll remain in the IDLE mode. He performs random actions, as shown in Figure 8-8. He also can randomly play some sound clips, such as "Need input," "Malfunction," and "Yeah! Johnny 5! That's cool!" If he sees an obstacle while in the presence of loud sounds, he'll lower his torso and aim the laser until the whole environment becomes calm again. When he simply sees something, he greets you and waits for you to press the orange button, to enter his menu.

JohnNXT's Menu

From the menu, you can access the *R/C, Line Following, Hand Following, Arms Control,* and *Show Off* modes. From the menu, you can also choose to come back to the autonomous mode (IDLE). When you are in the menu, if you don't press any button for a while, JohnNXT will come back into autonomous mode automatically.

R/C Mode

This functionality is enabled only if you've connected the remote control to the master NXT via Bluetooth before. In this mode, JohnNXT waits for commands from the remote and executes them. As you'll also see in Chapter 9, the remote device can access all JohnNXT's features.

The remote program for this particular robot works in two modes, toggled by pressing both remote buttons together. In the first mode, the joysticks control the treads and buttons that make the arms move to the open state (right trigger) or to the closed state (left trigger). In the second mode, the right joystick controls the head, the left joystick controls the torso, the right trigger makes JohnNXT play a random sound from his repertoire, and the left trigger arms or disarms the laser.

Line Following Mode

In this mode, you can make JohnNXT follow dark lines on light ground. The robot doesn't start going around at once: first, you are asked to sample the dark and light values from the bottom Light Sensor. The actual reading is shown on the NXT display. Place the JohnNXT line-tracking sensor on the line (dark) and press the left arrow button, then place it on the ground (light) and press the right arrow button. This way, the sampled values are stored and used to calibrate the line-following algorithm.

Press the orange button to start the line-following routine, and press it again to come back to the JohnNXT menu. If you don't calibrate the sensor readings, two default values for light and dark will be used.

Hand Following Mode

In *Hand Following* mode, JohnNXT centers the head and then swings it left, center, right, center, and so on continuously, while staying still in place. When the Ultrasonic Sensor detects your hand, the robot will drive towards you, going straight or turning according to the actual position of the head. If the hand is really near, the robot will drive away from you.

Arms Control Mode

In this mode, you can control the arms' position with sound pulses—for example, clapping your hands. When entering this mode, JohnNXT measures the ambient noise (so please keep silent for a short while) and folds its arms; then he waits for sharp sounds, which represent the commands you can give him:

- *One sound*: The arms are folded

- *Two sounds*: The arms are unfolded a bit, so they are vertical

- *Three sounds*: The arms are completely unfolded, but the hands are still closed

- *Four sounds*: The hands are open

- *Five sounds*: The wrists are rotated

Try clapping your hands and observe the text shown on the NXT screen: with every clap, a new arm state is chosen. If you stop clapping, the arms are moved into the state whose name is shown on the display. For example, consider starting with folded arms; clap two times and the arms are unfolded a bit; three claps unfold the arms, keeping the hands closed; and five claps (the maximum number) cause the hands to open and the wrists to rotate. A single clap brings the arms to their folded position again. So, you can go from every state to another.

Notice that you must produce the sound sequence with a constant timing, otherwise the robot won't behave as you would desire. For example, if you want to open the robot's hands starting from the state where the arms are folded, you must clap your hands five times. If you start clapping at a certain rate, but either the Sound Sensor fails to detect a clap, or you slow down the clapping rate too much, the robot will assume that the sequence is finished, and it will move the arms according to the number of sounds detected up till that moment. The procedure is simple and reliable, but it needs a bit of practice!

Show Off Mode

In this mode, JohnNXT performs a complete demonstration of its features. A sound loop is played, while JohnNXT moves right in time with it. It's a pity that I could not fit, in this small-scale model, a last feature that would be cool: making Johnny stand on his tread tips would make his dancing performance perfect!

Programming JohnNXT

It's time to make JohnNXT come alive! A pedantic, detailed description of more than 1,600 lines of NXC source code that make up the JohnNXT programs (master and slave) would be at the least boring—for me to write, but more so for you to read. For this reason, I'll focus only on the programs' outlines and on their interesting aspects. Many solutions adopted for the JohnNXT programs have already been explained in detail in the preceding chapters. I can say for certain that this chapter's programs are a big summary of all the programming techniques shown in this book. I won't go back to basics to discuss the FSM that implements the autonomous behavior, the servomotors automagic built-in limit switch technique that was mentioned before, the line-following routine (like the one seen in Chapter 6), and other minor trivial aspects. In particular, I'll spend some time discussing the overall program's structure and the sound counting routine, used to control the arm movements.

You can download the complete code for JohnNXT from the Source Code/Download area of the Apress web site at http://www.apress.com.

Panoramic View of the JohnNXT Software

When you are about to write a program for a complex project, the basic rule is to *divide et impera*, the Latin motto corresponding to "divide and conquer." To maintain the whole program easily, you should split it up into small parts; it is a good habit to split every program into many functions and subroutines. Of course, you already know that, but I mean that the program should also be divided into many files. So, you'll have an NXC file with the routines to manage head movements, another one devoted to remote control command reception, and so on. Then, in the main file, you just need to include the subfiles with the known preprocessor directive #include "filename.nxc".

The general working of JohnNXT is shown in Figure 8-8 and is described in the section "JohnNXT Behavior and Menu." Now, let's dive into the details. As you know, JohnNXT is controlled by two NXT bricks: the master, placed in the body, and the slave, the one built in the base. You need two different programs for these two NXTs. The FSM in Figure 8-8 is implemented in the master program, while the slave program's duty is just to receive and execute the commands from the master program. The whole slave NXT is just an interface to let the master control the three auxiliary motors attached to it: the torso, the arms, and the laser motors.

As said before, the two NXTs communicate through a standard 6-wire cable connecting their respective ports 4. So, I prepared a simple library to use this kind of communication, the High Speed Communication Library, implemented in the file HSlib.nxc. In the following section, you'll learn how to use this library, so you can also reuse it in your own two-NXT robots.

After that, I'll describe the two programs in an outline form, first starting from the slave, and then proceeding with the master, where we'll focus on the sound counting routine.

High Speed Communication Library

Exploiting the serial communication behind port 4 is made simple by this NXC library.

- To use the library, simply include it at the top of your program:

```
#include "HSlib.nxc"
```

■**Caution** The HSlib.nxc file must be located in the same folder of your program, otherwise the compiler won't be able to find it.

- At the beginning of the program, you can initialize port 4 by calling

```
SetHSPort();
```

This is enough to tell the NXT firmware to enable the RS485 chip for the serial communication.

- To send a string, simply call

```
SendHSString ( msg );
```

where msg is the string you want to send.

- To send a number, call

```
SendHSNumber ( num );
```

where num is the integer you want to send.

- To receive a string, make the following call:

```
result = ReceiveHSString ( msg );
```

After the call, the Boolean result will be true if the buffer is not empty, and the msg string will contain the received data. If the buffer is empty, or the data is equal to zero, the result value will be false.

- To receive an integer number, call

```
result = ReceiveHSNumber ( num );
```

As before, after the call, the Boolean result will be true if the buffer is not empty, and the num variable will contain the received data. If the buffer is empty, or the data is equal to zero, the result value will be false. This function, as does the preceding, features a timeout mechanism to avoid remaining stuck if the high-speed buffer is empty.

Next I'll describe the two programs in outline form, starting from the slave—the simpler— and proceeding with the master, where I'll focus on the sound counting routine.

Slave Program

To start dealing with the slave program, take a look at the program excerpt in Listing 8-1. Some parts, similar to the programs in the preceding chapters, are omitted. The purpose here is to give you an idea of what the program outline looks like.

Listing 8-1. *The JohnNXT Slave Program Code*

```
#include "J5Defs.nxc"
#include "HSlib.nxc"

//mechanical state variables
short torso_state, arms_state;

///////////////////////////////////////////////////////////////////////////////
//                              LASER                                         //
///////////////////////////////////////////////////////////////////////////////

sub Laser (short new_state)
{
   [...]
}

///////////////////////////////////////////////////////////////////////////////
//                              ARMS                                          //
///////////////////////////////////////////////////////////////////////////////

   [...]

sub Arms( short new_state )
{
   [...]
}

sub ArmsStepOpen()
{
   [...]
}

sub ArmsStepClose()
{
   [...]
}
```

```
//////////////////////////////////////////////////////////////////////////
//                              TORSO                                    //
//////////////////////////////////////////////////////////////////////////

   [...]

sub Torso( short new_state )
{
   [...]
}

sub TorsoStepUp()
{
   [...]
}

sub TorsoStepDown()
{
   [...]
}


//////////////////////////////////////////////////////////////////////////
//                              INIT                                     //
//////////////////////////////////////////////////////////////////////////

void J5_Init()
{
   SetHSPort();
   torso_state = UNKNOWN;
   arms_state = UNKNOWN;
   Torso(T_DOWN);
   Arms(A_FOLDED);
   Laser(L_UP);
}


//////////////////////////////////////////////////////////////////////////
//                              MAIN                                     //
//////////////////////////////////////////////////////////////////////////

// show a message to describe the command being executed
bool ShowRxCommand ( short s )
{
  [...]
   return error; //returns true if the command is unknown
}
```

```
// parse received command and execute it
void ExecuteCommand ( short command )
{
    if (abs(command)/10 == TORSO_ACTIONS)
    {
        if (command == T_STEPUP) TorsoStepUp();
        else if (command == T_STEPDOWN) TorsoStepDown();
        else Torso(command);
    }
    if (abs(command)/10 == ARMS_ACTIONS)
    {
        if (command == A_STEP_OPEN) ArmsStepOpen();
        else if (command == A_STEP_CLOSE) ArmsStepClose();
        else Arms(command);
    }
    if (abs(command)/10 == LASER_ACTIONS) Laser(command);
}

task main()
{
    KeepAliveType kaArgs;    // this structure is used to call SysKeepAlive
    int cmd;

    J5_Init();
    Torso(T_MID);
    // receive commands from master.
    // send an ack meaning "command received"
    // execute the command
    // send another ack meaning "command executed"
    SendHSNumber(ACK_RX);
    SendHSNumber(ACK_DONE);
    while(true)
    {
        if (ReceiveHSNumber(cmd))
        {
            TextOut(0,LCD_LINE3,"send rx ack  ");
            SendHSNumber(ACK_RX);
            ShowRxCommand(cmd);
            ExecuteCommand(cmd);
            TextOut(0,LCD_LINE3,"send exe ack  ");
            Wait(100);
            SendHSNumber(ACK_DONE);
        }
        else
        {
            TextOut(0,LCD_LINE3,"idle           ");
            SendHSNumber(ACK_ERR);
        }
```

```
    // keep the NXT alive: this system call
    // resets the sleep timer, to avoid having the NXT
    // turn off automatically when the program is running.
    SysKeepAlive(kaArgs);
  }
}
```

In Listing 8-1, you find the subroutines to actuate the three motors (torso, arms, and laser) using the decision tables (see Chapter 3). The J5_Init() function initializes the state variables torso_state and arms_state, and performs the routines to bring the moving parts into their zero position. The communication between the NXT bricks is set up simply by calling the function SetHSPort(), defined inside the High Speed Communication Library HSlib.nxc. At the top of the code, you can read the following preprocessor directives:

```
#include "J5Defs.nxc"
#include "HSlib.nxc"
```

With the first line, you tell the compiler to include the JohnNXT header file J5Defs.nxc, where all the robot constant definitions are specified: the motor ports; the sensor ports; and the opcodes for the various commands written in capital letters, such as A_FOLDED, T_DOWN, or UNKNOWN, for example. The other inclusion is for the communication library described earlier. After the initial definitions, the code goes on with the low-level routines for the mechanics.

The program starts executing the main task; here the J5_Init() function is called. After that, an infinite loop is started, to receive and execute the commands for the master NXT.

The incoming commands are received using the ReceiveHSNumber(cmd) function. Note that the ReceiveHSNumber function is called inside the parentheses of the if structure, and so the value returned by that function affects the subsequent working. If the result returned is true, it means that no error occurred when receiving the command, and the cmd variable, passed as an argument, contains the command sent by the master NXT; so, the first branch of the if structure is taken. The slave sends a first ack ACK_RX to the master, meaning "Hey, I got the message correctly!" Then it displays information onscreen by calling the ShowRxCommand(cmd) function, it executes the command with ExecuteCommand(cmd), and after that sends another ack ACK_DONE to the master, to say "I've executed your command!" The reason for using two different acks is to inform the master about both reception and execution of the command. So, the master can choose to wait for the remote operation's completion (signaled by the ACK_DONE ack), or to go on with its own task after having sent the command. To tell the master to repeat the last message, the slave can send a third kind of ack, ACK_ERR, if the ReceiveHSNumber function returned false, meaning that some error occurred (else branch). The Remote function (inside the J5_comm.nxc file), used by the master program to send commands to the slave, can thus exploit the information carried by these different acks to implement a simple error detection and correction protocol.

The last thing done before closing the loop in main is to invoke the system call SysKeepAlive. With that, you reset the firmware's sleep timer, and you can avoid the annoying issue that causes the NXT to turn off right in the middle of play, even if the program is running! I once heard about a LEGO sumo competition lost by a robot that had this kind of problem. You can solve it as shown, or manually change the sleep timer settings using the NXT on-brick menu.

This is the overall structure of the slave program. It isn't complicated. The subroutines to move the auxiliary motors are not reported here, but you can read those in the source code of JohnNXT; they are simple to understand once you've learned the theory behind them. The FSMs are explained in Chapter 3 and the practical example is in Chapter 4 (Listings 4-6 and 4-7, Tables 4-1 and 4-2).

Master Program

In Listing 8-2, I show the master JohnNXT program's outline. Even though the real code is replaced by explanatory comments, the listing is still very long. That's why I chose not to report the entire code.

Listing 8-2. *The Master Program Outline*

```nxc
#include "J5Defs.nxc"
#include "J5_comm.nxc"
#include "J5_head.nxc"
#include "J5_sounds.nxc"
#include "J5_lineflw.nxc"
#include "J5_handflw.nxc"
#include "J5_show.nxc"
#include "J5_remote.nxc"

// global state variable for JohnNXT behavior FSM
short J5_state;

void J5_Init()
{
   TextOut(0,LCD_LINE1,"Initializing...");
   SetHSPort();
   SetSensorLowspeed(EYES);
   SetSensorSound(MIC);
   Remote(L_UP,ACK_DONE);
   Remote(T_MID,ACK_DONE);
   Remote(A_FOLDED,ACK_DONE);
   head_state = UNKNOWN;
   J5_state = IDLE;
   Head(CENTER,1);
}

////////////////////////////////////////////////////////////////////////////
//                            MANIPULATION                                 //
////////////////////////////////////////////////////////////////////////////

// here is the code to control JohnNXT's arms using sound pulses

[...]
```

```
////////////////////////////////////////////////////////////////////////////
//                  SUBROUTINES FOR BEHAVIOR STATES                        //
////////////////////////////////////////////////////////////////////////////

sub J5_Armed()
{
    // lowers torso and laser
    // aiming it at whoever is present
    // when a loud noise occurs
}

sub J5_Greeting()
{
    // makes JohnNXT greet and then waits for someone
    // to click the orange button, to enter menu.
    // if nothing happens within 3 seconds
    // comes back to idle mode
}

sub Idle_treads()
{
    // called by J5_Random, moves treads
}

sub J5_Random()
{
    // performs random actions
}

sub J5_Idle()
{
    // Reads Ultrasonic Sensor and mic values:
    // if someone is near, enters GREETING mode,
    // but if there is also a loud noise,
    // enters ARMED mode.
    // Otherwise calls J5_Random,
    // then waits for a random amount of time
}

////////////////////////////////////////////////////////////////////////////
//                              MENU                                       //
////////////////////////////////////////////////////////////////////////////

[...] //menu opcodes definitions

short DisplayMenuItems(short item)
{
```

```
        //displays the specified menu item
}

short MenuEngine()
{
    //calls DisplayMenuItems to browse the menu and returns
    //the chosen item
}

sub J5_Menu()
{
    //calls MenuEngine() and
    //changes J5_state according to menu choice
}

////////////////////////////////////////////////////////////////////////
//                                MAIN                                 //
////////////////////////////////////////////////////////////////////////

task main()
{
    KeepAliveType kaArgs;
    J5_Init();
    J5_state = IDLE;
    // J5 behavior FSM
    while (true)
    {
        switch(J5_state)
        {
            case ARMED:
                J5_Armed();
                J5_state = IDLE;
                break;
            case GREETING:
                J5_Greeting();
                break;
            case HANDFOLLOW:
                J5_HandFollow();
                J5_state = MENU;
                break;
            case IDLE:
                J5_Idle();
                break;
            case LINEFOLLOW:
                J5_LineFollow();
                J5_state = MENU;
                break;
```

```
            case MANIPULATION:
                J5_Manipulation();
                J5_state = MENU;
                break;
            case MENU:
                J5_Menu();
                // next state is determined by user choice
                break;
            case SHOWOFF:
                J5_Show();
                Remote(T_MID,ACK_DONE);
                Remote(A_FOLDED,ACK_DONE);
                Remote(L_UP,ACK_DONE);
                J5_state = MENU;
                break;
            case REMOTE_CONTROL:
                if (BluetoothStatus(0)==NO_ERR)
                {
                // if the Bluetooth master NXT (remote control)
                // is connected, call J5_Remote_Control()
                    J5_Remote_Control();
                    Remote(T_MID,ACK_DONE);
                    Remote(A_FOLDED,ACK_DONE);
                    Remote(L_UP,ACK_DONE);
                }
                else
                {
                // show error message
                    ClearLine(3);
                    TextOut(0,LCD_LINE3,"Remote offline!");
                    Wait(1000);
                }
                J5_state = MENU;
                break;
        }
        // keep the NXT alive: this system call
        // resets the sleep timer, to avoid having the NXT
        // turn off automatically when the program is running.
        SysKeepAlive(kaArgs);
    }
}
```

The master program core is in the main task, where I implemented the FSM that regulates JohnNXT's behavior. The diagram of this FSM is shown in Figure 8-8. The structure of main is quite similar to the skeleton program in Listing 3-4, described in Chapter 3, in the section "FSM General Implementation." You can refer to that chapter to go over the FSM argument again, if you still have some doubts.

At a quick glance, the program looks modular: the working of every FSM state is implemented in a separate subroutine, to help the readability and maintainability of this big program. Also, notice the many NXC subfile inclusions at the top of the program.

The master program is not as complicated as you might think. It is long, but it uses many techniques and tricks that I have already presented throughout the book, with which you might feel familiar by now. Next, I'll discuss the part of the master program worthy of a detailed explanation: the FSM that allows you to control JohnNXT's arms with sounds.

Sound Counting FSM

As described in the section "JohnNXT User Guide," when you enter the Arms Control mode in JohnNXT's menu, you can control the position of its arms with sound pulses. Now, let's analyze the mechanism that makes this possible: the sound counting FSM, illustrated in the diagram in Figure 8-9.

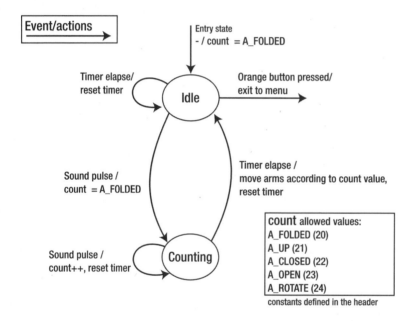

Figure 8-9. *The sound counting FSM diagram*

Its implementation code, whose outline was included in Listing 8-2, is reported in Listing 8-3.

Listing 8-3. *The Sound Counting FSM Implementation, to Control JohnNXT's Arms with Sounds*

```
/////////////////////////////////////////////////////////////////////////////
//                          MANIPULATION                                     //
/////////////////////////////////////////////////////////////////////////////

#define E_EXIT 1
#define E_TRIGGER 2
#define E_ELAPSE 3
#define E_TIMEOUT 1300
#define FSM_IDLE 0
#define FSM_COUNTING 1

int MeasureNoise ()
{
  int n;
  //estimate ambient noise by averaging 10 readings
  n = 0;
  repeat(10)
  {
    n += Sensor(MIC);
    Wait(20);
  }
  n /= 10;
  return n;
}


// this function waits for one of three events:
//  - someone clicks the orange button
//  - the timer elapses
//  - a loud sound pulse occurs
// and returns a number to describe which event
// occurred first
short WaitEvent(short noise, unsigned long timer)
{
   short event = 0;
   while ( event==0 )
   {
      if (ButtonPressed(BTNCENTER,true)==1)
      {
         event = E_EXIT;
         while(ButtonPressed(BTNCENTER,true)==1);
         TextOut(5,LCD_LINE6,"Button");
      }
      else if (CurrentTick() > timer + E_TIMEOUT)
      {
         event = E_ELAPSE;
         TextOut(5,LCD_LINE6,"Elapse");
```

```
      }
      else if (Sensor(MIC)>noise+50)
      {
         event = E_TRIGGER;
         TextOut(5,LCD_LINE6,"*");
         until(Sensor(MIC)<noise+40);
         Wait(10);
      }
   }
   ClearLine(6);
   return event;
}
// this subroutine shows the actual state of the arms FSM
sub ShowArmsState(short state, short line)
{
   ClearLine(line);
   switch(state)
   {
      case A_FOLDED: TextOut(5,(8-line)*8,"Folded"); break;
      case A_UP: TextOut(5,(8-line)*8,"Up"); break;
      case A_CLOSED: TextOut(5,(8-line)*8,"Hands closed"); break;
      case A_OPEN: TextOut(5,(8-line)*8,"Hands open"); break;
      case A_ROTATE: TextOut(5,(8-line)*8,"Wrist rotate"); break;
   }
}


// this subroutine manages the arms FSM, to command the arms with
// sound pulses
sub J5_Manipulation()
{
   unsigned long soundFSMtimer;
   short count = A_FOLDED;
   short state = FSM_IDLE;
   short event;
   bool exit;
   short noise;
   ClearScreen();
   TextOut(0,LCD_LINE1,"Arms control");
   // measure background noise
   noise = MeasureNoise();
   Remote(A_FOLDED,ACK_DONE);
   // the sound counting FSM is implemented as follows
   until(exit)
   {
      if (state == FSM_IDLE)
      {
```

```
        // wait for an event
        event = WaitEvent(noise,soundFSMtimer);
        // perform the actions for this state
        if (event == E_TRIGGER)
        {
            state = FSM_COUNTING;
            count = A_FOLDED;
        }
        else if (event == E_ELAPSE)
        {
            // reset the timer
            soundFSMtimer = CurrentTick();
        }
        else if (event == E_EXIT) exit = true;
    }
    else if (state == FSM_COUNTING)
    {
        // displays information onscreen line 3
        ShowArmsState(count,3);
        // wait for an event
        event = WaitEvent(noise,soundFSMtimer);
        // perform the actions for this state
        if (event == E_TRIGGER)
        {
            count++;
            if (count>A_ROTATE) count = A_ROTATE;
            // reset the timer
            soundFSMtimer = CurrentTick();
        }
        else if (event == E_ELAPSE)
        {
            // reset the timer
            soundFSMtimer = CurrentTick();
            Remote(count,ACK_DONE);
            state = FSM_IDLE;
        }
        else if (event == E_EXIT) exit = true;
    }
  }
}
```

The J5_Manipulation() subroutine is called by the principal JohnNXT FSM from the main task, when you choose the Arms Control item from the JohnNXT menu. This subroutine starts measuring the average ambient noise by calling the MeasureNoise() function, which reads the Sound Sensor ten times and then computes the arithmetic average.

> **Tip** Averaging many measurements over time is useful for lowering the uncertainty of the whole measurement. For example, imagine making a single measurement of the sound level, right when an unpredictable loud noise occurs. You would get a bad estimation of the real environment's background noise: in fact, you expected to get a low percentage value, but your single measurement has returned a high value, because of that sudden loud noise. In robotics, it's a bad habit to trust a single measurement. To avoid having a single measurement corrupt your estimation with its high uncertainty, it's common use to average many measurements over time. Every time you make a new measurement, it contributes to lowering the estimation's uncertainty.

To compute the average value, you simply sum these ten readings in the variable n (initially set to zero) and then divide it by ten. This noise measurement is then used as a threshold to detect loud sounds, such as hand claps or whistles.

As previously said, the FSM in Figure 8-9 is implemented in the J5_Manipulation() subroutine. The code's meaning is straightforward. In both the two states, the WaitEvent function detects the events. This function waits for one of three kinds of events, by returning the corresponding opcode to the FSM: the orange NXT button click that causes the whole routine to exit, the timer elapsing, or a loud sound's detection.

In the beginning, the FSM is in IDLE mode, and there it remains until a loud sound is detected. The count variable is initialized with the A_FOLDED value. The first sound detected is an event that causes the state to switch from IDLE to COUNTING, and the count variable to assume the value A_FOLDED, which is the first value among the constants that describe the arms' state.

While in the COUNTING state, a new sound detection is an event that causes the count variable to be incremented by one (limited by the maximum value of A_ROTATE) and the timer to be reset. If you stop clapping, the timer elapses, and the arms are actuated according to the count variable's value. The master actuates the arms by calling the Remote(count, ACK_DONE) function, which sends the count variable value as a command to the slave NXT. The count variable can assume one of the values of the possible commands for the arms: remember that the constants in capital letters are indeed aliases for numerical values, declared in JohnNXT's header file J5Defs.nxc. So, by passing count to the Remote function, you're just telling the FSM implemented in the slave NXT program to bring the arms into one of their possible states. After the arms' actuation, the state comes back to IDLE and the timer is reset. If the timer elapses while the FSM is in IDLE mode, it does not cause any action.

If you were paying attention, you would notice that the code that implements the timer is the same as I described in Chapter 6, using the soundFSMtimer variable and the CurrentTick() NXC API function. Now you know the internals of the sound counting FSM.

JohnNXT Programming Guide

The programs provided are just a start! You can write your own custom programs for JohnNXT, to make him do whatever you want. You could develop an articulated master program to give JohnNXT a real autonomous behavior, or you could use this elegant hardware platform to attempt some new software experimentation. To help you in this task, I have provided here a short programming guide, to let you exploit all the ready-to-use functions to make JohnNXT's parts move, so you won't have to worry about the low-level mechanical hassles. Whatever you write, keep in mind that you don't need to modify the slave program.

Your work can be focused on the master program by following some directions. First of all, you must have the files shown in Table 8-1 in the same folder; you must include them in the master program's code using the #include directive. You can compile and run some sub-files as stand-alone, because they contain a main task that is compiled only when the file is not included in the JohnNXT master program.

Table 8-1. *The Subfiles That Must Always Be Included in the Master NXT Program*

File	Functions Provided	Can Run As Stand-Alone
J5Defs.nxc	Contains all the definitions and macros for JohnNXT	No
HSlib.nxc	This is the High Speed Communication Library to use high-speed wired communication	No
J5_head.nxc	Contains the FSM to manage head movements	Yes
J5_comm.nxc	Contains the Remote function to send commands to the slave NXT	No
J5_handflw.nxc	Contains the hand-following algorithm	Yes
J5_lineflw.nxc	Contains the line-following algorithm	Yes
J5_remote.nxc	Receives commands from the remote control	Yes
J5_show.nxc	Performs the show, featuring all the actions available	Yes
J5_sounds.nxc	Plays the sound files containing J5 phrases	No

You can use Table 8-2 as a quick guide for the master NXT Input/Output devices' aliases defined in the JohnNXT header file (J5Defs.nxc). Table 8-4 contains the definitions for the slave NXT. If you have any doubts about constants or ports, please check the JohnNXT definitions header file.

Table 8-2. *Master NXT Constant Definitions for Motors and Sensors*

Device	Port	Alias
Right tread motor	OUT_A	R_TREAD
Left tread motor	OUT_C	L_TREAD
Both treads	OUT_AC	TREADS
Head motor	OUT_B	HEAD
Sound Sensor	IN_1	MIC
Line-tracking sensor	IN_2	LIGHT
Ultrasonic Sensor	IN_3	EYES
High-speed serial port	IN_4	COMM

While reading the following paragraphs, I recommend you have a look at the source code of the various subfiles. The code to control the treads is the master program; to know where to find the code that controls a particular feature, check Table 8-1.

Moving the Treads

The tread motors are connected to the master NXT and are the simplest to use. You can control them by using the common OnRev and OnRevSync statements to let JohnNXT go forward and turn, or the OnFwd and OnFwdSync statements to go in reverse. The inversion of directions is due to the particular motor's position and gearing. To stop the treads, just use Off or Float, to brake or to stop them gently, respectively.

Moving the Head

The head motor is connected to the master NXT. To move the head, I advise you against directly turning the motor on and off, but to use instead the FSM-regulated function that I wrote. In fact, if you moved the head with the basic OnFwd/OnRev functions, you would lose control of the head's position, and you wouldn't know if the neck had reached its turning limits. You can use the Head function after having included the file J5_head.nxc.

To move the head, use the following code, where direction can be CENTER, RIGHT, or LEFT, and the scale_factor can be a small integer number (normally 1):

```
Head ( direction, scale_factor)
```

The scale_factor is a number used as a divisor to turn the head less than the normal angle. For example, a scale_factor equal to 1 makes the head rotate by the total range, while a scale_factor equal to 2 makes the head rotate at an angle that is half the total excursion. Unless you need small movements, always keep this number equal to 1.

To reset the head to the center at the beginning of a program, write the following code:

```
head_state = UNKNOWN;
Head(CENTER,1);
```

The head_state variable is the one that is used to keep track of the position of the head. So, you must not assign it a value directly in your programs, as you would mess up the way the head FSM works. As the only exception to this rule, you need to change the head_state value explicitly when you want to center the head using the torque sensing limit switch. In fact, if the state is UNKNOWN when the Head(CENTER,1) is called, this function uses the procedure to center the head based on motor torque sensing. It turns the head to the right, until the motor feels blocked, and then rotates the head back to the center. After this initial reset, the Head subroutine itself changes the head_state variable, so you don't have to change it manually anymore. To turn the head left or right, simply use Head(LEFT,1) or Head(RIGHT,1), respectively. By calling Head(CENTER,1) again, the head is brought to the center without using the reset routine, because the head_state variable is assigned a value different from UNKNOWN. The head is rotated by a precise number of degrees, according to the head_angles decision table.

Playing Sounds

You must download sound files for JohnNXT into the master NXT by using BricxCC (see Appendix A). To play sounds, use

```
Sound (sound, wait_completion)
```

where sound is one of the constants in Table 8-3 and where the wait_completion can be true (the program waits until the sound has been completely executed) or false (the program starts the sound and continues at once).

Table 8-3. *Opcodes to Play JohnNXT Sounds*

Action	Constant
Play "Number Five is alive!"	S_ALIVE1
Play "I am alive."	S_ALIVE2
Play "Yeah! Johnny 5! That's cool!"	S_COOL
Play "Hello, bozos!"	S_HELLO
Play "Need input!"	S_INPUT
Play "Malfunction!"	S_MALFUNCTION
Play soundtrack loop	S_LOOP
Stop sounds	S_NONE
Play one of the preceding sounds randomly	S_RANDOM

Moving the Slave NXT Motors

The torso, arms, and laser motors are connected to the slave NXT on the ports specified in Table 8-4.

Table 8-4. *Slave NXT Constant Definitions for Motors and Sensors*

Device	Port	Alias
Torso motor	OUT_A	TORSO
Arms' motor	OUT_B	ARMS
Laser treads	OUT_C	LASER
Laser-tip Light Sensor	IN_1	LASER_TIP

You can control those motors by calling the following function (implemented inside J5_comm.nxc) within JohnNXT's master program:

```
Remote (opcode, ack)
```

opcode is one of the constants in Table 8-5, and ack can be either ACK_RX or ACK_DONE. With ACK_RX, the master program just waits for the slave to receive the command, while with ACK_DONE, the master program hangs on until the slave has finished the action it was told to do. The constants listed in Table 8-5 are used in the slave program both as commands to be executed and as state descriptions.

Table 8-5. *Constant Definitions to Move Torso, Arms, and Laser*

Output Device	Action	Constant
Torso motor	Lower torso to downmost position using torque sensing	T_DOWN
Torso motor	Bring torso to middle position	T_MID
Torso motor	Bring torso to up position	T_UP
Torso motor	Bring torso to upmost position	T_UPMOST
Torso motor	Move torso a step up	T_STEPUP
Torso motor	Move torso a step down	T_STEPDOWN
Arms motor	Fold the arms	A_FOLDED
Arms motor	Move forearms up	A_UP
Arms motor	Close hands	A_CLOSED
Arms motor	Open hands	A_OPEN
Arms motor	Rotate wrists	A_ROTATE
Arms motor	Step towards open hands state	A_STEP_OPEN
Arms motor	Step towards folded arms state	A_STEP_CLOSE
Laser motor	Raise laser	L_UP
Laser motor	Lower laser	L_DOWN
Laser light	Turn laser tip on	L_ON
Laser light	Turn laser tip off	L_OFF
Laser light	Blink laser tip	L_BLINK

This concludes the programming guide, a sort of handy Software Development Kit (SDK) intended for those who want to write custom programs for JohnNXT. Now that you know what's running inside JohnNXT's brain, it's time to put him together.

Building JohnNXT

Constructing JohnNXT takes quite a long time and more than a thousand LEGO elements. As stated at the beginning of this chapter, you need more than two NXT sets' parts, because many of them are not included in the standard set—just to name a few, the neck pistons, the tread links, and the arms' chain links. The complete bill of materials is shown in Figure 8-10, and the textual list in Table 8-6.

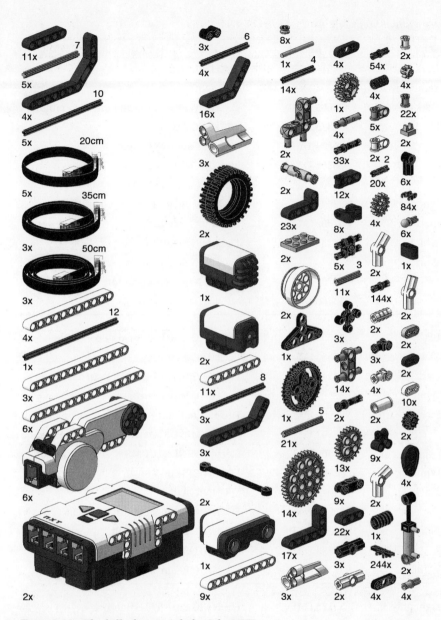

Figure 8-10. *The bill of materials for JohnNXT*

Table 8-6. *JohnNXT Bill of Materials*

Quantity	Color	Part Number	Part Name
11	Dark gray	32316.DAT	TECHNIC Beam 5
5	Light gray	44294.DAT	TECHNIC Axle 7
4	Dark gray	32009.DAT	TECHNIC Beam Liftarm Bent 45 Double
5	Black	3737.DAT	TECHNIC Axle 10
5		55804.DAT	Electric Cable NXT 20cm
3		55805.DAT	Electric Cable NXT 35cm
3		55806.DAT	Electric Cable NXT 50cm
11	White	32525.DAT	TECHNIC Beam 11
1	Black	3708.DAT	TECHNIC Axle 12
3	White	41239.DAT	TECHNIC Beam 13
6	White	32278.DAT	TECHNIC Beam 15
6		53787.DAT	MINDSTORMS NXT Motor
2		53788.DAT	MINDSTORMS NXT
3	Black	45590.DAT	TECHNIC Axle Joiner Double Flexible
4	Black	3706.DAT	TECHNIC Axle 6
16	Dark gray	32348.DAT	TECHNIC Beam 7 Liftarm Bent 53.5 (4:4)
3	White	32527.DAT	TECHNIC Panel Fairing #5
2	Black	2696.DAT	Tire Model Team
1		55963.DAT	Electric MINDSTORMS NXT Sound Sensor
2		55969.DAT	Electric MINDSTORMS NXT Light Sensor
11	White	32524.DAT	TECHNIC Beam 7
3	Black	3707.DAT	TECHNIC Axle 8
1	Dark gray	32271.DAT	TECHNIC Beam 9 Liftarm Bent 53.5 (7:3)
2	Black	32293.DAT	TECHNIC Steering Link 9L
1		53792.DAT	MINDSTORMS NXT Ultrasonic Sensor
9	White	40490.DAT	TECHNIC Beam 9
8	Light gray	32123.DAT	TECHNIC Bush 1/2 Smooth
1	Light gray	30374.DAT	Bar 4L Light Saber Blade
14	Black	3705.DAT	TECHNIC Axle 4
2	Light gray	55615.DAT	TECHNIC Beam 5 Bent 90 with 4 Pins
2	Light gray	9244.DAT	TECHNIC Universal Joint
23	Dark gray	32140.DAT	TECHNIC Beam 5 Liftarm Bent 90 (4:2)
2	Light gray	3021.DAT	Plate 2×3
2	White	2695.DAT	Wheel Model Team
1	Black	2905.DAT	TECHNIC Liftarm Triangle

Quantity	Color	Part Number	Part Name
1	Black	X344.DAT	TECHNIC Gear 36 Tooth Double Bevel
21	Light gray	32073.DAT	TECHNIC Axle 5
14	Light gray	3649.DAT	TECHNIC Gear 40 Tooth
17	Dark gray	32526.DAT	TECHNIC Beam 7 Bent 90 (5:3)
3	White	32528.DAT	TECHNIC Panel Fairing #6
4	Dark gray	6632.DAT	TECHNIC Beam 3 × 0.5 Liftarm
1	Light gray	32269.DAT	TECHNIC Gear 20 Tooth Double Bevel
4	Light gray	32556.DAT	TECHNIC Pin Long
33	Black	6558.DAT	TECHNIC Pin Long with Friction and Slot
12	Dark gray	42003.DAT	TECHNIC Axle Joiner Perp. with 2 Holes
8	Dark gray	41678.DAT	TECHNIC Axle Joiner Perp. Double Split
5	Black	32136.DAT	TECHNIC Pin 3L Double
11	Light gray	4519.DAT	TECHNIC Axle 3
3	Black	32072.DAT	TECHNIC Knob Wheel
14	Light gray	48989.DAT	TECHNIC Axle Joiner Perp. with 4 Pins
2	Black	32054.DAT	TECHNIC Pin Long with Stop Bush
13	Light gray	3648.DAT	TECHNIC Gear 24 Tooth
9	Black	32184.DAT	TECHNIC Axle Joiner Perpendicular 3L
22	Dark gray	32523.DAT	TECHNIC Beam 3
3	Black	32034.DAT	TECHNIC Angle Connector #2
2	Black	32034.DAT	TECHNIC Angle Connector #2
1	White	6536.DAT	TECHNIC Axle Joiner Perpendicular
54	Blue	43093.DAT	TECHNIC Axle Pin with Friction
4	Light gray		TECHNIC Hose 2L
5	Light gray	6536.DAT	TECHNIC Axle Joiner Perpendicular
2	White	6536.DAT	TECHNIC Axle Joiner Perpendicular
20	Black	32062.DAT	TECHNIC Axle 2 Notched
4	Light gray	4019.DAT	TECHNIC Gear 16 Tooth
2	White	32192.DAT	TECHNIC Angle Connector #4 (135 degree)
144	Black	2780.DAT	TECHNIC Pin with Friction and Slots
2	White	6538B.DAT	TECHNIC Axle Joiner Offset
3	Black	32039.DAT	TECHNIC Connector with Axlehole
4	White	32039.DAT	TECHNIC Connector with Axlehole
2	White	75535.DAT	TECHNIC Pin Joiner Round
9	Dark gray	32291.DAT	TECHNIC Axle Joiner Perp. Double

Continued

Table 8-6. *Continued*

Quantity	Color	Part Number	Part Name
2	White	32015.DAT	TECHNIC Angle Conn. #5 (112.5 degree)
1	Black	4716.DAT	TECHNIC Worm Screw
244	Black	3873.DAT	TECHNIC Chain Tread
4	Dark gray	6632.DAT	TECHNIC Beam 3 × 0.5 Liftarm
2	White	3713.DAT	TECHNIC Bush
4	Light gray	3647.DAT	TECHNIC Gear 8 Tooth
22	Light gray	3713.DAT	TECHNIC Bush
2	Light gray	2555.DAT	Tile 1 × 1 with Clip
6	Black	32013.DAT	TECHNIC Angle Connector #1
84	Black	3711.DAT	TECHNIC Chain Link
6	Light gray	2736.DAT	TECHNIC Axle Towball
1	Dark gray	43857.DAT	TECHNIC Beam 2
2	White	32016.DAT	TECHNIC Angle Conn. #3 (157.5 degree)
2	Light gray	41677.DAT	TECHNIC Beam 2 × 0.5 Liftarm
2	Dark gray	41677.DAT	TECHNIC Beam 2 × 0.5 Liftarm
10	White	41677.DAT	TECHNIC Beam 2 × 0.5 Liftarm
2	Black	32270.DAT	TECHNIC Gear 12 Tooth Double Bevel
4	Dark gray	6575.DAT	TECHNIC Cam
2		x253.DAT	TECHNIC Pneumatic Cylinder Small
4	Tan	3749.DAT	TECHNIC Axle Pin

1,042 parts total (more than two NXT retail set parts are needed)

You can obtain LEGO spare parts from LEGO Education (http://www.legoeducation.com/global.aspx), BrickLink (http://www.bricklink.com/), and LEGO Factory Pick a Brick (http://us.factory.lego.com/), even though the TECHNIC section is not well furnished at the moment. Also, a good place to find LEGO spares remains eBay (http://www.ebay.com). For those who live in Italy, a good resource is CampuStore (http://www.campustore.it/lego).

This time, the building phase is more challenging than for the other robots in this book, but once finished, it will give you great satisfaction. Every JohnNXT subassembly will reveal many interesting mechanical aspects for you, and each one will teach you something.

- The torso motor subassembly shows you how to get a liftarm to rotate with a huge torque, to raise heavy loads, such as JohnNXT's body. Here symmetry is important, because loading an axle (or a gear) on just one side would twist it and you could run the risk of breaking it. In this assembly, notice that the geartrain is repeated on both sides of the motor. Also, to avoid ungearings, all the axle-bearing gears that are subject to high torque are kept together by beams.

- The torso subassembly shows you how to use a servomotor as an integral part of a robot. Here, the motor shaft not only drives the arms' mechanism, but also is the pivot for the whole shoulders' frame. The lever system to raise the whole body shows you how to transmit a translational movement beyond a narrow bent structure (the lower body's top joint with the torso).

- The treads' frames teach you how to build extremely strong structures. Triangular frames are in fact crushproof, contrary to the rectangular ones.

- The arms feature the double-drive mechanism explained in the section "Johnnicle: My LEGO Johnny 5 Chronicle" to fold the forearm and grab objects. The poseable shoulder shows how you can use a LEGO universal joint to transmit motion through a bendable joint, on the condition that the hinge is aligned with the universal (cardan) core.

- The parallelogram frame of the upper body shows how to keep complex moving structures always vertical with respect to the ground.

- The laser levers system shows you how to obtain a combined rotational and translational movement.

You must insert two LEGO yellow rubber bands in the elbows as shown in Figure 8-11 (steps *a* through *f*). There, you can see the left elbow montage; repeat the same procedure for the right elbow before attaching the arms to the shoulders. Make sure to align the forearms' levers before adding the chain to the gears. If their position is not correct, the final result will be asymmetrical once they are attached to the shoulders' driving axle.

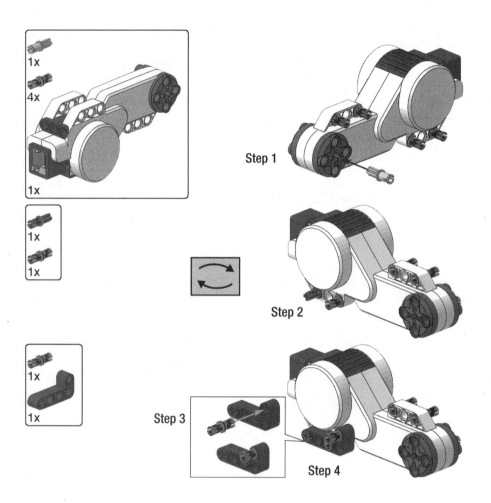

Start building the treads' motors subassembly. In Step 1, insert a tan axle pin in the motor shaft.

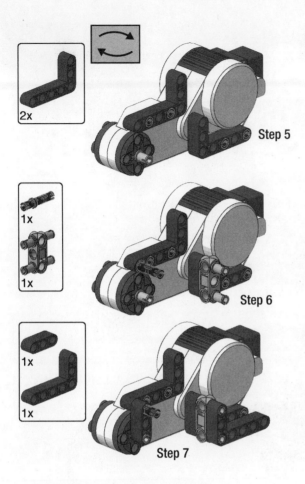

Step 5

Step 6

Step 7

Build the spacer between the motors.

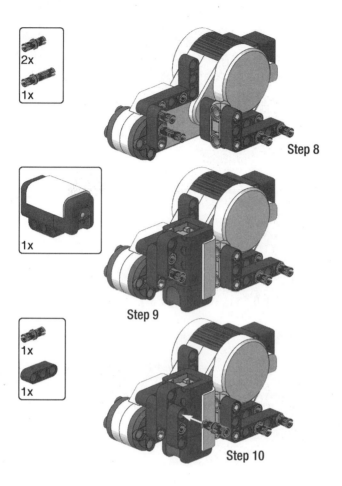

Step 8

Step 9

Step 10

Add the Light Sensor pointing downwards; it's used to follow lines on the ground.

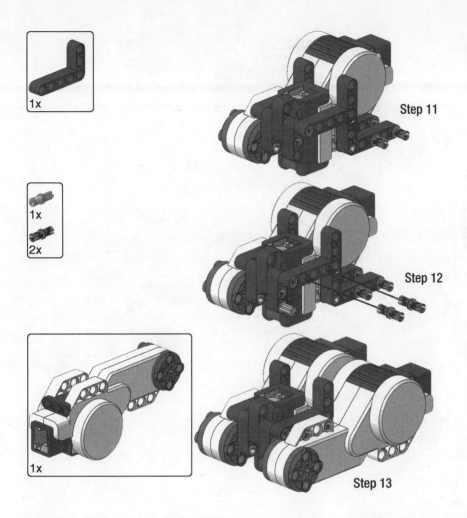

Step 11

Step 12

Step 13

Finish the sensor holder and add the left tread motor. In Step 12, add two black pins and a tan axle pin.

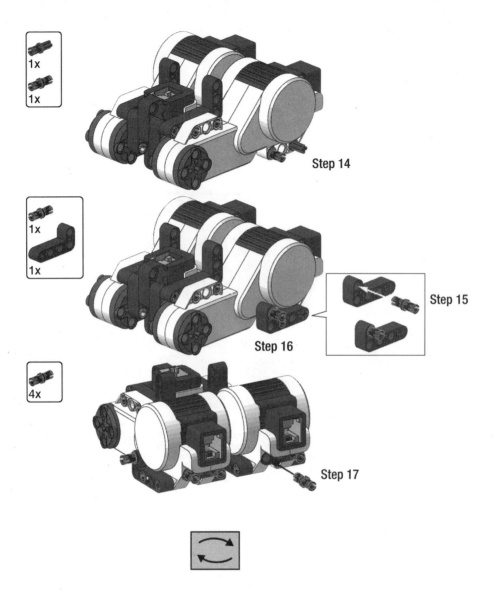

Step 14

Step 15

Step 16

Step 17

In Step 17, add four black pins in the back of the motors.

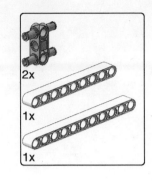

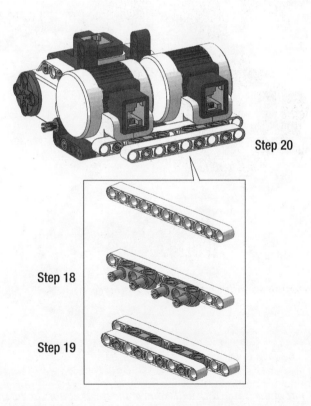

Step 20

Step 18

Step 19

Add an 11-hole beam and a 9-hole beam, attaching them with the gray Axle Joiners Perpendicular with 4 Pins.

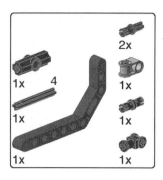

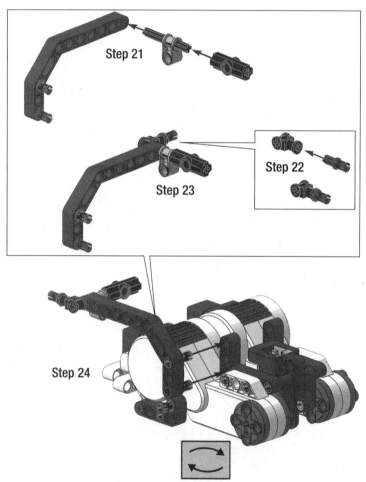

Add the right part of the frame that will connect the tread motors to the slave NXT.

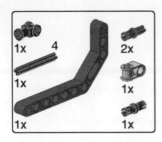

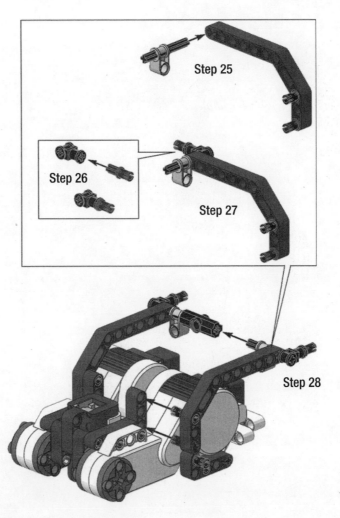

Complete the frame with its left part.

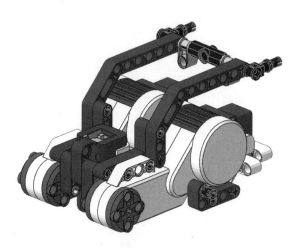

The treads' motors' subassembly is complete.

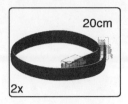

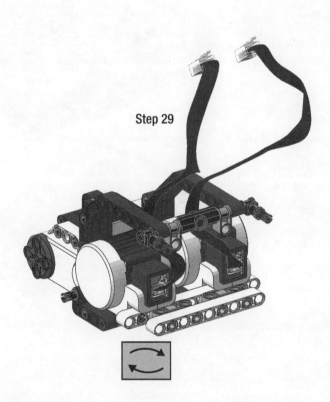

Step 29

Add two 20cm (8 inch) cables.

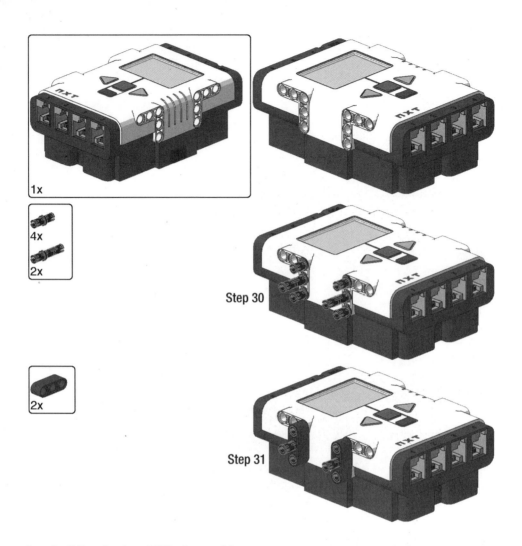

Step 30

Step 31

Start building the slave NXT subassembly.

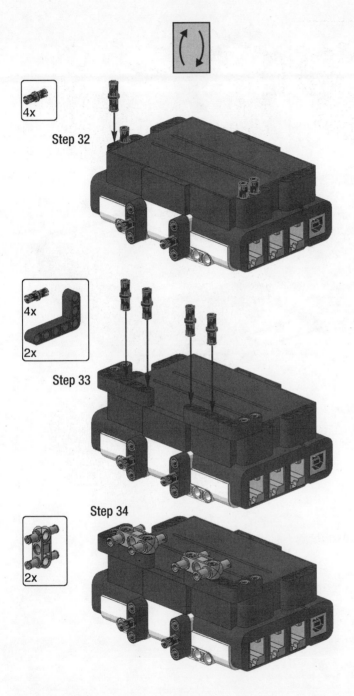

Step 32

Step 33

Step 34

Turn the NXT upside down and add the parts that will be connected to the rest of the base.

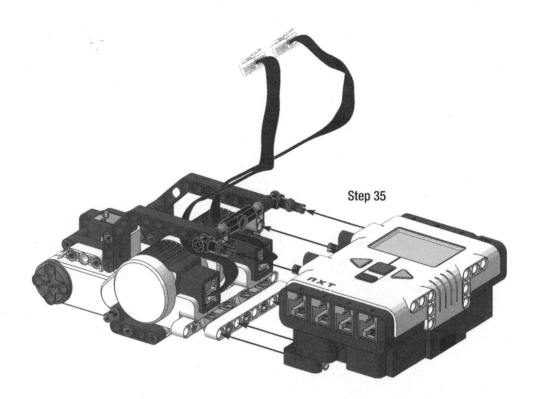

Step 35

Attach the NXT to the treads' motors' assembly.

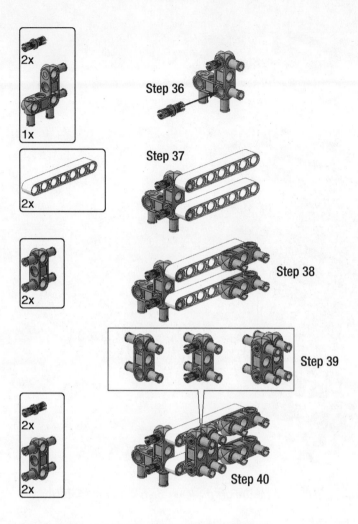

Step 36

Step 37

Step 38

Step 39

Step 40

Start building the passive wheel holder assembly.

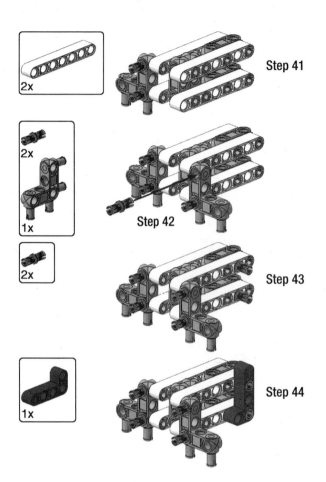

In Step 44, add the first beam that will be used to support the lower body's lifter mechanism.

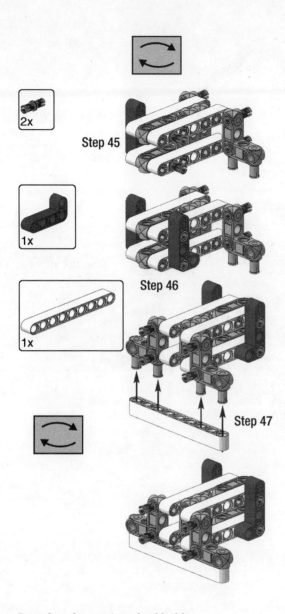

Step 45

Step 46

Step 47

Complete the passive wheel holder.

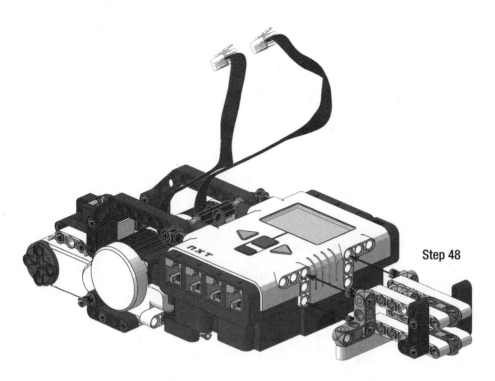

Step 48

Attach the passive wheel holder to the rest of the base.

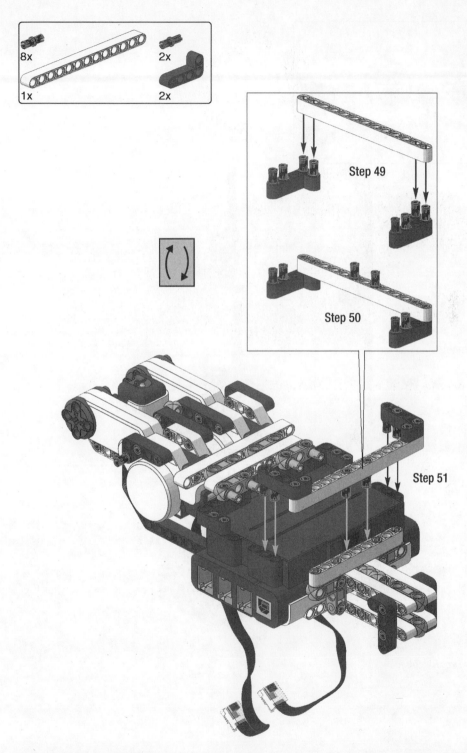

Step 49

Step 50

Step 51

Turn the model upside down and build the frame to hold the passive wheel holder firmly with the NXT. Use a 13-long beam.

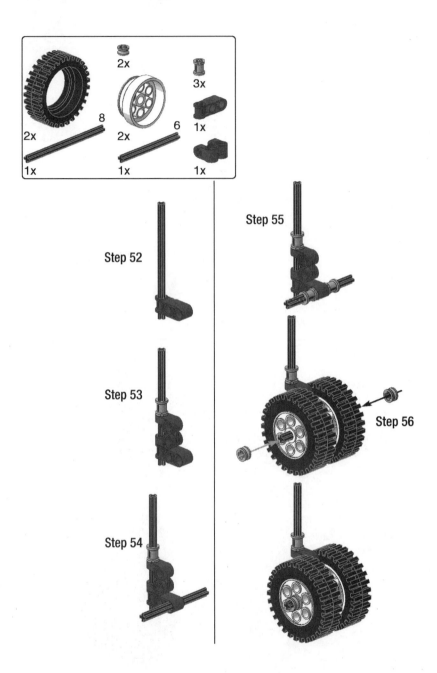

Step 52

Step 53

Step 54

Step 55

Step 56

Build the passive wheel.

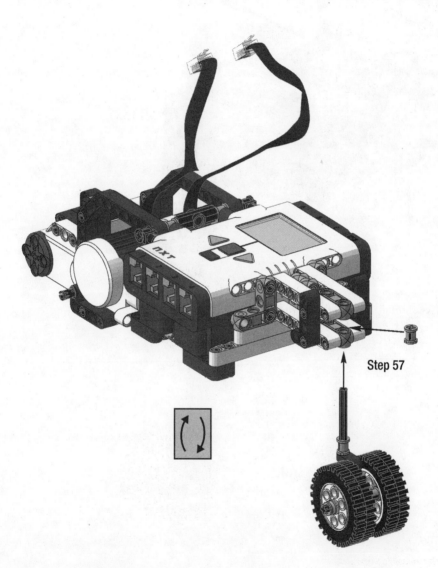

Step 57

Insert the passive wheel in place, holding it in place with a bush.

The base assembly of JohnNXT is complete.

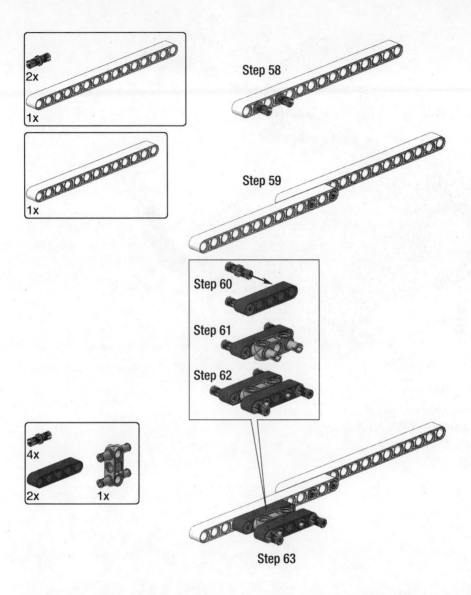

Step 58

Step 59

Step 60

Step 61

Step 62

Step 63

Start building the right part of the lower body. Attach the 15-long beam to the 13-long beam as shown.

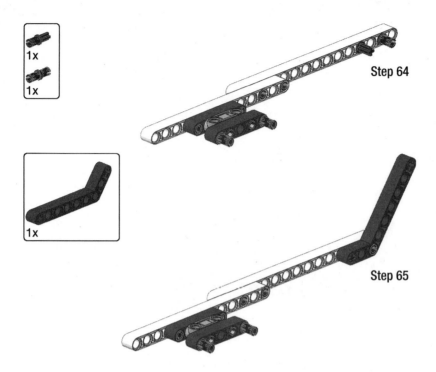

Complete the right part of the lower body.

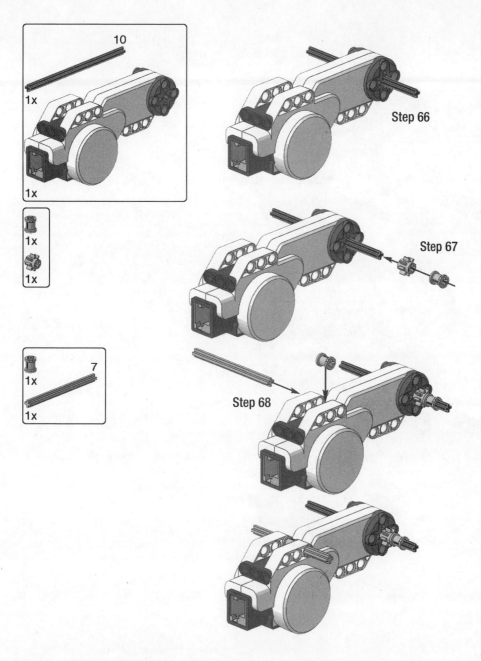

Start building the torso's lifter mechanism.

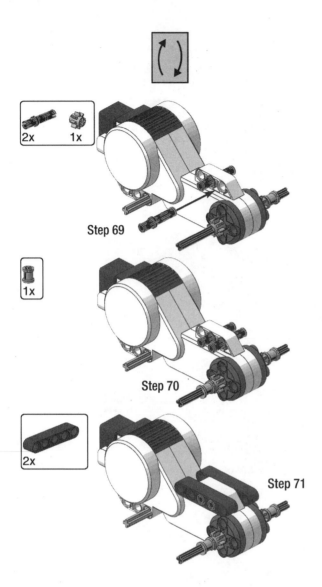

Step 69

Step 70

Step 71

Turn the motor as shown.

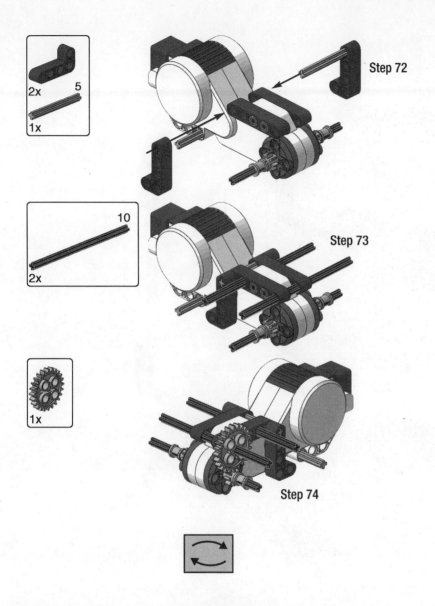

Step 72

Step 73

Step 74

Continue building the torso's lifter mechanism.

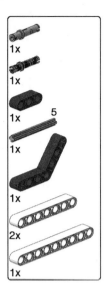

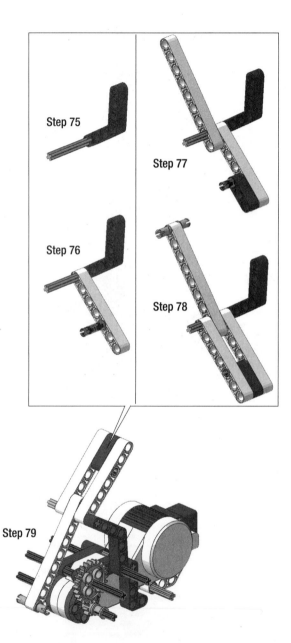

Build the levers' structure that will lift the whole JohnNXT body. Use two 7-long beams and a 9-long beam.

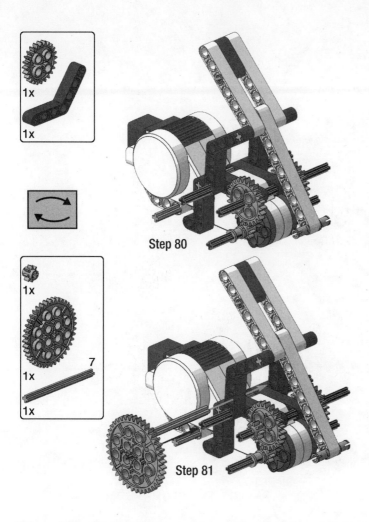

Step 80

Step 81

When adding the 40-tooth gear, make sure that the 7-long axle is correctly inserted in one of the gear's axleholes.

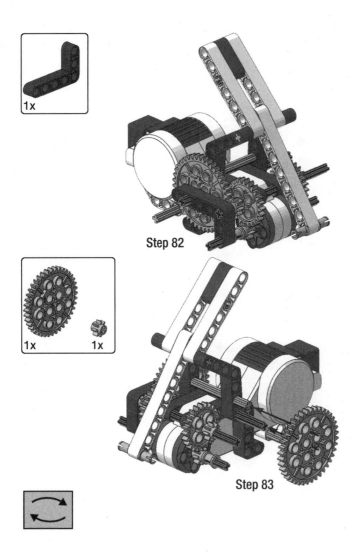

Step 82

Step 83

Add the bent beam that cross-braces the geartrain axles, to avoid gear scratching. Add the symmetric 40-tooth gear and 8-tooth gear to complete the geartrain.

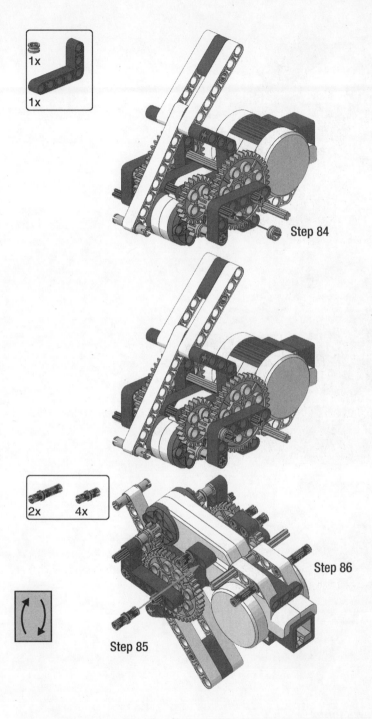

Step 84

Step 86

Step 85

Add the other cross-bracing beam. Then turn the model and add the pins where shown.

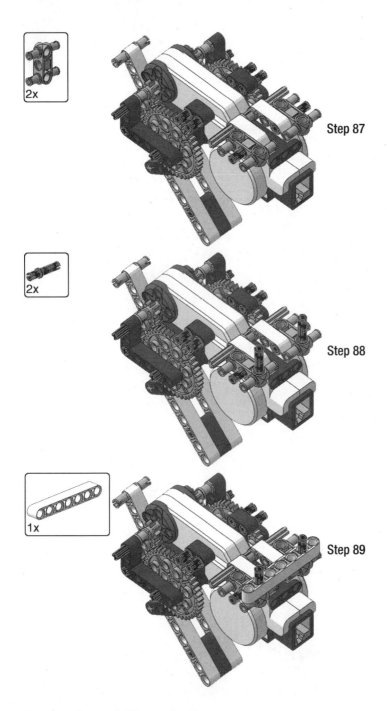

Step 87

Step 88

Step 89

Complete the torso's lifter mechanism.

Step 90

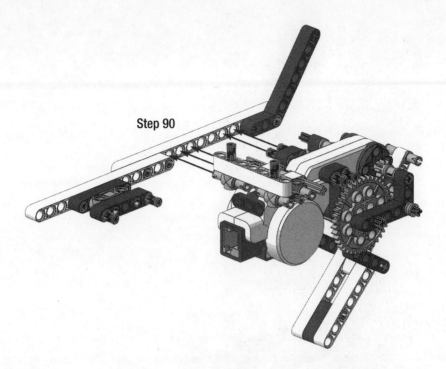

Attach the subassembly you just finished to the right part of the lower body.

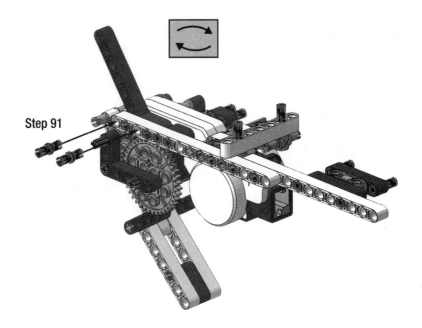

Step 91

Turn the model and add two black pins.

Step 92

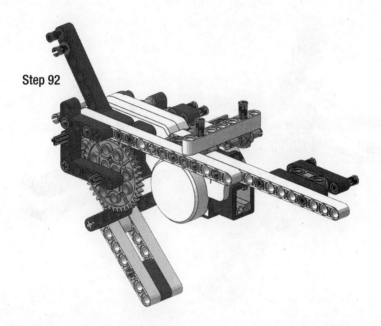

Add a blue axle pin in the top hole of the bent beam, just over the black pin. Add the liftarm that will be used to hold the cable of the arms' motor.

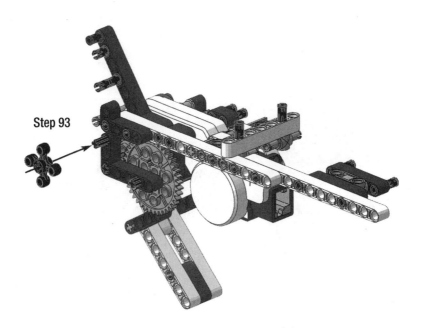

Step 93

The knob wheel is used to move the torso manually.

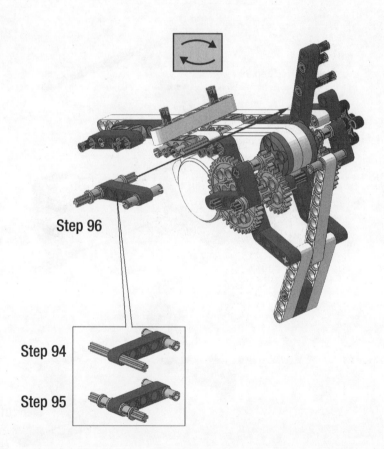

Step 96

Step 94

Step 95

Turn the model and add the auxiliary lever. Use a long gray pin.

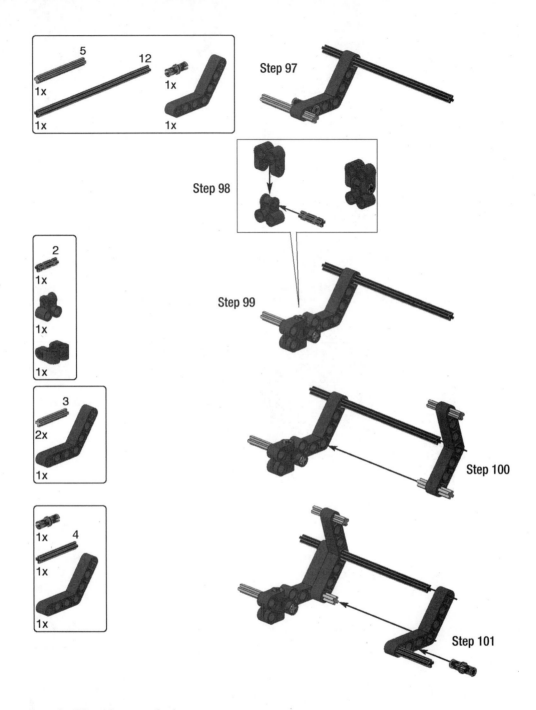

Start building the upper body.

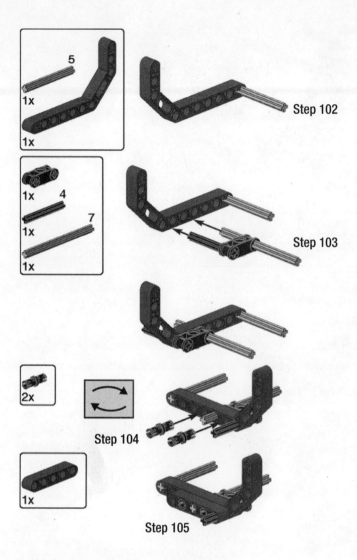

Step 102

Step 103

Step 104

Step 105

Build the right part of the upper body.

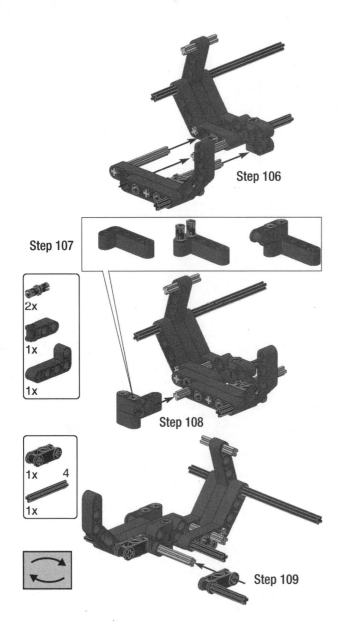

Step 106

Step 107

Step 108

Step 109

Attach the two submodels together.

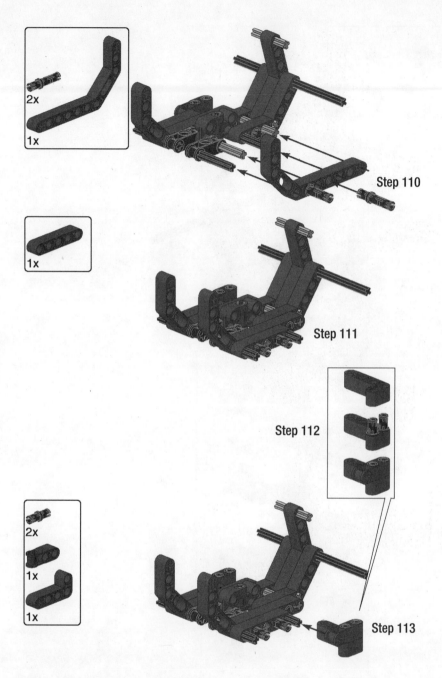

Step 110

Step 111

Step 112

Step 113

Build the left part of the upper body.

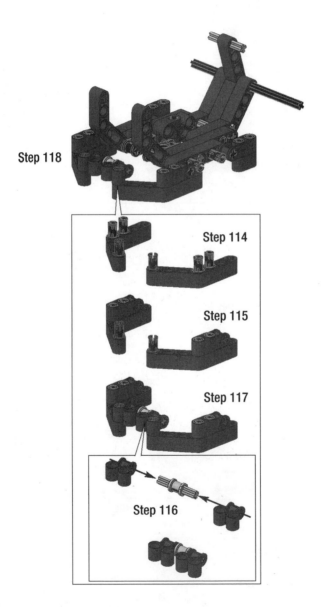

Complete the upper body's lid shape.

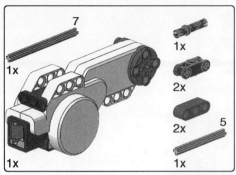

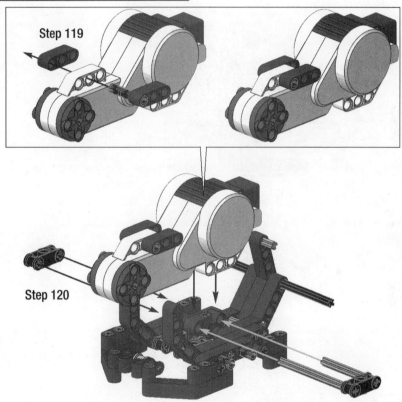

Add the arms' motor.

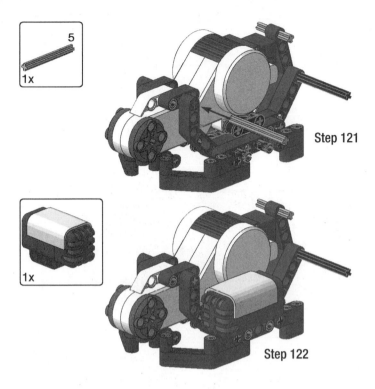

Step 121

Step 122

Hold the motor in place with the 5-long axle and add the Sound Sensor.

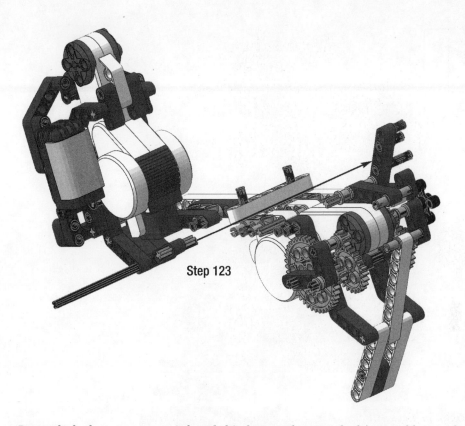

Step 123

Rotate the body so you can see it from behind. Insert the upper body's assembly onto the rest of the body.

2x

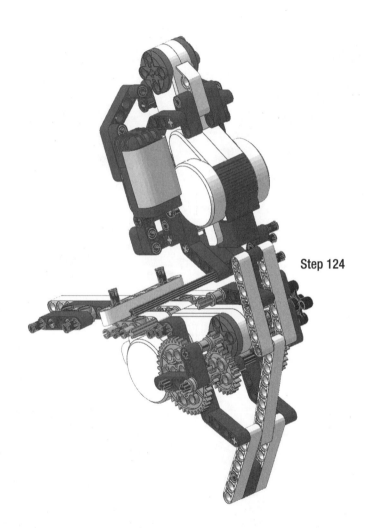

Step 124

Add two 7-long beams.

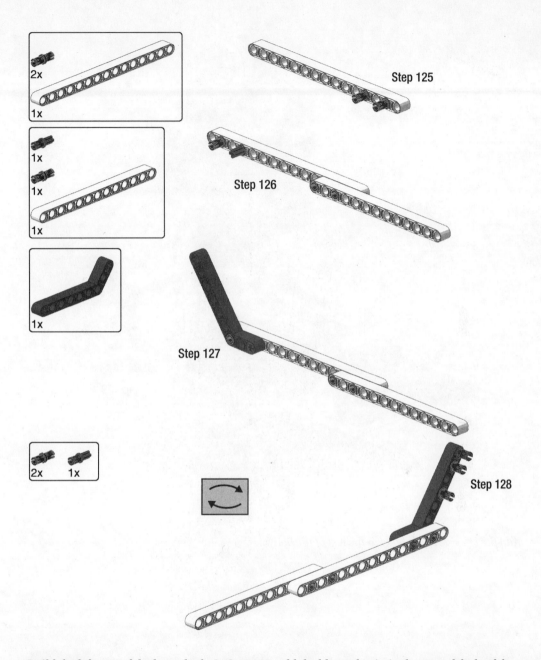

Build the left part of the lower body. In Step 128, add the blue axle pin in the top axlehole of the bent beam.

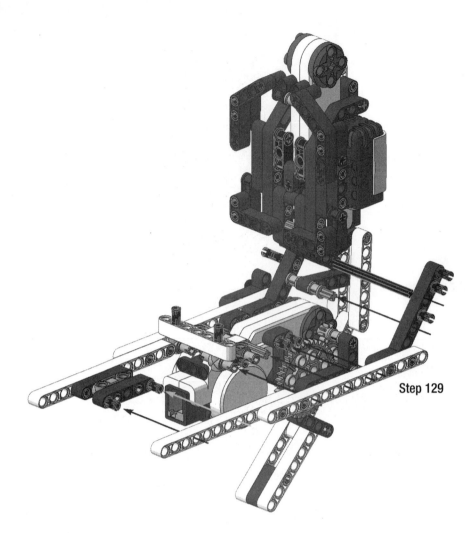

Step 129

Add the left side of the body to the rest of the body.

The body is complete.

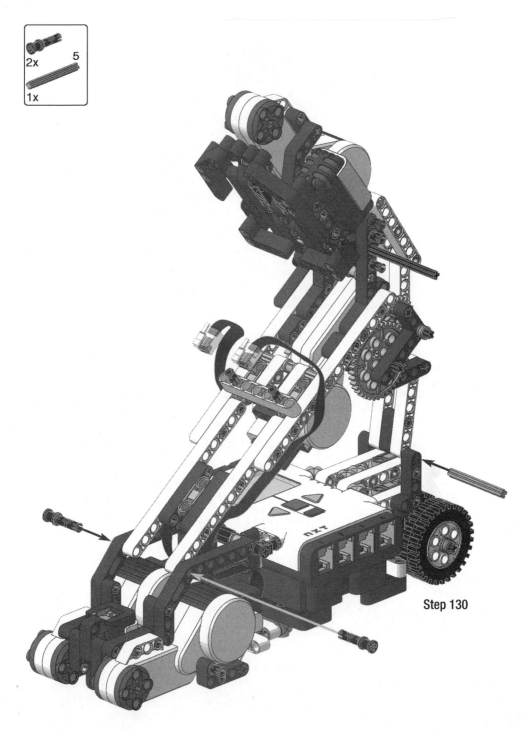

Step 130

Attach the body to the base and block it with two long pins with a stop bush and a 5-long axle in the back.

Try turning the knob wheel on the lifter's motor shaft to test whether the body's lifter mechanism is working.

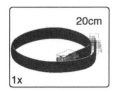

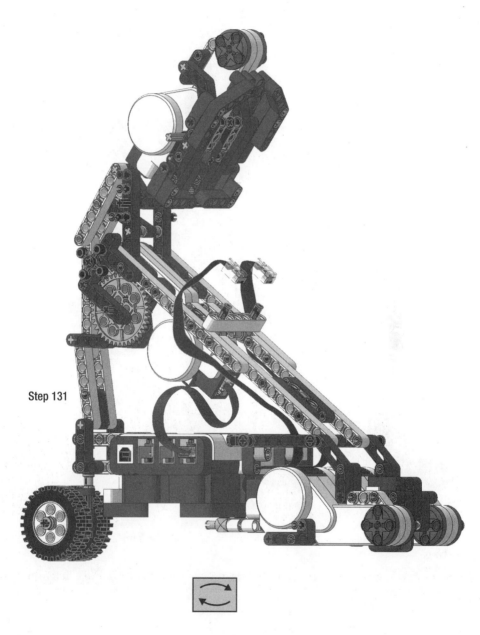

Step 131

Turn the model and attach the torso's lifter motor to slave NXT port A using a 20cm (8 inch) cable.

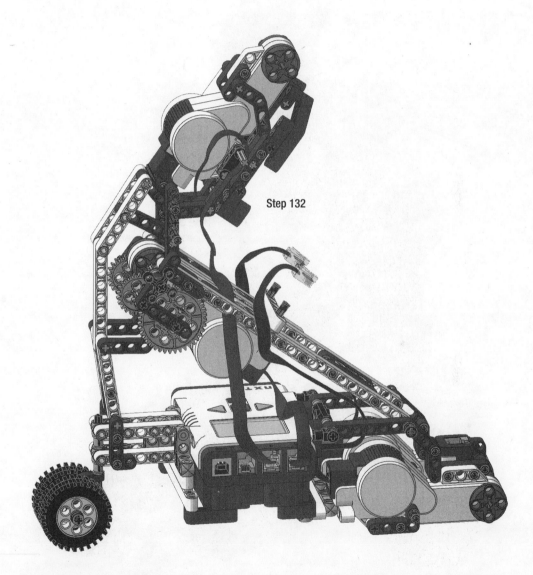

Step 132

Attach the arms' motor to slave NXT port B using a 35cm (14 inch) cable. Make sure to pass the cable where shown.

1x

Step 133

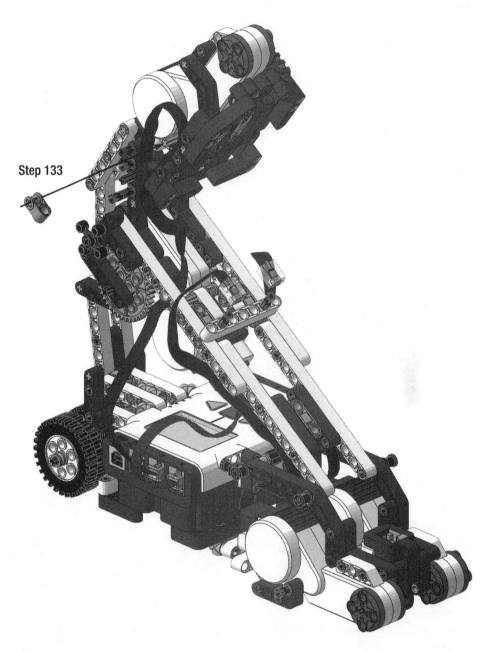

Add the axle joiner to hold the cable in place.

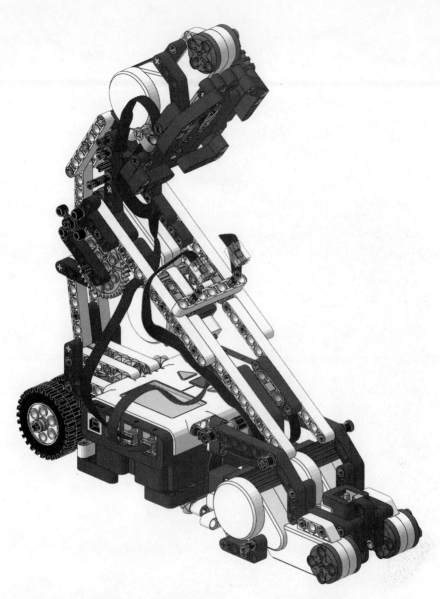

Check if all the cables are placed correctly.

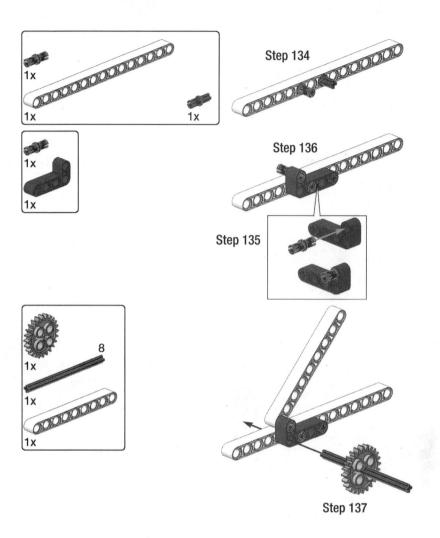

Step 134

Step 136

Step 135

Step 137

Start building the right tread's assembly. Use a 15-long beam and a 9-long beam.

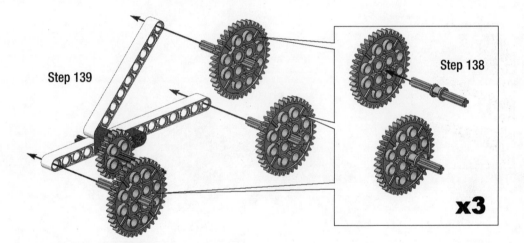

Step 139

Step 138

x3

Insert the three 40-tooth gears, used as hubs.

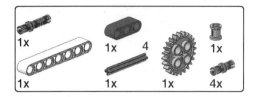

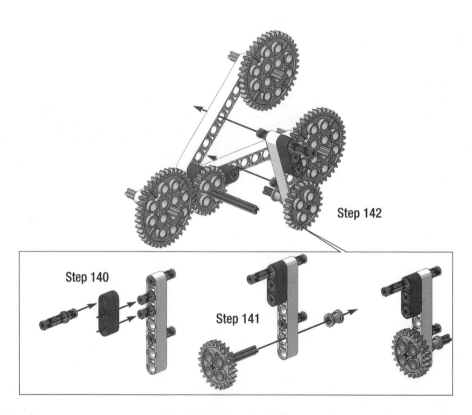

Build the assembly that helps to form the strong triangular shape of the tread.

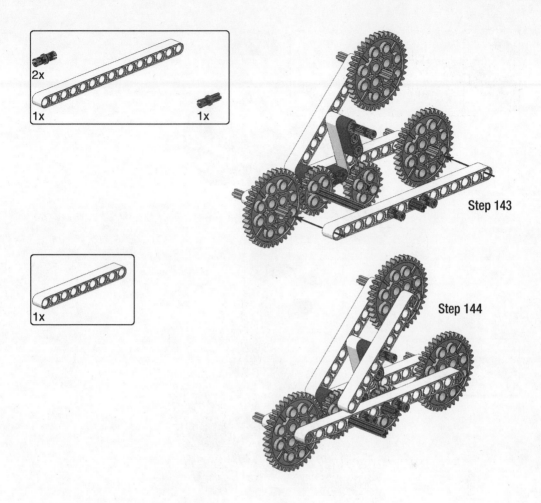

Step 143

Step 144

Add a 15-long beam and a 9-long beam.

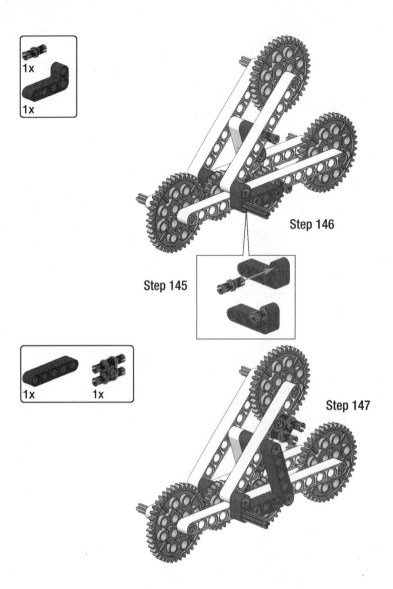

Step 146

Step 145

Step 147

Complete the triangular frame.

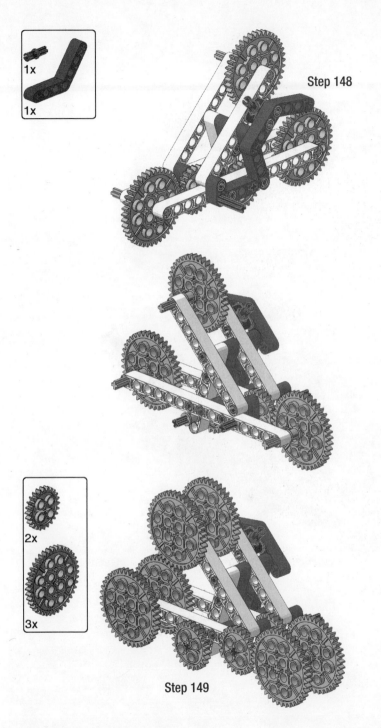

Step 148

Step 149

Add a blue axle pin in the black joiner. Turn the model and add three 40-tooth gears and two 24-tooth gears.

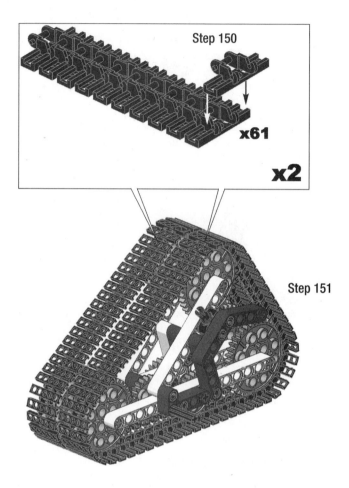

Build 2 treads of 61 links each. Close them around the large gears. The right tread assembly is complete.

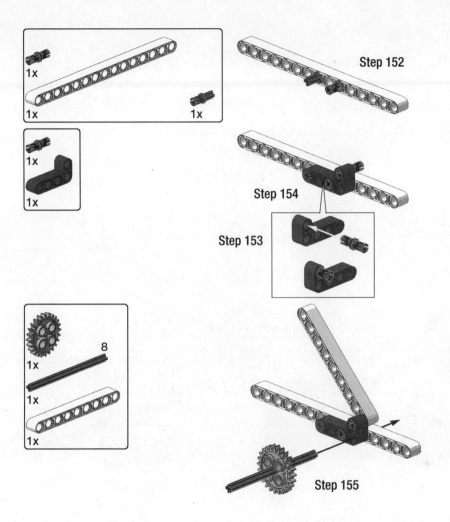

Step 152

Step 154

Step 153

Step 155

8

Start building the left tread assembly. Use a 15-long beam and a 9-long beam.

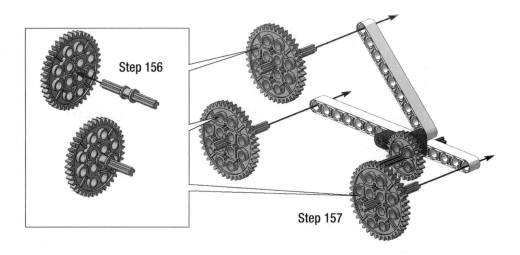

Insert the three 40-tooth gears, used as hubs.

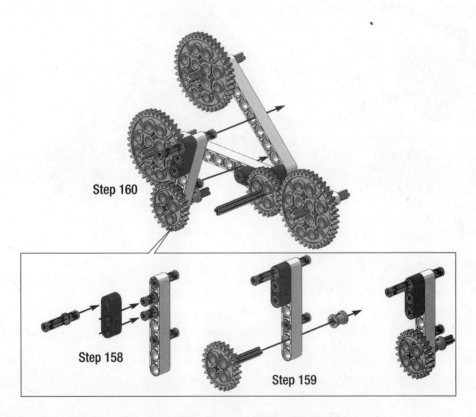

Build the assembly that helps form the strong triangular shape of the tread.

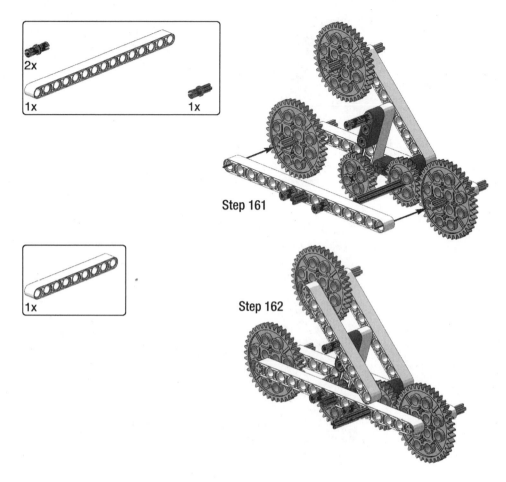

Step 161

Step 162

Add a 15-long beam and a 9-long beam.

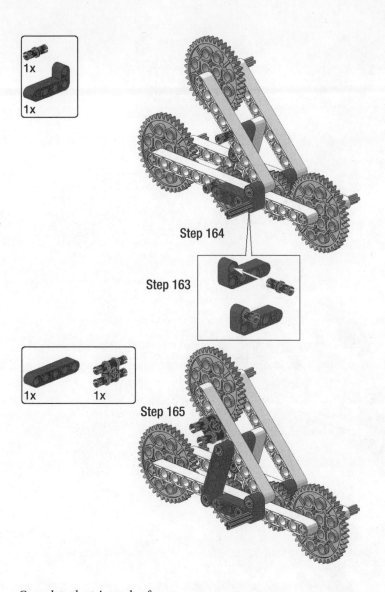

Step 164

Step 163

Step 165

Complete the triangular frame.

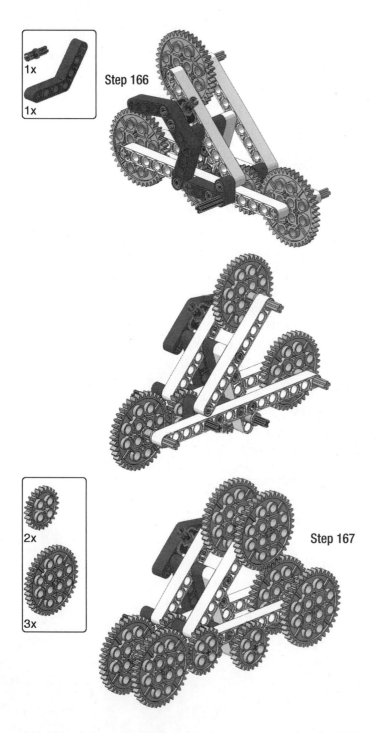

Step 166

Step 167

Add a blue axle pin in the black joiner. Turn the model and add three 40-tooth gears and two 24-tooth gears.

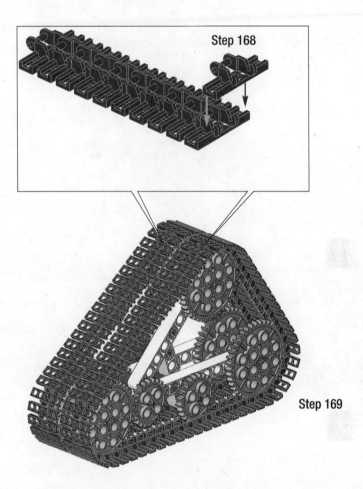

Build 2 treads of 61 links each. Close them around the large gears. The left tread assembly is complete.

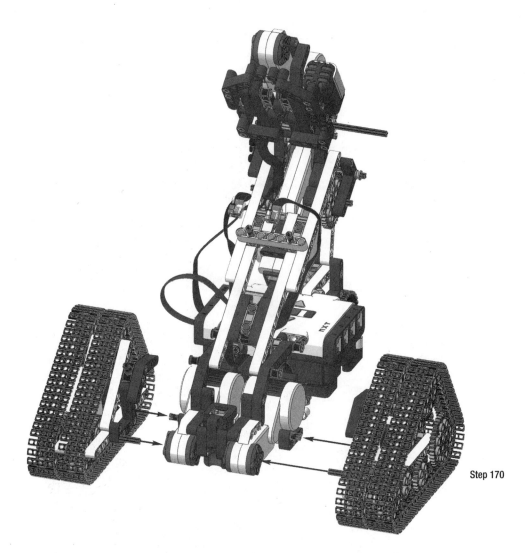

Step 170

Attach both treads in place. The driving axles go in the motor shafts, while the black pins go in the corresponding holes in the 15-long beams.

Step 171

Attach a 50cm (20 inch) cable to the Sound Sensor. Leave the other end floating; you'll attach it in the next steps.

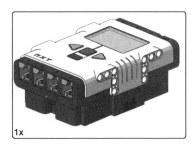

Step 172

Insert the master NXT brick in place. Notice that the two long pins go in the holes on the NXT's back. Attach the Sound Sensor cable to port 1. Attach the left tread's motor to port C and the right tread's motor to port A.

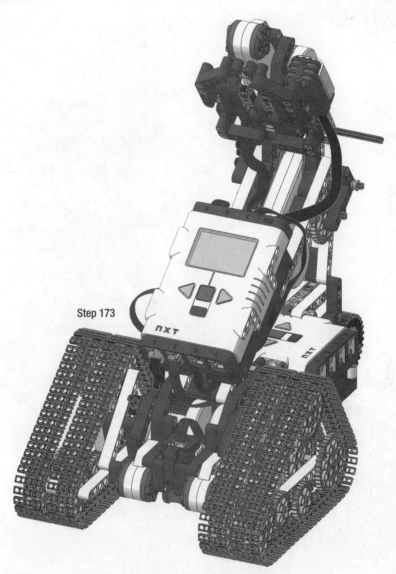

Step 173

Attach the line-tracking Light Sensor to master NXT input port 2, using a 20cm (8 inch) cable.

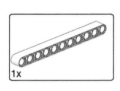

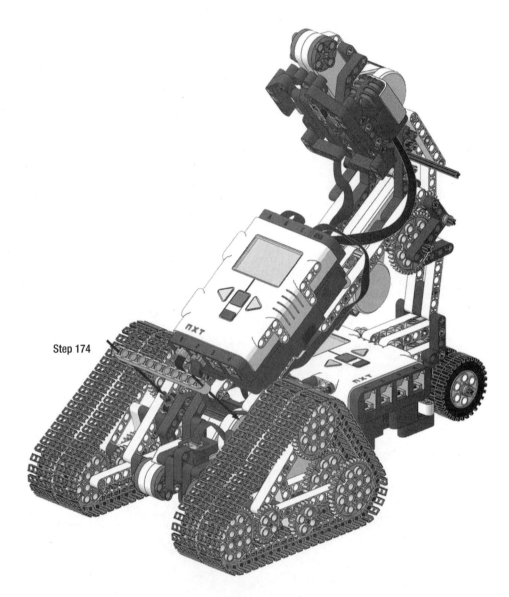

Step 174

Add a 13-long beam to hold the treads' assemblies together.

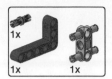

Step 176

Step 175

Turn the model and block the NXT with the assembly shown.

The Sound Sensor cable must pass between the NXT and the block just added.

The base and body assemblies are complete. The master NXT is attached to the body, leaving the space necessary for the Li-Ion battery pack.

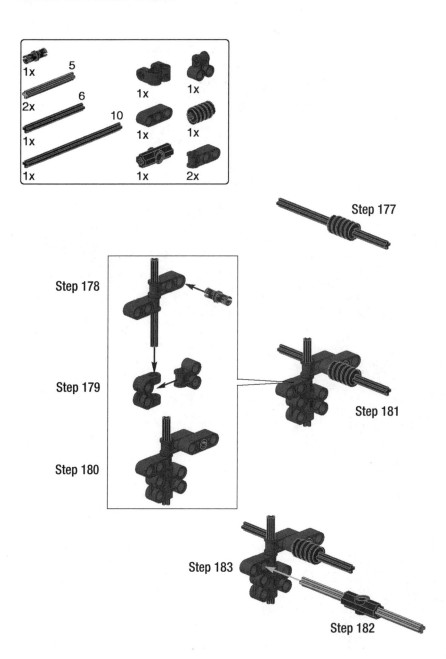

Step 177

Step 178

Step 179

Step 180

Step 181

Step 183

Step 182

Start building the shoulders.

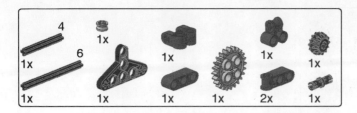

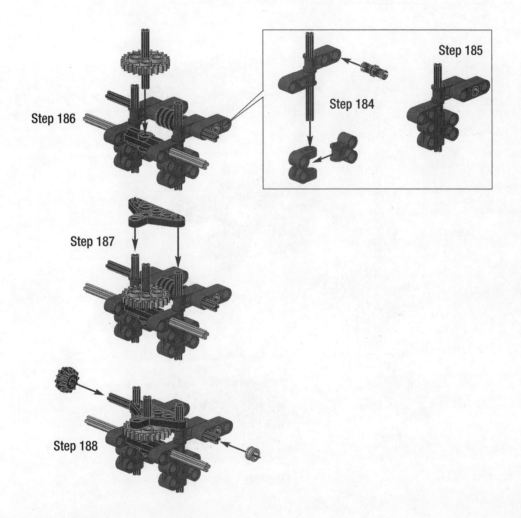

You're building the mechanism to turn the neck.

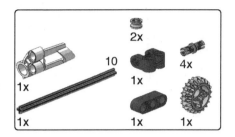

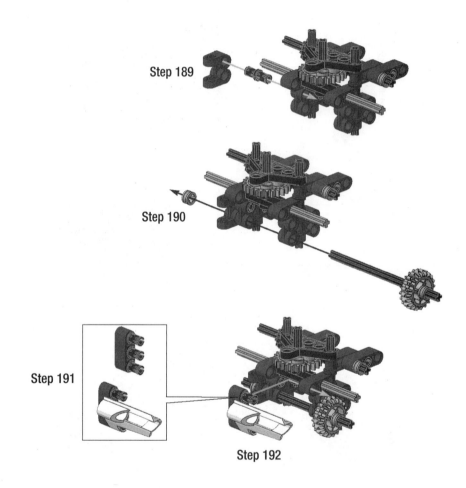

Step 189

Step 190

Step 191

Step 192

Add the axle and the gear for moving the arms. Add the fairing panel #6.

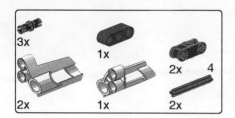

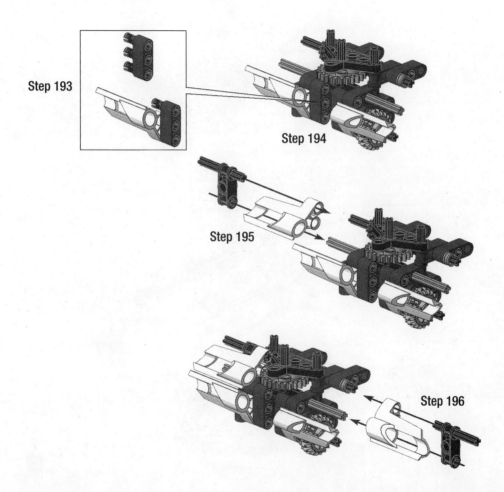

Step 193

Step 194

Step 195

Step 196

Add the symmetric panel #5 and another couple panels #5 and #6 to shape the round shoulders of JohnNXT.

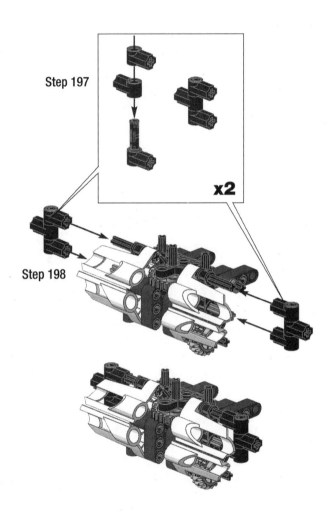

Step 197

x2

Step 198

Build the hinges for the arms.

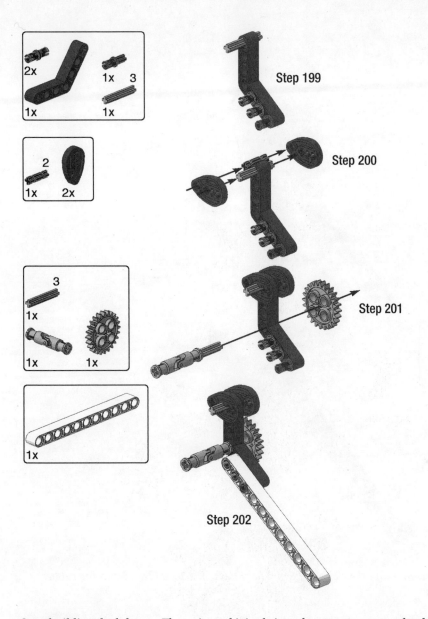

Step 199

Step 200

Step 201

Step 202

Start building the left arm. The universal joint brings the movement over the shoulder hinge.
Add an 11-long beam.

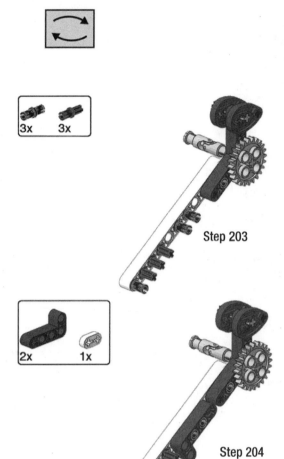

Step 203

Step 204

Add three blue axle pins and the elbow liftarm. The small white 1 × 2 beam holds the rubber band on the elbow.

Step 205

Add the 16-tooth gear that keeps the arm chain in tension.

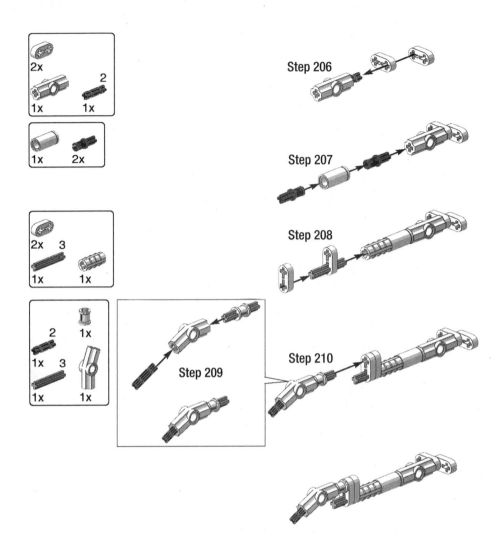

Build the left forearm. In step 207, add two blue axle pins.

Step 211

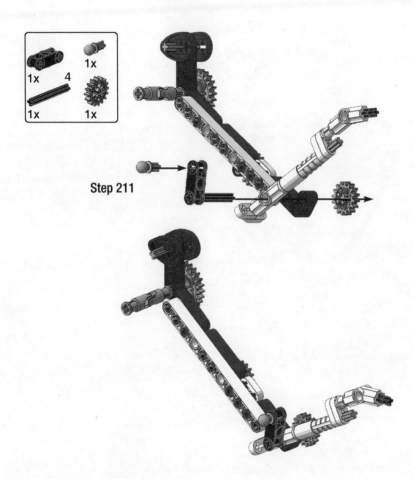

Attach the forearm to the arm.

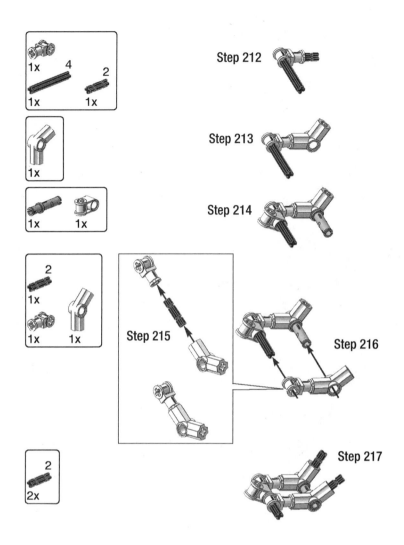

Step 212

Step 213

Step 214

Step 215

Step 216

Step 217

Build the left hand.

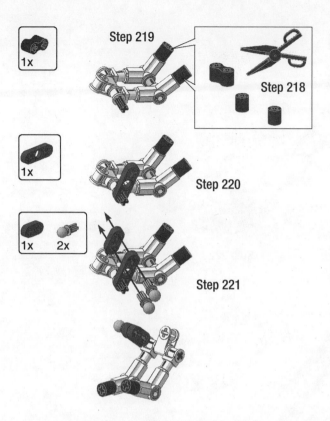

If splitting a rubber joiner in two does not bother you, prepare the finger grippers as shown. Otherwise, skip this step; the hand won't have friction on grasped objects.

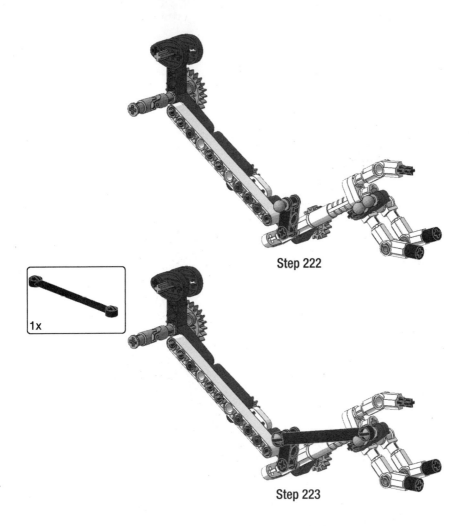

Step 222

Step 223

Attach the hand to the forearm and add a long steering link.

42x

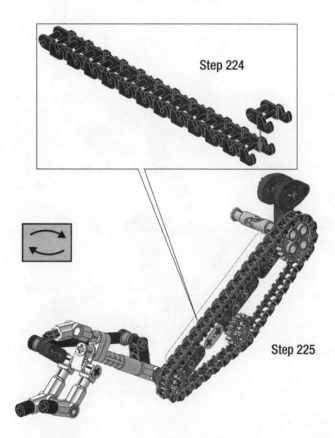

Step 224

Step 225

Attach 42 chain links and wrap them on the arms' gears as shown. The left arm is complete.

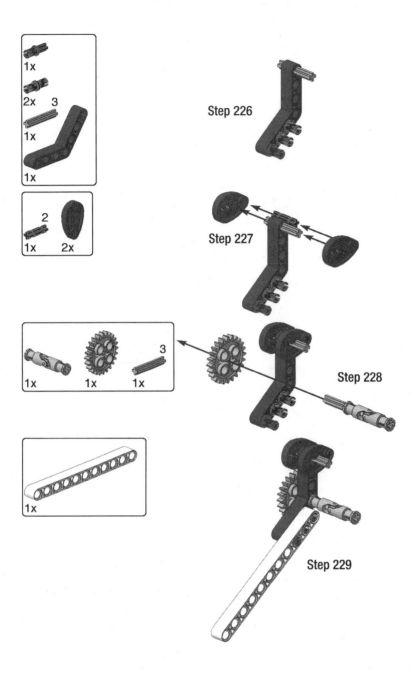

Step 226

Step 227

Step 228

Step 229

Start building the right arm. The cardan joint brings the movement over the shoulder hinge. Add an 11-long beam.

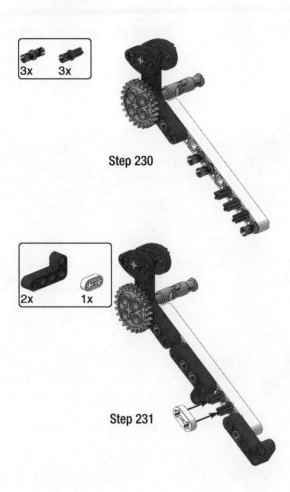

Step 230

Step 231

Add three blue axle pins and the elbow liftarm. The small white 1 × 2 beam holds the rubber band on the elbow.

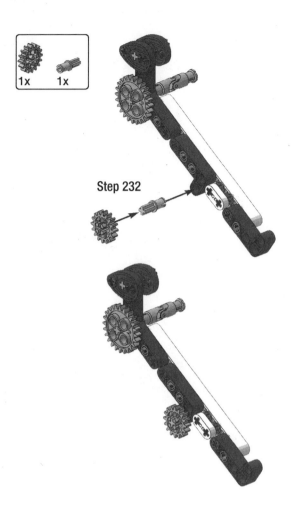

Step 232

Add the 16-tooth gear that keeps the arm chain in tension.

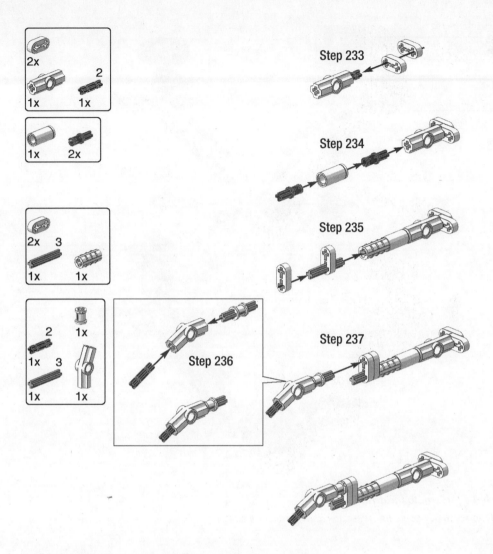

Build the right forearm. In Step 234, add two blue axle pins.

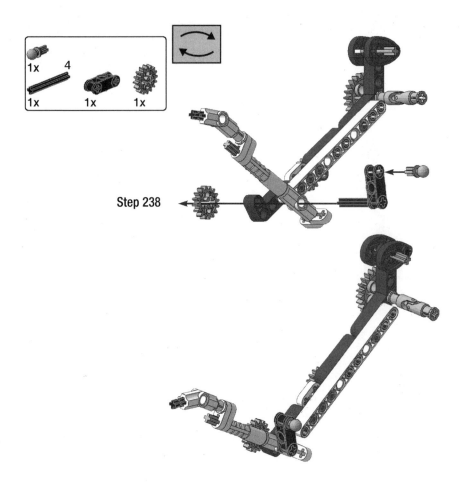

Step 238

Attach the forearm to the arm.

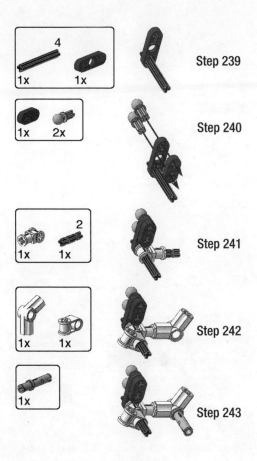

Step 239

Step 240

Step 241

Step 242

Step 243

Start building the right hand.

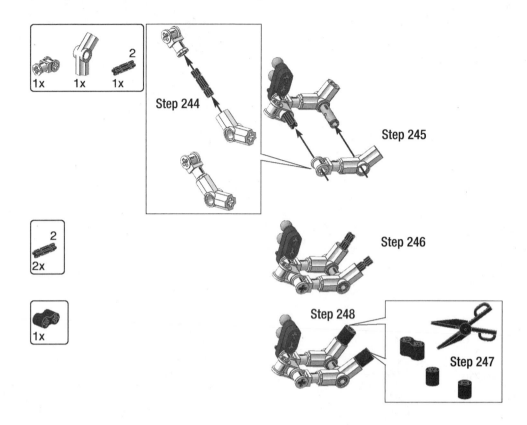

Again, if cutting LEGO parts does not bother you, prepare the finger grippers, splitting the rubber joiner as shown. Otherwise, skip this step; the hand won't have friction on grasped objects.

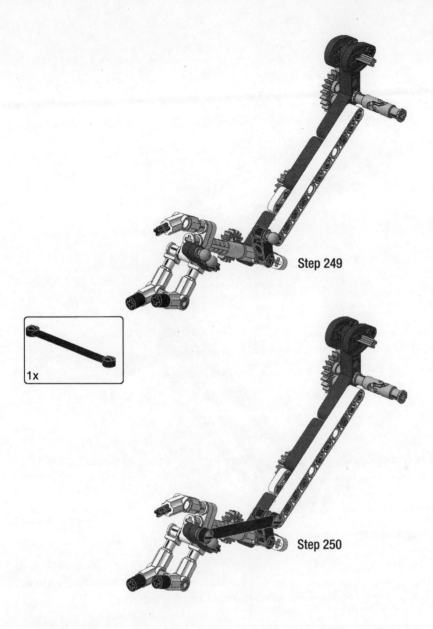

Step 249

1x

Step 250

Attach the hand to the forearm and add a long steering link.

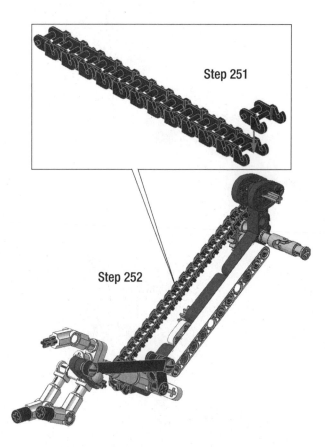

Step 251

Step 252

Join 42 chain links and wrap them on the arms' gears as shown. Make sure to align the forearm to the left one before adding the chain to the gears. The right arm is complete.

Step 253

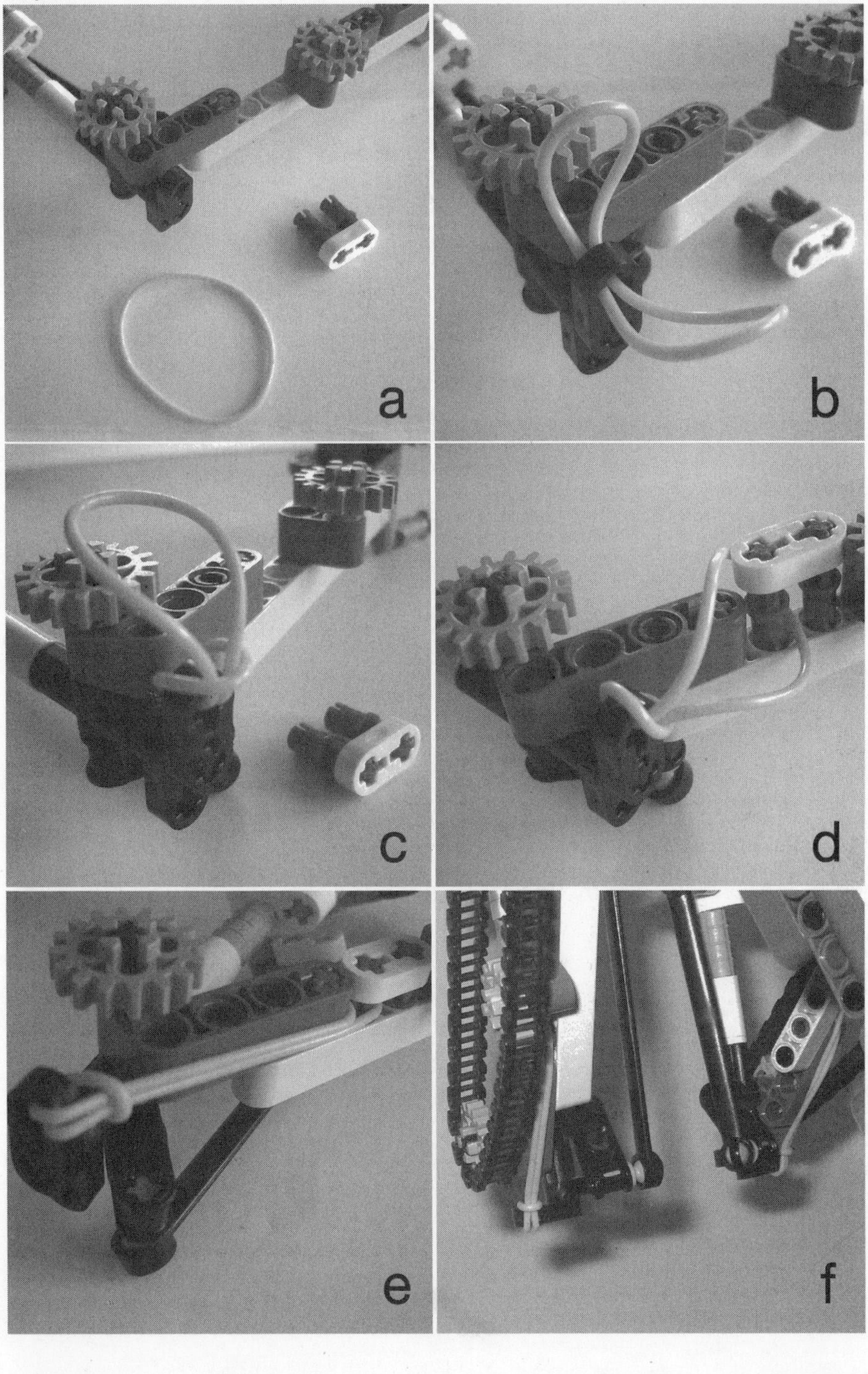

Figure 8-11. *This composite figure shows how to insert a LEGO yellow rubber band in the left elbow. Repeat this procedure also for the right elbow, before attaching the arms to the shoulders.*

Step 254

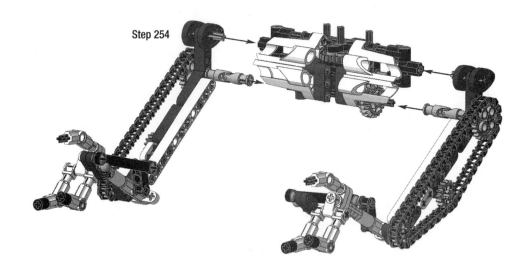

Attach both arms to the shoulders.

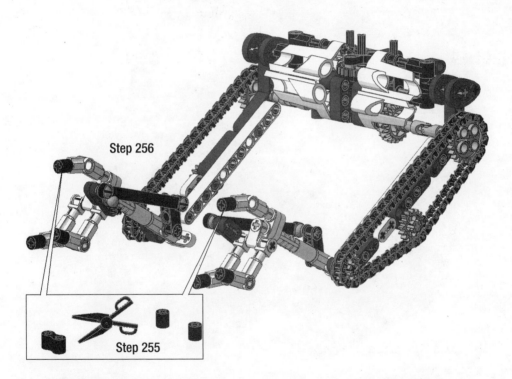

Step 256

Step 255

This is the last nerve-wracking rubber joiner cutting. Again, you can avoid this step.

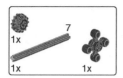

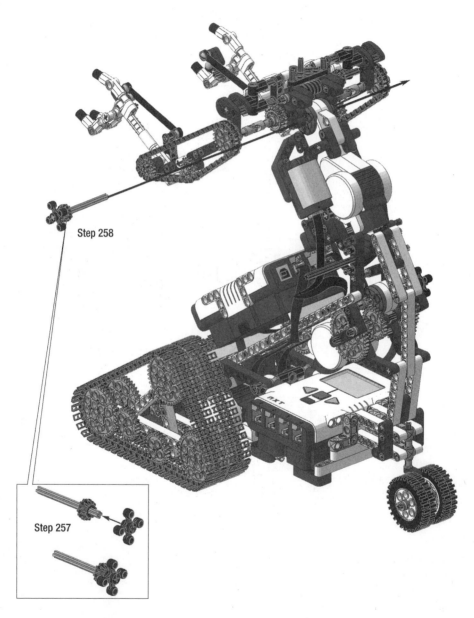

Step 258

Step 257

Attach the shoulders to the whole model, aligning the bottom holes with the motor shaft. Insert the axle that brings the movement to the arms and blocks the shoulders in place. You can turn the knob to move the arms manually.

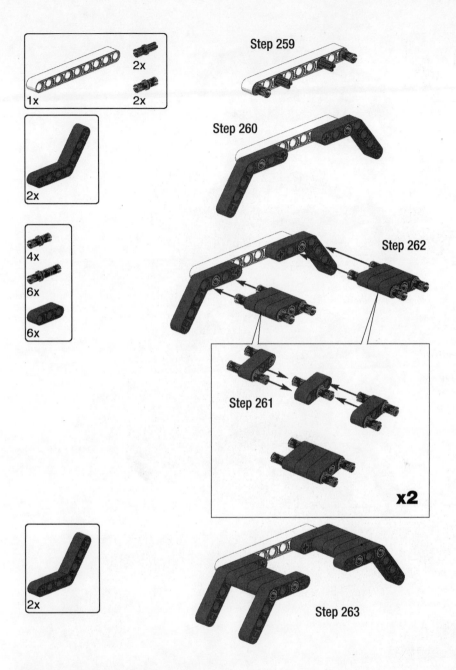

Step 259

Step 260

Step 262

Step 261

x2

Step 263

Start building the back of JohnNXT.

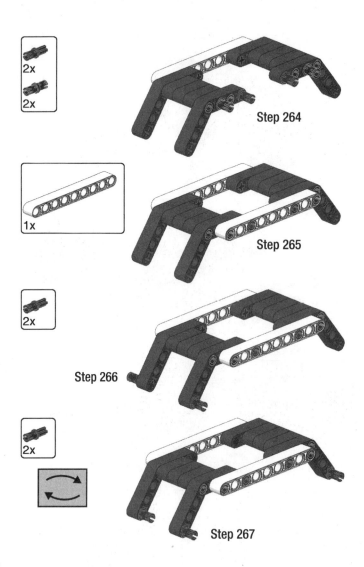

Step 264

Step 265

Step 266

Step 267

Complete the back of the robot.

Step 268

Attach the back assembly to the shoulders.

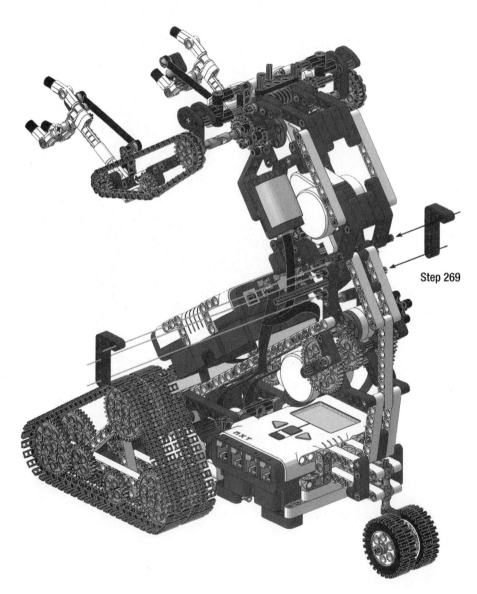

Step 269

These two bent beams complete the upper body's structure.

The upper body is a parallelogram structure. This way, the shoulders can move up and down, keeping the same inclination with respect to the ground.

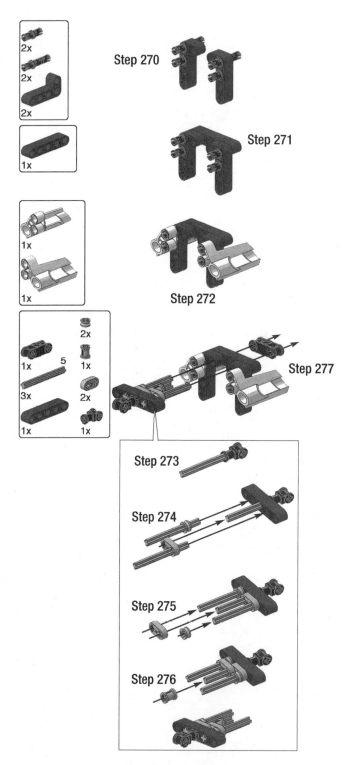

Step 270

Step 271

Step 272

Step 277

Step 273

Step 274

Step 275

Step 276

Start building JohnNXT's head. Add fairing panels #5 and #6.

Step 278

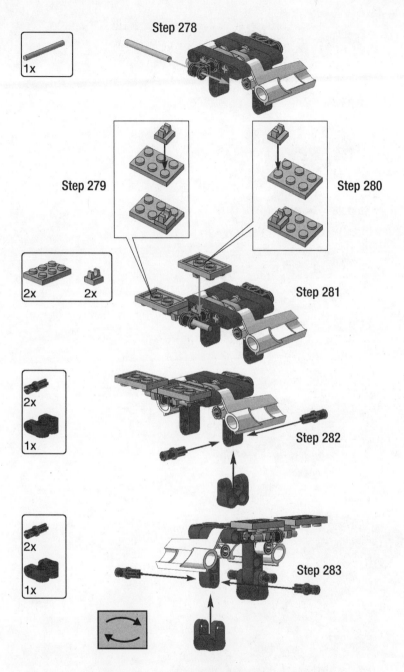

Step 279

Step 280

Step 281

Step 282

Step 283

Add a 4-long bar (like the minifigure's saber blades). Build the eyelids.

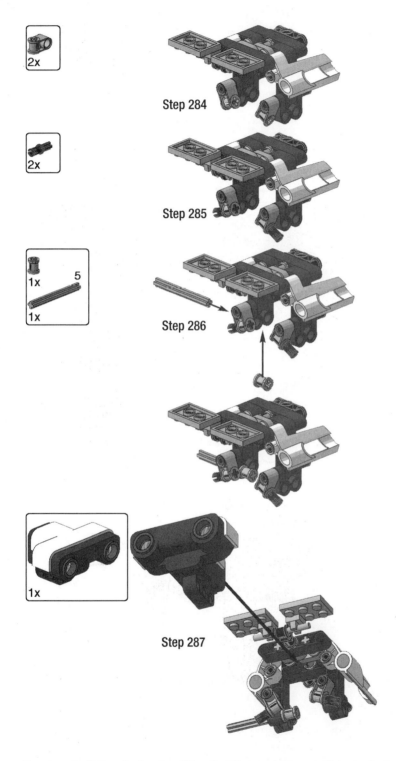

Step 284

Step 285

Step 286

Step 287

Continue building the head, adding the Ultrasonic Sensor. This one is similar to J5's own head!

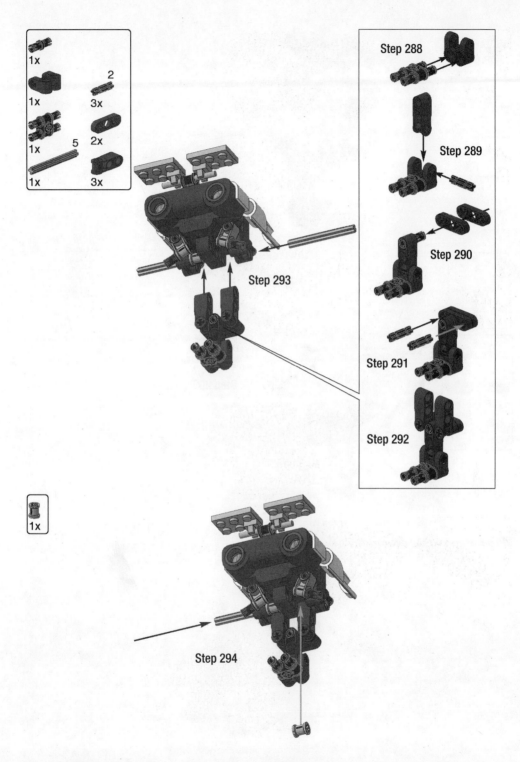

Step 288

Step 289

Step 290

Step 291

Step 292

Step 293

Step 294

Build the neck. Add a bush and push the axle to lock the sensor to the rest of the head.

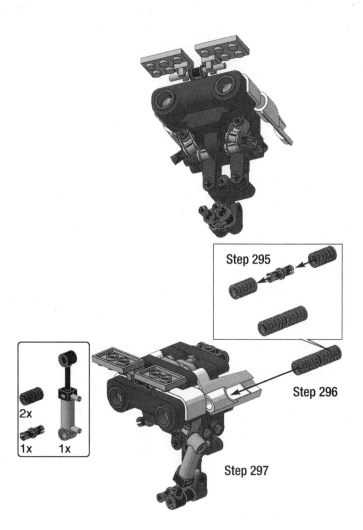

Step 295

Step 296

Step 297

Add a piston and the decorative hoses.

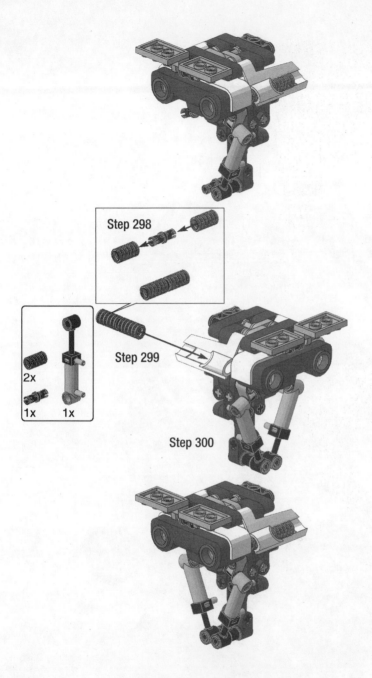

Step 298

Step 299

2x

1x   1x

Step 300

Complete the head, adding the other piston and hoses.

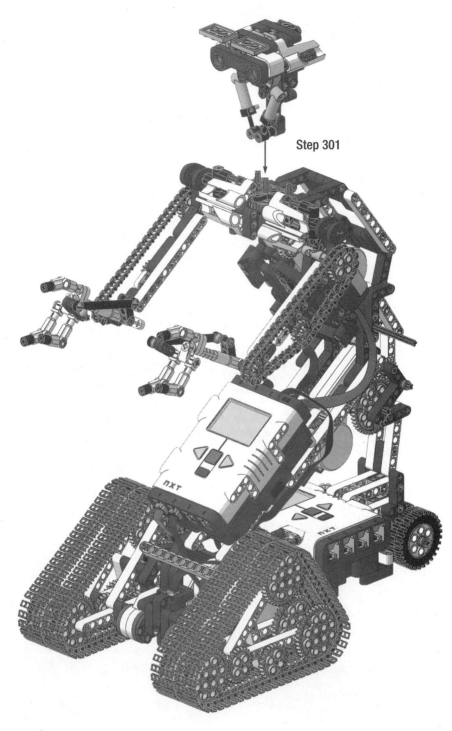

Step 301

Attach the head to the axle.

35cm

1x

Step 302

Attach a 35cm (14 inch) cable between the respective ports 4 of both NXTs. This cable is used for high-speed serial communication.

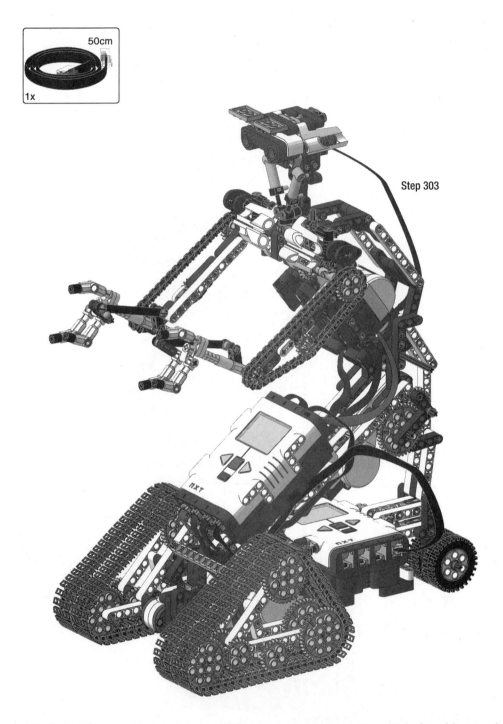

Step 303

Attach the Ultrasonic Sensor to master NXT input port 3 using a 50cm (20 inch) cable. Pass the cable where shown under the white 7-long beam to which the NXT is attached. Try to keep the cable central. Pull it to get the maximum length sticking out the back, so that it is free to move together with the head.

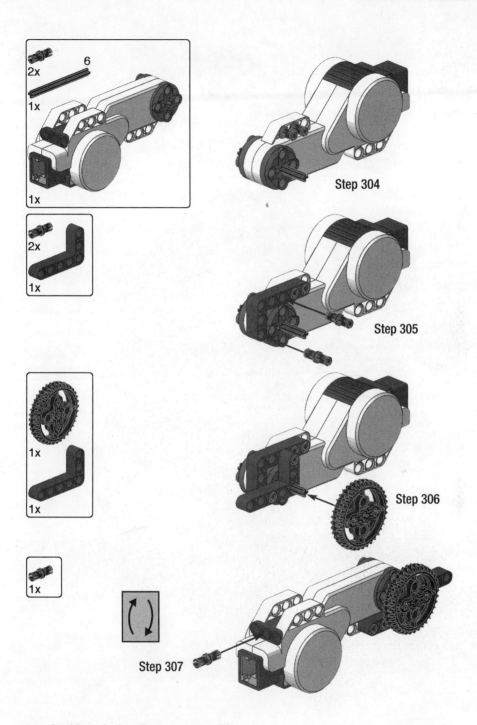

Step 304

Step 305

Step 306

Step 307

Start building the head's motor assembly.

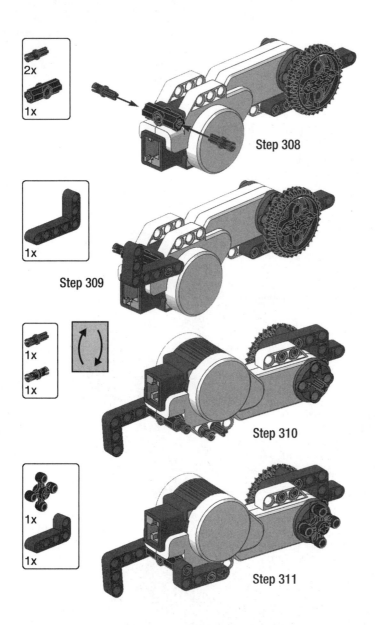

Step 308

Step 309

Step 310

Step 311

Complete the head's motor assembly.

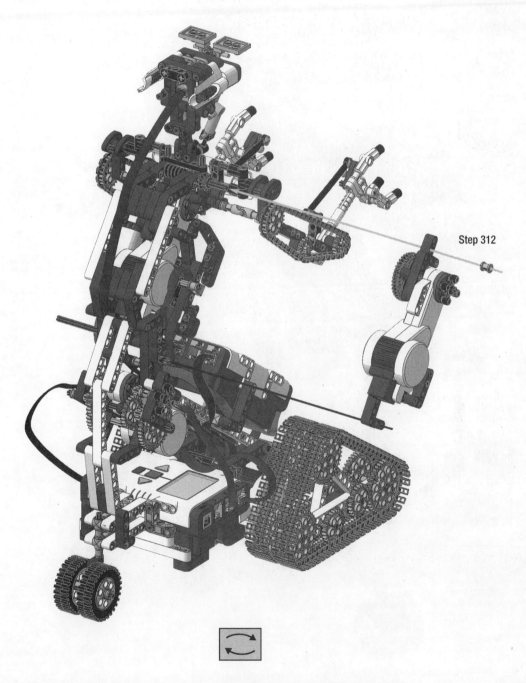

Step 312

Attach this motor to the rest of the robot, blocking it in place with a bush.

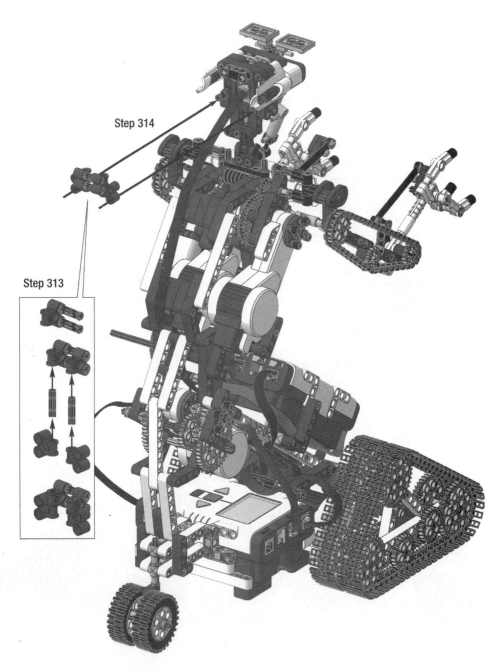

Step 314

Step 313

Build the back of the head.

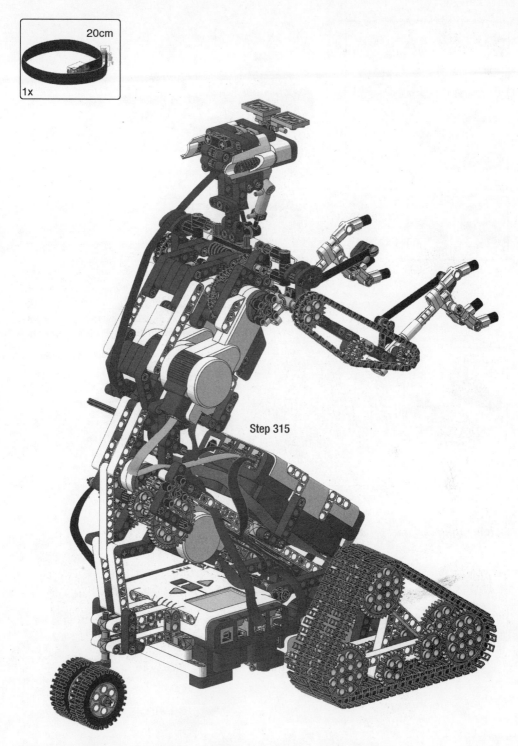

Step 315

Attach the head's motor to master NXT port B using a 20cm (8 inch) cable.

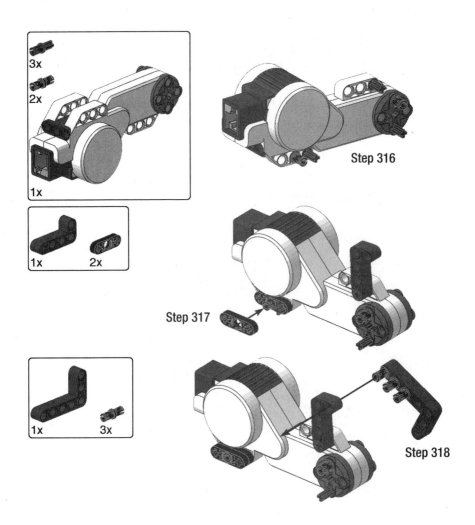

Step 316

Step 317

Step 318

Start building the laser's assembly.

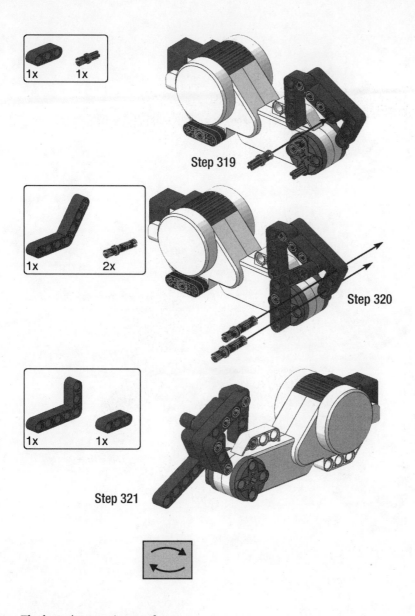

Step 319

Step 320

Step 321

The levers' system is complete.

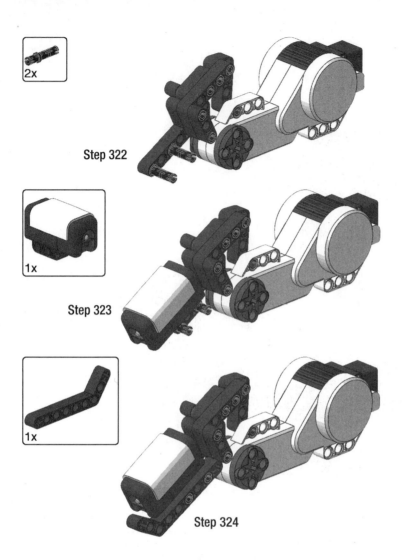

Step 322

Step 323

Step 324

Add the Light Sensor that simulates the laser blinking.

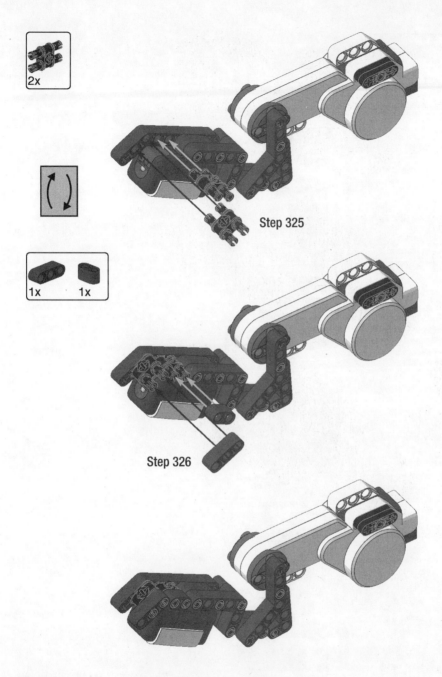

Step 325

Step 326

Turn the model and complete the laser weapon.

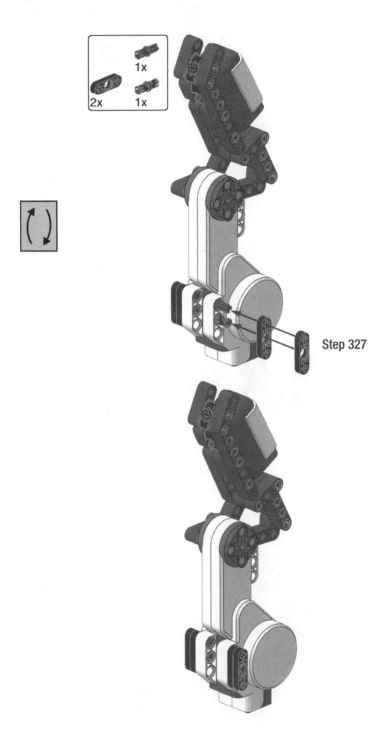

Step 327

Turn the laser and complete the assembly.

Step 328

Attach the laser in place, on the 12-long axle. The laser moves with the torso.

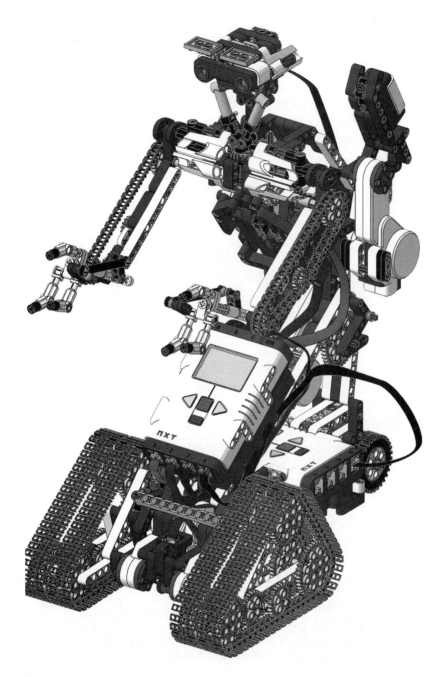

Here's how the model looks once the laser is attached.

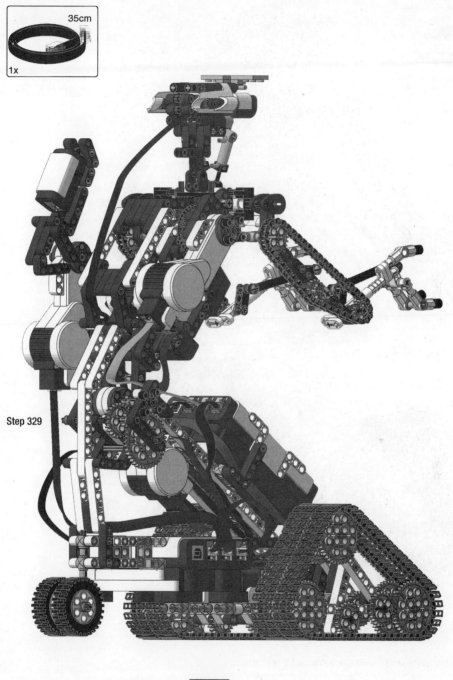

35cm
1x

Step 329

Turn the model and attach the laser's motor to slave NXT port C using a 35cm (14 inch) cable.

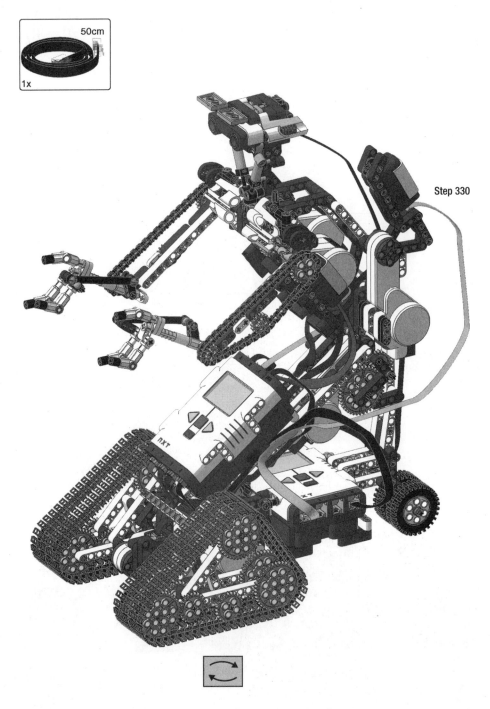

Step 330

Turn the model again and attach the Light Sensor of the laser to slave NXT port 1 using a 50cm (20 inch) cable.

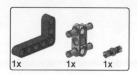

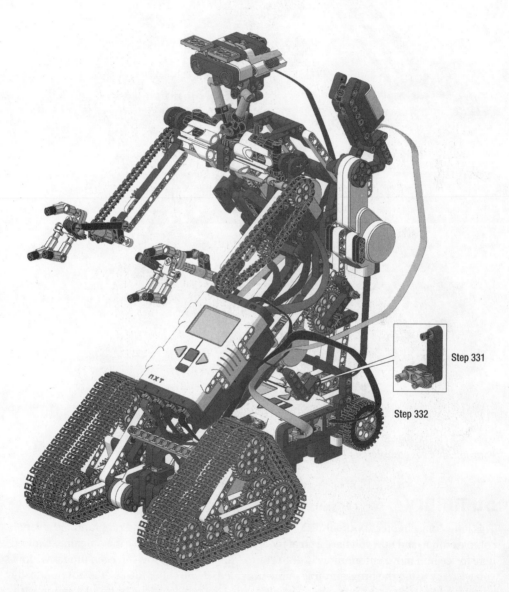

Step 331

Step 332

Build the assembly that blocks the NXT in place. This block must hold the cable for the laser sensor and for the high-speed communication.

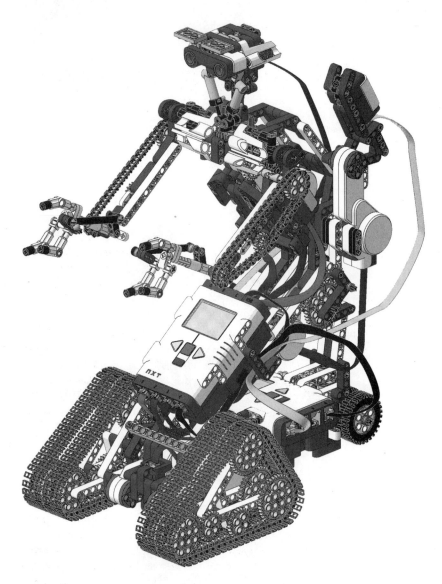

Your JohnNXT is completed.

Summary

This long, long chapter about JohnNXT is at an end. You have built and programmed a very complex robot, and now you have a great model to play with. You can use the program I showed here to see him move autonomously or to control him remotely. You can even program him as you wish, by using the programming guide provided. If you think the laser is not politically correct, you can do as Johnny did in *Short Circuit 2*, by replacing the harmful weapon with something else: a hang glider, a parachute, or an umbrella (weird!).

CHAPTER 9

■ ■ ■

Need Input! Building a Remote Control Device

Whatever you might do with LEGO MINDSTORMS NXT (autonomous vehicles, balancing walkers, brick sorters, line followers, and so on), one thing that still provides the most fun is controlling your creations remotely—at least for me. So, after having built an amazing model like JohnNXT, featuring any kind of functionality imaginable, I had to provide him with the "input" that he needed and that he was always looking for.

In this chapter, you'll build a Bluetooth remote control (R/C) for any differential drive robot (with two independent-driven wheels or two rows of legs). This remote also features two handy buttons to control functions other than mere locomotion. This R/C will be perfect to control the Tribot, the first robot you should have built with your NXT set, as well as the retail set scorpion Spike—not to mention the robots in this book, such as the Omni-Biped, the NXT Turtle, the Mine Sweeper, and finally, JohnNXT. For every robot, you should modify the sender and receiver programs to fit the application to have total control over every mechanism.

The Remote Control Design

First, I would like to say a few words about the design. In Figure 9-1, you can see how the R/C looks once it is built. For the most part, its volume is made up of the NXT brick and two motors. This quite ergonomic remote has just two analog inputs (the joysticks) and two digital inputs (the buttons). Please excuse me for the improper use of the term "analog"—even if the motors' encoders are digital—to point out that the joysticks can control the robot's wheels with a speed that is proportional to the joystick's displacement from the vertical rest position. It's not at all different from the PlayStation joysticks! On the other hand, the Touch Sensors are "digital" because their state can be only one (pressed) and zero (not pressed).

Adding a third motor or other sensors would make the whole remote too heavy and bulky. You must grasp it to get your thumbs on the joysticks (the dark gray beams attached to the motors' shafts), so that your forefingers can easily reach the Touch Sensors and you can read the NXT screen correctly. Also, notice that using the Touch Sensors is preferable to the NXT brick buttons for ergonomic purposes. It's designed so that you can push the sensors with your forefingers, without taking your thumbs off the joysticks.

Figure 9-1. *The Bluetooth R/C*

As you can see from the picture in Figure 9-1, there are no rubber bands or other weird mechanisms to keep the joysticks centered. The servomotors are used instead to bring the joysticks into their rest position, every time you release them.

Bluetooth Autoconnection Library

Before continuing with the R/C programs, you should know how to connect two NXTs via Bluetooth programmatically, without having to set up the connection manually with the NXT on-brick menu. This is handy, because you can avoid the annoying connection procedure every time you turn on the two NXT bricks: that would be done automatically inside the program.

Unfortunately, this is not possible using the actual NXT firmware version 1.05. John Hansen, the author of our beloved NXC and BricxCC, made this possible. He wrote a custom enhanced firmware for the NXT, giving your programs the capability to manage the Bluetooth connections, as you would do manually using the NXT menu.

■**Caution** I replaced the standard firmware with the custom enhanced firmware safely, and no NXT got damaged in any way. However, let me state here that, by updating the firmware, you do so at your own risk, and neither I nor John Hansen is responsible if your NXT gets damaged (also because the risk does not really exist). If you encounter any problem, you can always put the NXT in boot mode, pressing and holding the hidden button in the hole under the USB socket. Nothing weird will ever happen, but I had to inform you. In the future, LEGO might release an official update to implement these Bluetooth-related functionalities into the standard NXT firmware. This is a possibility, not a certainty.

I prepared a ready-to-use NXC library (`autoconnect.nxc`), which you can obtain from the Source Code/Download area of the Apress web site at `http://www.apress.com`. Once included in your programs, this library allows you to connect a slave NXT with a specified name on the specified Bluetooth channel (1, 2, or 3) using the following function:

```
bool ConnectNXT ( const string name , byte channel )
```

This function returns `true` if the connection was successfully established, `false` otherwise. For the autoconnection function to work properly, the slave NXT called `name` must be present in the Bluetooth contacts list of the master NXT (My Contacts, under the Bluetooth on-brick menu). To do that, you must connect the NXT manually, at least the first time. Follow these steps to let two NXT bricks use the Bluetooth Autoconnection Library:

1. Download the NXT enhanced firmware from `http://bricxcc.sourceforge.net/lms_arm_jch.zip`. Unzip it into the BricxCC main folder, or in the folder where the other official firmware files should be, for example, C:\Program Files\LEGO Software\LEGO MINDSTORMS NXT\engine\Firmware.

2. Download the enhanced firmware file `lms_arm_jch.rfw` to the master NXT using BricxCC; to do this, select Tools ➤ Download Firmware (see Appendix A for details). Repeat this for every NXT that you want to use as the master in a Bluetooth communication. If the NXT display is behaving strangely, you can remove the batteries and then put them in again. This enhanced firmware does not contain the sound files that you normally find on the NXT once you download the standard firmware. So, you have to download them manually. Use the NXT Explorer feature of BricxCC to download to the NXT the sound files ! Click.rso, ! Attention.rso, and ! Startup.rso, which are located, for example, in the folder C:\Program Files\LEGO Software\LEGO MINDSTORMS NXT\engine\Sounds.

3. Now you should let every NXT know the other one exists. That means you must let them exchange their passkeys. I'll explain how to do it for a master/slave couple, then you can repeat the same actions on other NXTs you might have.

4. Take the master NXT. Browse its menu to find and select the Bluetooth item. Select My Contacts to check if the slave NXT is already listed there. If its name is already known to the master NXT, you're done.

5. If the slave NXT name does not appear among the master NXT contacts, go back in the Bluetooth menu and select Search, making sure that all other NXTs around have Bluetooth radio turned on. After a while, the menu should show the Bluetooth devices found. Select the slave NXT you want to connect, and choose one of the three channels available.

6. Both NXTs (master and slave) should now play a sound and ask you to enter the passkey. Leave the default 1234 value and press the orange button on both NXTs.

7. Your NXTs should now be connected. Even if you turn them off, they now know each other, because they have updated their Bluetooth contact list. Later, you can connect them automatically within your programs, using the Autoconnection Library.

R/C: A Program for Every Need

The software that you are going to write for it is what makes this remote special. To fulfill any need in terms of control, I had to think about a fast and easy way to reach all the features not only for a simple three-motor robot, but also for a complex remote-controlled model such as JohnNXT.

Next, I'll show two different versions of the R/C sender/receiver programs. You can use the first basic version to control simple robots, such as the Tribot. The joysticks control the wheels and treads, while the two triggers activate other functions, related to the third motor.

Then, I'll discuss the second multimodal program's version—the one you'll use to control JohnNXT remotely. Finally, you'll be instructed how to modify the provided programs so you can adapt them to your own custom remote-controlled robots.

Simple R/C Programs

The simple version of the program can control a differential drive robot such as the Tribot, equipped with a motor per wheel and a third motor for some additional features. However, nothing stops you from bending the retail set scorpion Spike to your command! The way its legs are driven makes it a differential drive walking robot.

The joysticks control the wheels' turning speed and direction; you use the two Touch Sensors to send three commands to the robot, so you can activate three additional functions. Pressing the right trigger, the command sent activates the first function; pressing the left trigger, the second function is activated; finally, pressing both triggers together activates a third function on the robot.

Simple Sender Program (to Be Run on the Remote Control)

First, I'll describe the sender program; you can read its code in Listing 9-1.

Listing 9-1. *The Simple Version of the Remote Control Sender Program*

```
// include Bluetooth Autoconnection Library
#include "autoconnect.nxc"

// I/O devices' ports
#define R_JOYSTICK OUT_C
#define L_JOYSTICK OUT_A
#define JOYSTICKS OUT_AC
#define R_TOUCH IN_4
#define L_TOUCH IN_1
#define BT_CONN 1

// change this constant according to your slave NXT name
#define SLAVE_NXT "D_NXT2"
// this is the name of the slave program to be started
#define SLAVE_PROGRAM "remote_slave.rxe"
```

```
// position of the graphics onscreen
#define L_INFO_PX 25
#define R_INFO_PX 75

// commands' constant definitions
#define STOP    0
#define FWD1    1
#define FWD2    2
#define FWD3    3
#define FWD4    4
#define REV1    5
#define REV2    6
#define REV3    7
#define REV4    8

// joystick angle thresholds
#define THR0    3
#define THR1    5
#define THR2    10
#define THR3    15
#define THR4    20


#define TORQUE 7

// joysticks' related global variables
int Lpos, Rpos, Lzero, Rzero;
mutex motor_sem;

// this function returns true if the
// Bluetooth connection with the robot exists;
// otherwise it tries to make the connection
// using the Autoconnection Library;
// if even this fails,
// it displays some instructions
// and returns false
bool BTConnection(byte conn, const string name)
{
   bool connection_exists;
   if (BluetoothStatus(conn)==NO_ERR)
   {
      connection_exists = true;
   }
   else
   {
      // call the Autoconnection Library function
```

```
    if (ConnectNXT(name,conn)==true)
    {
        // if connection was successful
        // the function returns true
        PlayTone(2000,20);
        connection_exists = true;
    }
    else
    {
        ClearScreen();
        TextOut(0,LCD_LINE1,"You must connect");
        TextOut(0,LCD_LINE2,"the slave NXT on");
        TextOut(0,LCD_LINE3,"BT channel 1");
        TextOut(0,LCD_LINE4,"using the menu");
        TextOut(0,LCD_LINE5,"of this NXT.");
        Wait(4000);
        connection_exists = false;
    }
    }
    return connection_exists;
}


// this subroutine brings the joystick, whose motor
// is attached to the specified port, to the central
// position.
inline sub ZeroJoyStick(byte port)
{
    int t;
    t = MotorRotationCount(port);
    // start motor
    OnRev(port,50);
    Wait(80);
    // until a stall is detected
    while( abs(t-MotorRotationCount(port))>5 )
    {
        t = MotorRotationCount(port);
        Wait(20);
    }
    // stop motor
    Off(port);
}


// this function returns
// 1 if right sensor is pressed,
// 2 if left sensor is pressed,
// 3 if both sensors are pressed
byte GetTriggers()
{
```

```
    byte triggers;
    // combine right and left sensor Boolean readings
    triggers = 2*Sensor(L_TOUCH) + Sensor(R_TOUCH);
    return triggers;
}


// this function converts the position of the joystick,
// passed as an argument, into a command value
// applying a series of thresholds
short AngleToCommand (short pos)
{
    if ( pos <  -THR4 ) return FWD4;
    if ( pos >= -THR4 && pos < -THR3 ) return FWD3;
    if ( pos >= -THR3 && pos < -THR2 ) return FWD2;
    if ( pos >= -THR2 && pos < -THR1 ) return FWD1;
    if ( pos >= -THR1 && pos <  THR1 ) return STOP;
    if ( pos >=  THR1 && pos <  THR2 ) return REV1;
    if ( pos >=  THR2 && pos <  THR3 ) return REV2;
    if ( pos >=  THR3 && pos <  THR4 ) return REV3;
    if ( pos >=  THR4 ) return REV4;
}


//  this subroutine displays information
// about the command being sent
sub ShowCommands(byte Lc, byte Rc, byte trig)
{
    string arrows[];
    string Rstring, Lstring;
    // fill the arrows array with the listed strings
    ArrayBuild(arrows,"o",">",">>",">>>",">>>>","<","<<","<<<","<<<<");
    ClearScreen();
    // prepare the Xstring to be shown,
    // according to the right and left command values.
    // The Xstring is an element of the arrows array.
    Rstring = arrows[Rc];
    Lstring = arrows[Lc];
    // show the string on the screen.
    TextOut(R_INFO_PX,LCD_LINE2,Rstring);
    TextOut(L_INFO_PX-5*StrLen(Lstring),LCD_LINE2,Lstring);
    if (trig&1) TextOut(R_INFO_PX-5,LCD_LINE3,"*");
    if (trig&2) TextOut(L_INFO_PX-5,LCD_LINE3,"*");
}


// this function builds the command to be sent
// encoding all the information in a single number
// and sends the command via Bluetooth
void SendCommand(byte Lcmd, byte Rcmd, byte triggers)
{
```

```
    short out;
        // 100s: analog channel 1
        // 10s: analog channel 2
        // 1s: digital channels 3 and 4
    out = Lcmd*100 + Rcmd*10 + triggers;
    SendRemoteNumber(BT_CONN,1,out);
}

task main()
{
    // initialize sensors
    SetSensorTouch(R_TOUCH);
    SetSensorTouch(L_TOUCH);

    TextOut(0,LCD_LINE2,"Connecting...");
    if (BTConnection(BT_CONN,SLAVE_NXT)==false)
    {
        // if BT connection with robot
        // is not established, stop the whole program
        Stop(true);
    }
    else
    {
        ClearScreen();
        // start the selected program on slave NXT
        RemoteStartProgram(BT_CONN,SLAVE_PROGRAM);
    }
    // main ends, leaving execution to the other tasks
}

// bring right joystick to its limit position
task RightJoystickLimit()
{
    Follows(main);
    ZeroJoyStick(R_JOYSTICK);
}

// bring left joystick to its limit position
task LeftJoystickLimit()
{
    Follows(main);
    ZeroJoyStick(L_JOYSTICK);
}

// this task reads the joystick positions continuously
// and produces the feedback to keep them vertical
task RemoteEngine()
{
```

```
short command, Rcmd, Lcmd;
byte triggers;

// wait for these tasks to end
Follows(main,RightJoystickLimit,LeftJoystickLimit);

// rotate the motors by 110 degrees to bring the joystick vertical
RotateMotorPID(JOYSTICKS,70,110,70,40,70);
// store the current position (central) into the Xzero variable
Rzero = MotorRotationCount(R_JOYSTICK);
Lzero = MotorRotationCount(L_JOYSTICK);
while(true)
{
    // read the joysticks' angle from the central position
    Rpos = MotorRotationCount(R_JOYSTICK) - Rzero;
    Lpos = MotorRotationCount(L_JOYSTICK) - Lzero;
    // actuate the feedback on joysticks
    // to bring them to the center again
    OnRev(R_JOYSTICK,sign(Rpos)*TORQUE);
    OnRev(L_JOYSTICK,sign(Lpos)*TORQUE);
    // if the angle is about 0, then float the motors
    if (-THRO <= Rpos && Rpos <= THRO)  Float(R_JOYSTICK);
    if (-THRO <= Lpos && Lpos <= THRO)  Float(L_JOYSTICK);
    // convert the joysticks' angle to speed commands
    Lcmd = AngleToCommand(Lpos);
    Rcmd = AngleToCommand(Rpos);
    // read the triggers' state
    triggers = GetTriggers();
    // show various information onscreen
    ShowCommands(Lcmd, Rcmd, triggers);
    // send the command using Bluetooth
    SendCommand(Lcmd,Rcmd,triggers);
    Wait(50);
}
}
```

At the top of the listing, you can find the constant definitions and the statement to include the Bluetooth Autoconnection Library. Including the file autoconnect.nxc, you can connect the remote to the robot automatically.

At program startup, the first code to be executed is the one inside the main task. After the usual sensor initialization, the BTConnection function is called. This function, in turn, checks if the connection with the slave exists; if not, it calls the Autoconnection Library's ConnectNXT function. If the connection cannot be made, because the slave is off or its radio is off, the BTConnection function returns false; this condition causes the main task to call the Stop(true) NXC function to stop the whole program. If the connection is established successfully, main calls the RemoteStartProgram NXC function to start the slave NXT program. This way, once you have turned on your remote (master) and your robot (slave), you just have to start this program to get the connection—and the program—to start automatically. Not bad, is it? Of course, the remote robot's NXT must have the right program in its memory, or the whole thing won't work. To be sure that everything goes fine, change the two definitions at the top of the listing so that the SLAVE_NXT string matches your slave NXT name and the SLAVE_PROGRAM string matches the slave program's name:

```
// change this constant according to your slave NXT name
#define SLAVE_NXT "D_NXT2"
// this is the name of the slave program to be started
#define SLAVE_PROGRAM "remote_slave.rxe"
```

Make sure to append the .rxe extension to the program name string.

After the slave has been connected, the main ends, and the execution passes to the other tasks. The first to go into execution are the RightJoystickLimit and LeftJoystickLimit tasks, because they contain the statement Follows(main). These tasks run together, bringing both joysticks to their limit position at the same time; this is done by calling the ZeroJoyStick subroutine.

This subroutine is marked inline. This means that, at compilation time, its code is copied for every time it is called. In this case, it is repeated two times, when the RightJoystickLimit and LeftJoystickLimit tasks call it. If that subroutine wasn't marked inline, its code would be reported only once in the compiled program, and would be shared between the two tasks that had called it. This would result in a weird behavior, meaning that each joystick's shared position realignment would fail.

Inside the ZeroJoyStick subroutine, you find an old acquaintance: the so-called *servomotors automagic built-in limit switch* technique that was described in detail in Chapter 4. The servomotor shaft is rotated until a beam blocks the joystick. The servomotor "feels" this stall and stops. If the stall is detected too early, you can tweak the algorithm settings. In particular, you can decrease the angle threshold from 5 to 3, or increase the milliseconds to wait from 20 to 40: in both cases, you are setting the algorithm to stop the motor only when the speed of the shaft is very low.

```
while( abs(t-MotorRotationCount(port))>5 )
{
    t = MotorRotationCount(port);
    Wait(20);
}
```

The RemoteEngine task can begin its execution only when the preceding tasks end, because it contains the Follows(main,RightJoystickLimit,LeftJoystickLimit) statement; that instruction tells the NXT scheduler to start the RemoteEngine task only after all the tasks listed in the parentheses have ended. This task brings the joysticks orthogonal with respect to the NXT, and saves the servomotors' angles into the Rzero and Lzero variables. These angle values are used later to calculate how much every joystick has been displaced from its resting vertical position.

Now, RemoteEngine is the only task in execution. Inside this task there's an infinite loop, where the sensors (Touch Sensors and servomotors position) are read, and the output command is packed and sent. Let's see how. In every loop, the joystick's position is computed as the difference between the actual angle reading and the offset saved before (remember the Rzero and Lzero variables), and it is stored in the Rpos and Lpos variables. To provide the joysticks with a self-centering mechanism, the motors are started at a low speed to reach the position they had at startup, using this code:

```
OnRev(R_JOYSTICK,sign(Rpos)*TORQUE);
OnRev(L_JOYSTICK,sign(Lpos)*TORQUE);
```

When they get inside the center zone with a ±3 degrees tolerance around 0, the servon are stopped with Float. Using Off would make them too hard to move with the thumbs. TORQUE constant value passed to the OnFwd functions shown earlier equals a speed of just 7, ideal to keep the joysticks reactive, but still soft enough to move from the center. The factor sign(Xpos) is used to move the joystick in the opposite direction, with respect to the one you are pushing.

This way, you can obtain the self-centering joysticks feature. Because you are dealing with precise servomotors (giving you a one-degree resolution angle measure), you can drive the robot at a variable speed, with the common convention that the more the joysticks are displaced, the faster the robot will go. It is not practical to associate every degree step to one-hundredth of the motor's full speed. It would be impossible to control a robot just to go straight! Four incremental speeds are more than sufficient, so I defined some angle thresholds, as shown in Figure 9-2.

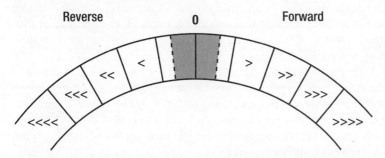

Figure 9-2. *The analog joystick sectors used to achieve gradual speed control*

When the joystick lies inside one of those sectors, the corresponding speed is used. This is done by the AngleToCommand function, which accepts the relative joystick angle as an argument pos and returns one of the speed levels defined at the beginning of the program. Then, the GetTriggers function reads the status of the Touch Sensors and stores it into the triggers variable.

The following statement packs the status of both triggers into the triggers variable:

```
triggers = 2*Sensor(L_TOUCH) + Sensor(R_TOUCH);
```

This variable can assume the following values:

```
No Trigger Pressed        triggers = 0 (base 10) = 00 (base 2)
Left Trigger Pressed      triggers = 2 (base 10) = 10 (base 2)
Right Trigger Pressed     triggers = 1 (base 10) = 01 (base 2)
Both Triggers Pressed     triggers = 3 (base 10) = 11 (base 2)
```

After all the measurements are done, the ShowCommands subroutine is called. This subroutine has just the aesthetic purpose to show, on the NXT screen, the actual commands that are sent to the robot. It provides you with visual feedback on the actual speed level on both analog channels, by drawing many arrows > (forward) or < (reverse), according to the actual speed level, depending on the joysticks' displacement from the center. A circle is drawn when the joysticks are in the center.

When a trigger is pressed, the corresponding asterisk is drawn by the following two lines of code:

```
if (trig&1) TextOut(R_INFO_PX-5,LCD_LINE3,"*");
if (trig&2) TextOut(L_INFO_PX-5,LCD_LINE3,"*");
```

The condition trig&1 controls if the right trigger was pressed, by checking if the *bitwise AND* operation between trig and 1 returns a number different from 0 (that means true) or not (false). Remembering that the Boolean AND operation returns true only if both operands are true, the trig&1 operation can be expanded as follows:

```
00 & 01 = 00 (false)
01 & 01 = 01 (true)
10 & 01 = 00 (false)
11 & 01 = 01 (true)      (numbers represented in base 2)
```

You use the trig&2 condition to check if the left trigger was pressed. The operation explicitly yields the following result:

```
00 & 10 = 00 (false)
01 & 10 = 00 (false)
10 & 10 = 10 (true)
11 & 10 = 10 (true)      (numbers represented in base 2)
```

For example, when the triggers are pressed together, the trig value is 3 (11 base 2), and both asterisks are drawn. For the left asterisk to be drawn, trig must be 2 or 3 (10 or 11 in base 2); for the right one to be drawn, trig must be 1 or 3 (01 or 11 in base 2).

The three variables Rcmd, Lcmd, and triggers have to be packed into a single number to be sent to the robot. The SendCommand function does this. The command format is simple: a three-digit decimal number is enough to encode the speed for the wheels and the Touch Sensors' status. Both Rcmd and Lcmd are represented by single-digit numbers from 0 to 8, as well as the triggers variable.

Look at the following statement:

```
out = Lcmd*100 + Rcmd*10 + triggers;
```

The out variable is the command to be sent out via Bluetooth. Lcmd is multiplied by 100 and summed to Rcmd multiplied by 10. The unit digit is filled with the information from the Touch Sensors. To fix this situation, consider the following examples, while having a look at the program definitions at the beginning of Listing 9-1.

```
Left Joystick >>>, Right Joystick >>>>, Right touch pressed :     command = 341
Left Joystick <, Right Joystick >>, Left touch pressed :          command = 522
Left Joystick centered, Right Joystick <<<<, none pressed :       command = 080
Left Joystick >>>, Right Joystick <<<, both pressed :             command = 373
```

The SendCommand function sends away the command obtained in this manner using the SendRemoteNumber(BT_CONN,1,out) statement. The RemoteEngine task loop starts from the beginning after catching a 50ms breath.

I tried to keep this explanation as essential as possible, yet complete. This program provided an occasion to discuss many interesting things, such as the self-centering joysticks feature, and the command encoding.

Simple Receiver Program (to Be Run on the Robot)

Now it's time to see how the command is decoded by the receiver program, whose code is shown in Listing 9-2. I'll focus just on the important parts of this code: the main task and the Move function, because the rest of the code is pretty much the same as before.

Listing 9-2. *The Program for the Remote-Controlled Robot (As Tribot)*

```
// I/O devices' ports
#define R_WHEEL OUT_B
#define L_WHEEL OUT_C
#define WHEELS OUT_BC
#define TOOL OUT_A

// position of the graphics onscreen
#define L_INFO_PX 25
#define R_INFO_PX 75

// possible speed values
#define SPEED1 (20)
#define SPEED2 (50)
#define SPEED3 (70)
#define SPEED4 (100)

// commands' constant definitions
#define STOP   0
#define FWD1   1
#define FWD2   2
#define FWD3   3
#define FWD4   4
#define REV1   5
#define REV2   6
#define REV3   7
#define REV4   8

// change this constant
// to get the robot going forward
// when getting a FWD command
// (allowed values are 1 or -1)
#define DIRECTION -1
```

```
// this function returns true if the
// Bluetooth connection with the robot exists,
// otherwise it displays some instructions
// and returns false
bool CheckBTConnection(int conn)
{
   bool connection_exists;
   if (BluetoothStatus(conn)==NO_ERR)
   {
      connection_exists = true;
   }
   else
   {
      ClearScreen();
      TextOut(0,LCD_LINE1,"You must connect");
      TextOut(0,LCD_LINE2,"this NXT on");
      TextOut(0,LCD_LINE3,"BT channel 1");
      TextOut(0,LCD_LINE4,"using the menu");
      TextOut(0,LCD_LINE5,"of the remote");
      TextOut(0,LCD_LINE6,"control NXT.");
      Wait(4000);
      connection_exists = false;
   }
   return connection_exists;
}

// this function converts the received command
// opcode into the corresponding motor speed
short DecodeSpeed(short cmd)
{
   short speed;
   if ( cmd == STOP ) speed = 0;
   if ( cmd == FWD1 ) speed = SPEED1;
   if ( cmd == FWD2 ) speed = SPEED2;
   if ( cmd == FWD3 ) speed = SPEED3;
   if ( cmd == FWD4 ) speed = SPEED4;
   if ( cmd == REV1 ) speed = -SPEED1;
   if ( cmd == REV2 ) speed = -SPEED2;
   if ( cmd == REV3 ) speed = -SPEED3;
   if ( cmd == REV4 ) speed = -SPEED4;
   return speed*sign(DIRECTION);
}

// this subroutine actuates the command received:
// if continuous is true, the TOOL motor is run
// while the remote buttons are pressed,
// if continuous is false, the TOOL motor is run stepping
```

```
// only if the function is different from the old one,
// which holds the preceding value of the function
sub Move(byte Lcmd, byte Rcmd, byte function, byte old, bool continuous)
{
    // float wheels if both Xcmd are equal to STOP
    if (Rcmd == STOP) Float(R_WHEEL);
    if (Lcmd == STOP) Float(L_WHEEL);
    if (Rcmd == Lcmd)
    {
        // if the speed of the wheels is the same,
        // run motors in sync
        OnFwdSync(WHEELS,DecodeSpeed(Rcmd),0);
    }
    else
    {
        // else run motor at the speed
        // given by the DecodeSpeed function
        OnFwd(R_WHEEL,DecodeSpeed(Rcmd));
        OnFwd(L_WHEEL,DecodeSpeed(Lcmd));
    }
    // if the commands can be continuous
    if (continuous)
    {
        switch (function)
        {
            case 0:
                Off(TOOL);
            break;
            case 1:
                OnFwd(TOOL,50);
            break;

            case 2:
                OnFwd(TOOL,100);
            break;

            case 3:
                OnRev(TOOL,100);
            break;
        }
    }
    // if the commands are one-shot
    else if (function!=old)
    {
```

```
        switch (function)
        {
            case 1:
                PlayTone(1000,10);
                RotateMotorPID(TOOL,100,180,50,30,70);
            break;

            case 2:
                PlayTone(2000,10);
                RotateMotorPID(TOOL,100,45,50,30,70);
            break;

            case 3:
                PlayFile("! Attention.rso");
                RotateMotorPID(TOOL,100,-360,50,30,70);
            break;
        }
    }
}

//  this subroutine displays information
// about the command received
sub ShowCommands(byte Lc, byte Rc, byte trig, short command)
{
    [...]
}

task main ()
{
    short command;
    byte Rcmd, Lcmd, function, oldfunction;
    if (!CheckBTConnection(0))
    {
        // if Bluetooth connection with remote control
        // is not established, stop the whole program
        Stop(true);
    }
    // loop forever
    while(true)
    {
        // if mailbox 1 is not empty, process command
        if (ReceiveRemoteNumber(1,true,command) != STAT_MSG_EMPTY_MAILBOX)
        {
            // decode the left command (100s)
            Lcmd = (command/100);
            // decode the right command (10s)
            Rcmd = (command/10)%10;
```

```
    // decode the function (1s)
    function = (command%10);
    // show various information onscreen
    ShowCommands(Lcmd,Rcmd,function,command);
    // actuate command
    Move(Lcmd,Rcmd,function,oldfunction,false);
    oldfunction = function;
  }
  Wait(50);
}
}
```

This program has only the main task running. At the beginning, it checks if the Bluetooth connection with the master exists (the connection numbered 0). The commands are received, decoded, and executed inside an infinite loop. If the condition if(ReceiveRemoteNumber(1,true,command) != STAT_MSG_EMPTY_MAILBOX) is true, that means that the mailbox contains something. If so, this something is put in the command variable. Unpacking the information from the received command is easy. It just takes a few lines of code, as follows:

```
    Rcmd = (command/10)%10;
    Lcmd = (command/100);
    function = (command%10);
```

The Rcmd (the speed level for the right wheel) is extracted by dividing the command by 10, and using the modulo operator (%) to take the remainder from the integer division of the number by 10. For example, consider the command 523: Divide it by 10, and it yields 52, and the modulo operation result is 2—exactly what you wanted. The speed level for the left wheel (Lcmd) is simply obtained by dividing the command by 100 into 523, and you get 5.

The function variable receives the code produced by the Touch Sensors pressed in the remote. The number is obtained by using the modulo operator (%) to get the remainder from the integer division by 10. For example, from 523 you get 3, because 10 is contained 52 times in 523, and 3 is the remainder. Once main has decoded these three variables, the functions ShowCommands() and Move() are invoked.

The Move function works straightforwardly. It uses the decoded variables to drive the motors in the following way: if both Rcmd and Lcmd are equal to STOP, the wheels are stopped. If these variables have the same value (different from STOP), the wheels are started with OnFwdSync by using 0 as a turning percentage, so the robot can proceed straight ahead. For any other value of these variables, the wheels are driven with the speed level returned by the DecodeSpeed function, which accepts the command code (a number from 0 to 8) as an argument, and returns one of the four speed levels defined at the top of the program. You can set the DIRECTION constant to 1 or -1, to get the robot going forward when receiving the command to go forward. This might seem obvious, but doesn't come free: the robot structure could vary from one robot to another, and the motors of the wheels could be placed so that the robot goes in reverse if they are running forward. So, you can change the DIRECTION constant to compensate for that inversion.

Finally, the program accomplishes the action corresponding to one of the three allowed values of the function variable by calling the Move subroutine. If the parameter continuous is true, the triggers can control the third motor in a continuous way: the motor runs until one of the triggers is pressed, and stops when it is released. If the parameter `continuous` is `false`, the third function is activated only once per trigger press, and the motor rotates only if the variable `old` is different from `function`. Because `old` holds the preceding value of the `function` variable, this trick allows you to avoid the machine-gun effect. The third motor action is performed only once when a trigger is pressed, so to repeat that action, you must release the trigger and then press it again.

This concludes the description of the simple version of the remote couple of programs. Next, you'll see how you can expand this basic program to feature multiple working modes.

Advanced Program

Complex multi-NXT robots such as JohnNXT have too many motors to be completely controlled with just two joysticks and two triggers. You would need more inputs to activate every feature. How should you do it with the hardware provided? The convenient position of the Touch Sensors is the answer. Your remote will have multiple working modes, activated sequentially by pressing them together.

At startup, the remote is in the basic mode. The joysticks control the motion of the wheels, or treads. The buttons, pressed one at a time, control the robot's other mechanisms. Pressing the two buttons together toggles the successive mode. In this mode, you can control different functions other than the ones of the first mode. You can design the program to have as many modes as you need.

Another problem remains if the robot to be controlled remotely uses multiple NXTs: if you connect the robot's NXTs using Bluetooth to exchange data, you would prevent the R/C from being used. This is because a limitation of the NXT firmware allows only one connection with a master at a time; also, an NXT is prevented from being both master and slave at the same time. For this reason, in JohnNXT, I connected the two NXTs using a standard 6-wire cable on port 4. This port is not just any input port: you can use it for high-speed serial communication with another NXT. Using this trick, the double NXT local system of JohnNXT is not using Bluetooth anymore, thus allowing you to use your remote.

You can slightly modify the preceding programs to expand a lot of your R/C capabilities. Let's see how, by starting from the sender program and continuing with the receiver program, as before. I'll discuss only the parts of code that differ from the preceding programs.

Advanced Sender Program (Remote Control)

Look at Listing 9-3. You can see the modified parts of the program running on the remote control NXT.

Listing 9-3. *The Advanced Sender Program, Omitting Similar Code from Before*

```
// include Bluetooth Autoconnection Library
#include "autoconnect.nxc"

[...]

// possible modes
#define MODE0 0
#define MODE1 1
```

```
#define MODE2 2
#define MODE3 3
#define MODE4 4
#define MODE5 5
#define MODE6 6
#define MODE7 7
#define MODE8 8
#define MODE9 9

// change MODE_LAST to set the number of modes:
// setting it to MODE1, the remote will have 2 modes
// setting it to MODE4, the remote will have 5 modes
// ...
// setting it to MODE9, the remote will have 10 modes
#define MODE_LAST MODE1

// joysticks' related global variables
int Lpos, Rpos, Lzero, Rzero;
mutex motor_sem;
byte mode = MODE0;

bool BTConnection(byte conn, const string name)
{
    [...]
}

[...]

inline sub ZeroJoyStick(byte port)
{
    [...]
}

// this function increases the mode value
// and resets it if it reaches the max allowed value
void ChangeMode()
{
    mode++;
    if (mode>MODE_LAST) mode = MODE0;
}

// this function returns
// 1 if right sensor is pressed,
// 2 if left sensor is pressed,
// 0 if both sensors are pressed, and changes mode
```

```
byte GetTriggers()
{
    byte triggers;
    // combine right and left sensor Boolean readings
    triggers = 2*Sensor(L_TOUCH) + Sensor(R_TOUCH);
    if (triggers == 3)
    {
        PlayFile("! Attention.rso");
        ChangeMode();
        triggers = 0;
        // wait for the user to release the triggers
        // to avoid machine-gun effect
        while(Sensor(L_TOUCH) || Sensor(R_TOUCH));
    }
    else return triggers;
}

short AngleToCommand (short pos)
{
    [...]
}

sub ShowCommands(byte Lc, byte Rc, byte trig)
{
    [...]
}

// this function builds the command to be sent
// encoding all the information in a single number
// and sends the command via Bluetooth
void SendCommand(byte Lcmd, byte Rcmd, byte triggers)
{
    short out;
            // 1000s: remote mode
            // 100s: analog channel 1
            // 10s: analog channel 2
            // 1s: digital channels 3 and 4
    out = mode*1000 + Lcmd*100 + Rcmd*10 + triggers;
    TextOut(0,LCD_LINE6,"                    ");
    NumOut(0,LCD_LINE6,out);
    SendRemoteNumber(BT_CONN,1,out);
}

task main()
{
    [...]
}
```

```
task RightJoystickLimit()
{
    [...]
}

task LeftJoystickLimit()
{
    [...]
}

task RemoteEngine()
{
    [...]
}
```

In the preceding listing, the code that is identical to the simple sender program has been omitted. Let's see how to give your remote multiple working modes. The GetTriggers function is the same as before, but in addition is responsible for mode changing. If both sensors are *pressed together*, GetTriggers does not activate any action in the robot, but it plays an acknowledgement sound and calls the ChangeMode() function. This last function simply increments the mode variable until it reaches the MODE_LAST value (here corresponding to MODE2). In this case, it is assigned the first mode's value. The mode variable is global, and initially assigned the MODE0 value. You can change the MODE_LAST definition, assigning the MODEx values, so you can have up to ten modes.

Now, let's see the new SendCommand function. To also include the information about the remote's actual mode, the out variable is now a four-digit number, where the thousands digit describes the mode. With 1 digit at your disposal, you can have 10 modes on your remote (from 0 to 9, sufficient for any big model). Nevertheless, you can choose to use a 5-digit number to support up to 100 modes (from 0 to 99). However, such a number is much exaggerated.

Advanced Receiver Program (JohnNXT)

The receiver program we're discussing is just a part of the whole JohnNXT master NXT program you saw in Chapter 8. The master JohnNXT program includes the code you see in Listing 9-4, as would normally be done with any header file, with the preprocessor statement #include "J5_remote.nxc".

Listing 9-4. *The Relevant Parts of the JohnNXT Remote Receiver Program*

```
#include "J5Defs.nxc"
#include "J5_sounds.nxc"
#include "J5_head.nxc"
#include "HSlib.nxc"
#include "J5_comm.nxc"

#define L_INFO_PX 20
#define R_INFO_PX 70
```

```
#define SPEED1 (25)
#define SPEED2 (50)
#define SPEED3 (80)
#define SPEED4 (100)

#define STOP   0
#define FWD1   1
#define FWD2   2
#define FWD3   3
#define FWD4   4
#define REV1   5
#define REV2   6
#define REV3   7
#define REV4   8

#define MODE0 0
#define MODE1 1

sub ShowCommands(byte Lcmd, byte Rcmd, byte triggers)
{
    [...]
}

// this function converts the received command
// opcode into the corresponding motor speed
short DecodeSpeed(short cmd)
{
   if ( cmd == STOP ) return 0;
   if ( cmd == FWD1 ) return SPEED1;
   if ( cmd == FWD2 ) return SPEED2;
   if ( cmd == FWD3 ) return SPEED3;
   if ( cmd == FWD4 ) return SPEED4;
   if ( cmd == REV1 ) return -SPEED1;
   if ( cmd == REV2 ) return -SPEED2;
   if ( cmd == REV3 ) return -SPEED3;
   if ( cmd == REV4 ) return -SPEED4;
}

// this function converts the received command
// opcode into the corresponding direction.
// This is handy for using joysticks as one-shot digital controls
short DecodeDir(short cmd)
{
   if ( cmd == STOP ) return 0;
   if ( cmd == FWD1 ) return 1;
   if ( cmd == FWD2 ) return 1;
   if ( cmd == FWD3 ) return 1;
```

```
    if ( cmd == FWD4 ) return 1;
    if ( cmd == REV1 ) return -1;
    if ( cmd == REV2 ) return -1;
    if ( cmd == REV3 ) return -1;
    if ( cmd == REV4 ) return -1;
}

// control movements of the first mode (treads and arms)
sub Mode_zero_actions(short Lcmd, short Rcmd, byte function)
{
    if (Rcmd == STOP) Float(R_TREAD);
    if (Lcmd == STOP) Float(L_TREAD);
    if (Rcmd == Lcmd)
    {
        OnRevSync(TREADS,DecodeSpeed(Rcmd),0);
    }
    else
    {
        OnRev(R_TREAD,DecodeSpeed(Rcmd));
        OnRev(L_TREAD,DecodeSpeed(Lcmd));
    }
    if ( function == 1 )
    {
        Remote(A_STEP_OPEN,ACK_DONE);
    }
    if ( function == 2 )
    {
        Remote(A_STEP_CLOSE,ACK_DONE);
    }
}

// these variables contain the old received commmand
// to avoid the machine-gun effect
byte Rold, Lold, Fold;

// this is a bi-stable state variable to toggle the laser
bool laser_FF;

// control movements of the second mode (head, torso, laser, and speech)
sub Mode_one_actions(byte Lcmd, byte Rcmd, byte function)
{
    // this macro (defined in J5Defs) clears a text line onscreen
    ClearLine(2);
    short R_action, L_action;
    // get the displacement direction of the joysticks
    R_action = DecodeDir(Rcmd);
    L_action = DecodeDir(Lcmd);
```

```
// activate one-shot movements, only if the actual Xaction value
// is different from before: this eliminates the machine-gun effect.
// To activate the same function again,
// you must release the trigger of the joystick.
if (R_action!=Rold)
{
    if (R_action>0)
    {
        TextOut(0,LCD_LINE2,"Head Left"); //R jstk fwd
        StepHead(RIGHT);
    }
    if (R_action<0)
    {
        TextOut(0,LCD_LINE2,"Head Right"); //R jstk rev
        StepHead(LEFT);
    }
}
if (L_action!=Lold)
{
    if (L_action>0)
    {
        TextOut(0,LCD_LINE2,"Raise Torso"); //L jstk fwd
        Remote(T_STEPUP,ACK_DONE);
    }
    if (L_action<0)
    {
        TextOut(0,LCD_LINE2,"Lower Torso"); //L jstk rev
        Remote(T_STEPDOWN,ACK_DONE);
    }
}
ClearLine(3);
if ( function==1 && function!=Fold)
{
    TextOut(0,LCD_LINE3,"Speech");
    // Play a random phrase without waiting for completion
    Sound(S_RANDOM,false);
}
if ( function==2 && function!=Fold)
{
    if ( laser_FF )
    {
        TextOut(0,LCD_LINE3,"Laser disarmed");
        Remote(L_OFF,ACK_DONE);
        Remote(L_UP,ACK_DONE);
    }
    else
    {
```

```
            TextOut(0,LCD_LINE3,"Laser armed  ");
            Remote(L_DOWN,ACK_DONE);
            Remote(L_ON,ACK_DONE);
        }
        laser_FF = !laser_FF;
    }
    // update the old commands
    Fold = function;
    Rold = R_action;
    Lold = L_action;
}

// this subroutine is called by JohnNXT master program
sub J5_Remote_Control()
{
    short Rcmd, Lcmd, function, mode;
    int command;
    head_state = UNKNOWN;
    Head(CENTER,1);
    laser_FF = false;
    bool exit = false;
    ClearScreen();
    TextOut(10,LCD_LINE1,"JohnNXT R/C");
    // repeat until the exit variable becomes true
    until (exit)
    {
        // if the Bluetooth buffer is not empty
        if (ReceiveRemoteNumber(1,true,command) != STAT_MSG_EMPTY_MAILBOX) {
                // decode command
                mode = (command/1000);
                Rcmd = (command/10)%10;
                Lcmd = (command/100)%10;
                function = (command%10);
            // move the robot according to the mode
            if (mode == MODE0)
            {
                ShowCommands(Lcmd,Rcmd,function);
                Mode_zero_actions(Lcmd,Rcmd,function);
            }
            if (mode == MODE1)
            {
                Mode_one_actions(Lcmd,Rcmd,function);
            }
        }
        Wait(50);
        // if the orange NXT button is pressed, exit is set to true,
        // and the next loop will be aborted
```

```
        if (ButtonPressed(BTNCENTER,true)) exit = true;
    }
    // wait for the orange button to be released
    while(ButtonPressed(BTNCENTER,true));
}
[...]
```

The receiver's main body is in the J5_Remote_Control() subroutine, which the JohnNXT master program calls using the JohnNXT menu (see Chapter 8). Here, the receiver loop does not run forever, but can be interrupted by pressing the NXT's orange button, so that you can exit the JohnNXT remote control mode and come back to its menu. You can implement this with an until loop, waiting for the exit Boolean variable to become true. The only way to make it true is to press the orange button:

```
if(ButtonPressed(BTNCENTER,true)) exit = true;
```

Here, you need slightly different code to extract the remote mode information from the received packet, which is formed by using a four-digit number:

```
        mode = (command/1000);
        Rcmd = (command/10)%10;
        Lcmd = (command/100)%10;
        function = (command%10);
```

As previously explained, mode assumes the value of the thousands digit, Rcmd assumes the tens digit value, Lcmd the hundreds, and function the unit's value. Then, the Mode_zero_actions or Mode_one_actions function is called, according to the value of the mode variable.

In the first mode, the joysticks control the treads, and the buttons make the arms step towards the open state (right trigger) or the closed state (left trigger). In the second mode, the right joystick drives the head, the left joystick drives the torso, the right trigger makes JohnNXT play a random sound, and the left trigger arms or disarms the laser. Remember that you can switch from one mode to another by pressing both triggers together.

In the simple program, the old variable avoided the machine-gun effect of the auxiliary function; here three variables Rold, Lold, and Fold are used to activate the one-shot functions. The one-shot actions are performed only if the actual function value is different from the value it had before, stored in one of those variables.

This is a particularly advanced receiver program, written to control all the JohnNXT features. In the following section, I'll show you a couple skeleton programs that you can use as you start to write your own custom remote sender/receiver programs.

Remote Control Template Programs

Now, I'll provide you with a sort of development guide to write custom sender and receiver programs. To speed up your work, you can copy and modify the skeleton programs that follow.

Sender Program Template

I start with the sender program that, while almost identical to the advanced sender program of Listing 9-3, is generalized in some aspects. The program runs on the remote NXT, so that the initial port definitions don't change. The only customizations you have to be concerned with are the number of modes you want your remote to have and the onscreen textual help for the remote user.

To set the maximum quantity of modes available, you can change the MODE_LAST definition that is found in the program header (see Listing 9-5). For example, if you plan for your remote to have five total modes, replace the definition with the following:

```
#define MODE_LAST MODE4
```

Otherwise, to have just two modes, leave the following definition:

```
#define MODE_LAST MODE1
```

Listing 9-5. *The Modes Definition in the Sender Program Header*

```
#define MODE0 0
#define MODE1 1
#define MODE2 2
#define MODE3 3
#define MODE4 4
#define MODE5 5
#define MODE6 6
#define MODE7 7
#define MODE8 8
#define MODE9 9
#define MODE_LAST MODE1  //<-----Change this one
```

The MODE_LAST constant is used by the ChangeMode() function (that is called in its turn by the GetTriggers() function), when both Touch Sensors are pressed together. The ChangeMode function code is shown in Listing 9-6 just to clarify the MODE_LAST constant function.

Listing 9-6. *The ChangeMode Function Called When Both Triggers Are Pressed*

```
void ChangeMode()
{
    mode++;
    if (mode>MODE_LAST) mode = MODE0;
}
```

The mode variable is a global one that is initialized to MODE0 at the beginning of the main task. Then, every time the ChangeMode function is called, the mode variable is incremented by one, and eventually reset back to MODE0, if the mode variable value has exceeded the MODE_LAST value. So, by setting MODE_LAST to MODE1, the mode variable will assume just the values MODE0 and MODE1. Because it will be incremented up to the MODE2 value (actually yielding 2), it will be changed back to MODE0. Got it? Now, Listing 9-7 shows the second customizable part of the program.

Listing 9-7. *Fill This Empty ShowCommands() Function Frame with Onscreen Contextual Help*

```
sub ShowCommands()
{
    // add text output on NXT screen to guide the user
    if (mode == MODE0)
    {
        //help for mode 0
    }
    if (mode == MODE1)
    {
        //help for mode 1
    }
    if (mode == MODE2)
    {
        //help for mode 2
    }
    //code to display the joystick position omitted
    [...]
}
```

The `ShowCommands()` function is called at every iteration of the infinite loop of the `JoySticksMonitor` task. On LCD line 2, it displays the arrows to indicate the current joysticks' position, so that you can exploit the rest of the display (lines 3 through 8) to write some short hints to help the user know what can be done in the actual remote mode.

You should use the `ClearLine(int line)` macro (defined in the file `J5Defs.nxc`) to clear only one line of the display at a time. For example, use `ClearLine(2)` to clear just the second line of the screen. Usually, it is better to use a macro such as this instead of the `ClearScreen()` NXC function to avoid erasing the other information that other subroutines or tasks could write on the screen. This way, you can clear just the line you are going to use. Recall that you can write text on the NXT screen by using the `TextOut(int x,int y,string text)` function, replacing the comments *//help for mode N*. You can also add other `if` blocks to manage all the modes that help the system (up to ten in this case).

Receiver Program Template

In the preceding program, there was little to change. The part that you can stir up is the receiver program. I'll describe how to customize this after having discussed the skeleton code in Listing 9-8.

Listing 9-8. *The Receiver Program Template to Be Customized*

```
// I/O devices' ports
#define R_WHEEL OUT_B
#define L_WHEEL OUT_C
#define WHEELS OUT_BC
#define TOOL OUT_A
#define BT_CONN 1
```

```
// position of the graphics onscreen
#define L_INFO_PX 25
#define R_INFO_PX 75

// possible speed values
#define SPEED1 (20)
#define SPEED2 (50)
#define SPEED3 (70)
#define SPEED4 (100)

// commands' constant definitions
#define STOP    0
#define FWD1    1
#define FWD2    2
#define FWD3    3
#define FWD4    4
#define REV1    5
#define REV2    6
#define REV3    7
#define REV4    8

// change this constant
// to get the robot going forward
// when getting a FWD command
// (allowed values are 1 or -1)
#define DIRECTION -1

// this function returns true if the
// Bluetooth connection with the robot exists,
// otherwise it displays some instructions
// and returns false
bool CheckBTConnection(int conn)
{
    [...]
}

// this function converts the received command
// opcode into the corresponding motor speed
short DecodeSpeed(short cmd)
{
    short speed;
    if ( cmd == STOP ) speed = 0;
    if ( cmd == FWD1 ) speed = SPEED1;
    if ( cmd == FWD2 ) speed = SPEED2;
    if ( cmd == FWD3 ) speed = SPEED3;
    if ( cmd == FWD4 ) speed = SPEED4;
    if ( cmd == REV1 ) speed = -SPEED1;
```

```
   if ( cmd == REV2 ) speed = -SPEED2;
   if ( cmd == REV3 ) speed = -SPEED3;
   if ( cmd == REV4 ) speed = -SPEED4;
   return speed*sign(DIRECTION);
}

// this function converts the received command
// opcode into the corresponding direction.
// This is handy for using joysticks as one-shot digital controls
short DecodeDir(short cmd)
{
   if ( cmd == STOP ) return 0;
   if ( cmd == FWD1 ) return 1;
   if ( cmd == FWD2 ) return 1;
   if ( cmd == FWD3 ) return 1;
   if ( cmd == FWD4 ) return 1;
   if ( cmd == REV1 ) return -1;
   if ( cmd == REV2 ) return -1;
   if ( cmd == REV3 ) return -1;
   if ( cmd == REV4 ) return -1;
}

// this subroutine actuates the command received
// * if continuous is true, the TOOL motor is run
// while the remote buttons are pressed,
// * if continuous is false, the TOOL motor is run stepping
sub Mode0Actions(byte Lc, byte Rc, byte fun, bool continuous)
{
   // float wheels if both Xc are equal to STOP
   if (Rc == STOP) Float(R_WHEEL);
   if (Lc == STOP) Float(L_WHEEL);
   if (Rc == Lc)
   {
      // if the speed of the wheels is the same,
      // run motors in sync
      OnFwdSync(WHEELS,DecodeSpeed(Rc),0);
   }
   else
   {
      // else run motor at the speed
      // given by the DecodeSpeed function
      OnFwd(R_WHEEL,DecodeSpeed(Rc));
      OnFwd(L_WHEEL,DecodeSpeed(Lc));
   }
   // if the commands can be continuous
   if (continuous)
   {
```

```
        switch (fun)
        {
            case 0:
                Off(TOOL);
            break;
            case 1:
                OnFwd(TOOL,50);
            break;

            case 2:
                OnRev(TOOL,100);
            break;
        }
    }
    // if the commands are one-shot
    else
    {
        switch (fun)
        {
            case 1:
                PlayTone(1000,10);
                RotateMotorPID(TOOL,100,180,50,30,70);
            break;

            case 2:
                PlayTone(2000,10);
                RotateMotorPID(TOOL,100,-360,50,30,70);
            break;
        }
    }
}

// these are a kind of state variables to allow the one-shot
// functions' activation (avoid machine-gun effect)
short oldRf,oldLf;

// similar to Mode0Actions, but you can use joysticks
// to perform one-shot functions, as you do with the triggers

sub Mode1Actions(byte Lc, byte Rc, byte fun, bool continuous)
{
    short R_action, L_action;
    R_action = DecodeDir(Rc);
    L_action = DecodeDir(Lc);
    // function activated by the right joystick
    // can be one-shot or continuous
    if ( (R_action!=oldRf) || continuous )
```

```
    {
       if (R_action>0)
       {
          PlayTone(1000,10);
       }
       if (R_action<0)
       {
          PlayTone(1500,10);
       }
    }
    // function activated by the left joystick
    // can be one-shot or continuous
    if ( (L_action!=oldLf) || continuous )
    {
       if (L_action>0)
       {
          PlayTone(2000,10);
       }
       if (L_action<0)
       {
          PlayTone(3000,10);
       }
    }
    oldRf = R_action;
    oldLf = L_action;

    // if the commands can be continuous
    if (continuous)
    {
       switch (fun)
       {
          case 0:
             Off(TOOL);
          break;
          case 1:
             OnFwd(TOOL,50);
          break;

          case 2:
             OnRev(TOOL,50);
          break;
       }
    }
    // if the commands are one-shot
    else
    {
       switch (fun)
```

```
        {
            case 1:
                RotateMotorPID(TOOL,100,180,50,30,70);
            break;

            case 2:
                RotateMotorPID(TOOL,100,-360,50,30,70);
            break;
        }
    }
}


sub Mode2Actions(byte Lc, byte Rc, byte fun, bool continuous)
{
  // ...
}


//  this subroutine displays information
// about the command received
sub ShowCommands(byte Lc, byte Rc, byte trig, byte command, byte mode)
{
    [...]
}

task main ()
{
    short command;
    byte Rcmd, Lcmd, function, mode;
    if (!CheckBTConnection(0))
    {
        // if Bluetooth connection with remote control
        // is not established, stop the whole program
        Stop(true);
    }
    // loop forever
    while(true)
    {
        // if the mailbox 1 is not empty, process command
        if (ReceiveRemoteNumber(1,true,command) != STAT_MSG_EMPTY_MAILBOX)
        {
            // decode remote control working mode (1000s)
            mode = (command/1000);
            // decode the left command (100s)
            Rcmd = (command/10)%10;
            // decode the right command (10s)
            Lcmd = (command/100)%10;
            // decode the function (1s)
```

```
        function = ((command%1000)%100)%10;
        // show various information onscreen
        ShowCommands(Lcmd,Rcmd,function,command,mode);
        // actuate commands

        switch(mode)
        {
            case 0:    Mode0Actions(Lcmd,Rcmd,function,true);   break;
            case 1:    Mode1Actions(Lcmd,Rcmd,function,false);  break;
        // case 2:    Mode2Actions(Lcmd,Rcmd,function,false);  break;
        //   ...
        // case 9:    Mode9Actions(Lcmd,Rcmd,function,false);  break;
        }
    }
    Wait(50);
  }
}
```

Now, let's proceed in order. At the top of the program, you can edit the port alias definitions and the DIRECTION constant to fit your particular robot's hardware configuration. Also, you can change the four speed levels. The main task checks if the Bluetooth connection with the master exists (connection number 0); if so, it enters the infinite loop that checks for incoming commands and dispatches them. After the command has been unpacked, the Rcmd, Lcmd, function, and mode variables are filled with the values sent by the remote. According to the mode variable value, different subroutines are called inside the switch structure. For example, if mode is equal to MODE0, then Mode0Actions is called. You can add other routines as Mode1Actions and so on (up to Mode9Actions, because the total number of available modes is ten). Of course, you can also use more imaginative names for your routines!

Inside the Mode0Actions routine (meant to be the default one), the wheels are driven as in the Move() subroutine of the simple program in Listing 9-2. Also, the two functions can be activated by pressing the two Touch Sensors on the remote control.

The other subroutines, from Mode1Actions to Mode9Actions(), have a similar structure. The joysticks, which control the wheels in the MODE0, can be used in the other modes to activate other functions than the wheel movement, as you do with the triggers. However, you can plan to use the multiple modes to change just the triggers' functions, and to have the joysticks always control the wheels. If you're going to use the joysticks to trigger discrete functions (that don't need the "analog" feature), you'll want to avoid a machine-gun effect. In other words, you should wait for the joystick to be released and centered before triggering another action, just like you did before for the triggers.

Listing 9-9 shows the code excerpt of the solution adopted in the Mode1Actions subroutine to avoid the machine-gun effect for the right joystick. You can read the similar code for the left joystick in Listing 9-8.

Listing 9-9. *Avoiding Machine-Gun Effects When Using Joysticks to Trigger Discrete Commands*

```
R_action = DecodeDir(R_cmd);
if ( (R_action!=oldRf) || continuous )
{
   if (R_action>0)
   {
      //do something
   }
   if (R_action<0)
   {
      //do something else
   }
}
oldRf = R_action;
```

First, the DecodeDir function calculates the direction of the joystick displacement (the right one in the example), by returning just 1, 0, or -1 and not a speed level. Then, the action corresponding to the joystick inclination is performed only if the actual R_action is different from the one saved before in the oldRf variable, and updated with the current R_action value only after the desired action has been performed. This way, no action will be retriggered until the joystick has returned to its center position, so that the DecodeDir function will return a value different from before. Notice that, if the continuous variable is true, the logical OR || function will force the whole condition ((R_action!=oldRf) || continuous) to be true, and some action will be performed anyway, no matter if R_action is equal to oldRf or not.

For example, if the right joystick is moved forward, the DecodeDir function will return 1, thus triggering the action inside the if(R_action>0) {...} block. This block becomes unreachable if the (R_action!=R_old) condition is false, until the joystick does not return to its center (DecodeDir thus returns 0). This trick is necessary because the Mode1Actions function is called about 20 times per second—notice that the loop calls Wait(50)—and not only when the joysticks are moved. That said, you should now know how to bend the receiver program's template to your will.

Building the Remote Control

Now let's get building! The construction is simple, because it just uses a bunch of parts from the NXT retail set. You need two NXT retail sets to build the robot and the R/C. To build the remote shown here, you need an extra Touch Sensor and an extra 20cm (8 inch) cable. You can replace the extra short cable with a longer spare one you have in the set.

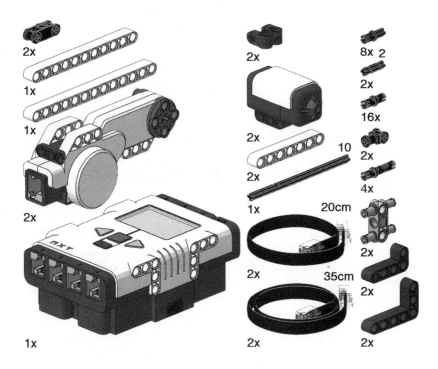

Figure 9-3. *The Bluetooth remote bill of materials*

Table 9-1. *The Bluetooth Remote Bill of Materials*

Quantity	Color	Part Number	Part Name
2	Black	32184.DAT	TECHNIC Axle Joiner Perpendicular 3L
1	White	32525.DAT	TECHNIC Beam 11
1	White	41239.DAT	TECHNIC Beam 13
2		53787.DAT	Electric MINDSTORMS NXT Motor
1		53788.DAT	Electric MINDSTORMS NXT
2	Dark gray	41678.DAT	TECHNIC Axle Joiner Perpendicular Double Split
2	Dark gray	53793.DAT	Electric MINDSTORMS NXT Touch Sensor
2	White	32524.DAT	TECHNIC Beam 7
1	Black	3737.DAT	TECHNIC Axle 10
2		55804.DAT	Electric Cable NXT 20cm
2		55805.DAT	Electric Cable NXT 35cm
8	Blue	43093.DAT	TECHNIC Axle Pin with Friction
2	Black	32062.DAT	TECHNIC Axle 2 Notched
16	Black	2780.DAT	TECHNIC Pin with Friction and Slots
2	Black	32039.DAT	TECHNIC Connector with Axlehole
4	Black	6558.DAT	TECHNIC Pin Long with Friction and Slot
2	Light gray	48989.DAT	TECHNIC Axle Joiner Perpendicular 1×3×3 with 4 Pins
2	Dark gray	32140.DAT	TECHNIC Beam 5 Liftarm Bent 90 (4:2)
2	Dark gray	32526.DAT	TECHNIC Beam 7 Bent 90 (5:3)

56 parts total (all included in NXT retail set, except for one Touch Sensor and one 20cm cable)

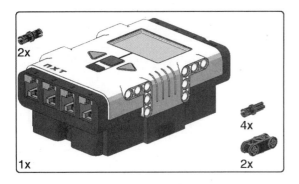

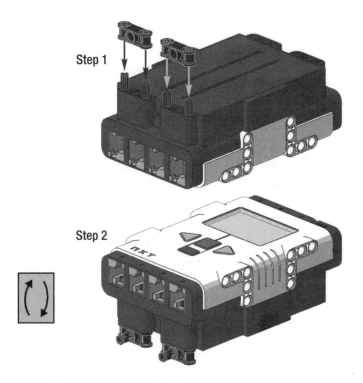

Step 1

Step 2

Rotate the NXT upside down and attach the black joiners to the blue axle pins. Rotate the NXT and add two black pins.

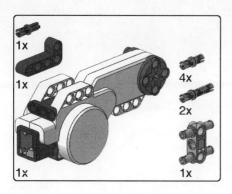

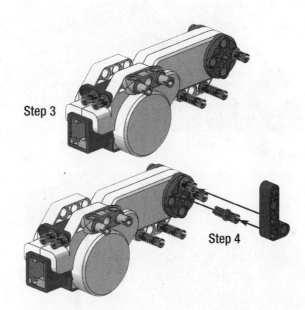

Step 3

Step 4

Start building the left joystick control. You must insert two pins in the holes in the back of the motor. Then attach two black pins, a blue axle pin, and the lever to the motor shaft.

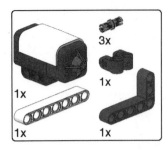

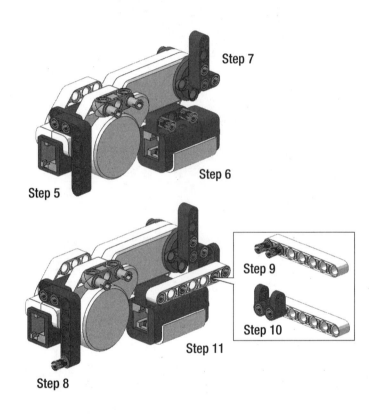

Add a Touch Sensor and the blocking beam subassembly.

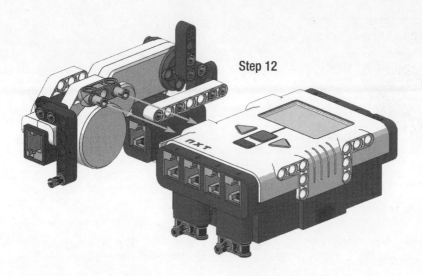

Step 12

Connect the left control to the NXT.

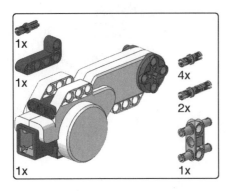

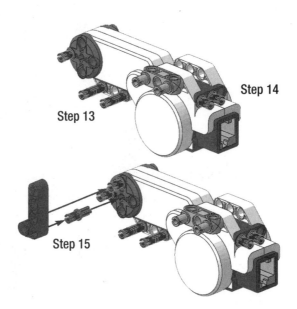

Start building the right joystick control. You must insert two pins in the holes in the back of the motor. Then attach two black pins, a blue axle pin, and the lever to the motor shaft.

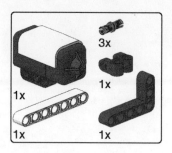

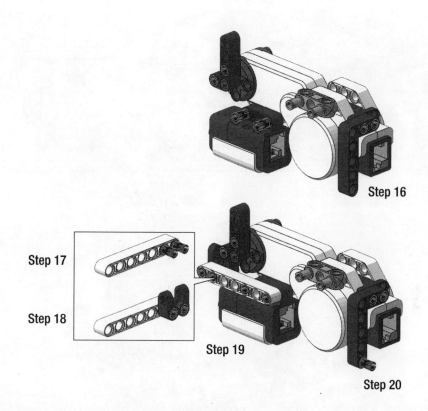

Add another Touch Sensor and the blocking beam subassembly.

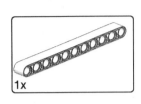

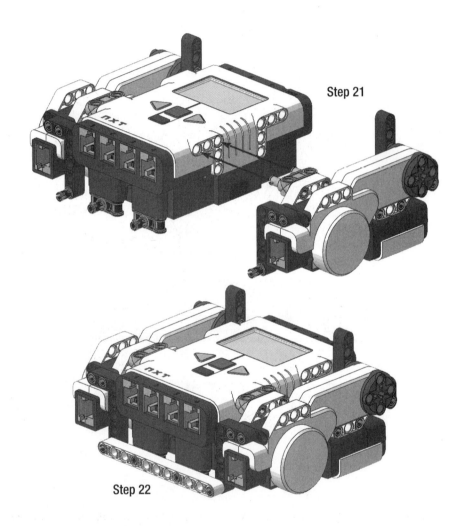

Step 21

Step 22

Connect the right control to the NXT. Attach an 11 holes-long beam to hold the controls together with the NXT. Notice that here the cross-bracing technique is used.

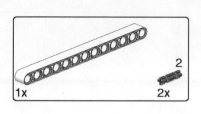

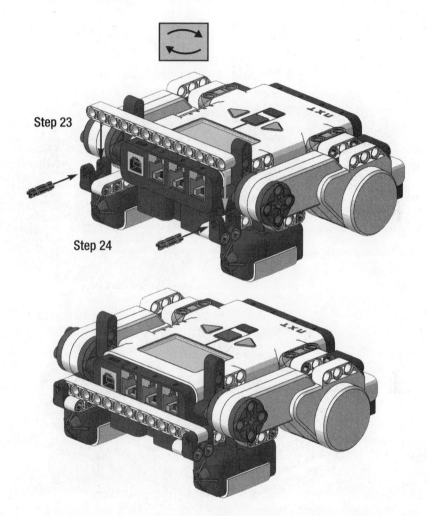

Rotate the whole model, insert a 13-long beam into the perpendicular joiners, and attach it by inserting two 2-long axles.

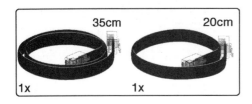

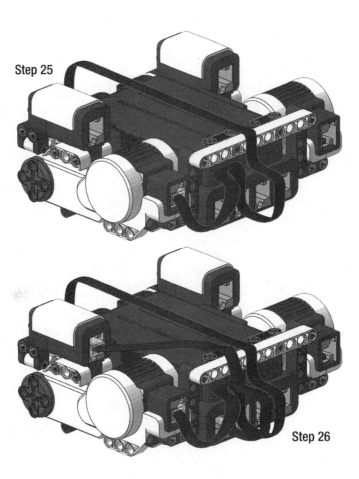

Rotate the model upside down and attach the right motor to NXT output port C with a 35cm (14 inch) cable. Attach the right Touch Sensor to NXT input port 4 with a 20cm (8 inch) cable.

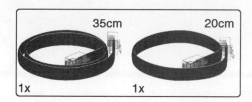

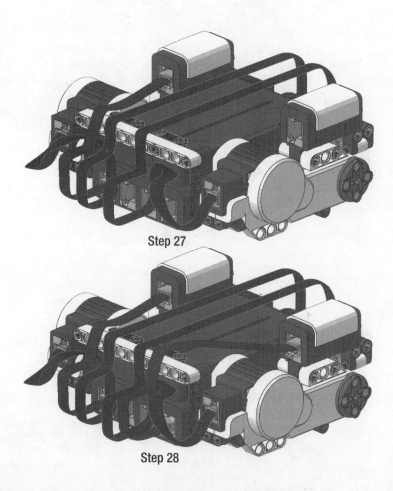

Step 27

Step 28

Rotate the model and attach the left motor to NXT output port A with a 35cm (14 inch) cable. Attach the left Touch Sensor to NXT input port 1 with a 20cm (8 inch) cable.

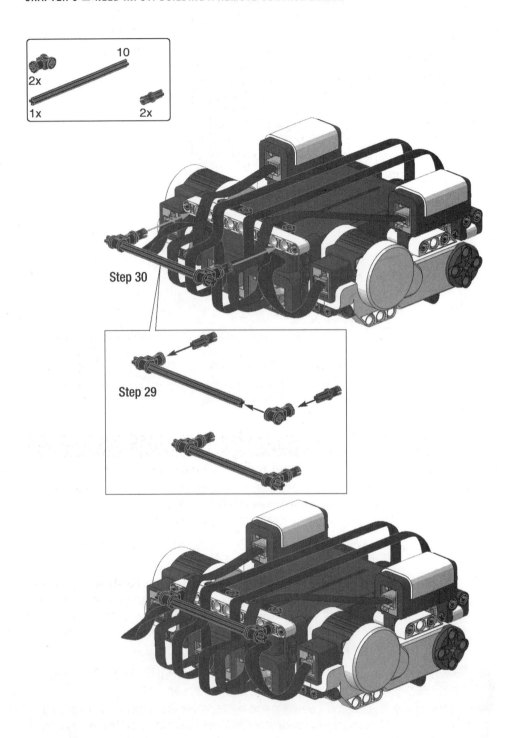

Add the bar subassembly to contain the cables.

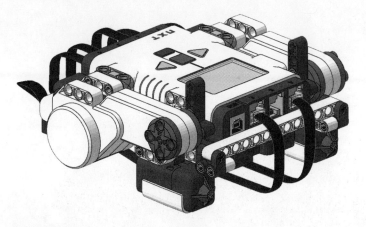

The remote is completed.

Summary

In this chapter, you learned how to send your robots remote input. In particular, I described the remote control system of JohnNXT (kept in suspense from Chapter 8). You saw how to create a self-centering mechanism by using the NXT servomotors, instead of using rubber bands or springs. In addition, you also have two template programs to use for any custom remote-controlled robot you could imagine.

Exercise 9-1. Further Ideas

As stated at the beginning of the chapter, you can use the R/C to command many of the robots discussed in this book. For example, try modifying the template programs to control the following robots remotely, by looking at the following suggestions. Usually, the sender program does not need many modifications. On the contrary though, you should modify the receiver program and integrate it with care in the other existing programs:

- You can just drive Quasimodo straight at different speeds, and you can use the other controls to make it play sounds.

- The AT-ST receiver program is quite a challenge to modify! You should integrate the AT-ST walking routines seen in Chapter 4 with the receiver program template. Also, you should adopt a semaphore system to make the robot finish its current walking routine before performing the new received action. Because the robot can only walk and turn forward, you could use the triggers instead of the joysticks to pilot the movements, and the robot will walk while you keep them pressed.

- Omni-Biped is another nontrivial robot to control. The receiver program should behave like the AT-ST one, waiting for the legs' realignment before starting a turn (see Chapter 5).

- The NXT Turtle is simple to control: the rows of legs work just like wheels of a differential drive robot, and the head is a mechanism that can have two stable states (in or out), ideal to be controlled with remote triggers, like the JohnNXT laser.

- The Mine Sweeper is a wheeled robot, so it is the simplest to control remotely. Use the remote triggers to grab and release objects.

■ ■ ■

Introduction to BricxCC and NXC Programming

This appendix is a tutorial about Bricx Command Center (BricxCC), the IDE (Integrated Development Environment) that is used to write, compile, and test the NXC programs in this book. This IDE is handy, because it includes many utilities for the LEGO programmable bricks and for the NXT in particular: a file browser, a sound converter to translate WAV files into RSO files, a panel to monitor the brick's sensors and outputs, a screen-capture utility, and so on.

The BricxCC program was originally written by Mark Overmars, and is now magnificently maintained and improved by John Hansen, who is also the creator of the NXC language. BricxCC was born as the IDE to write Not Quite C (NQC) programs for the RCX, so it inherits many features of the NQC language, created by Dave Baum. Through the years, many new functions have been built inside BricxCC, to let it manage the new NXC language and the NXT brick itself. I worked together with John Hansen to produce an NXC language tutorial that is now available on the Web. My tutorial, together with the well-done NXC programming guide by John Hansen, makes a comprehensive manual to learn this textual programming language for the NXT.

I learned NXC using that guide, and I have also made contributions to fix some of the Bluetooth API functions. Many people worldwide have already started writing NXC programs successfully by reading my tutorial. I suggest that you read it too, to learn the basics of NXC.

Given that this tutorial is not made to replace the BricxCC guide (to which you must refer for the doubts that could arise), let's get started! You should download and install the *latest release* of BricxCC that now includes a built-in version of the NeXT Byte Codes (NBC) compiler.

You can find the following information and software online:

- All the software needed to get started at http://bricxcc.sourceforge.net/

- The NXC manual at http://bricxcc.sourceforge.net/nbc/nxcdoc/NXC_Guide.pdf

- My tutorial at http://bricxcc.sourceforge.net/nbc/nxcdoc/NXC_tutorial.pdf

First, I'll show you how to write, compile, and download your first NXC program to the NXT, using BricxCC. Next, I'll briefly analyze the BricxCC menu functions, followed by tracking the advanced NXT-dedicated utilities.

Getting Connected with BricxCC

Here, I assume you've already used the LEGO NXT-G programming software, so you know how to rename your NXT and how to make and download simple NXT-G programs. Also, I assume you have the NXT turned on and connected to the PC via USB (later I'll explain how to use Bluetooth). Open BricxCC by double-clicking its desktop icon or by clicking the icon installed in the Start menu.

At startup, the Find Brick form shows up (see Figure A-1). This dialog asks which kind of brick you're going to use (notice that BricxCC can manage all kinds of programmable bricks produced by LEGO through the years), and how the brick should be connected.

Figure A-1. *The Find Brick form that shows up when you open BricxCC*

To use the NXT, you must first choose NXT from the drop-down list at the right, and Automatic from the left drop-down list. You don't have to worry about the Firmware radio buttons, because these options are meant for the RCX. Click OK and the IDE should find the brick; if everything went fine, no error message appears and the toolbar icons are lit up with their normal colors (otherwise they would look grayed—compare Figures A-2 and A-3).

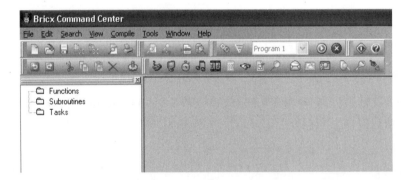

Figure A-2. *The BricxCC IDE with buttons enabled, when the NXT is connected*

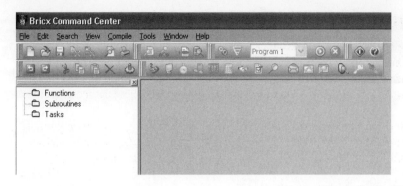

Figure A-3. *The BricxCC IDE with buttons disabled, meaning no brick is connected*

Connecting the NXT via Bluetooth is a bit more complicated. Follow these steps to get connected without encountering any problems:

1. Be sure to have Bluetooth enabled on your laptop or a Bluetooth dongle connected and correctly installed on your PC. Also, make sure you have your NXT brick turned on, with Bluetooth on and visible. When choosing the settings in the Find Brick form (see Figure A-1 again), select Automatic as before, and check the Bluetooth check box. Then click OK. BricxCC starts searching for Bluetooth-enabled NXTs, but it will eventually hang.

   Don't lose heart! Go on with the steps that, once done, let BricxCC find your NXT fast.

Caution This step of the procedure might cause BricxCC to hang up. So, you need to force it to close by pressing Ctrl+Alt+Del, which terminates the process from the Task Manager.

---

2. You must introduce every NXT you're going to use to your PC by using the Bluetooth Devices dialog (a feature present in Windows XP) once you have a Bluetooth dongle installed. To make them meet each other, open the Bluetooth Devices panel from the Control Panel or by double-clicking the icon you should have among the tray icons in the Windows application bar at the bottom of the screen, near the clock.

   In Figure A-4, you can see how my Bluetooth Devices dialog looks. You might have some items in yours, or none.

Figure A-4. *The Bluetooth Devices dialog in Windows XP*

3. Click the Add button in the lower left of the panel and follow the instructions to make your NXT meet the PC and exchange greetings (see Figures A-5 and A-6). In those screens, click Next to proceed.

Figure A-5. *The first step of the Add Bluetooth Device Wizard*

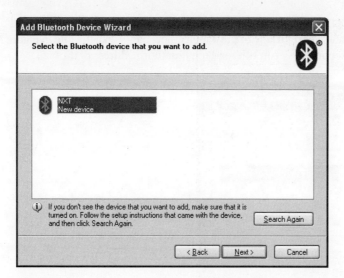

Figure A-6. *The Wizard found a new NXT device (named NXT).*

4. You're then asked for a passkey. Just type in **1234**—the default for any NXT brick (see Figure A-7)—and click Next. Finally, click Finish in the last screen. At this point, your NXT (with the name you gave it) should be listed in the Bluetooth Devices (Devices tab).

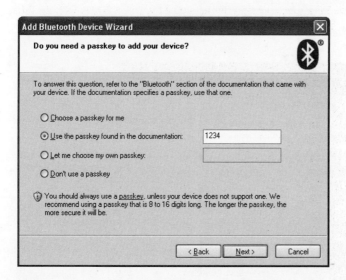

Figure A-7. *In this step of the Add Bluetooth Device Wizard, you must type in the passkey.*

5. Next, select the NXT name just added to the list (NXT in Figure A-8), and click the Properties button in the lower right side of the panel. A new panel (like the one in Figure A-9) shows up. In the second line, you can read the Bluetooth address of the NXT.

Figure A-8. *The Bluetooth Devices dialog shows the newly connected NXT.*

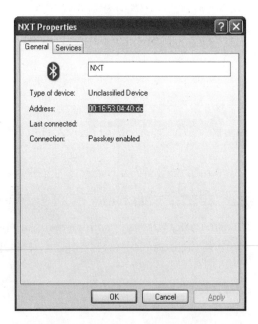

Figure A-9. *The NXT Properties, where you can copy its address*

6. Now, select and copy the address with Ctrl+C. Then, close this dialog by clicking OK. In the Bluetooth Devices dialog, select the COM Ports tab and make note of the COM port number of your NXT that's marked as incoming (COM4 in Figure A-10).

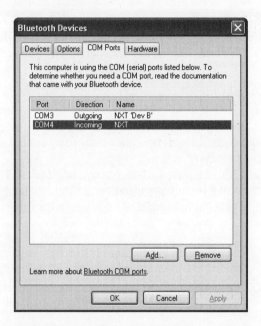

Figure A-10. *The NXT device's allotted COM ports*

7. Now, open the file browser by pressing Windows+E, and browse to the BricxCC install folder (for example, C:\Program Files\BricxCC\). Here, you should find a file named nxt.dat; if not, create it. Open it with Notepad or any other text editor you prefer. Add the following line to this file:

`alias = BTH::nxt_name::bt_address::com_port`

You have to fill in the preceding fields like so:

- `alias`: The name you desire for your NXT to be shown in the BricxCC Find the Brick drop-down list

- `nxt_name`: The NXT brick name as shown in the Bluetooth Devices Peripherals tab

- `bt_address`: The hexadecimal address you copied before from the Properties panel

- `com_port`: The input COM port you noted before

8. Be careful to put the double colon :: in the right places. For example, my entry looks like this:

`NXT_BT = BTH::NXT::00:16:53:04:40:dc::4`

9. Save and close this file; also close the file browser and the Bluetooth Devices dialog. If you have BricxCC open, close it and reopen it. Now, you should find the newly connected NXT in the left drop-down list in the Find Brick form. Click OK and BricxCC will get connected to your NXT in just a few seconds.

It was laborious, but your efforts will be repaid! This time it takes just a moment to connect your NXT via Bluetooth. You can repeat the whole procedure to add all the NXT devices you want. At this point, you are online with your brick. Let me show you what can be done now.

Ready to Go

The IDE's main form should be empty and the toolbar buttons filled with their colors (meaning you are connected to the NXT). You can usually do every operation in three equivalent ways: using a keyboard shortcut, a menu item, or a toolbar button.

You can create a new file in many ways: you can press Ctrl+N, you can select File ➤ New from the menu, or you can just click the "New file" button on the toolbar. An untitled file is then created; you can now double-click the file's title bar to expand it. Now type in the following trivial NXC program:

```
task main ()
{
    TextOut (10,LCD_LINE4,"Hello, World!");
    Wait (SEC_2);
}
```

You can save the file by pressing Ctrl+S, or by selecting File ➤ Save, or by clicking the "Save file" icon on the toolbar (the third icon from the left—the one showing the floppy disk). You're then asked for a name and location to save the file. Name it tutorial1.nxc and save it wherever you want by clicking OK. Now that your file has the NXC extension, you can compile it. To do this, you can press F5, or select Compile ➤ Compile from the menu, or click the "Compile program" button on the toolbar. If no compile error occurs, nothing visible will happen. BricxCC can compile the program using the right compiler (NBC, in this case) corresponding to the program file extension and the initial connection settings. The latest BricxCC release has a built-in NBC compiler, so the external one using the DOS shell won't be used. You can enable this built-in compiler by opening the Preferences dialog (Edit Preferences toolbar button, or Edit ➤ Preferences from the menu). Now go to the Compiler tab and select the NXC/NBC subtab; check the "Use internal compiler" box. Just to be sure about which version you are using, click the Version button. You should have at least NBC compiler version 1.0.1.34. Because you are here, select the 0 Optimization level from the drop-down menu (no optimization), and click OK.

The program is now ready to be downloaded to the NXT. To download it without starting it, press F6, or select Compile ➤ Download, or click the Download button. To download and start it at once, press Ctrl+F5, or select Compile ➤ Download and Run from the menu. The appropriate toolbar button to start the program isn't missing, of course!

The NXT should beep and start the program that simply shows the text (traditional for programming tutorials) "Hello, World!" You can find other commands to start and stop the program in the same Compile menu. If you ever feel lost, just hover the mouse on a toolbar icon to get the pop-up tip, or consult the BricxCC online guide. I leave to you the exercise of opening an existing file, because it is a simple activity. What's been discussed up until now should be enough to open, compile, and download to the NXT any program that comes with this book.

BricxCC Menu

Now you'll take just a fleeting glance at the text editing capabilities of the BricxCC IDE. I'll introduce briefly the menu items, starting from the left. Remember that almost any function is also reachable from the toolbar buttons.

- *File menu*: From here, you can create, open, save, save as, or close the files. BricxCC also allows you to print your listings. At the bottom of the menu, you can find the handy list of recently opened files.

- *Edit menu*: As in any text editor, here you find the undo and redo functions, as well as the cut, copy, and paste ones. The Copy special feature allows you to copy not just the text, but also the formatting, including fonts, colors, and bold and italic shaping. You use the "Next field" function (F10) to highlight the next text inside quotation marks. You can use this feature together with the Templates (F9) to speed up the program writing. Double-clicking an item in the template panel puts the corresponding skeleton code into your file. For example, by double-clicking the Programs ➤ Task item from the Template panel, you get the skeleton code of a task. Also, pressing F10 highlights the "name" and "body" fields, to replace the code promptly. Finally, you can open the Preferences panel from the Edit menu.

- *Search menu*: From here, you can find and replace text in your program (as you would do in any other text editor). Also, you can go to a precise line number or open the procedure list.

- *View menu*: You use this menu to toggle the visibility of all the panels and toolbars of the IDE. A useful window is the Code/Error listing (F12). Here, you can see the translated assembly code of your compiled program (if successfully compiled) or the exact lines where the compiler found errors, if any.

- *Compile menu*: I already described this menu earlier. From here, you can compile, download, start, and stop your program.

- *Tools menu*: This menu is worth the whole next section.

- *Window menu*: Here, you can arrange the subwindows, and even save and load their position.

- *Help menu*: From here, you can open the online guide; the old NQC guide; the About box; and the official BricxCC web page, where you can get updates, samples, and documents.

BricxCC Tools

The tools are what make the BricxCC IDE so special and precious. The tools for the NXT are made by John Hansen, so thanks to him again! Many utilities are provided, so let's see them in order:

- *Direct Control*: Here, you can turn motors on and off in both directions at any speed. This utility is meant to be used for debugging purposes. You use the Sensors dialog to set the sensors' type and mode of working.

- *Diagnostics*: This utility tells you all information available about the NXT connected: the firmware version, the battery voltage, the way the NXT is connected to the PC (USB or Bluetooth), its name, its Bluetooth address (remember the preceding procedure?), the free amount of memory in bytes, and so on.

- *Watching the Brick*: This utility is a fully comprehensive dialog from which you can get information about the NXT sensor readings, the servomotor parameters, messages, and more. You can even trace graphs of a monitored event!

- *Brick Piano*: The musicians among you can use this tool to write melodies for any programmable brick and export the code to play the tune just composed.

- *Joystick*: With this tool, you can control a differential drive robot (such as Tribot, JohnNXT, or the Turtle of this book). You can also drive a steering vehicle around, with one motor driving the wheels and the other turning the steering.

- *Configurable Watch*: This tool has a similar function to the Watching the Brick panel, except that you have to manually add the monitors of the chosen sources.

- *NXT Explorer*: This tool is a file browser for the NXT flash memory. Here, you can manage the files, upload and download them, delete them to free space, and even defragment the memory. From here, you can play a selected sound file, or you can start a compiled program (with the RXE extension).

- *NXT Screen*: This utility allows you to visualize and capture the content of the NXT screen on your PC. It is useful for having a look at an unreachable NXT screen, or for pressing the NXT buttons remotely.

- *MIDI Conversion and Sound Conversion*: These tools are used to convert a MIDI file or a WAV file into a piece of code or into an RSO file, respectively. Before converting a WAV file, you should resample it to get a mono (only one channel), 8-bit 8KHz file. You can compress the RSO file to save space on the NXT, but only firmware 1.05 or later can read it.

- *Find Brick/Turn Brick Off/Close Communication*: The functionality of these items is self-explanatory. Find Brick opens the startup panel where you can choose how to connect the NXT, while Close Communication releases the connection and corresponding drivers. You can guess what the Turn Brick Off function does.

- *Download Firmware*: This tool allows you to update the NXT firmware. You have to browse to find it. A probable place can be C:\Program Files\LEGO Software\LEGO MINDSTORMS NXT\engine\Firmware\.

- *Configure Tools*: Here, you can set up BricxCC to execute macros and external programs.

Perhaps some utility has been left out of the preceding discussion. However, these are the most important at the time of writing this tutorial.

Summary

Now, you should have an idea of how to use the BricxCC IDE to open, compile, and download the programs' source code provided with this book. You should also know how to write your own programs, and monitor the NXT screen, motors, and sensors.

In this appendix, you also learned a useful procedure to connect the NXT via Bluetooth quickly. You also learned how an appropriate WAV file (8KHz, 8 bit, mono) can become an RSO sound file that the NXT loudspeaker can play.

Index

Symbols & Numerics

& (ampersand) before argument name, 147

   & (bitwise AND operator), 528

&& (AND Boolean operator), 213

{} (braces) in NXC code, 23

#define directive, 63

/* */ (forward slash, asterisk, asterisk, forward slash) comments in NXC code, 24

// (forward slash, forward slash) commented line in NXC code, 23

#include "NXCDefs.h" statement, 22

% (modulo operator), 152

! (negation Boolean operator), 23, 213

|| (OR Boolean operator), 213

; (semicolon) in NXC code, 23

A

Acquire (mutex_name) statement, 147

actions, associating conditions with, 57

actuators, JohnNXT, 354–356

Add Bluetooth Device Wizard, 570–572

Advanced COG Biped, 9

aesthetic add-ons, AT-ST, 74

aligning cams horizontally, 12

AlignRightLeg() task, Omni-Biped multitask program, 161

All Terrain Armored Transport (AT-AT), 60

All Terrain Scout Transport. *See* AT-ST

Alpha Rex, history of, 144

ampersand (&) before argument name, 147

AND operator (&&), 213

ankles

   reinforcers for, AT-ST, 86

   rotating, motorized, 9

arguments, macro and, 63

arms

   JohnNXT, 465–469, 474–478

   Mine Sweeper, 282–284, 309–316

   Omni-Biped, 197

   robotic, decision table to manage, 56–58

Arms Control mode (JohnNXT), 356–360

associating conditions with actions, 57

asynchronous protocol, 358

AT-AT (All Terrain Armored Transport), 60

AT-ST (All Terrain Scout Transport)

   ankle reinforcers, 86

   bill of materials, 74

building, 71–74, 141

cannons for, 136

description of, 7, 59–60

early prototype of, 61

face, 135–137

feet

   external, 87

   foot blades, 90

   foot pads, 88

   internal, 89

head

   attaching to neck, 125–128

   link to hold, 139

   NXT as, 124

   Sound Sensor assembly for, 132

   Touch Sensor assembly for, 130

   Ultrasonic Sensor assembly for, 134

hips

   decorative parts of, building, 77

   left, building, 75

in jerky COG shifting category, 62

leg beams, 84

legs

   beam to hold firmly, 120

   black spots on, 83

   building, 78

   decorative parts of, building, 80–82

   hip assembly and, 85

   inserting beam and brick assembly, 110

   joining completed, 109

   left, completed, 91

motors

   attaching subassembly for, 116

   axles for, 115

   gears for, 123

   subassembly for, 113–114

neck assembly, 117

parts for aesthetic add-ons, 74

programming, 62–71

reproducing, 61–62

retail set parts only, 111

Atmel ARM7 processor, 16

ATST_init() function, 64

Autoconnection Library (Bluetooth), 518–519

autonomous behavior

   JohnNXT, 358

   NXT Turtle, 217–219, 232–233

averaging measurements over time, 374

B

You Need the Companion eBook

Your purchase of this book entitles you to buy the companion PDF-version eBook for only $10. Take the weightless companion with you anywhere.

We believe this Apress title will prove so indispensable that you'll want to carry it with you everywhere, which is why we are offering the companion eBook (in PDF format) for $10 to customers who purchase this book now. Convenient and fully searchable, the PDF version of any content-rich, page-heavy Apress book makes a valuable addition to your programming library. You can easily find and copy code—or perform examples by quickly toggling between instructions and the application. Even simultaneously tackling a donut, diet soda, and complex code becomes simplified with hands-free eBooks!

Once you purchase your book, getting the $10 companion eBook is simple:

❶ Visit **www.apress.com/promo/tendollars/**.

❷ Complete a basic registration form to receive a randomly generated question about this title.

❸ Answer the question correctly in 60 seconds, and you will receive a promotional code to redeem for the $10.00 eBook.

 THE EXPERT'S VOICE™

 eBookshop

2855 TELEGRAPH AVENUE │ SUITE 600 │ BERKELEY, CA 94705

Offer valid through 10/08.